A
DRAMA IN MUSLIN

A REALISTIC NOVEL

by
George Moore

with an Introduction by
A. Norman Jeffares

COLIN SMYTHE
Gerrards Cross

Introduction copyright © 1981 A. Norman Jeffares

First Published in 1886

This edition first published in 1981 by Colin Smythe Ltd
P.O. Box 6, Gerrards Cross, Buckinghamshire
reprinted 1993

British Library Cataloguing in Publication Data

Moore, George, *b*. 1852
   A drama in muslin
   I. Title
   823'.8   PR5042.M/
   ISBN 0-86140-055-0
   ISBN 0-86140-056-9 Pbk

Printed in Great Britain

INTRODUCTION.

A Drama in Muslin (1886) is ostensibly about education: the emergence of five girls from a convent school into the world and their subsequent fates in what Moore called the marriage mart. But it is also much more than that: it is a portrayal of a disturbed country, an artificial society, and a simmering conflict between riches and poverty rooted in the question of the ownership of the land. In this novel Moore is portraying his native country in the period of the Land League.

The eighteen-seventies had begun well in Ireland. The crops were good, so were the prices, and, as a result, rents went up. But with the coming of cheap wheat from North America in the mid-seventies prices went down. Gladstone's Land Act of 1870 had not settled the matter of fair rents, nor did it protect from eviction those tenants who were in arrears with their rents. Evictions had enabled landlords after the devastating, debilitating mid-nineteenth century famine to use land for grazing rather than tillage. As evictions increased so did agrarian crime: landlords and their agents were shot. Michael Davitt began to organise the tenants in County Mayo in 1879. A vast meeting held at Irishtown in April led to a reduction of local rents by a Father Burke (the inheritor of a property with twenty-two tenants) who also withdrew his action to evict the tenants. Another meeting at Westport in June was addressed by Parnell, who advised the tenants to hold a firm grip of their homesteads. After this came the formation of the Land League of Mayo, which quickly became the Irish National Land League, with Parnell elected as its president in October. By 1880 the League had two hundred thousand members in Ireland, with its overseas membership growing to match this formidable total.

Parnell, supported by the Fenians, got to the nub of the question: after Gladstone's compensation for Disturbances Bill (to compensate tenants evicted for not paying rent) was rejected by the House of Lords in August, he made a speech at Ennis in County Clare in September. He told his audience that military force could never subdue the half million tenant farmers if they struck against the ten thousand landlords of Ireland. He asked his audience what they should do to a tenant who made a bid for a farm from which his neighbour had been evicted. To the cries of "kill him" and "shoot him" he suggested that such a person should be left severely alone to realise how his action was viewed by his neighbours. This speech led to the famous reaction against Captain Boycott. And as the boycotting spread, evictions declined. Then a Coercion Act was passed in February 1881. Davitt was re-arrested, and agrarian crimes increased. Gladstone produced another Land Act, with land courts to determine a fair rent. Parnell suggested that the Land League should prepare trial cases to see how the Land Commissioners would behave. He himself was arrested, and placed in Kilmainham jail in Dublin, and the agrarian disturbances multiplied while evictions continued. The Land Courts reduced rents slightly; the Land League's offensive, based on a call for a general non-payment of rent, collapsed; and Parnell and Gladstone reached the agreement known as the Kilmainham Treaty, in which Parnell accepted the 1881 Land Act and Gladstone abandoned the Coercion policy.

To Parnell it seemed as if things were on the eve of Home Rule. He was, however, deeply disturbed by the violence in Ireland, and the murder in May 1882 of the new Chief Secretary Lord Frederick Cavendish and Thomas Burke, the permanent undersecretary, as they were walking in the Phoenix Park in Dublin, at first shattered him; he was able to persuade Davitt and other leaders that the Land agitation should be replaced by the movement for Home Rule, the Land League changed into the National League.

Further Irish Land Acts were put through the Westminster Parliament in 1885, 1887, 1891 and 1896 by the Tory government, but it took a meeting between landlords and the leaders of the agrarian movement called by Captain John Shawe-Taylor, Lady Gregory's nephew, to suggest a solution to the whole corrosive problem of land tenure. This was the crucial watershed. George Wyndham, the chief secretary, agreed to the ideas put forward, and the Wyndham Land Act was passed in 1903. This meant that the British government bought up the land-purchase debt; it was to be repaid over sixty-two and a half years by the tenants who thus became proprietors. While the landlords lost the bulk of their land, they obtained their money immediately. This measure changed the whole situation; in effect, by removing the landlords from the political scene and giving the peasant farmer tenure of the land he worked, it shaped most of Ireland into a land of small landowning farmers.

Moore realised the way that events were moving. He was himself a landlord, having succeeded in 1870 to a property of nearly thirteen thousand acres, most of it in County Mayo. He studied in London and once he was twenty-one set off for Paris in 1873 to become, he hoped, an artist. Once in Paris he relied on his agent, his uncle, Joe Blake, to collect his rents. He was very shaken when he received a letter in 1880 from Blake refusing to act any longer. Prices, his uncle wrote, had come down, the tenants were refusing to pay their rents and he ran the risk of being shot. Moore had drawn money but this had not come in from rents and now Blake wanted to be repaid the sum of three thousand pounds. Moore found the refusal of his tenants to pay rents "terrible". "What does it mean", he asked in his reply to Blake, "Communism?" And he went on to say that if he had never looked into his business, at all events he had never committed any follies. He had never spent more than five hundred pounds a year, "and I was told when I came into the properties I had ever so much".

He promptly went to London to meet Blake, fully realised the serious nature of his position, and arranged for his effects in Paris to be sold. In the summer his uncle pressed him for the three thousand pounds he was owed. Moore spent the winter of 1880 at Moore Hall. He repaid Joe Blake by raising a mortgage, sold some timber to keep himself, and appointed a young untried agent Tom Routledge:

With his new agent he made a tour of inspection of his
property, a distressing experience which brought him up
the desolate slopes of the Tourmakeady Mountains and
across water-logged plains where farms were rented at five
shillings an acre. Tenants' deputations, headed by the local
politician, called at Moore Hall, and instructed him in the
grievance of the confiscations and in the history of Irish
land tenure, explaining why no rents were being paid.[1]

Moore was not in physical danger himself: his father had not
evicted tenants, and nor did he. But he had visited Captain
Boycott and saw him protected by two thousand troops while
some Orangemen brought in his harvest, and he realised very
clearly that the peasants had good reason for alarm and for
action. "I am a landlord to-day, but I will recognise it as a
fact that had not Davitt organised the Land League in '78, a
great clearance of peasants would have been again made in '78".[2]

Moore also understood that life in Ireland had changed and
would change still further, and he probably realised this the
more objectively through the distancing provided by his seven
years' residence in France. He thought that he had been
born in feudalism and argued that the eighteenth century,
which ended in England in 1830, lasted on in Ireland till 1870.[3]
In 1881 he moved to London, to Cecil Street in the Strand
(where he stayed for about two years), to set up as a writer,
horrified by the prospect of debt, thinking that he would never
be paid rents again. He wrote A Modern Lover (3 vols., 1883),
followed it with A Mummer's Wife (1885) and had a polemic
joust at Mudie's Library in Literature at Nurse, or Circulating
Morals (1885).

During this time Moore continued to contemplate the new,
changed Ireland, where he spent the winter of 1883–84 while
working on A Mummer's Wife and that of 1884–5 while collect-
ing material for A Drama in Muslin. He became acutely
aware of the melancholia and despair of the west, and the
sketches in Terre d'Irlande (1887), later published in English as
Parnell and his Island (1887), reveal him in a sardonic mood,
selecting, as befitted "Zola's richochet", sordid details of dirt

---

[1] Joseph Hone, The Life of George Moore, 1936, p. 85.
[2] George Moore, Parnell and his Island, 1887, p. 89.
[3] Joseph Hone, The Life of George Moore, p. 86.

and decay, in his portrayal of a poverty-stricken and priest-ruled peasantry. His estimates of the Anglo-Irish gentry were equally negative. As his biographer Joseph Hone put it, "he is himself the poet who returns to Ireland with Verlaine and Mallarmé in his pocket and finds people who take his word for it that Wagner was a first rate cattle-dealer". These essays contain a powerful account of an eviction; they convey atmospherically the feeling of desolation of the often deserted landscape. And they are steeped in Moore's consciousness that the social order in Ireland is about to change, his fore-boding that the land is going to be re-occupied by the Catholic Irish in America, busily financing the Fenians and the Land League and the National League. *Parnell and his Island* should be seen as a companion piece to *A Drama in Muslin* where the doom that hangs over the landlords is equally present.

This awareness of coming change remains the background to the novel, however continually conscious of it the reader is made by Moore. In the foreground are the girls in the marriage market hoping to attract a husband with at least a thousand pounds a year, and they are Moore's major concern. He disliked intensely what he saw in social as well as political life in Ireland in the eighteen-eighties. He intended, he said, a study of "unmarried girls, the poor muslin martyrs", for he regarded intelligent women in a society as deserving more than mere domestic status. Thus Alice Barton, his heroine, through whose awakening eyes we see much of the contrast between poverty and riches, seeks a life in which she can fulfil herself. She begins to write, she marries a dispensary doctor who is socially "beneath" her, but actually a man worthy of her love. They leave for England, looking for independence, and their last act in Ireland is symbolically to pay the rent of a family being evicted.

Moore knew his countryside from boyhood; in the winter of 1883–4 he went to Dublin, stayed at the Shelbourne Hotel and attended the Levee, the State Ball at the Castle, and a Calico Ball at the Rotunda. He visited the drawing rooms; he danced; he even flirted with an heiress, Maud Browne, effectively frightened by an aunt who disapproved heartily of Moore. "Marriage is of course the ruling topic of conversation", he told his mother in a letter of 17 February 1884, in which he announced that all was over between Maud and himself, and described his reactions to the State Ball at the Castle—"very grand and imposing"—and to the Calico Ball at the Rotunda— "Never did I see anything so low, so vile, so dirty".

The following winter he was working hard on *A Drama in Muslin*; he left Moore Hall for Dublin and, obviously feeling the need for more naturalistic detail, wrote to Colonel Dease:

I am actively engaged on a book, in the interests of which I came to Dublin last year to attend the Levee, the Drawing Rooms and the Castle balls. I was not fortunate enough to receive an invitation for a State dinner party. Now, as my book deals with the social and political power of the Castle in Modern Ireland, I should be glad to attend the Levee in February, if I could make sure of being asked to one of the big dinner parties. My books, as you are probably aware, are extensively read; this particular one will attract a good deal of attention. It would therefore be well to render my picture as complete, as true, as vivid as possible.[1]

Eventually he sent notes to the Castle by messenger, and, once he was finally told the lists were "at present closed", he capitalised on his own awkward situation by publishing the correspondence in the *Freeman's Journal*:

The "at present" is amiable. Who are the people entitled to share in the entertainments given in Dublin Castle? Every year large sums are voted in Parliament for the maintenance of this court. Surely this is not done solely for the purpose of feasting and feting—and—I am of course unable as I am unwilling to argue that my social position entitles me to be asked to the Castle, but I cannot refrain from saying that Lord Fingall and Col. Dease would find it difficult to show I was not. Be that as it may, it was as a man of letters, it was for the purpose of studying, not of amusing myself, that I applied for an invitation. Was that the reason I was refused? One would feel almost inclined to think so . . . It would be presumptuous on my part to hope to unearth any fresh crime, the lists of shame are already filled . . . The Opinions I hold on the subject [of the Castle]

[1] Joseph Hone, *The Life of George Moore*, p. 107.

will be found in my next novel, my writing table is covered with human documents—fragments of conversations overheard, notes on character, anecdotes of all kinds. I came to the Castle, not as a patriot nor as a place hunter, but as the passionless observer, who, unbiassed by political creed, comments impartially on the matter submitted to him for analysis. I confess I would have liked to have seen one of the State dinner parties, but we cannot have all things, and I am not sure that Lord Fingall was not right to refuse my application. Fame comes to us in unexpected ways, and I believe that when this somnolent earl is overtaken by that sleep which overtakes us all, and for which, it appears, he is qualifying himself daily as well as nightly, his claim to be remembered will be that he refused to invite me to dinner at the Castle.[1]

Out of his experience of the glitter and tinsel of Dublin society came the famous decorative passages: the dressmaker's shop where Alice Barton and Olive, her beautiful sister, are prepared for the Castle Ball; the Castle Drawing Room itself, with the shoulders of the girls described in terms of exotic flowers. On this battlefield Mrs. Barton manoeuvers her troops, but the prize, Lord Kilcarney, falls for another of the girls, Violet Scully, whose mother watches from afar. Moore manages to differentiate skilfully between the five girls, Alice and Olive Barton, May Gould who has an illegitimate child and is secretly supported by Alice, and Cecilia Cullen, the cripple, who resents sensuous life from a religious point of view that is matched by the nature of the language she uses in a highly intense, hysterical way.

A sense of contrast is ever present throughout the novel: Alice and Olive, different in appearance, are also very different in character, as their conversations show. Their scheming, powerful mother treats them differently, and their lives turn out very differently indeed, with Olive failing to elope, whereas Alice has the courage to defy her mother, and leaves for a happy marriage. But while Olive seems at first to accept the social conventions of the time, another ironic contrast occurs when Moore gives alternate descriptions of Mrs. Barton dismis-

[1] Joseph Hone, *The Life of George Moore*, p. 108.

sing Captain Hibbert as an unsuitable suitor for Olive, while outside the landlord and his agent are arguing with the peasants over rents.

All through the story Moore has an Ibsen-like sense of restrictive life, to which these intelligent Irish girls seem doomed. He sees, too, the ineffectiveness of the landlords, the boredom of the long evenings and the tediousness of the political conversations in the country. Dublin seems seedy, with its echoing of last year's London, and always in the background is the contrast of wealth and poverty between cabin and castle— a hundred little houses working to keep one big one in sloth and luxury, as Alice Barton puts it. There is a feeling that the system is doomed, worn-out, ripe for retribution to fall on it: and yet Moore does not fancy a peasant-dominated society, however clearly he realises the injustice, the inegality, the inhumanity which causes the festering violence of the eighties. It is all there in the novel: murders, evictions, outrages, Coercion Acts, the Phoenix Park murders, the Bill for the Prevention of Crime, the Land League suddenly vanished "as a card up the sleeve of a skilful conjurer".

Moore too was divided: he remained deterministically a landlord. Despite all his worries about having no money—he was, after all, only twenty-one when he had to realise his apparently steady income was in abeyance perhaps for ever— in the end he sold his estate to the Land Commission, and, after paying off mortgages, had between twenty-five and thirty thousand pounds; he retained Moore Hall and five hundred acres. This big house was burned down by the Republicans in 1923 because Moore's brother, Colonel Maurice Moore, was loyal to the Irish Free State of which he was a senator. Moore received £7000 in compensation but the loss of Moore Hall grieved him deeply. Yet as well as being a landlord he was liberal in his attitudes. The contradictions are there in *A Drama in Muslin*. He wanted to show readers outside Ireland what it was like. He had not, however, fully learned the objectivity that he sought after all: his own feelings break through, notably the humanitarianism he affected to despise.

Moore was uneven in his presentation of his material (his delight in Huysmans affected his style in places); he was moving forward, away from Zola's influence, to what he achieved in the melodic line of *The Lake*, just as in *Parnell and His Island* he was also preparing material for the lucidity and the irony of the stories of *The Untilled Field* (1903). But the unevenness, the occasional purple passages, don't spoil the novel; on the other hand what makes it so readable is the mixture of main narrative, the skilfully imagined development of Alice Barton as a thoughtful, independent character who, seeing through pretence, defends her own kind of integrity, and the effective, economical presentation of the troubled country in which Alice has successfully discovered her own identity.

The reader who has enjoyed *A Drama in Muslin* should next read the Preface to *Muslin*, the revised edition published in 1915, in which Moore discusses what he had done. He describes how thirty years after *A Drama in Muslin* had been in print he re-read it.

> A comedy novel written with sprightliness and wit, I said, as I turned to the twentieth page, and it needs hardly any editing. A mere retying of a few bows that the effluxion of time has untied, or were never tied by the author, who, if I remember right, used to be less careful of his literary appearance than his prefacer, neglecting to examine his sentences, and to scan them as often as one might expect from an admirer, not to say disciple, of Walter Pater.[1]

He asks when the author of *A Drama in Muslin* disappeared from literature:

> His next book was *Confessions of a Young Man*. It was followed by *Spring Days*; he must have died in the last pages of that story, for we find no trace of him in *Esther Waters*! And my thoughts, dropping away from the books he had written, began to take pleasure in the ridiculous appearance that the author of *A Drama in Muslin* presented in the mirrors of Dublin Castle as he tripped down the staircases in early morning. And a smile played round my lips as I recalled his lank yellow hair (often standing on end), his sloping shoulders and his female hands—a strange appear-

---

[1] George Moore, *Muslin*, 1915, p. 111.

ance which a certain vivacity of mind sometimes rendered
engaging.

He goes on to wonder how the critics of the eighteen-eighties
could have been blind enough to call him an imitator of Zola.

"A soul searcher, if ever there was one", I continued,
"whose desire to write well is apparent on every page, a
headlong, eager, uncertain style (a young hound yelping at
every trace of scent), but if we look beneath the style we
catch sight of the young man's true self, a real interest in
religious questions and a hatred as lively as Ibsen's of the
social conventions that drive women into the marriage
market . . ."[1]

The theme of *A Drama in Muslin*, he continued, is the same as
that of *A Doll's House*.

When halfway through writing his novel he had been read a
translation of Ibsen's play. He had objected to Ibsen making
a woman first in a sensual and then transferring her into an
educational mould: he himself, he had said at the time, was
writing of a puritan, "but not a sexless puritan, and if women
cannot win their freedom without leaving their sin behind they
had better remain slaves, for a slave with his sex is better than
a free eunuch".

The Preface moves into a sketch of Violet Scully's life as the
marchioness and her lovers, a story the younger Moore, says
the older, might well have written. Moore had written a
strong condemnation of *A Drama in Muslin*, in a letter to T.
Fisher Unwin, 14 January 1902, as "perhaps the best subject I
have ever had excepting *Esther Waters* and . . . the worst
written".[2] He had mellowed in his judgement of it by his
sixties and rightly so, for *A Drama in Muslin* remains with its
mixture of satire and sympathy, objectivity and panoramic
range of vision one of its creator's most intelligent insights into
human life.

Stirling 1980   A. Norman Jeffares

[1] George Moore, *Muslin*, 1915, p. 111.
[2] Quoted in *George Moore in Transition: Letters to T. Fisher Unwin
and Lena Milman*, 1894–1910, ed. H. E. Gerber, Detroit, 1968, p. 245.

A Note on the Text

A Drama in Muslin first appeared in the *Court and Society Review*, January 1886. It was prefaced by an advertisement (written by Moore himself) praising its actuality, its complete picture of Ireland "painted by an Irishman". The first edition, *A Drama in Muslin. A Realistic Novel*, was published by Vizetelly & Co., London, in 1886. The copy text used in the preparation of the present edition is that of the 7th printing, published by William Heinemann, London. The text of the first seven 'editions' was not changed. The revised version of the novel, *Muslin*, was published by William Heinemann, London, in 1915. The alterations made by Moore, largely a cutting of the more lyrical passages, have been listed in an unpublished Ph.D. thesis written by Graham Owens for the University of Leeds.

A DRAMA IN MUSLIN.

BOOK I.

CHAPTER I.

THE grey stone cross of the convent-church was scarcely seen in the dimness of the sun-smitten sky. The convent occupied an entire hilltop, and it overlooked the sea.

All around was a beautiful garden, and the white dresses of the girls fluttered through the verdurous vistas like the snowy plumage of a hundred doves. Obeying a sudden impulse, a flock of little ones would race through a deluge of leaf-entangled rays towards a pet companion. You see her at the end of a gravel-walk, examining the flower she has just picked : the sunlight glancing along little white legs, proudly and charmingly advanced. The elder girls in their longer skirts were more dignified, but when sight was caught of a favourite sister, they too ran forward, and then retreated timidly, as if afraid of committing an indiscretion.

It was prize-day in the Convent of the Holy Child, and since early morning all had been busy preparing for the arrival of the Bishop. His throne had been set at one end of the school-hall, and at the other the carpenters had erected a stage for the performance of " King Cophetua," a musical sketch written by Miss Alice Barton for the occasion. But now a pause had come in the labour of the day ; the luncheon, that all had been too excited to partake of, was over; and for the next half-hour, straying over the green swards, or clustered round a garden-bench, the girls talked of the many expectations that the coming hours of the afternoon would

1

set at rest. Their faces were animated with discussion. They
spoke of the parts they would play; of the dresses they
would wear; of the probable winners of the prizes; of the joys
and ambitions that even now absorbed their lives. A charming and infantile peace slept on land and sea. In the distance
the grey girdle of water glittered as with the leaping silver of
a myriad fishes; between the chimneys, under the hill, a fleet
of fishing-boats basked in the sun like sparrows. It was
almost blinding to lift the eyes, so intense was the radiation
of the light; and the downy whiteness of the sky was un-
relieved by any splash of blue. Suddenly, a rearrangement
of figures on the terrace made one group of girls the centre
of the vast panorama. They seemed like a piece of finished
sculpture ready to be taken from the peace and meditation
of the studio and placed in the noise and staring of the
galleries.

Then a nun called from the sward where the children
were playing, and two girls rose from the bench. Their
places were quickly appropriated, and the five remaining
girls drew together, forming a new and more harmonious
group.

Alice Barton was what is commonly known as a plain girl.
At home, during the holidays, she often heard that the dressmaker could not fit her, that her eyes were not so large nor
so sweet as her sister's. But the clear, sweet mind was so
often revealed in those grey eyes, that the want of beauty
was forgotten in love of her personality. Although her
shoulders were narrow and prim, her arms long and
almost awkward, there was a character about the figure that
commanded attention. Alice was now turned twenty, she
was the eldest, the best-beloved, and the cleverest girl in the
school. It was not, therefore, on account of any backward-
ness in her education that she had been kept so long out of
society; but because Mrs. Barton thought that, as her two
girls were so different in appearance, it would be well for them
to come out together. Against this decision Alice said
nothing, and, like a tall arum lily, she had grown in the
convent from girl to womanhood. To her the little children
ran to be comforted; and to walk with her in the garden was
considered an honour and a pleasure that even the reverend
mother was glad to participate in.

Lady Cecilia Cullen sat next to Alice. At a glance you

saw she was a hunchback; but in a standing position her deformity would have appeared less marked than it did at present. It lay principally in her right shoulder, which was higher than her left—now she was seen at her worst. Cecilia was the wonder and enigma of the convent. Of a nature more than delicate and sensitive, she shrank from the normal pleasures and loves of life as from the sight of a too coarse display of food; often an ordinary look, or word, or gesture shocked her, and so deeply that she would remain for hours sitting apart, refusing all consolation. A spot on the table-cloth, or the presence of one repellent to her, was sufficient to extinguish a delight or an appetite. Her fancies were so abrupt and obscure that none could ever be certain what would please or offend her. In one thing only was she constant—she loved Alice. There was love in those wilful brown eyes—love that was wild and visionary, and perhaps scarcely sane. And the intensity of this affection had given rise to conjecturing. When other girls spoke of men and admirers, her lip curled: had it not been for her deformity she would have expressed her abhorrence. At home she was considered wayward, if not a little queer, and her wish, therefore, to remain at school met with no opposition.

Violet Scully occupied the other end of the garden-bench. She was very thin, but withal elegantly made. Her face was neat and delicate, and it was set with light blue eyes that sparkled as did the misted glitter of the sea. When she was not restlessly changing her place, or looking round as if she fancied someone was approaching, when she was still (which was seldom), a rigidity of feature, and an almost complete want of bosom, gave her the appearance of a convalescent boy. The small aristocratic head was beautifully poised on the swaying neck; faint, wavy, brown tresses cast light shadows over the small but finely-shaped temples, behind which it was easy to see that a sharp but narrow intelligence was at work—an intelligence that would always dominate weak natures, and triumph in a battle of mean interests.

May Gould, who stood at the back, her hand leaning affectionately on Alice's shoulder, was a very different type of girl. Had she been three inches taller she would have been a magnificent woman—but for her height, which was five feet four, her features were too massive. Although only seventeen, all the characteristics of her sex were in her distinctly

marked, and her sensuous nature was reflected in the violet
fluidity of her eyes.   Her hair was not of an inherited tint.
It was of that shade of red that is only seen in the children
of dark-haired parents.   In great coils it rolled over the
dimpled cream of her neck, sweeping with copper threads the
vermilion-hued curves of her ear.   With the exception of
Alice, May was the cleverest girl in the school.   For public
inspection she made large water-coloured drawings of Swiss
scenery; for private view, pen-and-ink sketches of officers
sitting in conservatories with young ladies.   The former were
admired by the nuns, the latter occasioned a vast deal of
excitement amid a select few.

Olive Barton lay on the grass, her arms thrown over her
sister's knees.   The pose recalled that of Venus in Titian's
picture of " Venus and Adonis "; but of the material beauty
of the pagan world there was nothing in Olive's face.   It was
the mild and timid loveliness that is the fruit of eighteen
hundred years of Christianity.   Even now the uplifted throat
recalled that of an adoring angel.   Olive's hair was the colour
of primroses.   Her face, with its pronounced nose, was full of
all the pseudo-classicality of a cameo.   Now the action of
listening had distended the limbs, and the skirt was cast into
folds that made clear the movement of the body; the arms
and bosom were moulded into amorous plenitudes, and the
extremities flowed into chaste slendernesses, that the white
stocking and loose convent-shoe could not distort.   In the
beautiful framework nothing was wanting but a mind.   She
was, in a word, a human flower—a rose—a carnation that a
wicked magician had endowed with the power of speech.

"I don't see, Alice, why you couldn't have made King
Cophetua marry the Princess.   Who ever heard of a King
marrying a beggar-maid?   It seems to me most unnatural.
Besides, I hear that lots of people are going to be present,
and to be jilted before them all is not very pleasant.   I am
sure mamma wouldn't like it."

" But you are not jilted, my dear Olive; you do not like
the King, and you show your nobleness of mind by refusing
him."

"I don't see that; who ever refused a king?"

"Well, what do you want?" exclaimed May, "I never saw
anyone so selfish in all my life; you would not be satisfied
unless you played the whole piece by yourself.   First you

would have your sister beg the nuns to allow you to play the beggar-maid, then you didn't like the part and refused to go on with it; and hadn't Violet very kindly consented to give the Princess up to you—which she would have played beautifully—and agreed to act the beggar-maid, I don't know what we should have done."

Olive would probably have made a petulant and passionate reply, but at that moment the sound of laughter was heard. It was a man's voice, and the merriment was vapid and loud.

The girls started to their feet, and, looking past the green garden, they watched a party of visitors who were coming up the drive.

"'Tis papa," cried Olive, and, instantly forgetting her troubles, she rushed forward, laughing as she went.

"And he is with mamma," said Violet, and with an air of satisfaction she tripped after Olive. The three remaining girls lingered, then advanced shyly. From where they were they could see that someone was attracting a good deal of attention. Presently a tall, handsome man escaped from the two priests who were walking on either side of him, and, after kissing Olive, held her at arm's length and admired her somewhat boisterously. The high aquiline nose which the daughter had inherited made the likeness obvious. Mr. Barton wore a flowing beard, his hair was long, and both were the colour of pale *café au lait*. His appearance was, therefore, somewhat romantic, and he spoke as if he were trying to speak up to it.

"Here is learning, and here is beauty, what could any father desire more?" he exclaimed, after he had bestowed a kiss upon Alice. "I used to kiss you all in old times, but I suppose you are too big now. How strange! how strange! There you are, a row of brunettes and blondes, who, before many days are over, will be charming the hearts of all the young men in Galway. And I suppose it was in talking of such things you spent the morning?"

"Our young charges have been, I assure you, very busy all the morning. We are not as idle as you think, Mr. Barton," said the nun, in a tone of voice that showed that she thought the remark extremely ill-considered. "We have been arranging the stage for the representation of a little play that your daughter Alice composed."

"Oh, yes, I know, she wrote to me about it; 'King Cophetua' is the name, isn't it? I am very curious indeed, for I have set Tennyson's ballad to music myself. I sing it to the guitar—have not had time to have it written down. Life is so hurried, and I keep my thoughts fixed on one thing, or I should have sent it to you. However—however we are all going home to-morrow. I have promised to take charge of Cecilia, and Mrs. Scully is going to look after May."

"Oh, how nice, how nice that will be!" cried Olive, and, catching Violet by the hands, she romped with her for glee.

Then the nun, taking advantage of this break in the conversation, said:

"Come now, young ladies, it is after two o'clock, we shall never be ready in time if you don't make haste—and it won't do to keep the Bishop waiting."

The priests smiled blandly, and, like a hen gathering her chickens, the Sister hurried away with Violet, Olive, and May.

"How happy they seem in this beautiful retreat!" said Mrs. Scully, drawing her black lace shawl about her huge grey-silk shoulders. "How little they know of the troubles of the world! I am afraid it would be hard to persuade them to leave their convent if they knew the trials that await them."

"We cannot escape our trials, they are given to us that we may overcome them," said one of the Fathers, who thought that Mrs. Scully's remark called for a word of comment.

"I suppose so, indeed," said Mrs. Scully; and, trying to find consolation in the remark, she sighed deeply. Then the other reverend gentleman, as if fearing further religious shop from his *confrère*, informed Mr. Barton, in a cheerful tone of voice, that he had heard he was a great painter.

"I don't know—I don't know," replied Mr. Barton, " painting is, after all, only dreaming—I should like to be put at the head of an army, and sent to conquer Africa—my affairs keep me in Ireland—but when I am seized with an idea I have to rush to put it down."

Finding no appropriate answer to these somewhat erratic remarks, the priest joined in a discussion that had been started, concerning the action taken by the Church during the present agrarian agitation. Mr. Barton, who was weary of the subject, stepped away, and, sitting on one of the terrace-benches between Cecilia and Alice, he feasted his eyes on the colour-changes that came over the sea, and, in long-drawn-out and disconnected phrases, explained his views on nature and art, until the bell was rung for the children to assemble in the school-hall.

It was a large room with six windows; these had been covered over with red cloth, and the wall opposite was decorated with plates, flowers, and wreaths woven out of branches of evergreen, oak, and holly. Chairs for the visitors had been arranged in a semicircle around the Bishop's throne—a great square chair approached by steps, and rendered still more imposing by the canopy, whose voluminous folds fell on either side like those of a corpulent woman's dress. Opposite was the stage. The footlights were turned down, but the blue mountains and brown palm-trees of the drop-curtain, painted by one of the nuns, loomed through the red obscurity of the room. Benches had been set along both walls; between them a strip of carpet, worked with roses and lilies, down which the girls advanced when called to receive their prizes, stretched its blue and slender length.

As the girls entered, their voices reminded you of a tree full of April-talking birds. Alice was in great requisition. A kind of place of honour had been made for her, and those who sat next her were looked upon enviously. In the excitement of the moment it was forgotten they were going to lose her. For her, every heart was full of admiration; and many were the mental calculations made as to the number of prizes she would have carried off, had she not, for the last year, been placed by herself, outside of the school classes. There was a suspicion afloat that some special sign of approbation would be made to her; the form that it would take none ventured to predict; but it was thought that the usual blue ribbon for good conduct, in so exceptional a case as Alice's, would not be considered sufficient. Then, as a breeze in a garden suddenly blows the flowers different ways, the conversation would change, and, leaning together, groups and couples discussed passionately their chances of obtaining rewards for their year's labours. The little children were pushed out of the way, and they sat on the back benches, conscious of their inferiority in point of age. The youngest was a child of eight; but there were many of eleven and thirteen, and, like nurses, these, their narrow shoulders raised, lectured the little ones, all the while arranging their blue sashes for them. It was a pretty sight. The vague, sexless stare of infancy contrasted with the quick glances of the elder girls, whose sharp features hinted at a budding feminality.

Then, suddenly, a nun entered, and, in a voice full of trepidation and expectancy, announced that the Bishop was coming. The babbling of voices ceased, and, hurriedly, four girls hastened to the pianos placed on either side of the stage—two left-hands struck a series of chords in the bass, the treble notes replied, the eight hands went rattling over the keys; and, to the gallant measure of a French polka, a stately prelate entered. Everyone was on her feet in a moment, and the soft clapping of feminine palms resounded through the rooms, drowning for a moment even the slangy strains of the polka.

But, when the Bishop was seated on his high throne, the back of which extended some feet above his head, and when the crowd of visitors had been accommodated with chairs around him, a nun made her way through the room, seeking anxiously among the girls. She carried in her hand a basket filled with programmes, all rolled and neatly tied with pieces of different coloured ribbon. These she distributed to the ten tiniest little children she could find, and, advancing five from either side, they formed in a line and courtesied to the Bishop. One little dot, whose hair hung about her head like a golden mist, nearly lost her balance; she was, however, saved from falling by a companion, and then, like a group of kittens, they tripped down the blue strip of carpet, and handed the programmes to the guests, who leaned forward as if anxious to touch their hands—to stroke their shining hair. The play was now ready to begin, and Alice felt she was going from hot to cold, for when the announcement printed on the programme, that she was the author of the comedy of " King Cophetua," had been read, all eyes were fixed upon her : the Bishop, after eyeing her intently, bent towards the Reverend Mother and whispered to her. Doubtless it was very trying; Cecilia clasped Alice's hand, and said, as the nun who had written the introductory music played the last bars, " You must not be afraid, dear, I know it will be all right."

And the little play was as charming as it was guileless. The old legend had been arranged—as might have been expected from a schoolgirl—simply and unaffectedly. The scene opened in a room in the palace of the King, and when a chorus, sup-posed to be sung by the townspeople, was over, a minister entered hurriedly. The little children uttered a cry of delight; they did not recognise their companion in her strange disguise. A large wig, with brown curls hanging over the shoulders, almost hid the face that had been made to look quite aged by a few clever touches of the pencil about the eyes and mouth. She was dressed in a long garment, something between an ulster and a dressing-gown; it fell just below her knees, for it had been decided by the Reverend Mother that it were better that there should be a slight display of ankles than the least suspicion of trousers. The subject was a delicate one, and for some weeks past a look of alarm had not left the face of the nun in charge of the wardrobe. But these considerations only amused the girls, and now, delighted at the novelty of her garments, the minister strutted manfully about the stage. Bitterly she complained of the temper of the dowager Queen. "Who could help it if the King wouldn't marry? Who could make him leave his poetry and music for a pretty face if he didn't care to do so? He had already refused blue eyes, black eyes, brown eyes. However, the new Princess was a very beautiful person, and ought, all things considered, to be accepted by the King. She must be passing through the city at the moment." On this the Queen entered. Alice's face contracted with apprehension, for the little girl who played the part had shown such timidity at rehearsal that it was impossible to say that now, in the presence of an audience, she might not grow utterly disconcerted, and fly crying from the stage. The first words she spoke were inaudible, but, gathering courage as she went on, she trailed her white satin, with its large brocaded pattern, in true queenly fashion, and questioned the minister as to his opinion of the looks of the new Princess. But she gave no point to her words. The scene was, fortunately, a short one, and no sooner had they disappeared than a young man entered. He held a lute in his left hand, and with his right he twanged the strings idly. He was King Cophetua. This was the crucial point of the play, and not many words had been spoken before Alice saw her expectations fade, and a bitter sense of disappointment filled her mind. Many times during rehearsal Alice had warned May of the error she was falling into, but May did not seem able to accommodate herself to the author's view of the character, and, after a few minutes, fell back into her old swagger. And now this was more exaggerated than it had ever been before. Excited by the presence of an audience, by the footlights, by the long coat under which she knew her large well-shaped legs could be seen, she forgot her promises, and strolled about like a man— as she had seen young Scully saunter about the stable-yard at home. She looked, no doubt, very handsome, and, conscious of the fact, she addressed her speeches to a group of young men, who, for no ostensible reason except to get as far away as possible from the Bishop, had crowded into the left-hand corner of the hall.

And so great was May's misreading of the character, that Alice could hardly realise that she was listening to her own piece. Instead of speaking the sentence, ' My dear mother, I could not marry anyone I did not love; besides, am I not already wedded to music and poetry ? ' slowly, dreamily, May emphasised the words so jauntily, that they seemed to be poetic equivalents for wine and tobacco. There was no doubt that things were going too far; the Reverend Mother frowned, and shifted her position in her chair uneasily ; the Bishop crossed his legs and took snuff methodically.

But at this moment the attention of the audience was diverted by the entrance of the Princess. May's misbehaviour was forgotten, and a murmur of warm admiration rose through the red twilight. Dressed in a tight-fitting gown of pale blue, opening in front, and finishing in a train held up by the smallest child in the school, Olive moved across the stage like a beautiful bird. Taking a wreath of white roses from her hair, she presented them to the King. He had then to kiss her hand, and with much courtly grace he led her to a chair. In the scene that followed, Alice had striven to be intensely pathetic. She had intended that the King, by a series of kindly-put questions, should gradually win the Princess's confidence, and induce her to tell the truth ; that her affections had already been won by a knight at her father's Court, that she could love none other. Touched by her candour, and interested in her story, the King in turn grows sentimental.

King: But if this knight did not exist; if you had never seen him, you would, I suppose, have accepted my hand?

Princess: You will not be offended if I tell you the truth?

King: No, I promise you.

Princess: Well, then, I could never have listened to your love.

King (rising hastily): Am I then so ugly, so horrible, so vile, that even if your heart were not engaged elsewhere you could not have listened to me?

Princess: You are neither horrible, nor vile, King Cophetua; but again promise me secrecy, and I will tell you the whole truth.

King: I promise you.

Princess: You are loved by a maiden far more beautiful than I; she is dying of love for your sake! she has suffered much for her love; she is suffering still.

King: And who is this maiden?

Princess: Ah! She is no more than a beggar-girl; she lives on charity, the songs she sings, and the flowers she sells in the streets. And now she is poorer than ever, for your royal mother has caused her to be driven out of the city.

Here the King weeps—he is supposed to be deeply touched by the Princess's account of the wrongs done to the beggar-girl—and it is finally arranged between him and the Princess that they shall pretend to have come to some violent misunderstanding, and that, in their war of words, they shall insult each other's parents so grossly that all possibilities of a marriage will be for ever at an end. Throwing aside a chair so as to bring the Queen within ear-shot, the King declares that his royal neighbour is an old dunce, and that there is not enough money in his treasury to pay the Court bootmaker; the Princess retaliates by saying that the royal mother of the crowned head she is addressing is an old cat, who paints her face and beats her maids of honour.

The play, that up to this point had been considered a little tedious, now riveted the attention of the audience, and when the Queen entered she was greeted with roars of laughter. Aghast, she stands on the threshold, unable to believe her ears, listening to the wild invective with which a powerful King and the Princess of a neighbouring State were attacking each other.

The applause was deafening. Olive had played her part better than had been expected, and all the white frocks trembled with excitement. The youths in the left-hand corner craned their heads forward so as not to lose a syllable of what was coming, the Bishop recrossed his legs in a manner that betokened his entire satisfaction; and, delighted, the mammas and papas whispered together. But the faces of the nuns betrayed the anxiety they felt. Inquiring glances passed beneath the black hoods; all the sleek faces grew alive and alarmed. May was now alone on the stage, and there was no saying what indiscretion she might not be guilty of.

The Reverend Mother, however, had anticipated the danger of the scene, and had sent round word to the nun in charge of the back of the stage, to tell Miss Gould that she was to set the crown straight on her head, and to take her hands out of her pockets. The effect of receiving such instructions from the wings was that May forgot one half her words, and spoke the other half so incorrectly that the passage Alice had counted on so much—"At last, thank Heaven, that tiresome trouble is over, and now I shall be free to return to music and poetry"—was rendered into nonsense, and the attention of the audience lost. Nor were matters set straight until a high soprano voice was heard singing:

> Buy, buy, who will buy roses of me?
> Roses to weave in your hair.
> A penny, only a penny for three,
> Roses a queen might wear!
>
> Roses! I gathered them far away
> In gardens, white and red.
> Roses! Make presents of roses to-day,
> And help me to earn my bread.

With the instinct of a true lover, the King at once divined that this must be the ballad-singer—the beggar-maid who loved him, who, by some secret emissaries of the Queen, had been driven away from the city, homeless and outcast; and, snatching his lute from the wall, he sang a few plaintive verses in response. The strain was instantly taken up, and then, on the current of a plain religious melody, the two voices were united, and, as two perfumes, they seemed to blend and become one.

Alice would have preferred something less ethereal, for the exigences of the situation demanded that the King should get out of the window and claim the hand of the beggar-maid in the public street. But the nun who had composed the music could not be brought to see this, and, after a comic scene between the Queen and the Chancellor, the King, followed by his Court and suite, entered, leading the beggar maid by the hand. In a short speech, he told how her sweetness, her devotion, and, above all, her beautiful voice, had won his heart, and that he intended to make her his Queen. Then a curtain was drawn aside. It disclosed a double throne; and as the young bride ascended the steps to take her place by the side of her royal husband, a joyful chorus was sung, in which allusion was made to a long reign and happy days.

Everyone was enchanted but Alice. She alone saw how the beauty of her thoughts had been turned into hideousness in the representation; the idea as it passed into reality had become polluted. She had wished to show how a man, in the trouble and bitterness of life, must yearn for the consoling sympathy of a woman, and how he may find the dove his heart is sighing for in the lowliest bracken; and, having found her and having recognised that she is the one, he should place her in his bosom, confident that her plumes are as fair and immaculate as those that glitter in the sunlight about the steps and terraces of the palace. Instead of this, she had seen a King who seemed to regard life as a sensual gratification; and a beggar-maid who looked upon her lover, not timidly, as a new-born flower upon the sun, but as a clever huckstress at a customer who had bought her goods at her valuing. But the audience did not see below the surface, and, in answer to clapping of hands and cries of *encore*, the curtain was raised once more, and King Cophetua, seated on his throne by the side of his beggar-maid, was shown to them again. Then every eye was radiant, and every lust delighted in the spectacle; fingers twitched nervously at the folds of serge habit and lace mantle. Even the hearts of the little children rejoiced in the materialisation of the idea, in the crudity of the living picture placed before them. In a vision each girl saw herself selected out of the multitude, crowned with orange-blossoms and led by a noble husband through the dim church, from an altar where the candles burnt like stars, to a life made of riches, adulation, amusement. Like warm vapour, one thought filled the entire hall. The expansive matrons, on whose bosoms had lain this white-frocked generation, leaned to the grey-headed fathers, worn with a life's toil, and sought to express the complete, the fathomless, content that had fallen upon them. It was a moment of delirium, even the nuns forgot themselves; and, their sex asserting itself through all their vows of celibacy, they gloried in having been, at least, the providers of the brides of men; and in imagination they assisted at the wedding of an entire epoch.

The excitement did not begin to calm until the *tableaux vivants* were ready. For, notwithstanding the worldliness of the day, it was thought that Heaven should not be forgotten. The convent being that of the Holy Child, something illustrative of the birth of Christ naturally suggested itself. No more touching or edifying subject than that of the Annunciation could be found. Violet's thin, elegant face seemed representative of an intelligent virginity, and in a long, white dress she knelt at a *prie-dieu.* Olive, with a pair of wings obtained from the local theatre, and her hair, blonde as an August harvesting, lying along her back, took the part of the Angel. She wore a star on her forehead.

Then, after an interval that allowed the company to recover their composure, and the carpenter to prepare the stage, the curtain was again raised. This time, the scene was a stable. At the back, in the right-hand corner, there was a manger to which was attached a stuffed donkey; Violet sat on a low stool and held the new-born Divinity in her arms; May, who for the part of Joseph had been permitted to wear a false beard, held a staff, and tried to assume the facial expression of a man who has just been blessed with a son. In the foreground knelt the three wise men from the East; with outstretched hands they held forth their offerings of frankincense and myrrh. The picture of the world's Redemption was depicted with such taste, that a murmur of pious admiration sighed throughout the hall. The dove, emblem of purity, was perched on the hayrack just above the cow's head, and so touchingly did the virgin· mother hold the child to her bosom, that every knee quivered, instinct with worship. The humanity of the Bethlehem mystery held the world in the nineteenth, as it had done in the first century. To Alice alone did the representation appear absurd, grotesque; her clear mind forced her to deny God's presence in a drama, so obviously one of human invention. The stuffed ox and ass were irresistibly comic, but knowing that Cecilia's wistful brown eyes were fixed upon her, she bit her lips and avoided a smile.

Soon after, a distribution of prizes began. At the end of the room next the stage, a nun stood, holding a large book like a ledger in her hands, and in the midst of a profound silence, she read out : " Miss Alice Barton not having taken part in the studies of the year, we are unable to award her any one of our ordinary prizes, but for the beautiful play of 'King Cophetua,' performed before you all to-day, the Reverend Mother and the Bishop of the Diocese present her with the entire works of Dr. Newman, and for the great example she has always set, by conduct and precept, during the long years she has been with us, she is likewise awarded the blue ribbon."

The ribbon had been looked upon by everyone from the first as a certainty ; but a special prize, given by the Reverend Mother and the Bishop, was so utterly without precedent in the convent-annals, that the announcement called forth the enthusiasm with which the victory of a favourite general is hailed. Among the girls there was not a pair of hands nor lips still, and as Alice walked back to her place, bearing with her as much as she could carry of the illustrious cardinal's works, her companions leaned forward to congratulate her. All the way down the line fragments of phrases were heard : " Oh ! Alice, I am so pleased, I am sure you deserve it, I know you deserve it ? " Cecilia could say nothing, she could only look with delight through the bright tears of pleasure that filled her eyes.

After this unexpected excitement, the distribution of the rest of the prizes went, necessarily, a little flat : but the Galway girls were uncommonly successful. Violet received a prize for French, May obtained one for Ancient History, Cecilia was awarded a blue ribbon for good conduct, and a book for English composition. In the general happiness, the poor bench-warmers, as the girls who obtained neither books nor ribbons were called, were forgotten. The heavy features of the parents rippled with household smiles, and they watched with delight the delicate features of their children growing grave, as they knelt before the benign Bishop to receive their rewards. In every lull of applause the unctuous voices of the priests were heard chiming : " I am sure she is a good girl. Now, do you not think she gives them a little trouble at home afterwards? "

Then there was benediction in the convent-church. A real young-girls' church : trim, delicate pillars rising like uplifted arms, arches gracefully turned as adolescent bosoms, an altar fanciful and light coloured as a toilet-table. And when the last sigh of the organ died in the stillness, and the Bishop turned the host to his white-robed congregation, from the bent heads white veils fell pendulously—immovable among draperies of the plaster angels that bowed in the niches.

This brought the business of the day to a close, and when the clock struck six the convent had assumed its customary aspect of peace and refinement. All leave-takings were over for the day; and only those who were to spend their vacation at St. Leonards, and the Irish girls—who did not start for home till the following morning—remained. These were again talking among themselves, watching, without seeing, the fishing-boats scattered over the rippling sea. The brown sails were now filled with the glories of the sunset; the air was full of languor and sorrow, and the evening had all the mystic charm of the corpse of a fragile maiden poetised by the ravages of a long malady, perfumed and prepared according to some antique rite, for a jewel-bespangled bier; eyelids and cheeks painted, hands set in sculptured poses— the finger-nails tinted with rose. Cloud draperies, striped with orange and garnished with crimson fringes, trailed as the pageant moved; and overhead the firmamental blue was stretched like a pall of turquoise-tinted silk. From the deeps of the sky the music of colour was chanted, and delicious but inaudible harmonies vibrated through the golden soul of the twilight. Soft and low and melancholy came the strain—it was the music of death, and the dark clouds that waited on either side, were as processional priestesses who, advancing, struck their lyres at each solemn step.

"And to think," said Alice, "that this is the very last evening we shall ever pass here!"

"I don't see why you should be so very sorry for that," replied May, "I should have thought that you must have had enough of the place; why, you have been here nearly ten years! I never would have consented to remain so long as that."

"I did not mind—we have been very happy here, and to say good-bye, and for ever, to friends we have known so long, and who have been so good to us, seems very sad—at least, it does to me."

"It is all very well for you," said Olive, "I daresay you

have been happy here, you have always been the petted and spoilt child of the school. Nothing was ever too good for Alice; no matter who was wrong or what was done, Alice was sure to be right."

"I never knew anyone so unreasonable," said Cecilia. "You grumble at everything, and you are always dying of jealousy of your sister."

"That's not true, and you haven't much to talk of; after beating your brains out, you only just got the prize for composition. Besides, if you like the convent as much as I daresay you do, although you aren't a Catholic, you had better stop here with my sister."

"Oh! Olive, how can you speak to Cecilia in that horrid way? I am ashamed of you."

"So you are going to turn against me, Alice; but that's your way—I shan't stay here."

And in the pale light, the retreating figure of the young girl stood out in beautiful distinctness. Behind her the soft evening swept the sea, effacing with azure the brown sails of the fishing-boats; in front of her the dresses of the girls flitted white through the sombre green of the garden.

"I am sorry," said Cecilia, "you spoke to her. She is put out because she didn't get a prize, and Sister Agnes told her that she nearly spoilt the play by the stupid way she played the Princess."

"She will find that that temper of hers will stand in her way if she does not learn to control it," said Violet; "but, now that she is gone, tell me, Alice, how do you think she played her part? As far as I can judge, she didn't seem to put any life into it. You meant the Princess to be a sharp, cunning woman of the world, didn't you?"

"No, not exactly; I can't describe my idea very well: but I agree with you that Olive didn't put life into it."

"Well, anyhow, the play was a great success, and you got, dear Alice, the handsomest prize that has ever been given in the school."

"And how do you think I did the King; did I make him look like a man? I tried to walk just as Mr. Scully does when he goes down to the stables."

"You did the part very well, May; but I think I should like him to have been more sentimental."

"I don't think men are sentimental—at least, not as you think they are. I tried to copy Mr. Scully."

"My part was a mere nothing. You must write me a something, Alice, one of these days; a coquettish girl, you know, who could twist a man round her fingers; a lot of *bavardage* in it."

"I suppose you'll never be able to speak English again, now you've got the prize for French conversation."

"Sour grapes!—you would like to have got it yourself. I worked hard for it, I was determined to get it; for ma says it is of great advantage in society for a girl to speak French well. You are a bit jealous."

"Jealous! I should like to know why I should be jealous. Of what? I got all I tried for. Beside, the truth about your French prize is, that you may consider yourself very fortunate, for if (she mentioned the name of one of her schoolfellows) had not been so shy and timid you would have come off second-best."

The rudeness of this retort drew a sharp answer from Violet; and then, in turn, but more often simultaneously, the girls discussed the justice of the distribution. The names of an infinite number of girls were mentioned, but when, in the babbling flow of convent-gossip, a favourite nun was spoken of, one of the chatterers would sigh, and for a moment be silent, absorbed by a sorrow as fragile and as lustral as the splendours that were fading, that were slowly moving away. The violet waters of the bay had darkened; and, like the separating banners of a homeward-moving procession, the colours of the sky went east and west. The girdle of rubies had melted, had become the pale red lining of a falling mantle; the large spaces of gold grew dim; orange and yellow streamers blended; lilac and blue pennons faded to deep greys; dark hoods and dark veils were drawn closer, purple was gathered like garments about the loins, and the night fell. The sky, now decorated with a crescent moon and a few stars, was filled with stillness and adoration; the day's death was exquisite, even human; and as she gazed on the beautiful corpse lowered amid the fumes of a thousand censers into an under-world, even Violet's egotism began to dream.

"The evening is lovely: I am glad: it is the last we shall pass here," said the girl, pensively, "and all good-byes are sad."

" Yes, we have been happy," said May, " and I too am sorry to leave, but then we couldn't spend our lives here. There are plenty of things to be done at home ; and I suppose we shall all get married one of these days ? And there will be balls and parties before we get married. I don't think that I'd care to get married all at once ; would you, Violet ? "

" I don't know, perhaps not, unless it was to someone very grand indeed."

" Oh, would you do that ? I don't think I could marry a man unless I loved him," said May.

" Yes, but you might love someone who was very grand as well as someone who wasn't."

" That's true enough—but then—" and May stopped, striving to readjust her ideas, which Violet's remark had suddenly disarranged. After a pause she said :

" But does your mother intend to bring you to Dublin for the season ? Are you going to be presented this year ? "

" I hope so ; mamma said I should be, last vacation."

" I shall take good care that I am ; the best part of the hunting will be over, and I wouldn't miss the Castle balls for anything. Do you like officers ? "

The crudity of the question startled Alice, and it was with difficulty she answered she didn't know—that she had not thought about the matter. As she spoke she felt Cecilia's hand press hers more closely. The poor girl knew that, at least for her, the world had neither marriage nor pleasure to give ; and that she was leaving the only place where she could find love—shelter from scornful pity.

But, unconscious of the pain they were giving, May and Violet continued the conversation ; and over the lingering waste of yellow, all that remained to tell where the sun had set, the night fell like a heavy, blinding dust, sadly, and regretfully, as the last handful of earth thrown upon a young girl's grave.

CHAPTER II.

On the following day the Irish girls, under the guidance of Mr. Barton and Mrs. Scully, started for Ireland. The journey was considered fatiguing, but on arriving in Dublin, they stopped at the "Shelbourne," where they were going to spend a few days, the girls having dresses to buy.

The first evening passed awkwardly, constrainedly; but on the second, all were on speaking terms. Mrs. Scully looked askance at the curious medley of people, and tried to withdraw her daughter from the society of the fireplace; but Mr. Barton, who had spoken of his pictures to everybody in the room, declared that it was here they should stay when they came to Dublin for the Castle season in February.

There was, however, little time for either considering or concluding. A letter had arrived from Mrs. Barton, saying that the girls were to attend at Mrs. Symond's, the celebrated dressmaker. As a favour, this lady had agreed to provide everything they would want. They were not even consulted regarding the shade of the ribbon that trimmed the front of their dresses: all had been arranged for them. Among other things, they were each supplied with a dozen pairs of different coloured thread stockings; but for Olive, there were six pairs in silk, and all prettily embroidered.

A still more marked distinction was observable in the dresses given to the two girls. Olive had a beautiful cherry-coloured dinner-dress; the skirt was in tulle, the bodice in stamped silk, trimmed with tulle; and from the waist, *en cascade*, fell rippling showers of tulle. The dressmaker seemed to recognise an inequality between the two sisters, and when she was trying on Olive a cream-coloured dinner-dress, trimmed with pale yellow satin, she explained volubly why it had been chosen; why the colour would set off the beautiful flaxen hair. An assistant showed Alice a black silk, trimmed with *passementerie*, relieved with a few bits of red ribbon, and a ball-dress in white corded silk. But it was not until Olive put on a dark green cashmere (a coquettish cape with a bow placed on the left shoulder), and Alice a terra-cotta serge, buttoned down the front, that the mother's partiality became too glaringly apparent. Then Olive and Alice might have passed for mistress and maid.

Alice was too sharp, too intelligent, not to estimate at its full value the injustice that had been done to her. But she argued in favour of the partiality shown to her sister, "it would be a pity not to make the most of Olive's good looks. Was she not the family beauty?" As they travelled down in the train they met many young men, who stared, and were anxious to be introduced to Olive. She laughed foolishly, but from her sweet lips silly remarks seemed to fall like pearls of wit, and Alice was surprised to find that in society her sister could talk better than she.

On arriving at their destination, they first went to Dungory Castle, where they left Lady Cecilia; they then drove to "Brookfield," which was a mile distant. The air was heavy with heat, and the leaves of the beeches that leaned over the high walls flecked with light shadows the dust-whitened roadway; and as the Dungory domain was passed by streaks of open country became visible. These were barren, rocky, and low-lying, and the cabins of the peasants came out in crude white spots upon the purple mountains.

In the tiny cornfields the reapers rose from their work to watch. The carriage was swiftly borne along. Mr. Barton commented on the disturbed state of the country. Olive asked if Mr. Parnell was good-looking. A railway-bridge was passed, and a pine-wood aglow with the sunset, and the footman got down to open a swinging iron gate.

This was Brookfield. Sheep grazed on the lawn, at the end of which, on a hill, beneath some chestnut-trees, was the house. It had been built by the late Mr. Barton, out of a farm-building, but the present man, after travelling in Italy,

inspired by a sentiment of the picturesque, had added a
verandah ; and for the same reason he had insisted on calling
his daughter Olive.

The rooms, except the bedrooms, were on the groundfloor,
and, to maintain a southern character, glass doors opened on
what was generally a mass of soaking gravel. But now, on
this burning August day, Brookfield was looking its best, and
wore its most Italian air. Every breeze was redolent with the
pungent odour of hay, the laburnums were folded in flowery
mantles of yellow, and in the fragrant shadows of the
chestnut trees, Mrs. Barton was seen waving her white hands
at some little compliment that Lord Dungory had just paid
her.

" Oh ! there's mamma ! " cried Olive.

Mrs. Barton received her girls with many protestations of
affection. She trifled with, as if anxious to set straight, their
newly-bought *foulards*, inquired in brief phrases after their
health, their delight at returning home, and the fatigues of
the journey.

" But you must be starving, my dears, and I am afraid the
saffron buns are cold. Milord brought us over such a large
packet to-day ; we must have some heated up, they won't be
a minute."

" Oh ! mamma, I assure you I am not in the least hungry,"
cried Olive.

" *La beauté n'a jamais faim, elle se nourrit d'elle même,*"
replied Lord Dungory, in his most youthful and most gallant
manner.

A thrush was pouring forth his soul into the ear of the
evening, but his song was less melting than Mrs. Barton's
laugh.

" You see, you find Milord the same as ever ; *toujours
galant ;* always thinking of *la beauté, et les femmes.*"

In looking at Mrs. Barton, you wondered if she were forty.
Her hair was touched with dye sufficiently to give it a golden
tinge in places where it might be suspected of turning grey ;
it was parted in the middle, and was worn, drawn back over
the ears, and slightly puffed on each side, in accordance with
a fashion that came in with the Empress Eugénie.

Her face was more than oval—it was heart-shaped. The
eyes, long brown almond eyes, attracted attention at once,
as would those of a beauty of the last century, sketched by

Romney in pastel. Mrs. Barton resembled the celebrated portrait of Lady Hamilton.

Time had, however, affected her figure more than her face. It was thin, a little bent, and even in youth it had probably resembled Alice's rather than Olive's, which was obviously a heritage that had come to her from her father.

But Mrs. Barton's figure was singularly in keeping with her moral character; both were elegant, refined, supple. When she walked, no movement of her limbs was ever visible; she glided when she crossed a room; she seemed by preference to avoid the middle of the floor, and to pass as close to the wall as possible. She, therefore, suggested the idea of one who had worked her way through life by means of numberless bye-paths, all lying a little to the left of the main road along which the torrent of men and women poured, and who had been known to them only at intervals as she passed furtively down the end of a vista, or hurriedly crossed an unexpected glade.

The bent shoulders hinted at a capacity for stooping under awkward branches and passing through difficult places. There was about Mrs. Barton's whole person an air of falseness, as indescribable as it was bewitching.

The waves of her white hands, with which she accompanied all her pretty speeches, seduced, if they did not deceive you. Her artificiality was her charm.

Never had she been known to weary an acquaintance or a friend with accounts of her troubles, her pains, her hopes; and when you entered her presence, your own disappointments evaporated in the fumes of the incense she burned in your honour.

The compliments she paid were often wanting in *finesse*; but when accused of this by a wit her defence was profoundly philosophical: "What does it matter? Nineteen people out of twenty believe them, and even the twentieth, who does not, is pleased to hear that he is very nice, and clever, and that all women are in love with him.' And similar wise sayings were often scattered through Mrs Barton's conversation, for she knew well, although her chatter was always *en omelette soufflée*, a little seasoning thought would not come amiss, even to the lightest appetite.

Her views of life were practical ones, and, had she ever had affections or illusions, she had found pleasure in them only as

long as it had suited her aims and interests to do so. Conscience
with her seemed to be merged entirely in the idea of expediency.

On suitable occasions she would say, sighing, letting the
white hand fall negligently over the arm of the chair : " But
what are we here for, if it is not to try to get a good place in
the next world ? Our great aim should be to live respectably
without coming to grief in any conspicuous way, and does not
religion help us to do this ? Religion is all that is respectable,
'tis you, 'tis me, it is the future of our children. Society
could not hold together a moment without religion."

Lord Dungory was the kind of man that is often seen with
the Mrs. Barton type of woman. He was sixty-seven, but he
did not look more than sixty. He was about the medium
height, and his portly figure was buttoned into a tightly-fitting
frock-coat; a shooting-jacket would have been too youthful.
A high silk hat in the country would have called attention to
his age, so the difficulty of costume was ingeniously compromised by a tall felt—a cross between a pot and a chimney-
pot.

For collars, a balance had been struck between the jaw
scrapers of old time and the nearest modern equivalent; and
in the tying of the large cravat there was a reminiscence, but
nothing more, of the past generation.

It is easy to read the marking on this shell. Lord Dungory was a concession, and he compromised now with time,
as he had compromised before in politics, in racing, in friendship. At different periods he had passed for a man of ability,
but, through powerlessness to stand by an idea, he had never
achieved anything very tangible.

In the course of conversation you gathered that he was on
terms of intimacy with the chiefs of the Liberal party, such
as Lord Granville and Lord Hartington, and if the listener
was credited with any erudition, allusion was made to the
most celebrated artists and authors, and to their works.
There was a celebrated Boucher in Dungory Castle, which
Milord, it was hinted, had bought for some very small sum,
many years ago on the Continent ; there was also a cabinet by
Buhl and a statue supposed to be a Jean Gougon. The story
and the proofs of their authenticity were sometimes spoken of
after a set dinner-party. Lord Dungory spoke with consider-
able urbanity, and, on all questions of taste, his opinion was
eagerly sought for. He gave a tone to the ideas put forward

in the surrounding country-houses, and it was through him that Mr. Barton held the title of "Genius gone wrong."

Milord found his artistic sympathies invaluable: they helped to maintain the amenities of his life at Brookfield. It is not an exaggeration to say that for the last ten years he had lived there.

Half an hour before lunch the carriage drove up to the door; in the afternoon he went out to drive, or sat in the drawing-room with Mrs. Barton; four times in the week he remained to dinner, and did not return home until close on midnight.

Whether he ever made any return to Mrs. Barton for her hospitalities, and if so, in what form he repaid his obligations to her, was, when friends drew together, a favourite topic of conversation in the county of Galway. It had been remarked that the Bartons never dined at Dungory Castle except on state occasions, and it was well-known that the Ladies Cullen hated Mrs. Barton with a hatred as venomous as the poison hid in the fangs of adders.

But Lord Dungory knew how to charm his tame snakes. For fortune they had but five thousand pounds each, and, although freedom and a London lodging were often dreamed of, the flesh-pots of Dungory Castle continued to be purchased at the price of smiles and civil words exchanged with Mrs. Barton. Besides, as they grew old and ugly, the Ladies Cullen had developed an inordinate passion for the conversion of souls. They had started a school of their own in opposition to the National school, which was under the direction of the priest. To obtain a supply of scholars, and to induce the peasants to eat fat bacon on Friday, were good works that could not be undertaken without funds; and these were obtained, it was said, by the visits of the Ladies Cullen to Brookfield. Mrs. Gould declared she could estimate to a fraction the prosperity of Protestantism in the parish by the bows these ladies exchanged with Mrs. Barton when their carriages crossed on the roads.

Now, with face slanted in the pose of the picture of Lady Hamilton, Mrs. Barton distributed her coquettish glances. Olive, looking like a tall, white doe, tossed her fair head. Mr. Barton squared his shoulders, pulled at his flowing beard, and growled as if he were keeping at bay the deep emotions that were supposed to be continually throbbing within him.

Alice sat plain and demure ; her quick, intelligent eyes alone revealed her personality. To a stranger the scene would have appeared a picture of perfect domestic virtue.

The evening was immeasurably calm. The large sloping woods of the Lawler domain fell into masses of deep violet colour ; pale shadows filled the soft meadows that lay between, and from miles away the rooks came flying through the sunset. Overhead the clapping of their wings was heard continuously.

" And now, my dear children, if you have finished your tea, come, and I will show you your room."

Then Milord drew his chair closer to Mr. Barton, and, with a certain parade of interest, asked him if he had been to the Academy :

" Did you see anything, Arthur, that in design approached your picture of ' Julius Cæsar overturning the Altars of the Druids ? ' "

" There were some beautiful bits of painting there," replied Arthur, whose modesty forbade him to answer the question directly. " I saw some lovely landscapes, and there were some babies' frocks," he added satirically ; " in one of these pictures, I saw a rattle painted to perfection."

" Ah, yes, yes, you don't like the pettiness of family-feeling dragged into Art," replied the courtier. Then he added, with a sigh : " But if you would only condescend to take a little more notice of the *technique ;* the *technique* is after all—"

" I am carried along too rapidly by my feelings. I feel that I must get on—that I must get my idea on canvas. But when I was in London I saw such a lovely woman—one of the most exquisite creatures possible to imagine. Oh ! so sweet, and so feminine ! I have it all in my head. I shall do something like her to-morrow."

Here he began to sketch with his stick on the grass, and from his face it might be judged he was satisfied with the invisible result. At last he said :

" You needn't say anything about it, but she sent me some songs, with accompaniments written for the guitar ; she said she was most anxious to hear me play the guitar. You shall hear some of the songs to-night."

At this moment a bell rang ; Arthur growled in imitation of a lion, which was his humorous way of declaring he was hungry, and both men got up and walked towards the house.

The two tall wax-candles had just been lighted, and, under their red shades, the silver sparkled, the fruit grew luscious as in the glow of a southern sun. A deep, rich twilight fell from the high-hanging red curtains, and half concealed the painted forms of the women that, in a sort of nightmare nakedness and confusion, were intermingled with the roaring jaws and the dying struggles of many lions and tigers. *The Bridal of Triermain* was one of Mr. Barton's favourite subjects.

Olive was radiant with delight. She had been placed next to Milord, and the compliments of the old courtier, although imperfectly understood from their being in French, at once fevered and bewildered her. The delicately-turned phrases, the stock-in-trade of an old roué, epigrams faded in the dust, and torn in the racket of fifty years of usage, were new to her, and, in the bright atmosphere of new ideas, she fluttered like a sun-smitten butterfly.

" *La femme est comme une ombre: si vous la suivez, elle vous fuit; si vous fuyez, elle vous poursuit*," tickled the champagne-excited imagination of the girl, and she laughed with hysterical delight. But Milord had aphorisms for married women, as well as for young girls, and he often leaned over the table to whisper to Mrs. Barton. Once Alice heard him say, " *L'amour est la conscience du plaisir donné et reçu, la certitude de donner et de recevoir.*"

A little frightened, she bent her eyes on her plate, and, later on, she strove to understand when, in speaking of Olive's youth, beauty, and innocence, Milord said : " *Gardez bien vos illusions, mon enfant, car les illusions sont le miroir de l'amour.*"

" *Ah ! mais il ne faut pas couvrir trop l'abîme avec des fleurs*," said Mrs. Barton, as a sailor from his point of vantage might cry " rocks ahead ! "

Arthur only joined occasionally in the conversation, he seemed rapt in dreams. He gazed long and ardently on his daughter, and then sketched with his thumb-nail on the cloth. When they arose from the table, Mrs. Barton said :

" Now, now, I am not going to allow you gentlemen to spend any more time over your wine ; this is our first evening together; come into the drawing-room with us, and we shall have some music."

Like most men of an unevenly-balanced mind, Arthur

loved an eccentric costume, and soon after he appeared in a
long-tasselled cap and a strangely-coloured smoking jacket;
he wore a pair of high-heeled brocaded slippers, and, twanging
a guitar, hummed to himself plaintively. Then when he
thought he had been sufficiently admired, he sang "A che la
morte," "Il Balen" and several other Italian airs, in which
frequent allusion was made to the inconstancy of woman's
and the truth of man's affection. At every pause in the music
these sentiments were laughingly contested by Mrs Barton.
She appealed to Milord. He never had had anything to
complain of; was it not well-known that the poor woman had
been only too true to him? Finally, it was arranged there
should be a little dancing.

As Mrs. Barton said, it was of great importance to know if
Olive knew the right step, and who could put her up to all
the latest fashions as well as Milord? The old gentleman
replied in French, and settled his waistcoat, fearing the garment was doing him an injustice.

"But who is to play?" asked the poetical-looking Arthur,
who, on the highest point of the sofa, hummed and tuned his
guitar after true troubadour fashion.

"Alice will play us a waltz," said Mrs. Barton, winningly.

"Oh, yes, Alice dear, play us a waltz," cried Olive.

"You know how stupid I am; I can't play a note
without my music, and it is all locked up in my trunk,
upstairs."

"It won't take you a minute to get it out," said Mrs.
Barton, and moving, as if she were on wheels, towards her
daughter, she whispered: "Do as I tell you, run upstairs
at once, and get your music; make yourself useful."

Now that she was grown up Alice had hoped to find consideration, if not sympathy. She looked questioningly at her
mother and hesitated. But Mrs. Barton had a way of
compelling obedience, and the girl went upstairs, to return
soon after with a roll of music. At the best of times she had
little love of the art, but now, sick with disappointment, and
weary from a long railway journey, to spell through the
rhythm of the "My Queen" waltz, and the jangle of "L'Esprit
Français," was to her an odious, and, when the object of it was
considered, an abominable duty to perform. She had to
keep her whole attention fixed on the page before her: but

when she raised her eyes, the picture she saw engraved itself
on her mind. It was a long time before she could forget
Olive's blond, cameo-like profile seen leaning over the old
beau's fat shoulder. Mrs. Barton laughed and laughed again,
declaring the while that it was *la grâce et la beauté réunies.*
Mr. Barton shouted and twanged in measure, the excitement gaining on him until he rushed at his wife, and,
seizing her round the waist, whirled her and whirled her,
holding his guitar above her head. At last they bumped
against Milord, and shot the old man and his fair burden on
to the nearest sofa. Then Alice thought that her mission at
the piano was over; she rose to go, but Mrs. Barton ordered
her to resume her seat, and the dancing was continued till the
carriage came up the gravel-sweep to fetch Milord away. This
was generally about half-past eleven, and, as he muffled
himself up in overcoats, the girls were told to cram his
pockets with cigarettes and bonbons.

"Bedad, I think it is revolvers and policemen you ought
to be givin' me, not swatemates," he said, affecting a
brogue.

"Oh, yes, is it not dreadful?" exclaimed Mrs. Barton; "I
don't know what we shall do if the Government don't put
down the Land League; we shall all be shot in our beds,
some night. Did you hear of that murder the other
day?"

"And it is said there will be no rents collected this year,"
said Mr. Barton, as he tightened one of the strings of his
guitar.

"Oh! do cease that noise!" said Mrs. Barton: "And tell
me, Lord Dungory; will the Government refuse us soldiers,
and police, to put the people out?"

"If we go to the Castle, we shall want more money to buy
dresses," said Olive.

"*La mer a toujours son écume pour habiller ses déesses,*"
replied Milord, and he got into his carriage, amid pearly
peals of laughter from Mrs. Barton, intermingled with a few
high notes from Olive, who had already taken to mimicking
her mother.

While candles were being lighted, further remarks concerning the rights of property were made. Then parents and
children bid each other good night, and a few moments after
the girls found themselves alone in their room. Giving way to

a sudden burst of emotion, Olive threw herself into her sister's arms :

" Oh ! Alice, how glad I am to be at home again ! and is it not delightful to think that we shall never have to return to that horrid convent, to those cross nuns, with their lecturing and their lessons ? But what is the matter, dear ? How cross you look ! I never will say anything to you again. When I do, you always snub me. I can't help being glad I am not going back to St. Leonards. I don't want to spend my life learning lessons, if you do."

" I am not cross, Olive, and I don't see any harm in your being glad at being at home. I am a little tired, that's all, and my head aches."

" Tired, are you ? I am not a bit—I could go to a ball now—ta ra, ta ra, ta re ra, ta ra ra ra, ta re ra," she sang, as she waltzed round the room.

" Do you know that I think I look better in my stays than any other way ? and I am glad of it, for I want to look well in a ball-dress. It must be a funny sensation to walk into a room half-undressed, before a lot of men ; for, you know, we shall be just as .undressed in our ball-dresses as we are now. I am quite anxious to see how we shall all look. May's arms are too fat, and Violet's are too thin ; I think mine are about the best. I heard Lord Dungory saying something to mamma about ' décolletée,' but I could not quite make out what he said. He always talks half in French, which is very tiresome. I wish I knew the language like you. But what a nice man Lord Dungory is, and how he seems to admire mamma, and how complimentary he is to ladies ! I suppose all nice men are. But I do wish I had understood what he said about seeing me ' décolletée.' "

" Oh, Olive ! " exclaimed Alice, " you should not talk in that way ; it is not nice, and it must be very wrong."

" Why, I don't think I said anything really wrong, did I ? I am sure I didn't mean to. I am going to say my prayers now ; and you, Alice, you haven't said your prayers, and that is far more sinful, I am sure. I should never be able to go to sleep, if I didn't say my prayers."

Alice lay very still. Her eyes were closed, but, in the darkness, the events and the ideas of the day blazed with a star-like intensity. It seemed to her that she was looking on a picture traced in lines of flame on a black background : every angle, every perspective was lucent and precise, but there was no blending of tints, there was no delightful distance. All was so clear and so complete, that the whole was inexplicable. The girl remembered everything, and she understood nothing.

She remembered seeing, as they drove up the avenue, the tea-table set beneath the ample chestnut-tree, and her mother's hands waving as she talked to the stately old gentleman; again she saw her mother taking them upstairs, to show them their room, and the kind words she had used in explaining everything now splashed into the girl's mind, as stones drop in a well.

But the dinner-table laughs and artificial compliments, what did they mean? and the dancing after dinner? Her thoughts clamoured with a sense of insult. She had not been home for years; everything appeared so strange. Who was this Lord Dungory? Why was he always at their house? And her dislike for her mother's admirer grew momentarily more explicit in her mind.

Had he not a house, a great big castle! What did he want in their poor place? "Has he not children of his own?" the girl wailed; "then why does he not care for them? Dear little Cecilia, he scarcely asked after her, but seemed quite satisfied when told she was all right, and he had thanked papa for the trouble he had in looking after her. Poor dear papa!" and as she thought of her father, Alice's thoughts grew kinder, and she shut out the vision that arose; she would not see him dressed in his gaudy smoking-jacket, twanging his guitar, or bumping Lord Dungory and her sister all in a heap on the sofa, or chasing the embroidered slippers which had been sent skimming into different corners of the room. She preferred to imagine him as a great artist, painting noble pictures in his studio, and, fearing to mar her ideal, she refused to analyse the merits of those she had seen, but thought of them simply as beautiful conceptions. She saw him a blond-bearded dreamer, his head filled with pictorial fancies; and his wife, a pearly, laughing, world-loving woman, her mind never wandering further than the attainment of some social advantage. Then the figure of Lord Dungory again loomed in sight. Suspicion, dark, formless, and fragmentary, forced sleep from Alice's eyes, and a ray from the setting moon illumined the chamber. Raising herself in bed, she allowed her weary eyes to wander.

The room was a symbol of girlhood. By skilful arrangement, Mrs. Barton had created the idea of the playful purity
and the daisy-like candour which we so willingly assume as
representative of the mind of sweet seventeen. Innocence,
piety, and gaiety went, it would appear, trippingly hand-in-
hand. Just under the ceiling, some ten feet apart, there were
two bright brass crowns, and from them fell, in meek folds,
the white curtains.

Above each pillow, entwined with a rosary, there was a font
for holywater. The room was papered with a clear paper,
covered with light blue spots, relieved with a border in darker
blue, representing a sash. The two little hanging bookcases
were filled with suitable volumes; half-a-dozen novels by
writers acknowledged to understand the ways and usages of
good society, a history, a few elegantly-bound books that
looked like school-prizes, and a prayer-book or two. The
wardrobes were in white-painted wood. Alice's was next the
door, Olive's was at the opposite end of the room, facing the
beds. There was but one toilet-table, but it was prettily
adorned with flowing skirts, and furnished with tall wax-
candles. It stood under the window next the marble wash-
stand, with its double sets of basins, jugs and glasses. There
were but two pictures. " Le Printemps " was represented by
a laughing youth and a maiden, swinging amid budding trees
and blossoming flowers. The other showed a loving girl, carving her sweetheart's name on the grandest oak in her father's
domain.

Alice looked anxiously at her sister. The dark masses of
hair lying on the pillows were touched with gold. In a
beautiful abandonment of attitude the girl slept; delicate
shadows veiled her face, and from her lips, fresh as fruit,
seemed to rise the breath of a beautiful dream. The cover-
tures floated away in folds, that were melodies; not a line was
defined. Less human she was than a Titian, less precise than
a Raphael; she was, perhaps, like a figure set by Phidias in
a dream of eternal youth, or the nebulous birth of an angel,
unfolding its loveliness beneath the suscitating smiles of a
god. Olive had now all the beauty of inanimate Nature,
and, unconscious of all things, save the sense of living that a
rose may feel in the dew-time, she slept.

But in the beauty of perfect proportions no soul exists;
the soul asserts itself in certain bodily imperfections of form,

which, when understood, become irresistible charms. Let us
look at the elder sister.

A thin girl, pale from want of rest; her pointed shoulders
and long arms were not beautiful like Olive's, and she had
no thick tresses to scatter over the pillow; her brown hair
was rolled, and pinned with one hairpin into a small knot.
The forehead swept above the marked eyebrows in a wide,
clear path; the hands, although well-shaped, were sinewy and
strong. She had not a feature that was either regular or
attractive; but her face was one of interest to the critical
observer; for now, when the quick, uncertain thoughts swept
across her mind, the eyes, like a grey lake in a sudden sun,
were flooded with bright attractiveness, and the formless
features gained, through expression, a precision not their
own.

Both sisters had returned to a home they had not seen for
years, both were going to enter a world of which they knew
nothing : unanxious, one slept, her brain tranquil as the lines
of her own beautiful body; the other sat wakeful, watching the
greying space of window, all her corporal imperfections
illustrative of the keen, the yearning, the inquiring, the
doubting mind, that burned within. And now as the white
room grew whiter in the dawn, with the same thoughts still
grinding, still burning in her head—thoughts of her mother, of
Lord Dungory, of her father—amid the hoarse voices of shrill-
ing cocks, and the metallic voices of chirping birds, the tired
girl fell asleep.

CHAPTER III.

MR. BARTON, or Arthur, as he was usually called, always retired to his studio immediately after breakfast, and, as Mrs. Barton had domestic duties to attend to, the girls were left to themselves.

Alice was glad to be with her sister. The dark forebodings of the night were forgotten in the gaiety of the morning sunshine, and her thoughts were now but floating remembrances of home. For there are moments when intervening years render the past lucent, and she pictured the dead life of childhood as one looking through morning mists on a fair prospect—hills and hill-villages full of outline and colour—may picture the hopes and joys that are unfolding themselves there. The sweet girl by her side was her sister—the sister she had known since babyhood, and as they descended the stairs with their summer hats and sunshades, Alice stopped at the door of the schoolroom. It was here that, only a few years ago, she had interceded with the dear old governess, and aided Olive to master the difficulties against which the light brain could not contend singly—the hardships of striving to recall the number of continents the world possesses, the impossibility of learning to say definitely if seven times four made twenty-eight or thirty.

The map of the world still hung on the wall, but the furniture had been removed, and to turn over the dusty books and glance at the dog's-eared pages that they would never again be called upon to study, left a blankness in the heart.

This room was placed at the further end of a long passage where the children used to play for hours, building strange houses out of boxes of bricks, or dressing dolls in fantastic costumes. Olive had forgotten, but Alice remembered, and her thoughts wandered lovingly through the land of toys. The box of bricks had come from an aunt that was now dead;

the big doll, mother had brought from Dublin when she went to see the oculist about her eyes; and then there were other toys, that suggested nothing, and whose history was entirely forgotten. But the clock that stood in the passage was well remembered, and Alice thought how this old-fashioned time-piece used to be the regulator and confidant of all their joys and hopes. She saw herself again listening, amid her sums, for the welcome voice that would call her away; she saw herself again examining its grave face and striving to calculate, with childish eagerness, if she would have time to build another Tower of Babel or put another tack in the doll's frock before the ruthless iron tongue struck the fatal hour.

"Oh, Olive! how can you pass here without waiting a moment to look at the dear old clock? Do you not remember how we used to listen to it when we were children?"

"You are a funny girl, Alice, you remember everything. Fancy thinking of that old clock! I hate it, for it brought me in to lessons when it struck eleven."

"Yes, but it brought you out to play when it struck twelve. See! the hands are just on the hour; let us wait to hear it strike."

"Oh! come on, come on, I want to get out in the garden. I can't waste the whole day waiting for an old clock to strike. Besides, if it were going we should hear it ticking. How silly you are!"

The girls listened vainly for a sound; and Alice felt as if she had been apprised of the loss of a tried friend when one of the servants told them the clock had been broken some years ago.

The kitchen-windows looked on a street made by a line of buildings parallel with the house. These were the stables and outhouses, and they formed one of the walls of the garden that lay behind. It was sheltered on the north side by a thin curtain of beeches, filled every evening with roosting rooks. Then, coming round to the front of the house, were the chestnut-trees, the verandah and the rosary, where a little fountain played when visitors were present; and further back, taking in the chestnut-trees, a wooden paling defended the pleasure-ground from the cows that grazed in the generous expanse of grass extending up to the trees of the Lawler domain.

Brookfield was, therefore, a small place, but, manifolded in

dreams past and present, it extended indefinitely before Alice's
eyes, and, absorbed by the sad sweetness of retrospection, she
played lovingly with the golden tassels of the laburnum-tree,
or lingered over the weed-grown sun-dial, while Olive ran
through the rosary from the stables and back again, calling to
her sister, making the sunlight ring with her light laughter.
Alice was disappointed to find that Olive could feel nothing of
what she felt, and she reminded her vainly that it was here
they used to play with Nell, the old setter, and that it was
there they gave bread to the blind beggar. And when they
met the coachman in the yard, it was of the old brown mare
she inquired, with which they used to go for such delightful
drives, not of the sleek carriage horses that had lately been
bought to take them to balls and tennis parties.

Suddenly Mrs. Barton's voice was heard calling. Milord
had arrived, and they were to go into the garden and pick a
few flowers to make a buttonhole for him. Olive darted
off at once to execute the commission, and soon returned with
a rose set round with some sprays of stephanotis. The old
lord was seated in the dining-room, in an armchair which
Mrs. Barton had drawn up to the window so that he might
enjoy the air. She had placed a table by his side, and, with
many little cajoleries, was pouring him out a glass of sherry,
and complimenting him, with quite a flutter of words, on his
good looks and general appearance. He bowed ceremoniously,
smiled urbanely, and Alice, as she entered the room, heard
him say : " *Quand on aime on est toujours bien portant.*"

She stopped abruptly, and Mrs. Barton, who already
suspected her of secret criticism, whispered, as she glided
across the room :

"Now, you awkward girl, don't stand there looking foolish ;
go and talk to Milord and learn to make yourself agreeable."

The girl felt she was incapable of this, and it pained her to
listen to her sister's facile hilarity, and her mother's coaxing
observations.   Milord did not, however, neglect her ; he
made suitable remarks concerning her school successes, and
asked appropriate questions anent her little play of " King
Cophetua." But whatever interest the subject possessed was
found in the fact that Olive had taken the part of the Princess ;
and, rearranging the story a little, Mrs. Barton declared, with
a shower of little laughs, and many waves of the white hands,

that "my lady there had refused a king; a nice beginning, indeed, and a pleasant future for her chaperon."

The few books the house possessed lay on the drawing-room table, or were piled, in dusty confusion, in the bookcase in Mr. Barton's studio; and, thinking of them, Alice determined she would go and see her father. The thought brought a glow of warmth to the girl's chilling heart, and, full of expectation, she knocked at the door.

Instantly the loud baritone voice ceased singing " Il balen," and answered in a high falsetto, " Come in ! "

Under the window, a small rickety easel seemed to totter under the weight of an enormous canvas. Thereon was a blonde Titaness, who gathered to her bosom one of the doves the winged boy by her side had just shot in the green trees above her. Arthur was rushing backwards and forwards streaking crimson along the thighs of his lady, but, when he saw his daughter, he hurriedly turned the picture to the wall.

" Oh ! I beg your pardon, papa; I'm afraid I am interrupting you."

"Not at all—not at all, I assure you; come in. I will have a cigarette; there is nothing like reconsidering your work through the smoke of a cigarette. The most beautiful pictures I have ever seen I have seen in the smoke of a cigarette; nothing can beat those, particularly if you are lying back looking up at a dirty ceiling."

These remarks were not a little disconcerting to Alice, and for some moments she looked round the walls in silent wonder. There, each picture demonstrated how a something less or a something more would have made of a disordered intelligence a genius of the first class. War and women were the two poles of Arthur's mind. " Cain shielding his wife from wild beasts" had often been painted, numberless " Bridals of Triermain "; and, as for the " Rape of the Sabines," it seemed as if it could never be sufficiently accomplished. Opposite the door was a huge design representing Samson and Delilah; opposite the fireplace, " Julius Cæsar overturning the Altars of the Druids" occupied nearly the entire wall. Nymphs and tigers were scattered in between; canvases were also propped against almost every piece of furniture.

At last Alice's eyes were suddenly caught by a picture representing three women bathing. It was a very rough

sketch, but, before she had time to examine it, Arthur turned
it against the wall. Why he hid two pictures from her she
could not help wondering. It could not be for propriety's
sake for there were nudities on every side of her.

Then, lying upon the sofa, he explained how so-and-so had
told him, when he was a boy in London, that no one since
Michael Angelo had been able to design as he could; how he
had modelled a colossal statue of Lucifer before he was sixteen, how he had painted a picture of the battle of Arbela,
forty feet by twenty, before he was eighteen; but that was of
no use, the world nowadays only cared for execution, and he
could not wait until he had got the bit of ribbon in Delilah's
hair to look exactly like silk.

Alice listened. Her heart was as full of tenderness as
her eyes were of admiration, as she watched the blonde,
expressionless face—so like Olive's in its pseudo-Greek proportions. Nor did the similitude cease there; and it was
easy to see that, from the imaginative but constantly un-
hinging intelligence of the father, the next step downwards
was the weak, feather-brained daughter. In what secret
source, lost far back in the night of generations, was this
human river polluted? Will the pure waters of some tribu-
tary again make it clean, or will it grow more and more
tainted until finally lost in a shrieking sea of madness
whose tumult is heard in the far distance answering pro-
phetically the boasts of civilisation? These are the terrible
questions that an examination of the history of families
propounds, and to which the scientist can as yet make no
answer. Yet, how absolutely consequent are these laws of
heredity.

Mr. Barton's father had spent fifty years in his study,
imagining himself a Gibbon, and writing unpublishable
history and biography. The attics were full of his manuscripts. It was from him Alice had inherited her love of
books; her clear logical intelligence had come from her
mother—of her father's brain she had nothing, she was only
connected with him by those imaginative faculties that for
three generations had characterised the family.

And now, as she listened to her father babbling nonsense
about his artistic capabilities, her heart and her mind were
at variance. A want of knowledge of painting might blind
her to the defects of his pictures (there was in them all a

certain crude merit of design), but it was impossible to deceive herself into thinking his conversation more than a sort of mild folly. In turn he spoke of himself as a great hunter, a great painter, a great singer, and, fact curious to note, in what he said there were flashes of humour and intelligence. For, in common with hundreds of his countrymen, Arthur had a trick of never appearing to thoroughly believe in his follies, and he sometimes seemed purposely to laugh at himself, as if by so doing he might nip all hostile criticism in the bud. He was a little bewildering. Alice, nevertheless, spent a pleasant afternoon chatting of Rome and art, and she learned, before she went upstairs to dress for dinner, that he was better than her mother, who, under a coaxing manner, concealed a hard and even bitter disposition.

A week passed away. Mrs. Barton went out for long drives with Olive, and Alice lived alone and apparently forgotten. Then the dresses came down from Mrs. Symond's, and Lord Dungory announced that he was going to give a great dinner-party.

Arthur, who rarely dined out, handed the ladies into the carriage.

Mrs. Barton was beautifully dressed in black satin; jet ornaments were woven about her bosom and shoulders; a diamond star glittered in the golden-brown hair. Olive was lost in a mass of tulle, that fell like crimson foam about her. Alice wore a black silk trimmed with *passementerie* and red ribbons. It was a delicious evening, sweet with sunset and corn. Behind the Clare mountain the pale transitory colours of the hour faded, and the women, their bodies and their thoughts swayed together by the motion of the vehicle, listened to the irritating barking of the cottage-dog. Surlily a peasant, returning from his work, his frieze coat swung over one shoulder, stepped aside; a bare-legged woman, surrounded by her half-naked children, leaving the potato she was peeling in front of her door, gazed, like her husband, after the rolling vision of elegance that went by her, and her obtuse brain probably summed up the implacable decrees of Destiny in the phrase:

"Shure there misht be a gathering at the big house this evening."

"But tell me, mamma," said Olive after a long silence, "how much champagne ought I to drink at dinner? You know it is a long time since I have tasted it; indeed, I don't remember that I ever did taste it."

Mrs. Barton laughed softly:

"Well, dear, I don't think that two glasses could do you any harm; but I would not advise you to drink any more."

"And what shall I say to the man who takes me down to dinner? Shall I have to begin the conversation, or will he?"

"He will be sure to say something; you need not trouble yourself about that. I think we shall meet some nice men to-night. Captain Hibbert will be there; he is very handsome and well-connected. I hope he will take you down. Then there will be the Honourable Mr. Burke. He is a nice little man, but there's not much in him, and he hasn't a penny. His brother is Lord Kilcarney, a confirmed bachelor. Then there will be Mr. Adair; he is very well off. He has at least four thousand a year in the country; but it would seem that he does not care for women. He is very clever; he writes pamphlets. He used to sympathise with the Land League, but the outrages went against his conscience. You never know what he really does think. He admires Gladstone, and Gladstone says he can't do without him."

They had now passed the lodge-gates, and were driving through the park. Herds of fallow-deer moved away, but the broad bluff forms of the red-deer gazed steadfastly as lions from the crest of a hill. The house was not yet visible.

"Did you ever meet Lady Dungory, mamma?" asked Alice. "Is she dead?"

"No, dear, she is not dead, but it would be better perhaps if she were. She behaved very badly. Lord Dungory had to get separated from her. No one ever speaks of her now; mind, you are warned!"

At this moment the carriage stopped before a modern house, built between two massive Irish towers entirely covered with huge ivy. The plate-glass square windows and rose blinds were a strange anachronism.

"I am afraid we are a little late," said Mrs. Barton to the servant as he relieved them of their *sorties de bal.*

"Eight o'clock has just struck, ma'am."

"The two old things will make faces at us, I know," murmured Mrs. Barton as she ascended the steps.

On either side there were cases of stuffed birds, a fox lay

in wait for a pheasant on the right, an otter devoured a trout on the left. These attested the sporting tastes of a former generation; the white-marble statues of nymphs sleeping in the shadows of the different landings, and the Oriental draperies with which each cabinet was hung, suggested the dilettantism of the present owner.

Mrs. Barton walked on in front; the girls drew together like birds. They were amazed at the stateliness of the library; and they marvelled at the richness of the chandeliers and the curiously-assorted pictures. The company was assembled in a small room at the end of the suite.

Two tall, bony, high-nosed women advanced and shook hands menacingly with Mrs. Barton. They were dressed alike in beautiful gowns of gold-brown plush.

With a cutting stare, and a few cold conventional words, they welcomed Olive and Alice home to the country again. Lord Dungory whispered something to Mrs. Barton. Olive passed across the room, the black coats gave way, and, as a white rose in a blood-coloured glass, her shoulders rose out of the red tulle. Captain Hibbert twisted his brown-gold moustache, and, with the critical gaze of the connoisseur, examined the undulating lines of the arms, the delicate waist, and the sloping hips: her skirts seemed to fall before his looks.

Immediately after, the roaring of a gong was heard, and the form of the stately butler was seen approaching. Lord Dungory and Lady Jane exchanged looks; the former offered his arm to Mrs. Gould; the latter, her finger on her lips, in a movement expressive of profound meditation, said:

" Mr. Ryan, will you take down Mrs. Barton; Mr. Scully, will you take Miss Olive Barton; Mr. Adair, will you take Miss Gould; Mr. Lynch, will you take Miss Alice Barton; Mr. Burke, will you take my sister ? " Then, smiling at the thought that she had checkmated her father, who had ordered that Olive Barton should go down with Captain Hibbert, she took Captain Hibbert's arm, and followed the dinner-party. About the marble statues and stuffed birds on the staircase, flowed a murmur of amiability, and, during a pause, skirts were settled amid the chairs, which the powdered footmen drew back ceremoniously to make way for the guests to pass.

A copy of Murillo's Madonna presenting the Divine Child to St. Joseph hung over the fireplace; between the windows

another Madonna stood on a half-moon, and when Lord
Dungory said, "For what we are going to receive, the Lord
make us truly thankful," these pictures helped the company
to realise a suitable although momentary emotion.

Turtle-soup was handed round. The soft steaming fragrance mixed with the fresh perfume of the roses that bloomed
in a silver vase beneath the light of the red-shaded wax-
candles; a tree covered with azaleas spread notes of delicate
colour over the gold screen that hid the door by which the
servants came and went.

"Oh! Lady Sarah," exclaimed Mrs. Gould, "I do not
know how you have such beautiful flowers—and in this
wretched climate!"

"Yes, it is very trying, but then we have a great deal of
glass."

"Which do you prefer, roses or azaleas?" asked Mrs.
Barton.

"*Les roses sont les fleurs en corsage, mais les azalées sont les
fleurs en peignoir.*"

Lady Sarah and Lady Jane, who had both overheard the
remark, levelled indignant glances at their father, scornful
looks at Mrs. Barton, and, to avoid further amatory allusions,
Lady Sarah said:

"I do not think we shall soon have bread, much less
flowers, to place on our tables, if the Government do not step in
and put down the revolution that is going on in this country."

Everyone, except the young girls, looked questioningly at
each other, and the mutuality of their interests on this point
became at once apparent.

"Ah! Lord Dungory, do you think we shall be able to
collect our rents this year? What reduction do you intend
to give?"

Lord Dungory, who had no intention of showing his hand,
said:

"The Land League has, I believe, advised the people to
pay no more than Griffith's valuation; I do not know if your
lands are let very much above it?"

"If you have not seen the *Evening Mail* you have probably
not heard of the last terrible outrage," said Captain Hibbert;
and, amid a profound silence, he continued: "I do not know
if anybody here is acquainted with a Mr. Macnamara; he
ives in Meath."

"Oh! you don't say anything has happened to him? I knew his cousin," exclaimed Mrs. Gould.

Captain Hibbert looked round with his bland, good-looking stare, and, as no nearer relative appeared to be present, he resumed his story:

"He was, it seems, sitting smoking after dinner, when suddenly two shots were fired through the windows."

At this moment a champagne-cork slipped through the butler's fingers and went off with a bang.

"Oh! goodness me! what's that?" exclaimed Mrs. Gould, and, to pass off their own fears, everyone was glad to laugh at the old lady. It was not until Captain Hibbert told that Mr. Macnamara had been so severely wounded that his life was despaired of, that the chewing faces became grave again.

"And I hear that Macnamara had the foinest harses in Mathe," said Mr. Ryan; "I very nearly sold him one last year at the harse show."

Mr. Ryan was the laughing-stock of the country, and a list of the grotesque sayings he was supposed, on different occasions, to have been guilty of, was constantly in progress of development. He lived with his cousin, Mr. Lynch, and, in conjunction, they farmed large tracts of land. Mr. Ryan was short and thick; a sort of mixture between a herd and a huntsman. Mr. Lynch was taller and larger, and a pair of mutton-chop whiskers made his bloated face look bigger still. On either side of the white tablecloth their dirty hands fumbled at their shirt-studs that constantly threatened to fall through the worn buttonholes. They were, nevertheless, received everywhere, and Pathre, as Mr. Ryan was called by his friends, was permitted the licences that are usually granted to the buffoon. All eyes were now turned on him.

"Arrah!" he said, "I wouldn't moind the lague being hard on them who lives out of the counthry, spendin' their cash on liquor and theatres in London, but what can they have agin us who stops at home, mindin' our properties and riding our harses?"

This criticism of justice, as administered by the league, did not, however, seem to meet with the entire approval of those present. Mr. Adair looked grave; he evidently thought it was based on a superficial notion of political economy. Mr. Burke, a very young man with tiny red moustache and a curious habit of wriggling his long weak neck, feeling his

amusements were being unfairly attacked, broke the silence he
had till then preserved, and said :

" I haven't an acre of land in the world, but if my brother
chooses to live in London, I don't see why he should be
deprived of his rents.   For my part, I like the Gaiety Theatre,
and so does my brother.   Have you seen the ' Forty Thieves,'
Lady Jane?   Capital piece—I saw it twenty times."

" I think what Pathre, me cousin, means to say," said Mr.
Lynch, declining the venison the servant offered him, " is that
there are many in the country who don't deserve much consideration.   I am alluding to those who acquired their
property in the land courts, and the Cromwellians, and the—
I mean the rack-renters."

The sudden remembrance that Lord Dungory dated from the
time of James so upset Mr. Lynch, that he called back the servant and accepted the venison, which he failed, however, to eat.

" I do not see," said Lord Dungory, with the air of a man
whose words are conclusive, " why we should go back to the
time of Cromwell to discuss the rights of property, rather than
to that of the early Kings of Ireland.   If there be a returning,
why not at once put in a claim on the part of the Irish Elk ?
No ! there must be some finality in human affairs."   And on
this phrase the conversation came to a pause.

But if the opinions of those present were not in accord
concerning the rights of property, their tastes in what might
be considered agreeable conversation certainly differed as
widely.   The heavy jaws and flabby cheeks of age and middle-
age grew hopelessly dejected, and their vision of poverty had
become so intolerably distinct that they saw not the name of
the entrée on the menu, and the côtelettes à la réforme were
turned to porridge in their mouths.   Olive's white face
twitched from time to time with nervous annoyance.   Alice
looked up in a sort of mild despair as she strove to answer the
questions Mr. Lynch plied her with, under his whiskey-heated
breath.   May had fallen into a state of morose lassitude.   If
Mr. Adair would only leave her alone she would not so much
mind, but, whenever he gave up the hope of being able to
introduce his repudiation of Mr. Davitt's system for the
nationalisation of the land, he explained to her how successfully he had employed concrete in the construction of his
farm-buildings.   When this subject was exhausted, he fell
back upon his sawmill.

But the moment came when the girls' eyes met: it was like the meeting of friends in a wilderness ; and, more or less definitely according to their characters, their looks said : " Well, if this is society, we might as well have remained in our convent."

But at this moment Captain Hibbert looked so admiringly at Olive that she instantly forgot her disappointments; and, at the same time Mr. Scully succeeded in making May understand that he would infinitely prefer to be near her than Lady Sarah. In return for this expression of feeling the young lady determined to risk a remark across the table ; but she was cut short by Mrs. Gould, who pithily summed up the political situation in the words :

" The way I look at it is like this : Will the Government help us to get our rents, or will it not ? Mr. Forster's Act does not seem to be able to do that. There's May there who has been talking all the morning of Castle seasons, and London seasons, and I don't know what; really I don't see how it is to be done if the Land League—— "

" And Mr. Parnell's a gentleman, too. I wonder how he can ally himself with such blackguards," gently insinuated Mrs. Barton, who saw a husband lost in the politician.

" But the difficulty the Government find themselves in is that the Land League is apparently a legal organisation," said Lord Dungory in the midst of a profound silence.

" A society legal, that exists and holds its power through an organised system of outrage ! Mind you, as I have always said, the landlords have brought all their misfortunes upon themselves; they have often behaved disgracefully—but I would, nevertheless, put down the outrages; yes, I would put down the outrages, and at any cost."

" And what would yer do ? " asked Mr. Ryan. " De yer know that the herds are being coerced now ? we'd get on well enough were it not for that."

" In the beginning of this year Mr. Forster asked Parliament for special powers. How has he used those powers ? Without trial, five hundred people have been thrown into prison, and each fresh arrest is answered by a fresh outrage; and when the warrant is issued, and I suppose it will be issued sooner or later, for the arrest of Mr. Parnell, I should not be surprised to hear of a general strike being made against rent. The con- sequences of such an event will be terrific; but let these conse-

quences, I say, rest on Mr. Forster's head. I shall have no
word of pity for him. His government is a disgrace to
Liberalism, and I fear he has done much to prejudice our ideal
in the eyes of the world."

Lord Dungory and Lady Jane exchanged smiles ; and poor
crotchety Mr. Adair leaned forward his large, bald brow,
obscured by many obscure ideals, and sought for words.
After a pause he continued :

"But I was speaking of Flanders. From the time of
Charles the Fifth the most severe laws were enacted to put
down the outrages, but there was an undercurrent of
sympathy with the outragemonger which kept the system
alive until 1840. Then the Government took the matter in
hand, and treated outragemongering as what it is—an act
of war ; and quartered troops on the inhabitants and stamped
the disease out in a few years. Of course I could not, and
would not, advocate the employment of such drastic measures
in Ireland ; but I would put down the outrages with a firm
hand, and I would render them impossible in the future by
the creation of peasant-proprietors."

Then, amid the juicy odours of cut pineapple, and the
tepid flavours of Burgundy, Mr. Adair warmed to his subject,
and proceeded to explain that absolute property did not exist
in land in Ireland before 1600, and, illustrating his arguments
with quotations from Arthur Young, he spoke of the planta-
tion of Ulster, the leases of the eighteenth century, the Pro-
testants in the North, the employment of labour ; until, at last,
inebriated with theory, he asked the company what was the
end of government ?

This was too much, and, seeing the weary faces about him,
Lord Dungory determined to change the subject of conversation :

"The end of government ? " he said ; " I am afraid that
you would get many different answers to that question. Ask
these young ladies ; they will tell you, probably, that it is to
have *des beaux amants et des joyeuses amours,* and I am not sure
that they are not right."

Mrs. Barton's coaxing laugh was heard, and then reference
was made to the detachment of the Connaught Rangers
stationed at Galway, and the possibility of their giving a
dance was eagerly discussed. Mr. Ryan had a word to say
anent the hunting prospect, and, when May Gould declared

she was going to ride straight and not miss a meet, she completed the conquest of Mr. Scully, and encouraging glances were exchanged between them until Lady Sarah looked inquiringly round the table—then she pushed back her chair. All rose, and a moment after, through the twilight of the drawing-room, colour and nudity were scattered in picturesque confusion.

Every mind was occupied by one thought—how the pleasure of the dinner-party had been spoiled by that horrible Land League discussion. All wondered who had introduced the subject, and the blame was fixed upon Mr. Adair. Mrs. Gould, in her homely way, came to the point at once :

"People say he is so clever, but I am sure I can't see it. He has spent a fortune in building farmyards in concrete, and his sawmill, I hear, costs him twenty pounds a month dead loss, and he is always writing letters to the papers. I never can think much of a man who writes to the papers."

"A most superior man," said Lady Sarah, who, notwithstanding her thirty-five years, had not entirely given up hope. "He took honours at Trinity."

Then Mr. Burke and Lord Kilcarney were spoken of, and some new anecdotes were told of Mr. Ryan. The famous one —how he had asked a lady to show him her docket at the Galway ball, when she told him that she was engaged for all the dances, excited—as it never failed to do—a good deal of laughter. Mrs. Barton did not, however, join in the conversation ; she knew, if she did, that the Ladies Cullen would be as rude as the absence of Milord, and the fact that she was a guest in their house, would allow them to be. Mrs. Barton's mind was now occupied with one thought, and, leaning back in her chair, she yielded herself entirely to it. Although the dinner-party had been spoiled by Mr. Adair's uncontrollable desire to impart information, she had, nevertheless, noticed that Captain Hibbert had been very much struck with Olive's beauty. She was aware that her daughter was a beautiful girl, but whether men would want to marry her Mrs. Barton did not know. Captain Hibbert's conduct would help her to arrive at a decision. She certainly dreamed of a title for Olive. Lord Kilcarney was, alas ! not to be thought of. Ah ! if Mr. Burke were only Lord Kilcarney ! But he was not. However, Captain Hibbert would be a fairly good match. He was of excellent family, and had five hundred a year,

and in England;—but to snatch up the very first fish that
came by! There was no saying whom they would meet at
the Castle. Still, to encourage a flirtation could be no harm;
if they met anything better, it could be broken off; if they
did not, it would be a very nice match indeed. Besides,
there was no denying that Olive was a little too *naïve* in her
manner. Captain Hibbert's society would brush that off, and
Olive would go up to the Castle with the reputation of having
made a conquest.

Such were Mrs. Barton's thoughts as she sat, her hands
laid like china ornaments on her lap; her feet were tucked
under the black-pleated skirt, and she sometimes raised her
Greuze-like eyes and looked at her daughter.

The girls were grouped around a small table, on which
stood a feather-shaded lamp. In clear voices and clear
laughs they were talking of each other's dresses. May had
just stood up to show off her skirt. She was a superb
specimen of a fat girl; and in a glow of orange ribbons and
red hair she commanded admiration.

"And to think she is going to waste her time with that
dissipated young man, Mr. Scully!" thought Mrs. Barton.
Then Olive stood up: she was all rose, and when, laughing,
with a delicious movement of the arms she hitched back her
bustle, she lost her original air, and looked as might have
done the Fornarina when not sitting in immortality. It was
the battle of blonde tints: Olive, with primroses and corn;
May, with a cadmium yellow and red gold.

"And now, Alice, get up and let's see you!" she cried,
catching hold of her sister's arm.

Still resisting, Alice rose to her feet, and May, who was full
of good nature, made some judicious observations.

"And how different we all look from what we did at the
convent!—do you remember our white frocks?"

Alice's face lit up with a sudden remembrance, and she
said :

"But why, Lady Sarah, have we not seen Cecilia? I
have been thinking of her during dinner. I hope she is not
ill?"

"Oh! dear me, no; but poor Cecilia does not care to come
down when there is company."

"But can I not see her?"

"Oh, certainly; you will find her in her room. But you

do not know the way; I will ring for my maid, she will show you."

At this moment men's voices were heard on the staircase. The ladies all looked up; the light defining the corner of a forehead, the outline of a nose and chin, bathing a neck in warm shadow, modelling a shoulder with grey tints, sending a thousand rays flashing through the diamonds on the bosom, touching the finger-rings, and lastly dying away amid the folds of the dresses that trailed on the soft carpet. Mr. Ryan, walking with his habitual roll, and his hands in his pockets, entered—his tie was under his left ear. Mr. Lynch, haunted by the idea that he had not made himself agreeable to Alice during dinner, sat down beside her. Mr. Scully made a rush for May. Tall, handsome Captain Hibbert, with his air of conventional high-style, quitted Lord Dungory, and asked Olive what they had been saying since they left the dining-room. Mr. Burke tried to join in the conversation, but Mr. Ryan, thinking it would be as well not to let the occasion slip of speaking of a certain "bay harse who'd jump anythin'," took him confidentially by the sleeve.

"Now, look here, will yer," he began. The rest of his remarks were lost in the hum of the conversation, and, by well-bred transitions, observations were made on the dancing and hunting prospects of the season. Mr. Adair took no interest in such subjects, and, to everyone's relief, he remained silent. May and Fred Scully had withdrawn to a corner of the room where they could talk more at their ease; Captain Hibbert was conscious of nothing but Olive and her laughter, which rippled and tinkled through an odour of coffee.

Little by little she was gaining the attention of the room. Mr. Adair ceased to listen to Lord Dungory, who was explaining why Leonardo da Vinci was a greater painter than Titian. Mr. Lynch left off talking to Alice; the little blonde honourable looked sillier and sillier as his admiration grew upon him. Mrs. Barton, to hide her emotion, engaged in an ardent discussion, concerning the rearing of calves, with Mrs. Gould. Lady Sarah bit her lip, and, unable to endure her enemy's triumph any longer, she said in her most mellifluous tone:

"Want you to sing us something, Captain Hibbert."

"Well, really, Lady Sarah, I should be very glad, but I don't think, you know—I am not sure I could manage without my music."

"I shall be very glad to accompany you. I think I know "In the Gloaming," and I have heard you sing that."

Olive, at a sign from her mother, entreated, and when the gallant Captain rolled from under the brown-gold moustache the phrase, "Oh! my darling," all strove not to look at her, and when he dropped his voice to a whisper, and sang of his aching heart, a feeling prevailed that all were guilty of an indiscretion in listening to such an intimate avowal. Then he sang two songs more, equally filled with references to tears, blighted love, and the possibility of meeting in other years, and Olive hung down her head, overcome by the fine sentiments which she felt were addressed to her.

Meanwhile, Alice had been left listening, alone and unnoticed. She was aware that her sister was the object of all eyes and thoughts; she was gaining the triumph that men are agreed may be ambitioned without impropriety by women. Alice was a healthy-bodied girl, every organ in her functioned admirably, and the blood flowed as warm in her as in her beautiful sister. Certainly the men about her did not in the least correspond with her ideal, but this scarcely rendered the fact that they neglected her less bitter. Presently she asked Lady Sarah if she might go upstairs and see Cecilia.

She found the little cripple leaning over the bannisters listening to the sound of voices.

"Oh, my dear! is it you? I expected you to come to see me when you left the gentlemen in the dining-room."

"I couldn't come before, dear," said Alice, kissing her friend. "Just as I was asking Lady Sarah the way to your room we heard them coming."

"And how did you like the party? and which of the men did you think the nicest?"

"I did not care for any of them; and oh! that odious Mr. Lynch!"

Cecilia's eyes flashed with a momentary gleam of satisfaction. "Yes, aren't they horrid? and the way they leer at women, isn't it beastly?" Alice did not answer, and, without a transitional phrase, Cecilia spoke of a little excursion—a walk to the Brennans, who lived two miles distant—that she had been planning for the last few days.

In about twenty minutes Mrs. Barton was heard calling to Alice, and Lord Dungory, with a profusion of gracious words and compliments, put them into the carriage. Then, in the close intimacy of the brougham, of upheaved petticoats and skirts, conversation began :

"Oh, mamma! did you see how cross little Mr. Burke looked because he could not get near me? and tell me, do you think I looked well in my pink tulle? Captain Hibbert said something about my belying my name; that I ought to be called Rose or Lily. I really didn't know what he meant. I think Rose a hateful name. And what did you think of May—she looked very well in that black-net with yellow ribbons, did she not? And I think she likes Mr. Scully. He often looked up at me, but she wouldn't let him get away. Do you think he admired me?"

Then, after a pause, the thin arms and bosoms of the Ladies Cullen were ridiculed, the relative dirt of Messrs. Ryan and Lynch disputed, the tiresomeness of Mr. Adair alluded to, until the conversation returned again to the success that Olive had achieved, and the certainty that her dress became her to perfection.

Around them the barren country lay submerged in shadows; the ridge of the uplands melted into the drifting grey of the sky, and every moment the hearth-fire of a cabin started into or disappeared from sight. They burned, steadfast and solitary, in the dim wastes that stretched from hill to hill, or were seen in clusters between the dark blowing foliage of the roadside poplars; and as the carriage passed, on a doorway full of yellow light, the form of a man was often sketched in menacing black.

CHAPTER IV.

During the next three or four days, the girls' life at Brookfield settled down into certain grooves.

Now Alice knew that about half-past one o'clock she would hear the wheels of Lord Dungory's carriage roll up to the hall-doors. Mrs. Barton would be dressed to receive him ; the glass of sherry, the little table, the coaxing laughs, and the compliments would be all prepared and served out with automatic precision. Sometimes, however, they were interrupted by Captain Hibbert, who came riding over from Gort. Then Mrs. Barton would propose a walk in the shrubberies, and with surprising ease the old and the young couple fell in, and sympathised with each other's habits. From her window Alice often saw them, and in fancy heard the crisp, courtly compliments of the portly, but tightly buttoned-up old lord, and the drawled-out platitudes of the tall and handsome captain.

And to these arrangements Mr. Barton paid no heed whatever. Immediately after breakfast he retired to his studio. When he was in painting-humour, the baritone voice roared in imitation of a lion ; when he was in a musical mood, it shouted forth some old Italian air to the tinkling of the guitar. And the great room, with its strange pictures, its smell of tobacco, its litter of books and old newspapers—in a word, its air of candour, of idea—had for Alice, weary of the rest of the house, an indescribable fascination. Dearly she would have liked to have sat and talked, as he painted the story of the man-eater ; but it distressed her to listen to the languid nonsense he spoke of his genius, and she noticed that, being now engaged on many nudities, her presence embarrassed him. It was, therefore, essential for her to discover how the hours might best be filled, and in which of the things within her reach she was most interested.

Mrs. Barton had decided that the young ladies were to have a maid to themselves;—a maid who, in a certain sense, would be a companion, and who could rearrange, and, if necessary, copy a dress from the original model. Barnes was not what would be imagined; she was a large woman of forty, but she concealed her age under a light, smiling manner. Generally she was to be found sewing in the room that had once been the nursery, but which had lately been refurnished, and converted into a kind of plain sitting-room—a workroom, where the young ladies were supposed to read, embroider, and write their letters. Once, Captain Hibbert, with many reprimands for his indiscretion, was brought up to see this feminine nook.

Barnes received him with smiles of recognition; smiles that said: Oh! of you, sir, I have heard much from my young ladies—Miss Olive in particular.

These insidious agreeabilities soon won the younger sister's heart; and when not in the drawing-room with *him*, as he was now called, mistress and maid, the work-basket and the skirt of a dress between them, sat for hours whispering together. If Alice came into the room, the conversation came to a full stop, or lapsed into a series of giggles, or sometimes plucking up courage, and as if anxious to rid the room of her sister's presence, Olive told how Barnes was going out next Sunday with her young man. Alice revolted against the odours of the kitchen, which these conferences exhaled, and she would steal away to walk about the grounds by herself, or in the fragrant shadows of the chestnut-trees, sit for hours absorbed in the lofty charms of Sir Walter Scott's novels. They suited her present mood, and, until the day came when she was to meet Cecilia, she stood on ramparts with Amy Robsart, and, riding on palfreys, experienced all the passion and despair of Leicester's great betrayal.

The girls had given each other rendezvous at the gate of Dungory Castle. Lover was never more anxious to meet mistress than this little deformed girl to see her friend; and Alice could see her walking hurriedly up and down the gravel-sweep in front of the massive grey-stone Lodge.

"She will see me next time she turns," thought Alice, and immediately after Cecilia uttered a joyful cry and ran forward.

"Oh! so it is you, Alice. I am so glad. I thought you were going to disappoint me."

"And why, dear, did you think I was going to disappoint you ? " said Alice, stooping to kiss the wan, wistful face.

" I don't know—I can't say, but I fancied something would happen," (and the great brown eyes began to melt with tears of delight) "I had, you know, set my heart on this walk with you."

This confession of love was delicious.

" I am sure the pleasure is as much mine as yours ; and now, whither lies our way ? "

" Through the deer-park, through the oakwood, across the fields into the highroad, and then you are at the gate."

" Won't that be too far for you ? "

" Oh, not at all; it is not more than a mile-and-a-half, but for you, you had to come another mile-and-a-half. It is fully that from here to Brookfield. But tell me, dear," said Cecilia, clinging to her friend's arm, " why have you not been over to see me before ? It is not kind of you ; we have been home from school now over a fortnight, and, except on the night of the dinner-party, I haven't seen you once."

" I was coming over to see you last week, dear, but, to tell you the truth, mamma prevented me. I cannot think why, but somehow she does not seem to care that I should go to Dungory Castle. But for the matter of that, why did you not come and see me ? I have been expecting you every day. Why haven't you been ? "

" I couldn't come either. My sisters advised me—I mean, insisted on my stopping at home."

" And why ? "

" I really can't say," replied Cecilia.

And now Alice knew the Ladies Cullen hated Mrs. Barton for her intimacy with Lord Dungory. Shrinking with shame, she longed to talk the matter out, but dared not; while Cecilia regretted she had spoken ; for, with the quickness of the deformed, she knew that Alice had divined the truth of the family feud. The silence was irritating, and then, with their parasols slanting to the west, they talked of indifferent things.

The sun fell like lead upon the short grass of the deer-park, and the frizzled heads of the hawthorns. On the right, the green masses of the oakwood shut in the view, and the stately red-deer, lolling their high necks, marched away through the hillocks, as if offended at their solitude being disturbed. One poor crippled hind walked with a wretched sidling movement, and Alice hoped Cecilia would not notice it, lest it should remind her of her own misfortune.

"I am sure," she said, "we never knew finer weather than this in England. I don't think there could be finer weather, and still they say the tenants are worse off than ever; that no rent at all, at least nothing above Griffith's valuation, will be paid."

"Do they speak much of Griffith's valuation at Dungory Castle?"

"Oh! they never cease, and—and—I don't know whether I ought to say, but it won't matter with you? I suppose—mind, you must not breathe a word of this at Brookfield—the fact is my sisters' school—you know they have a school, and go in for trying to convert the people—well, this has got papa into a great deal of trouble. The Bishop has sent down another priest—I think they call it a mission—and we are going to be preached against, and papa received a threatening letter this morning. He is going, I believe, to apply for police."

"And is this on account of the proselytising?"

"Oh! no, not entirely; he has refused to give his tenants Griffith's valuation; but it makes one very unpopular to be denounced by the priest. I assure you, papa is very angry. He told Sarah and Jane this morning at breakfast that he'd have no more of it; that they had no right to go into the poor people's houses and pull the children from under the beds, and ask why they were not at school; that he didn't care of what religion they were as long as they paid the rent; and that he wasn't going to have his life endangered for such nonsense. There was an awful row at home this morning. For my own part, I must say I sympathise with papa. Besides the school, Sarah has, you know, a shop, where she sells bacon, sugar, and tea at cost price, and it is well-known that those who send their children to the school will never be asked to pay their bills. She wanted me to come and help to weigh out the meal, Jane being confined to her room with a sick headache, but I got out of it. I would not, if I could, convert those poor people. You know, I often fancy—I mean fear—I often sympathise too much with your creed. It was only at service last Sunday I was thinking of it; our religion seems so cold, so cheerless compared to yours. You remember the convent-church at St. Leonards—the incense, the vestments, the white-veiled congregation—oh, how beautiful it was; we shall never be so happy again!"

"Yes, indeed; and how cross we used to think those dear nuns. You remember Sister Mary, how she used to lecture Violet for getting up to look out of the windows. What used she to say? 'Do you want, miss, to be taken for a housemaid or scullery-maid, staring at people in that way as they pass?'"

"Yes, yes; that's exactly how she used to speak," exclaimed Cecilia, laughing. And, as the girls advanced through the oakwood, they helped each other through the briers and over the trunks of fallen trees, talking, the while, of their past life, which now seemed to them but one long, sweet joy. A reference to how May Gould used to gallop the pony round and round the field at the back of the convent was interrupted by the terrifying sound of a cock-pheasant getting up from some bracken under their very feet; and, amid the scurrying of rabbits in couples and half-dozens, modest allusion was made to the girls who had been expelled in '75. Absorbed in the sweetness of the past, the girls mused, until they emerged from the shade of the woods into the glare and dust of the highroad. Then came a view of rocky country, with harvesters working in tiny fields, and then the great blue background of the Clare Mountains was suddenly unfolded. A line and a bunch of trees indicated the Brennan domain. The gate-lodge was in ruins, and the weed-grown avenue was covered with cowdung.

"Which of the girls do you like best?" said Alice, who wished to cease thinking of the poverty in which the spinsters lived.

"Emily, I think; she does not say much, but she is more sensible than the other two. Gladys wearies me with her absurd affectations; Zoe is well enough, but what names!"

"Yes, Emily has certainly the best of the names," Alice replied, laughing.

"Are the Miss Brennans at home?" said Cecilia, when the maid opened the hall-door.

"Yes, miss—I mean your ladyship—will you walk in?"

"You'll see, they'll keep us waiting a good half-hour while they put on their best frocks," said Cecilia, as she sat down in a faded armchair in the middle of the room. A piano was rolled close against the wall, the two rosewood cabinets were symmetrically placed on either side of the further window; from brass rods the thick, green curtains hung in stiff folds, and, since the hanging of some water-colours, done by Zoe before leaving school, no alterations, except the removal of the linen covers from the furniture when visitors were expected, had been made in the arrangement of the room.

The Brennan family consisted of three girls—Gladys, Zoe, and Emily. Thirty-three, thirty-one, and thirty were their respective ages. Their father and mother, dead some ten or a dozen years, had left them joint proprietors of a small property of seven hundred a year. Gossip had magnified this to three thousand, and they were, therefore, known as the heiresses of Kinavarah. All three were dumpty and dark, and in snub-noses and blue eyes their Celtic blood was easily recognisable. Every year they went to spend a month at the Shelborne Hotel in Dublin, and they returned with quite a little trousseau. Gladys and Zoe always dressed alike, from the bow round the neck to the bow on the little shoe that they so artlessly withdrew when in the presence of *gentlemen*. Gladys' formula for receiving visitors never varied :

" Oh, how do you do—it is really too kind of you to give yourself all this trouble to come and see us."

Immediately after Zoe put out her hand. Her manner was more jocose :

" How d'ye do? We are, I am sure, delighted to see you. will you have a cup of tea? I know you will."

Emily, being considered too shy and silent, did not often come down to receive company. On her devolved the entire management of the house and servants; the two elder sisters killed time in the way they thought would give least offence to their neighbours.

Being all St. Leonards girls, the conversation immediately turned on convent-life. "Was madame this there? Had madame that left?" Garden, chapel, school, hall, dormitory, refectory were visited; every nun was passed in review, and, in the lightness and gaiety of the memories invoked, even the wrinkling faces of the spinsters flushed and looked fresh again. Then, sighing, they recalled the hopes that had withered, and the conversation came to a pause.

Allusion was made to the disturbed state of the country, and to a gentleman who, it was reported, was going to be

married. But, as Alice did not know the person whose antecedents were being called into question, she took an early
opportunity of asking Gladys if she cared for riding? "No,
they never went to ride now: they used to, but they came in
so fatigued that they could not talk to Emily; so they had
given up riding." Did they care for driving? "Yes, pretty
well; but there was no place to drive to except into Gort,
and as people had been unjust enough to say that there were
always to be seen in Gort, they had given up driving; unless,
of course, they went to call on friends." Then tea was
brought in; and, apropos of a casual reference to conventual
buttered toast, the five girls talked, until nearly six o'clock,
of their girlhood—of things that would never have any
further influence in their lives, of happiness they would never
experience again. At last Alice and Cecilia pleaded that they
must be getting home.

As they walked across the fields, the girls only spoke
occasionally. Alice strove to see clear, but her thoughts
were clouded, scattered, diffused. Force herself as she would,
still no conclusion seemed possible; all was vague and con-
tradictory. She had talked to these Brennans, seen how
they lived, could guess what their past was, what their future
must be. In that neat little house, their uneventful life
dribbled away in maiden idleness; neither hope nor despair
broke the cruel triviality of their days—and yet, was it their
fault? No; for what could they do if no one would marry
them?—a woman could do nothing without a husband. There
is a reason for the existence of a pack-horse, but none for
that of an unmarried woman. She can achieve nothing—she
has no duty but, by blotting herself out, to shield herself from
the attacks of ever-slandering friends. Alice had looked
forward to a husband and a home as the certain accomplishment of years; now she saw that a woman, independently of
her own will, may remain single.

"I wonder," she said, forgetting for the moment she was
speaking to Cecilia, "I wonder none of those Brennans get
married; you can't call them ugly girls, and they have some
money. How dreadfully lonely they must be living there by
themselves!"

"I think they are far happier as they are," said Cecilia,
and her brown eyes set in liquid-blue looked strangely at
Alice as she helped her over the low wall. The girls walked

in silence through the tomb-like stillness of the silver-firs; and their thoughts were sharp as the needles that scratched the pale sky. Cecilia continued:

"It may seem odd of me to say so—of course I would not say this to anyone but you—but I assure you, even if I were as nice as you are, dear, nothing would induce me to marry. I never took the slightest pleasure in any man's conversation, and the idea—— Oh! it seems to me too revolting, and we make so little of ourselves. Now at home it never ceases. Jane asks papa if he has seen the So-and-sos, and immediately Sarah chimes in: 'Well, they have been going out a long time now, and they don't seem to be pulling off anything. I never believed in her flirtation with such a man; they did their very best to hook him, but it was no go, he slipped through their fingers,' etc. Don't you agree with me, Alice? But no, I know you don't," she said, breaking off suddenly—"I know you like men; I feel you do. Don't you?"

"Well, since you put it so plainly, I confess I should like to know nice men. I do not care for those I have met hitherto, particularly those I saw at dinner the other night; but I believe there are nice men in the world."

"Oh! no there aren't."

"Well, Cecilia, I don't see how you can speak so positively as that; you have seen as yet very little of the world."

"Ah! yes, but I know it; I can guess it all, I know it instinctively, and I hate it."

"There is nothing else, so we must make the best of it."

"But there is something else—there is God, and the love of beautiful things. I spent all day yesterday playing Bach's Passion music, and the hours passed like a dream until my sisters came in from walking and began to talk about marriage and men. It made me feel sick—it was horrible; and it is such things that make me hate life—and I do hate it; it is the way we are brought back to earth, and forced to realise how vile and degraded we are. Society seems to me no better than a pigsty; but in the beautiful convent—that we shall, alas! never see again—it was not so. There, at least, life was pure—yes, and beautiful. Do you not remember that beautiful white church with all its white pillars and statues, and the dark-robed nuns, and the white-veiled girls, their veils falling from their bent heads? They often seemed to me like angels. I am sure that Heaven must be very much like that—pure, desireless, contemplative."

Amazed, Alice looked at her friend; she had never heard her speak like this before. But Cecilia did not see her; the prominent eyes of the mystic were veiled with strange glamour, and, with divine *gourmandise*, she savoured the ineffable sweetness of the vision, and as the sensuality of her nature revolted against the warmth of a lover's kiss, it yielded to the cold aisle made lovely with the white body of God set in gold above the distant altar. After a long silence, she said :

"I often wonder, Alice, how you can think as you do ; and, strange to say, no one suspects that you are an unbeliever ; you are so good in all except that one point."

"But surely, dear, it is not a merit to believe ; it is hardly a thing that we can call into existence."

"You should pray for faith."

"I don't see how I can pray if I have not faith."

"Oh ! you argue too well for me. You are too clever ; but I would ask you, Alice—you never told me—did you never believe in God, I mean when you were a little child ? "

"I suppose I must have, but, as well as I can remember, it was only in a very half-hearted way ; much as I believed in hobgoblins. Belief never touched me. I could never quite bring myself to credit that there was a Being far away, sitting behind a cloud, who kept his eye on all the different worlds, and looked after them just as a stationmaster looks after the arrival and departure of trains from some huge terminus."

"Alice ! how can you talk so ? Are you not afraid that something awful might happen to you for talking of the Creator of all things in that way ? "

"Why should I be afraid, and why should that Being, if he exists, be angry with me for my sincerity ? If he is all-powerful, it rests with Himself to make me believe."

They had now accomplished the greater part of their journey, and, a little tired, had sat down to rest on a portion of a tree left by the woodcutters. Gold rays slanted through the glades, enveloping and rounding off the tall smooth trunks that rose branchless to a height of thirty, even forty, feet ; and the pink clouds, seen through the arching dome of green, were vague as the picture on some dim cathedral-roof.

"In places like these, I wonder you don't feel God's presence."

"On the contrary, the charm of nature is broken when you introduce a ruling official."

"Alice! how can you—you who are so good—speak in that way?" At that moment a dead leaf rustled through the silence—"And do you think that we shall die like that leaf? That, like it, we shall become a part of the earth and be forgotten as utterly?"

"I am afraid I do. That frail, fluttering thing was once a bud; it lived the summer-life of a leaf: now it will decay through the winter, and perhaps the next, until it finally becomes part of the earth. Everything in nature I see pursuing the same course; why should I imagine myself an exception to the general rule?"

"What, then, is the meaning of life?"

"Alas! we know nothing; we are perhaps no more than a lot of flies struggling in a water-jug. It is a very cruel creed. The sense of annihilation is a black, a heavy burden to bear, and no one will ever know what I have suffered. I am isolated from the rest of the world. At home I am like a stranger; I have not a thought in common with anyone."

"Alice, you must not cry. Am I not your friend? Yes, I am more than a friend; I cannot tell you how I love you; I do not know myself, and I often feel afraid of my love, so strange does it seem."

"Oh! yes, Cecilia, I know you love me, and I am thankful that I have such a friend; without you I should not be able to bear up."

And, their souls longing for storms, tears, relief, effusion, the girls threw their arms round each other's necks and wept.

This outburst of feeling had long been preparing; for days it had lain aching on their hearts. After their convent—where, in an atmosphere of general sympathy, flower-like their lives had grown—the girls had found the world cold and heartrending, and, in the severance of ties, nought but their friendship had remained. Alice had accepted it at first from pity, and then had abandoned herself, overcome by the power of an all-giving love. But they who can always accept, think little of the worth; and until now she had not even dreamed the meaning of it. A moment of effusion had revealed it. Words were unnecessary, and, intent on their happiness, absorbed in

the dolorous felicities of their sensations, the girls walked
onward in silence. Ideas evaporated like perfumes, and only
the short sharp cry of a bird broke the mild calm of the
woods.

"Now, Alice," said Cecilia, when they reached the turning
that made parting inevitable, and there was something of the
passion of the lover in her voice, "promise me you will come
and see me soon again. You will not leave me so long, you
will write; I shall not be able to live if I do not hear from
you."

At that moment the sound of horse-hoofs was heard, and
a pair of cream-coloured ponies, with a florid woman driving
determinedly, came sweeping round the corner.

"What a strange person!" said Alice, watching the blue
veil and the brightly-dyed hair.

"Don't you know who she is?" said Cecilia; "that is your
neighbour, Mrs. Lawler."

"Oh! is it really? I have been so long at school that I
know nobody—I have been anxious to see her. Why, I
wonder, do people speak of her so mysteriously?"

"You must surely have heard that she is not visited?"

"Well, yes; but I did not quite understand. Your
father was saying something the other day about Mr.
Lawler's shooting-parties; then mamma looked at him;
he laughed and spoke of 'les colombes de Cythère.' I
intended to ask mamma what he meant, but somehow I
forgot."

"She is one of those. . . they call them bad women; women
that men give money to and disgrace. In the towns they walk
about the streets by night."

"Oh! really!" said Alice; and the conversation came
to a sudden pause. They had never spoken upon such
a subject before, and the presence of the deformed girl
rendered it a doubly painful one. In her embarrassment,
Alice said:

"Then I wonder Mr. Lawler married her. Was it his
fault that——?"

"Oh! I don't think so," Cecilia replied, scornfully: "but
what does it matter?—she was quite good enough for him.
Men are always the worst."

Alice did not dare to pursue the conversation. At every
moment a new Cecilia was revealing herself, the existence of

whom Alice had not even suspected in the old. She knew
that she herself was altered, that the last few weeks had
taught her much, had strangely modified her ideas of life and
things, but this was nothing to the transformation she thought
she perceived in her friend. In reality Cecilia was the least
changed. In her case circumstances had developed nothing;
it had merely unveiled a state of soul that had existed for
years in its present condition; and Alice, as she hurried home,
wondered if the minds of the other girls were the same as they
were at school. She confessed she could see but little change
in her sister: May she had scarcely spoken to since they left
school, and Violet she had not met since they parted at
Athenry for their different homes. When she entered the
house she heard Olive talking:

"He said, mamma, that I would be the handsomest girl at
the drawing-room."

"And what did you say, dear?"

"I asked him how he knew; was that right?"

"Quite right, and what did he say then?"

"He said, because he had never seen anybody so handsome,
and as he had seen everybody in London, he supposed—I forget the exact words, but they were very nice, I am sure he
admired my new hat; but you—you haven't told me how you
liked it. Do you think I should wear it down on my eyes, or
a bit back?"

"I think it very becoming as it is; but tell me more about
Captain Hibbert."

"He told me he was coming to meet us at mass; you know
he is a Roman Catholic."

"I know he is, dear, and am very glad."

"If he weren't, he wouldn't be able to meet us at mass."

At this proof of the superiority of Catholic over other forms
of worship Mrs. Barton laughed, and, when Alice came downstairs, the Captain Hibbert discussion was being continued in
the studio. According to old-established custom, on the
arrival of his family, Arthur had turned his nudities to the
wall, and now sitting, one leg tucked under him, on the sofa,
throwing back from time to time his long blonde locks, he
hummed an Italian air.

"Why, Alice," said Mrs. Barton, "how tired you look, dear!
Will you have a cup of tea? it will freshen you up, you have
been walking yourself to death."

"Thanks, mamma, I will have a cup of tea; Cecilia and I went to see the Brennans."

"And are any of them going to be married yet?" said Olive.

"I really don't know; I didn't ask them."

"Well, they ought to be doing something with themselves; they have been trying it on long enough. They have been going up to the Shelbourne for the last ten years. Did they show you the dresses they brought down this season? They haven't worn them yet—they keep them wrapped up in silver paper."

Amazed, Alice looked at her sister; whence had come this flow of bitter gossiping?

"And how did you hear all that?" she asked.

"Oh! one hears everything: I don't live with my nose buried in a book like you. That was all very well in the convent."

"But what have I done that you should speak to me in that way?"

"Now, Alice dear," said Mrs. Barton, coaxingly, "don't get angry. I assure you Olive didn't mean it."

"No, indeed, I did not," exclaimed the corn-coloured girl, holding her sister by the arms and forcing her back into the chair.

Arthur's attention, however, had been too deeply absorbed in the serenade in "Don Pasquale," to give heed to the feminine bickering with which his studio was ringing, until he was startled suddenly from his musical dreaming by an angry exclamation from his wife.

The picture of the bathers, which Alice had seen begun, had been only partially turned to the wall, and Mrs. Barton had caught sight of one of the faces of the women. After examining it for a few moments, she got up, and, without a word, she seized the picture. Olive uttered a cry, and, looking terrified, Arthur broke off in the middle of a bar. The two naked creatures who were taking a dip in the quiet, sunlit pool were Olive and Mrs. Barton; and, so grotesque were the likenesses, that Alice could not refrain from laughing.

"This is monstrous! this is disgraceful, sir; how often have I forbidden you to paint my face on any of your shameless pictures?" exclaimed Mrs. Barton, purple with rage; "and your daughter too—and just as she is coming out! Do you want to ruin us? I should like to know what anyone would think if—" and, unable to complete her sentence, either mentally or aloud, Mrs. Barton wheeled the easel, on which the larger picture stood, into the full light of the window.

If Arthur had wounded the susceptibilities of his family before, he had outraged them now. The great woman, who had gathered to her bosom one of the doves her naked son, Cupid, had knocked out of the trees with his bow and arrow, was Olive. The white face and its high nose, beautiful as a head by Canova is beautiful; the corn-like tresses, piled on the top of the absurdly small head, were, beyond mistaking, Olive. Mrs. Barton stammered for words; Olive burst into tears.

"Oh! papa, how could you disgrace me in that way? Oh! I am disgraced! there's no use in my going to the drawing-room now."

"My dear, my dear, I assure you I can change it with a flick of the brush," said the blond delinquent; "admiration carried away by idea—I promise you I'll change it."

"Come away, Olive, come away," said Mrs. Barton, casting a look of burning indignation at her husband. "If you cry like that, Olive, you won't be fit to be looked at, and Captain Hibbert is coming here to-night."

When they had left the room, Arthur looked inquiringly at Alice.

"This is very disagreeable," he said; "I really didn't think the likeness was so marked as all that; I assure you I didn't. I must do something to alter it—I might change the colour of the hair; but no, I can't do that, the entire scheme of colour depends upon that. It is a great pity, for it is one of my best things; the features I might alter, and yet it is very hard to do so, without losing the character. I wonder if I were to make the nose straighter—Alice, dear, would you mind turning your head this way?"

"Oh! no, no, no, papa dear! you aren't going to put my face upon it;" and she ran smothered with laughter from the room.

When this little quarrel was over and done, when Arthur had altered, beyond recognition, the faces in his picture, and Olive had ceased to consider herself a disgraced girl, the allusion that had been made to Mass as a means of meeting

Captain Hibbert remained like a sting in Alice's memory. It surprised her at all sorts of odd moments, and often forced her, under many different impulses of mind, to reconsider the religious problem more passionately and intensely than she had ever done before. She asked herself if she had ever believed? Perhaps in very early youth, in a sort of vague, half-hearted way she had taken for granted the usual traditional ideas of heaven and hell, but even then, she remembered, she used to wonder how it was that time was found for everything else but God. If he existed it seemed to her that monks and nuns, or puritans of the sternest type, were alone in the right. And yet she couldn't quite feel that they were right. She had always been intensely conscious of the grotesque contrast between a creed like that of the Christian, and having dancing and French lessons, and going to garden-parties, yes, and making wreaths and decorations for churches at Christmas-time. If one only believed, and had but a shilling, surely the only logical way of spending it was to give it to the poor, or a missionary— and yet nobody seemed to think so. Priests and bishops did not do so, she herself did not want to do so ; still, so long as Alice believed, she was unable to get rid of the idea. Teachers might say what they pleased, but the creed they taught spoke for itself, and prescribed an impossible ideal, an unsatisfactory ideal which aspired to no more than saving oneself after all.

This represents the religious struggle that had filled Alice's mind from her twelfth to her sixteenth year. Then a few books read : Darwin on the origin of Species, a History of the French Revolution, Byron, Shelley's Satires on the absurdity of Revelation, the Immaculate Conception, and belief in God, an all-seeing, all-powerful, and Eternal Governor of the Universe, burst, like a wind-filled bladder under the point of a pin. How, then, with this rectitude of soul, had she consented to live so many years conforming outwardly to all the tenets of a religion which she recognised as an absurdity? The explanation of this seeming anomaly is found in the last line of the preceding paragraph : "An unsatisfactory ideal, which aspires to no more than saving oneself after all." In every nature there is a dominating force, which decides victory or defeat on all occasions. In Alice, this took the form of supreme unselfishness ; she could not—it was impossible for her to do or say anything—when, by so doing, she knew she might cause suffering, or give pain to anyone, even an enemy. And it was this defect in Alice Barton's character that forced her pitilessly, against any will of her own, to enact, to live up to what she deemed a lie. Often she had longed, and longed again, until she was sick with grief and longing, to tell the truth and be saved the mummery of attending at Mass, of bowing her head at the elevation of the Host. But when she realised the consternation, the agony of mind, it would cause the nuns she loved, she held back the word—cowardly, treacherously if you will; but it was this treachery—this imperfection, that linked her to and made her of the same nature as the four other heroines of this story. Cecilia alone had guessed the truth, and, at the first hint, Alice had told her all. The confession was a supreme relief; but, while unable to accept the counsel to ruthlessly break the oneness of their lives, she had hoped, she had looked forward to acting independently, and living an individual life at home. But at home, as in the convent, her resolution failed her. Her courage sank in the terrible and chilling tides of loneliness that surged about her; and the ever-present sense of mental separateness frightened her from all confidences. Since she had been at home, all her ideas and sensations had received violent contradiction; not one of the many practical rectitudes of which she had so fondly dreamed, had been found; and, therefore, in the brutal overthrow and wreck of so many illusions and hopes, her religious convictions and projects had been more than usually forgotten.

But they had again become the acute strain in this symphony of suffering; and now the weekly exhibition of best clothes, silk hats, carriages, gravity, collectedness, public proof of the world's unworldliness: proof that all, no matter what the facts said, did possess an ideal, horrified this straight-souled girl, until she felt the life she was leading as a leprosy upon her. Twenty times she had determined to speak to her mother, twenty times something had occurred to prevent her. Friday and Saturday went by, and, as the hour approached when they should go to Mass to meet Captain Hibbert, the desire to say that her going to chapel was but a mockery, and to beg to be allowed to stay away, grew almost irresist-ible. It was only a foolish fear that such a declaration might interfere with her sister's prospects that stayed the words as they rose to her lips; and at last, her gloves on

and prayer-book in hand, she found herself packed into the
brougham, watching the expressionless church-going faces of
her family. From afar the clanging of a high swinging bell
was heard, and the harsh reverberations travelling over the
rocky townlands summoned the cottagers to God. The stone
pillars of the chapel-gateway stared with bright yellow pro-
clamations. The tenant-farmers were called upon to assemble
by thousands and assert their rights. Landlordism and
land-grabbing must be put down. Messrs. I. M. Brady, M.P.,
Matthew Hagan, and P. Flanagan would address the meeting.

The roadway was filled with young peasants in frieze
coats and pot-hats; they stood in silent groups, or leaned
in lines along the low wall that marked the precincts of
the chapel. A look of quiet cunning overspread their faces,
and showed that they guessed the annoyance the Land
League proclamation would cause the gentry. Here and
there was seen an old man in a traditional tail-coat and
knee-breeches, walking apart, mumbling his toothless gums,
evidently as incapable of thinking as of dressing up to
the ideas of the present generation. And, mimicking
modesty, came the girls—thick, short, fit for work in the
fields; some with rosy cheeks, nice, with their shawls
folded about their shoulders, their hair drawn into a knot,
and tied with a ribbon at the back of their heads; others
like nothing at all, in cheap millinery bought in the county-
towns—shapeless hats with ostrich feathers of nameless hues
—formless mantles. There was no giggling; only the very
shyest glance to see if their boys were near. The bell continued
to clang, and the servants from the different gentlemen's estab-
lishments passed in; they were a class in themselves, and were
sleek, cringing, bashful under the public gaze.

"Now, Arthur—do you hear?—you mustn't look at those
horrid papers!" Mrs. Barton whispered to her husband; "we
must pretend not to see them. I wonder how Father
Shannon can allow such a thing, making the house of God
into—into I don't know what, for the purpose of preaching
robbery and murder. Just look at the country-people, how
sour and wicked they look—don't they, Alice?"

"Well, I don't know that they do, mamma," said Alice,
who had already begun to see something wrong in each big
house being surrounded by a hundred small ones, all working
to keep it in sloth and luxury.

"I don't know how it is, you always contradict me, and you seem to take pleasure in holding opinions that no one else does."

Then they entered a large whitewashed building. In the middle of the earthen floor there was a stone basin filled with water, into which each person dipped a hand, and therewith blessed themselves.

A plaster angel knelt at each side of the altar; the chancel-window was made out of extensive squares of yellow and green glass, which, coming against the raw glare of whitewash, had a hideous effect. On the left-hand side, next to the communion-rails, half-a-dozen *prie-Dieu* and cushions had been set; and this one trace of comfort and aristocracy had a pert and curious look in this very rural church.

"Goodness me!" said Olive, "who in the world can those people be in our pew?"

Mrs. Barton trembled a little. Had the peasants seized the religious possessions of their oppressors? Dismissing the suspicion, she examined the backs indicated by Olive.

"Why, my dear, it is the Goulds; what can have brought them all this way?"

"I don't know; but isn't it nice of them to come?" The expected boredom of the service was forgotten, and Olive shook hands warmly with Mrs. Gould and May.

"Why, you must have driven fifteen miles; where are your horses?"

"We took the liberty of sending the carriage on to Brook-field, and we are coming on to lunch with you; that is to say, if you will let us?" cried May.

"Of course, of course; but how nice of you!"

"Oh! we have such news; but it was courageous of us to come all this way. Have you seen those terrible procla-mations?"

"Indeed we have. Just fancy a priest allowing his chapel to be turned into a political—political what shall I call it?"

"Bear-garden," suggested May.

"And Father Shannon is going to take the chair at the meeting; he wouldn't get his dues if he didn't."

"Hush, hush! they may hear you; but you were saying something about news."

"Oh! don't ask me," said Mrs. Gould; "that's May's affair—such work!"

"Say quickly! what is it, May?"

"Look here, girls, I can't explain everything now; but we are going to give a ball; that is to say, all the young girls are going to subscribe. It will only cost us about three pounds apiece—that is to say, if we can get forty subscribers —we have got twenty already, and we hope you will join us. It is going to be called the spinsters' ball. But there is such a lot to be done; the supper to be got together, the decorations of the room (splendid room, the old schoolhouse, you know). We are going to ask you to let us take Alice away with us."

The conversation was here interrupted by the appearance of the priest, a large fat man, whose new, thick-soled boots creaked terribly as he ascended the steps of the altar. He was preceded by two boys dressed in white and black surplices. They rang little brass bells furiously, and immediately a great trampling of feet was heard. The peasants came, coughing and grunting with monotonous, animal-like voices; and the sour odour of cabin-smoked frieze arose, and was almost visible in the great beams of light that poured through the eastern windows; and whiffs of unclean leather, mingled with a smell of a sick child, flaccid as the prayer of the mother who grovelled, beating her breast, before the third Station of the Cross; and Olive and May, exchanging looks of disgust, drew forth cambric pocket-handkerchiefs, and in unison the perfumes of white rose and eau d'opoponax evaporated softly.

Alice watched the ceremony of Mass, and the falseness of it jarred upon her terribly. The mumbled Latin, the by-play with the wine and water, the mumming of the uplifted hands, were so appallingly trivial, and, worse still, all realisation of the idea seemed impossible to the mind of the congregation. Passing by, without scorn, the belief that the white wafer the priest held above his head, in this lonely Irish chapel, was the Creator of the twenty millions of suns in the Milky Way, she mused on the faith as exhibited by those who came to worship, and that which would have, which must have, inspired them, were Christianity now, as it once was, a burning, a vital force in the world. Looking round, what did she see? Here, at her elbow, were the gentry. How elegantly they prayed, with what refinement! Their social position was as manifest in their religion as in their homes, their language, their food. The delicate eyelids were closed from time to time; the long slim fingers held the gilt missals with the same well-bred grace as they would a fan; their thoughts would have passed from one to the other without embarrassment. Clearly they considered one the complement of the other. At the Elevation, the delicate necks were bowed, and, had lovers been whispering in their ears, greater modesty could not have been shown.

They had come to be in the absolute presence of God, the Distributor of Eternal rewards and punishments—and yet they had taken advantage of this stupendous mystery to meet for the purpose of arranging the details of the ball.

The peasantry filled the body of the church. They prayed coarsely, ignorantly, with the same brutality as they lived. Just behind Alice a man groaned. He cleared his throat with loud guffaws: she listened to hear the saliva fall: it splashed on the earthen floor. Further away a circle of dried and yellowing faces bespoke centuries of damp cabins, brutalising toil, occasional starvation. They moaned and sighed, a prey to the gross superstition of the moment. One man, bent double, beat a ragged shirt with a clenched fist; the women of forty, with cloaks drawn over their foreheads and trailing on the ground in long black folds, crouched until only the lean hard-worked hands that held the rosary were seen over the bench-rail. The young men stared arrogantly, wearied by the length of the service.

They, too, had come to be in the absolute presence of God— the Distributor of Eternal rewards and punishments—and yet they had taken advantage of the occasion of this stupendous mystery to meet for the purpose of arranging a land meeting.

Alice was troubled, as if by the obscure sensations of a nightmare. Surely, if their belief—gentry and peasants, she put them together—was not a mockery, a mere familiar usage, they could not be so indifferent as they were. If they did realise that the white wafer was God—God the Creator! before whom all things are nothing—something more full of meaning, more worthy than this little Sunday mummery would be the result. The early Christians, forgetting their food, had died in starving ecstasy in the desert! Then Alice felt, more calmly than she had ever done before, that what she was now witnessing was but the dust of an old-world faith, the sweeping away of which had only been delayed because a man is idle, and "loves to lie abed in the unclean straw of his intellectual habits."

Soon after came the sermon—to Alice an incomprehensible
jargon of ideas. The Ladies Cullen were denounced for
proselytising. Instances were given : they had pursued one
poor boy until he took refuge in an empty house, the door of
which he was fortunately enabled to fasten against them;
they had sent a sick woman blankets, in which they had not
neglected to enclose some tracts; tracts that declared that
reading the Bible—the Bible being admittedly the word of
God—must be the way to know Him. Amateur shopkeeping,
winter clothing, wood, turf, presents of meal, wine, and
potatoes were all vigorously attacked as the wiles of the Evil
One to lead the faithful from the true Church.

In the frieze-clad crowd, the tall, thin young man, in broad-
cloth, probably a Land League organiser, ground his teeth as
the priest spoke. Evidently he saw political capital in what
was being said, and was turning it over in his mind, thinking
how he could make use of it at the meeting. The gentry
bent their heads meekly, seeing only, in the denunciation of
proselytising, another stick being handed to the national party,
with which the landlords would be attacked.

At last it was all over. The peasants tramped away to the
meeting where they would lay claim to the land that they
tilled; the young ladies would soon return to their fine house
to consider the skirts they would wear at the ball; and the
house of God, the plea that had brought together so many
conflicting interests, would remain forlorn and forgotten for
another week. As they walked out of chapel catechism-classes
were being formed, and, looking into the future, Alice saw
from the new seed only a scantier harvesting than that she
had just witnessed, sprung from a similar semination, but in a
less-impoverished soil.

A circle of children was formed ; a big boy or girl stood in
the middle, and he or she put the questions.

" Who made the world ? "

" God made the world ! "

" Who is God ? "

" God is the Creator and Sovereign Lord of Heaven, and
earth, and all things."

" How many Gods are there ? "

" There is but one God, who will reward the just and
punish the wicked," etcetera, etcetera.

CHAPTER V.

As they returned from church, a horseman was seen riding rapidly towards them. It was Captain Hibbert. The movement of his shoulders, as he reined in his mettlesome bay, was picturesque. Never was a batch of ladies more favourably impressed by his beauty. Their glances were enveloping and absorbing; and he was coaxingly and gushingly upbraided for neglect of his religious duties.

During lunch, curiosity rendered May and Mrs. Gould nearly speechless; but their carriage had not turned into the highroad, on its way home, when the latter melted into a shower of laudatory words and phrases:

"What a charming man Captain Hibbert is! no wonder you young ladies like the military. He is so good-looking—and such good manners. Do you not think so, Alice dear?"

"I think the Captain a very handsome man—indeed, I believe that there are not two opinions on the subject."

"And Olive—I do not remember that I ever saw a more beautiful girl. Such hair! and her figure so sylph-like! I do not know what the young ladies will do—she will cut everybody out at the Castle!"

"I don't know about that," said May, jauntily; "what one man will turn his nose up at, another will go wild after."

Mrs. Gould did not answer; but her lips twitched, and Alice guessed she was annoyed that May could not express herself less emphatically. In a few moments the conversation was continued:

"At any rate, Captain Hibbert seems to think there is no one like Olive; and they would make a handsome couple. What do you think, Alice? Is there any chance of there being a match?"

"I really can't tell you, Mrs. Gould. Olive, as you say, is a very beautiful girl, and I suppose Captain Hibbert admires her; but I don't think that either has, up to the present, thought of the matter more seriously."

"You must admit, Alice, that he seems a bit gone on her," said May, with a direct determination to annoy her mother.

"May, dear, you should not talk in that slangy way; you never used to, you have picked it up from Mr. Scully. Do you know Mr. Scully, Alice? Violet's brother."

"Yes, I met him the night we dined at Lord Dungory's."

"Oh, of course you did. Well, I admit I do not like him; but May does. They go out training horses together. I don't mind that; but I wish she would not imitate his way of talking. He has been a very wild young man."

"Now, mother dear, I wish you would leave off abusing Fred. I have repeatedly told you that I don't like it."

The acerbity of this remark was softened by May's manner, and, throwing her arms on her mother's shoulders, she commenced to coax and cajole her.

The Goulds were of an excellent county family. They had for certainly three generations lived in comfortable idleness, watching from their big square house the different collections of hamlets toiling and moiling, and paying their rents every gale day. It was said that some ancestor, whose portrait still existed, had gone to India and come back with the money that had purchased the greater part of the property. But, be this as it may, in Galway three generations of landlordism are considered sufficient repentance for shopkeeping in Gort, not to speak of Calcutta. Since then the family history had been stainless. Father and son had in turn put their horses out to grass in April, had begun to train them again in August, had boasted at the Dublin horse-show of having been out cub-hunting, had ridden and drunk hard from the age of twenty to seventy. But, by dying at fifty-five, the late squire had deviated slightly from the regular line, and the son and heir being only twelve, a pause had come in the hereditary life of the Goulds. In the interim, however, May had apparently resolved to keep up the traditions so far as her sex was supposed to allow her.

They lived in one of those box-like mansions, so many of which were built in Ireland under the Georges. On either side trees had been planted, and they stretched to the right and left like the wings of a theatre. In front there was a green lawn, at the back a sloppy stableyard. The latter was May's especial delight, and when Mr. Scully was with them it seemed impossible to induce her to leave it. Frequently this young man rode over to Beechgrove, and towards the end of the afternoon it became easy to persuade him to stay to dinner. Then, as the night darkened and the rain began to fall, the inhospitality of turning him out was insisted on by May, and Mrs. Gould sent up word that a room was to be prepared for him. Next morning he sent home for a change of things, and thus it was not infrequent for him to protract his visit to the extent of three or four days.

His great friend, Mrs. Manly—a lady who had jumped five feet, four months before the birth of her sixth child— had said that his was a " wasted life," and the phrase, summing up what most people thought of him, gained currency, and was now generally used whenever his conduct was criticised or impeached. After having been in London, where he spent some years in certain vague employments, and having contracted as much debt as his creditors would permit, and more than his father would pay, he had gone through the Bankruptcy Court, and returned home to wearily drag through life, through days and weeks so appallingly idle, that he often feared to get out of bed in the morning. At first his father had tried to make use of him in his agency business, and it was principally owing to Mr. Fred's bullying and insolent manners that Mr. Scully was now unable to leave his house unless accompanied by police.

Fred was about thirty years of age. His legs were long, his hands were bony, and stableyard was written in capital letters on his face. He carried a *Sportsman* under his arm, a penny and a half-crown jingled in his pocket; and as he walked he lashed the trousers and boots, whose elegance was an echo of the old Regent Street days, with an ash-plant.

Such was the physiology of this being; from it the psychology is easy to surmise : a complete powerlessness to understand that there was anything in life worth seeking except pleasure—and pleasure to Fred meant horses, women, eating—beyond these three gratifications he neither thought, felt, nor saw. Of earthly honour the greatest was to be well-known in an English hunting-county, and he was not averse to speaking of certain ladies of title, with whom he had been on intimate terms, and with whom, it was said, he corresponded. On occasions he would read or recite poems, cut from the pages of the Society Journals, to his lady friends.

May, however, saw nothing but the outside. The already peeling-off varnish of a few years of London life satisfied her. Given a certain versatility in turning a complimentary phrase, the abundant ease with which he explained, not his ideas, for he had none, but his tastes, which, although few, were pronounced, add to these the remnant of fashion that still lingered in his wardrobe—scarfs from the Burlington Arcade, scent from Bond Street, cracked patent-leather shoes and mended silk stockings—and it will be understood how May built something that did duty for an ideal out of this broken-down swell.

She was a girl of violent blood, and, excited by the large air of the hunting-field, she followed Fred's lead fearlessly: to feel the life of the horse throbbing underneath her, passioned and fevered her flesh until her mental exaltation reached the rushing of delirium. Then his evening agreeabilities fascinated her, and, as he leaned back smoking in the dining-room arm-chair, his patent-leather shoes propped up against the mantel-piece, he showed her glimpses of a wider world than she knew of—and the girl's eyes softened as she listened to his accounts of the great life he had led, the county-houses he had visited, and the legendary runs he had held his own in. She sympathised with him when he explained how hardly fate had dealt with him in not giving him £5,000 a year, to be spent, not in this God-forsaken country, but in London and North-amptonshire. Both were sensualists, if you will. The girl was now ruled by her appetites because she was young, strong, and healthy; but there was a higher nature underneath, which might assert itself when the first years of passionate youth were done. With the man, however, it was different. He was a sensualist because his nature was idle, gross, vulgar, selfish. For him no redemption was possible. He would dissipate to the end, descending yearly in the social scale.

After breakfast, he began to chatter. He cursed Ireland as the most hideous hole under the sun; he frightened Mrs. Gould by reiterated assurances that the Land League would leave them all beggars; and, having established this point, he proceeded to develop his plan for buying young horses, training them, and disposing of them in the English market. Eventually he dismissed his audience by taking up the news-paper and falling asleep with the stump of a burned-out cigarette between his lips. Nothing more was heard of him for an hour; then he was seen slouching through the laurels on his way to the stables. From the kitchen and the larder—where the girls were immersed in calculations anent the number of hams, tongues, and sirloins of beef that would be required—he could be seen passing; and as May stood on no ceremony with Alice, whistling to her dogs, and sticking both hands into the pockets of her blue dress, she rushed after him, the mud of the yard oozing through the loose, broken boots which she insisted on wearing. Behind the stables there was a small field that had lately been converted into an exercise-ground, and there the two would stand for hours, watching a couple of goat-like colts, mounted by country lads—still in corduroy and hobnails—walking round and round.

Mrs. Gould was clearly troubled by this very plain conduct. Once or twice she allowed a word of regret to escape her, and Alice could see that she lived in awe of her daughter. And May, there was no doubt, was a little lawless when Fred was about her skirts; but when he was gone she returned to her old, glad, affectionate ways.

Then unease, suspicion, dread, vanished, and were replaced by confidence and all the amenities of country-life. The girls delighted in each other's society, and the arrangements for their ball were to them a continual occupation. The number of letters that had to be written was endless. Sitting at either end of the table in the drawing-room, their pens scratched and their tongues rattled together; and, penetrated with the intimacy of home, all kinds of stories were told, and the whole country was passed in review.

"And do you know," said May, raising her eyes from the letter she was writing, "when this affair was first started mamma was afraid to go in for it; she said we'd find it hard to hunt up fifty spinsters in Galway."

"I said fifty who would subscribe—a very different thing indeed."

Oh, no you didn't, mamma; you said there weren't fifty

spinsters in Galway—a jolly lucky thing it would be if there weren't; wouldn't it, Alice?"

Heedless of the conversation, Alice was busy trying to disentangle a difficult sentence. Her startled face made May laugh.

"It isn't cheering, is it?"

"I did not hear what you were saying," she answered, a little vexed at being misunderstood. "But fifty, surely, is a great number; are there so many unmarried women in Galway?"

"I should think there are," replied May, as if glorying in the fact. "Who are there down your side of the country? Let's count. To begin with, there are the Brennans—there are three of them, and all three are out of the running, distanced."

"Now, May, how can you talk like that?" said Mrs. Gould, and she pulled up her skirt so that she could roast her fat thick legs more comfortably before the fire. There being no man present, she undid a button or two of her dress.

"You said so yourself the other day, mother."

"No, I didn't, May, and I wish you wouldn't vex me. What I say I stand by, and I merely wondered why girls with good fortunes like the Brennans didn't get married."

"You said the fact was there was on one to marry."

"May, I will not allow you to contradict me!" exclaimed Mrs. Gould; and she grew purple to the roots of her white hair. "I said that the Brennans looked too high, that they wanted gentlemen, eldest sons of county families, if you please; that if they had been content to marry in their own position of life they would have been married long ago."

"Well, mother dear, there's no use being angry about it; let the thing pass. You know the Brennans, Alice; they are neighbours of yours."

"Yes, Cecilia and I walked over to see them the other day; we had tea with them."

"Their great hunting-ground is the Shelbourne Hotel—they take it in turns, a couple of them go up every six months."

"How can you say such things, May? I will not allow it."

"I say it! I know nothing about it. I have only just come back from school; it is you who tell me these things when we are sitting here alone of an evening."

Mrs. Gould's face again became purple, and vehemently she protested: " I shall leave the room, May. I will not stand it one moment longer. I can't think how it is you dare speak to me in that way; and, what is worse, attribute to me such ill-natured remarks."

" Now, mother dear, don't bother, perhaps I did exaggerate. I am very sorry. But, there's a dear, sit down and we won't say any more about it."

" You do annoy one so, May, and I believe you do it on purpose. You know exactly what will be disagreeable to say, and you say it," replied Mrs. Gould; and she raised her skirt so as to let the heat of the fire into her petticoats.

" Thank God that's over," May whispered to Alice; " but what were we talking about ? "

" I think you were making out a list of the Galway spinsters," said Alice, who could not help feeling a little amused, notwithstanding the gravity of the situation.

" So we were," cried May; " we were speaking of the Brennans. Do you know their friends the Duffys ? There are five of them. That's a nice little covey of love-birds; I don't think they would fly away if they saw a sportsman coming into the field."

" I never heard a girl talk like that," murmured Mrs. Gould, without raising her face from the fire, " that wasn't punished for it. Perhaps, my lady, you will find it hard enough to suit yourself. Wait until you have done two or three Castle seasons. We'll see how you'll speak then."

Without paying any attention to these maternal forebodings, May continued :

" Then there are Lord Rosshill's seven daughters; they are all maidens, and are likely to remain so."

" Are they all unmarried ? " asked Alice.

" Of course they are ! " exclaimed Mrs. Gould; " how could they be anything else ? Did they not want all to marry people in their father's position ? and that was not possible. There are seven Honourable Miss Gores, and one Lord Rosshill— so they all remained in single blessedness."

" Who's making ill-natured remarks now ? " exclaimed May triumphantly.

" I am not making ill-natured remarks; I am only saying what's true. My advice to young girls is that they should be glad to have those who will take them. If they can't make a good marriage let them make a bad marriage; for, believe me, it is far better to be minding your own children than your sister's or your brother's children. And I can assure you, in these days of competition, it is no easy matter to get settled."

"It is the same now as ever it was, and there are plenty of nice young men. It does not prove, because a whole lot of old sticks of things can't get married, that I shan't."

"I didn't say you wouldn't get married, May; I am sure that any man would be only too glad to have you; but what I say is that these grand matches that girls dream of are not possible nowadays. Nice young men! I daresay; there are lots of them, I know them; young scamps without a shilling, who amuse themselves with a girl until they are tired of her, and then, off they go. Now, then, let's count up the good matches that are going in the county——"

At this moment the servant was heard at the door bringing in the tea.

"Oh! bother!" exclaimed Mrs. Gould, settling her dress hurriedly. The interval was full of secret irritation; and passionately the three woman watched the methodical butler place the urn on the table, turn up the lamp that was burning low, and bring chairs forward from the furthest corners. It seemed to them that he would never leave the room.

"On your side of the county," said Mrs. Gould, as soon as the door was closed, "there is our brace of baronets, as they are called. But poor Sir Richard—I am afraid he is a bad case—and yet he never took to drink until he was five-and-thirty; and as for Sir Charles—of course there are great advantages, he has a very fine property; but still many girls might—and I can quite understand their not liking to marry him."

"Why, Mrs. Gould, what is wrong with him?" Alice asked, innocently.

"Don't you know?" said May, winking. "Haven't you heard? But I forgot, he isn't your side of the county. He's married already; at least, so they say."

"It is very sad, very sad, indeed," murmured Mrs. Gould, 'he'd have been a great match."

"And to whom is he married?" said Alice, whose curiosity was awakened by the air of mystery with which the baronet was surrounded.

"Well, he's not exactly married," replied May, laughing, "but he has a large family."

"May, I will not allow it; it is very wrong of you, indeed, to talk like that——"

"Now, mother dear, don't get into a passion; where's the harm? The whole country knows it; Violet was talking of it to me only the other day. There isn't a man within a mile of us, so we needn't be on our Ps and Qs."

Alice looked up surprised. Was a woman's modesty nothing more than a veil of ignorance which she drew down her face when a man appeared in sight? It had not struck her quite in this light before.

"And who is the mother of all these children?" she asked, determinedly.

"A country-woman with whom he lives," said May. "Just fancy marrying a man with a little dirty crowd of illegitimate children running about the stableyard!"

"The usual thing in such cases is to emigrate them," said Mrs. Gould, philosophically; and she again distended herself before the fire.

"Emigrate them!" cried May; "if he emigrated them to the moon, I wouldn't marry such a man; would you, Alice?"

"I certainly would not like to," replied the girl; and her sense of humour being now tickled by the conversation, she added slyly, "but you were counting up the good matches in the county."

"Ah! so we were," said the old lady; "well, there is Mr. Adair. I am sure no girl would wish for a better husband."

"Oh, the old frump! why he must be forty if he's a day. You remember, Alice, it was he who took me down to dinner at Lord Dungory's. He precious near killed me with his pamphlet on the Amalgamation of the Unions, which was then in the hands of the printer; and the other, in which he had pulled Mr. Parnell's ears, "Ireland under the Land League," and the series of letters he was thinking of contributing to the *Irish Times* on high-farming *versus* peasant-proprietors. I shall never forget him. Just fancy, Alice, living with such a man as that!"

"Well, I don't know what you girls think," said Mrs. Gould, whose opinions were moods of mind rather than convictions; "but I assure you he passes for being the cleverest man in the county; and it is said that Gladstone is only waiting to give him a chance. But, as you like; he won't do, so let him pass. Then there is Mr. Ryan, he ought to be well off; he farms thousands of acres."

"Oh! you might as well marry a herd at once. Did you ever hear what he once said to a lady at a ball; you know, about the docket?"

Alice said that she had heard the story, and the conversation turned on Mr. Lynch. Mrs. Gould admitted that he was the worse of the two.

"He smells so dreadfully of whiskey," said Alice, timidly.

"Ah! you see she is coming out of her shell at last," exclaimed May. "I saw you weren't having a very good time of it when he took you down to dinner at Dungory Castle. I wonder they were asked. Fred told me that he had never heard of their having been there before."

"It is very difficult to make up a number sometimes," suggested Mrs. Gould; "but they are certainly very coarse. I hear, when Mr. Ryan and Mr. Lynch go to fairs, that they sleep with their herdsman, and in Mayo there is a bachelor's house where they have fine times—whiskey-drinking and dancing until three o'clock in the morning."

"And where do the ladies come from, May?" asked Alice; for she now looked on the girl as an inexhaustible fund of information.

"Plenty of ladies in the village," replied Mrs. Gould, rubbing her shins complacently; "that's what I used to hear of in my day, and I believe the custom is not even yet quite extinct."

"And are there no other beaux in the county? Does that exhaust the list?"

"Oh! no; but there's something against them all. There are a few landlords who live away, and whom nobody knows anything of. Then there are some boys at school; but they are too young; there is Mr. Reed, the dispensary doctor. Mr. Burke has only two hundred a year; but if his brother were to die he would be the Marquis of Kilcarney. He'd be a great match then, in point of position; but I hear the estates are terribly encumbered."

"Has the present Marquis no children?" said Alice.

"He's not married," said Mrs. Gould; "he's a confirmed old bachelor. Just fancy, there's twenty years between the brothers. I remember, in old times, the present Marquis used to be the great beau at the Castle. Oh! wasn't he hunted! I don't believe there was a girl in Dublin who didn't have a try at him. Then who else is there? I suppose I daren't mention the name of Mr. Fred Scully or May will fly at me."

"No, mother dear, I won't fly at you; but what is the use of abusing Fred?—we have known him all our lives. If he has spent his money he has done no worse than a hundred other young men. I know I can't marry him, and I am not in love with him; but I must amuse myself with something. I can't sit here all day listening to you lamenting over the Land League; and, after a certain number of hours, conjecturing whether Mickey Moran will or will not pay his rent becomes monotonous."

"Now don't vex me, May; for I won't stand it," said Mrs. Gould, getting angry. "When you ask me for a new dress you don't think of what you are saying now. It was only the other day you were speaking to me of refurnishing this room. I should like to know how that's to be done if there was no one to look after Mickey Moran's rent?"

It was a large, dull room, where the emaciated forms of narrow, antique sofas were seen dimly in the musty-smelling twilight. Screens worked in hideous red and green wools stood in the vicinity of the fireplace, the walls were lined with dismal pictures in the style of Poussin, and the floor, hidden in dark shadow and sunken in places, conveyed an instant idea of damp and mildew.

"I think that something ought to be done," said May. "Just look at these limp curtains! Did you ever see anything so dreary? Are they brown, or red, or chocolate?"

"They satisfied your betters," said Mrs. Gould, as she lighted her bedroom-candle. "Goodness me!" she added, glancing at the gilt clock that stood on the high, stucco, white-painted chimney-piece, amid a profusion of jingling glass candelabra, "it is really half-past twelve o'clock!"

"Gracious me! there's another evening wasted; we must really try and be more industrious. It is too late to do anything further to-night," said May. "Come on, Alice, it is time to go to bed."

During the whole of the next week, until the very night of the ball, the girls hadn't a moment they could call their own. It was impossible to say how time went. There were so many things to think of—to remind each other of. Nobody knew what they had done last, or what they should do next.

The principle on which the ball had been arranged was this : the forty-five spinsters who had agreed to bear the expense, which it was guaranteed would not exceed £3 10s. apiece, were supplied each with five tickets to be distributed among their friends.   To save money, the supper had been provided by the Goulds and Manlys, and day after day the rich smells of roast-beef and the salt vapours of boiling hams trailed along the passages, and ascended through the bannisters of the staircases in Beech Grove and Manly Park.   Fifty chickens had been killed ; presents of woodcock and snipe were received from all sides ; salmon had arrived from Galway ; cases of champagne from Dublin.   As a wit said, " Circe has prepared a banquet and is calling us in."

After much hesitation, a grammar-school, built by an enterprising landlord for an inappreciative population that had declined to support it, was selected as the most suitable location for the festivities.   It lay about a mile from the town, and this was in itself an advantage.   To the decoration of the rooms May and Fred diligently applied themselves.   Off they went every morning, the carriage filled with yards of red cloth, branches of evergreen, oak and holly, flags and Chinese lanterns.   You see them : Fred mounted on a high ladder, May and the maid striving to hand him a long garland which is to be hung between the windows.   You see them leaning over the counter of a hardware-shop, explaining how oblong and semicircular pieces of tin are to be provided with places for candles (the illumination of the room had remained an unsolved problem until ingenious Fred had hit upon this plan) ; you see them running up the narrow staircases, losing themselves in the twisty passages, calling for the housekeeper ; you see them trying to decide which is the gentlemen's cloakroom, which the ladies', and wondering if they will be able to hire enough furniture in the town to arrange a sitting-room for the chaperons.

As May said, " We shall have them hanging about our heels the whole evening if we don't try to make them comfortable."

At last the evening of the ball arrived, and, as the clocks were striking eight, dressed and ready to start, Alice knocked at May's door.

" What ! dressed already ? " said May, as she leaned towards the glass, illuminated on either side with wax-candles, and looked into the whiteness of her bosom.   She wore a costume of Prussian-blue velvet and silk; the bodice (entirely of velvet) was pointed back and front, and a berthe of moresque lace softened the contrast between it and the cream tints of the skin. These and the flame-coloured hair were the spirits of the shadowy bedchamber; whereas Alice, in her white corded-silk, her clear candid eyes, was the truer Madonna whose ancient and inferior prototype stood on her bracket in a forgotten corner.

"Oh! how nice you look!" exclaimed May; "I don't think I ever saw anyone look so pure."

Alice smiled; and, interpreting the smile, May said:

"I am afraid you don't think so much of me."

"I am sure, May, you look very nice indeed, and just as you would like to look.'

To May's excitable mind it was not difficult to suggest a new train of thought, and she immediately proceeded to explain why she had chosen her present dress.

"I knew that you, and Olive, and Violet, and Lord knows how many others would be in white, and, as we shall all have to wear white at the drawing-room, I thought I would appear in this. But isn't the whole thing delightful? I am engaged already for several dances, and I have been practising the step all day with Fred." Then, singing to herself, she waltzed in front of the glass at the immediate risk of falling into the bath.

"Five-and-forty spinsters baked in a pie !
When the pie was opened the maids began to sing,
Wasn't that a dainty dish to set before the King?"

"Oh! dear, there's my garter coming down!" and, dropping on to the sofa, the girl hitched up the treacherous article of dress. "And tell me what you think of my legs," she said, advancing a pair of stately calves. "Violet says they are too large."

"They seem to me to be all right; but, May dear, you haven't got a petticoat on."

"You can't wear petticoats with these tight dresses; one can't move one's legs as it is."

"But don't you think you'll feel cold—catch cold?"

"Not a bit of it; no danger of cold when you have shammy-leather drawers."

Then, overcome by her exuberant feelings, May began to

sing : "Five-and-forty spinsters baked in a pie," etc. "Five-and-forty," she said, breaking off, "have subscribed. I wonder how many will be married by this time next year. You know, I shouldn't care to be married all at once; I'd want to see the world a bit first. Even if I liked a man, I shouldn't care to marry him now; time enough in about three years' time, when one is beginning to get tired of flirtations and parties. I have often wondered what it must be like. Just fancy waking up and seeing a man's face on the pillow, or for——"

"No, no, May; I will not; you must not. I will not listen to these improper conversations!"

"Now, don't get angry, there's a dear, nice girl; you are worse than Violet, 'pon my word you are; but we must be off. It is a good half-hour's drive, and we shall want to be there before nine. The people will begin to come in about that time."

Mrs. Gould was asleep in the drawing-room, and, as they awoke her, the sound of wheels was heard on the gravel outside. The three women followed each other into the carriage. Blotted out in a far corner, Mrs. Gould thought vaguely of asking May not to dance more than three times with Fred Scully, and May chattered to Alice or looked impatiently through the misted windows for the familiar signs; the shadow of a tree on the sky, or the obscure outline of a farm-building that would tell how near they were to their destination. Suddenly the carriage turned to the right, and entered a sort of crescent. There were hedges on both sides, through which vague forms were seen scrambling, but May humorously explained that as no very unpopular landlord was going to be present, it was not thought that an attempt would be made to blow up the building : and, conscious of the beautiful night which hung like a blue mysterious flower above them, they passed through a narrow doorway draped with red-striped canvas. May called upon her mother to admire the decorations and approve of the different arrangements.

The school-hall and refectory had been transformed into ball and supper rooms, and the narrow passages intervening were hung with red cloth and green garlands of oak and holly. On crossing threads Chinese lanterns were wafted luminously.

"What taste Fred has!" said May, pointing to the huge arrangement that covered the end wall. "And haven't my tin candelabra turned out a success? There will be no grease, and the room couldn't be better lighted."

"But look!" said Alice, "look at all those poor people staring in at the window. Isn't it dreadful that they, in the dark and cold, should be watching us dancing in our beautiful dresses, and in our warm bright room?"

"You don't want to ask them in, do you?"

"Of course not, but it seems very sinister; does it not seem so to you?"

"I don't know what you mean by its being sinister; but sinister or not sinister, it couldn't be helped; for if we had nailed up every window we should have simply died of heat."

"I hope you won't think of opening the windows too soon," said Mrs. Gould. "You must think of us poor chaperons, who will be sitting still all night."

Then, in the gaping silence, the three ladies listened to the melancholy harper, and the lachrymose fiddlers who, on the *estrade* in the far corner, sat tuning their instruments. At last the people began to come in. The first were a few stray black-coats, then feminine voices were heard in the passages, and necks and arms, green toilettes and white satin shoes, were seen passing and taking seats. Two Miss Duffys, the fattest of the four, were with their famous sister Bertha. Bertha was rarely seen in Galway; she lived with an aunt in Dublin, where her terrible tongue was dreaded by the *débutantes* at the Castle. Now, in a yellow dress as loud and as hard as her voice, she stood explaining that she had come down expressly for the ball. Opposite, the Honourable Miss Gores made a group of five; and a few men who preferred consideration to amusement made their way towards them. The Brennans—Gladys and Zoe—as soon as they saw Alice, asked after Lord Dungory; and all the girls were anxious to see Violet.

Hers was the charm of an infinite fragility. The bosom, whose curves were so faint that they were epicene, was set in a bodice of white *broché*, joining a skirt of white satin, with an overskirt of tulle, and the only touch of colour was a bunch of pink and white azaleas worn on the left-shoulder. And how irresistibly suggestive of an Indian carved ivory were the wee foot, the thin arm, the slender cheek!

"How sweet you look, Violet," said Alice, with frank admiration in her eyes.

"Thanks for saying so; 'tisn't often we girls pay each other compliments; but you, you do look ever so nice in that white silk. It becomes you perfectly."

In a few moments they were talking of the nuns they had so lately quitted. Violet had spoken also of the little play, "King Cophetua," and of her desire to act in theatricals; but she could not keep her attention fixed, and she said abruptly:

"Do you see Mr. Burke over there? If his brother died he would be a marquis. Do you know him?"

"Yes, I met him at dinner at Dungory Castle."

"Well, introduce him to me if you get a chance."

"I am afraid you will find him stupid."

"Oh! that doesn't matter; 'tis good form to be seen dancing with an Honourable. Do you know many men in the room?"

Alice admitted she knew no one, and, lapsing into silence, the girls scanned the ranks for possible partners. Poor Sir Richard, already very drunk, his necktie twisted under his right-ear, was vainly attempting to say something to those whom he knew, or fancied he knew. Sir Charles, forgetful of the family at home, was flirting with a young girl whose mother was probably formulating the details of a new emigration scheme. Dirty Mr. Ryan, his hands thrust deep into the pockets of his baggy trousers, whispered words of counsel to Mr. Lynch: a rumour had gone abroad that Captain Hibbert was going to hunt that season in Galway, and would want a couple of horses. Mr. Adair was making grotesque attempts to talk to a lady of dancing. On every side voices were heard speaking of the distances they had achieved: some had driven twenty, some thirty miles.

Already the first notes of the waltz had been shrieked out by the fiddle, and Mr. Fred Scully, with May's red tresses on his shoulder, was about to start, when Mrs. Barton and Olive entered. She was in white silk, so tightly drawn back that every line of her supple thighs, and every plumpness of the superb haunches was seen; and the double garland of geraniums that encircled the tulle veiling seemed like flowers of blood scattered on virgin snow. Her beauty imposed admiration; and, murmuring assent, the dancers involuntarily drew into lines, and this pale uncoloured loveliness, her high nose seen, and her silly laugh heard, by the side of her sharp brown-eyed mother, passed down the room. Lord Dungory and Lord Rosshill advanced to meet them; a moment after Captain Hibbert and Mr. Burke came up to ask for dances; a waltz was accorded to each. The triumph was complete. Such was the picture that a circling crowd of black-coats instantly absorbed; the violinist scraped, and the harper twanged intermittently; a band of foxhunters arrived; girls had been chosen, and in the small space of floor that remained the white skirts and red tail coats passed and repassed, borne along by the indomitable rhythm of Strauss.

An hour passed: perspiration had begun to loosen the work of the curling-tongs; dust had thickened the voices, but the joy of exercise was in every head and limb. A couple would rush off for a cup of tea, or an ice, and then, pale and breathless, return to the fray. Mrs. Manly was the gayest. Pushing her children out of her skirts, she called upon May:

"Now then, May, have you got a partner? We are going to have a real romp—we are going to have Kitchen Lancers. I'll undertake to see everybody through them."

A select few, by signs, winks, and natural instinct, were drawn towards this convivial circle; but, notwithstanding all her efforts to make herself understood, Mrs. Manly was sadly hampered by the presence of a tub-like old lady who, with a small boy, was seeking a *vis-à-vis*.

"My dear May, we can't have her here, we are going to romp, anyone can see that. Tell her we are going to dance Kitchen Lancers."

But the old lady could not be made to understand, and it was with difficulty that she was disentangled from the sixteen. At that moment the appearance of a waiter with a telegram caused the dancers to pause. Mr. Burke's name was whispered in front of the messenger; but he who, until that evening, had been Mr. Burke, was now the Marquis of Kilcarney. The smiling mouth drooped to an expression of fear as he tore open the envelope. One glance was enough; he looked about the room like one dazed; then, as his eyes fell upon the vague faces seen looking through the wet November pane, he muttered. "Oh! you brutes! you brutes! so you have shot my brother!"

Unchecked, the harper twanged and the fiddler scraped out the tune of their lancers. Few really knew what had

happened, and the newly-made marquis had to fight his way
through women who, in skin-tight dresses, danced with
wantoning movements of the hips, and threw themselves
into the arms of men to be, in true kitchen-fashion, whirled
round and round with prodigious violence.

Nevertheless, Lord Dungory and Lord Rosshill could not
conceal their annoyance ; both felt keenly that they had compromised themselves by remaining in the room after the news
of so dreadful a catastrophe. But, as Mrs. Barton was anxious
that her daughter's success should not be interfered with,
nothing could be done but to express sympathy in appropriate words. Nobody, Lord Dungory declared, could regret
the dastardly outrage that had been committed more than he.
He had known Lord Kilcarney many years, and he had always
found him a man whom no one could fail to esteem. The
earldom was one of the oldest in Ireland, but the marquisate
did not go back further than the last few years. Beaconsfield
had given him a step in the peerage ; no one knew why.
Most curious man—most retiring—hated society. Then Lord
Rosshill related an anecdote concerning an enormous water-
jump that he and Lord Kilcarney had taken together ; and he
also spoke of the late Marquis's aversion to matrimony, and
hinted that he had once refused a match which would have
relieved the estates of all debt. But he could not be persuaded ; indeed, he had never been known to pay any woman
the slightest attention.

"It is to be hoped the present Marquis won't prove so
difficult to please," said Mrs. Gould. The remark was an unfortunate one, and the chaperons present resented this viola-
tion of their secret thoughts. Mrs. Barton and Mrs. Scully
suddenly withdrew their eyes, which till then had been gently
following their daughters through the figures of the dance,
and, forgetting what they foresaw would be the cause of future
enmity, united in condemning Mrs. Gould. Obeying a glance
of the Lady Hamilton eyes, Lord Dungory said :

"*On cherche l'amour dans les boudoirs, non pas dans les
cimetières, madame.*" Then he added (but this time only for
the private ear of Mrs. Barton) : "*La mer ne rend pas ses morts,
mais la tombe nous donne souvent les écussons.*"

"Ha! ha! ha!" laughed Mrs. Barton, "*ce Milord, il trouve
l'esprit partout ;*" and her light coaxing laugh dissipated this
moment of ballroom gloom.

And Alice? Although conscious of her deficiency in the *trois temps*, determined not to give in without an effort, she had allowed May to introduce her to a couple of officers; but to execute the step she knew theoretically, or to talk to her partner when he had dragged her, breathless, out of the bumping dances, she found to be equally impossible. Too clearly did she see that he thought her a plain girl, too keenly did she feel that, knowing nothing of hunting or of London theatres, and having read only one book of Ouida's, it would be vain for her to hope to interest him. An impassable gulf yawned between his ideas and hers. Yet everyone else seemed happy as building birds. Behind screens, under staircases, at the end of dark passages, there were cooing couples. Girls she had known at St. Leonards as incapable of learning, or even understanding the simplest lessons, seemed suddenly to have grown bright, clever, agreeable—capable, in a word, of fulfilling that only duty which falls to the lot of women : of amusing men. But she could not do this, and must, therefore, resign herself to an aimless life of idleness, and be content in a few years to take a place amid the Miss Brennans, the Ladies Cullen, the Miss Duffys, the Honourable Miss Gores, whom she saw sitting round the walls " waiting to be asked," as did the women in the old Babylonian Temple.

Such • was the attitude of Alice's mind as she sat wearily answering Mrs. Gould's tiresome questions, not daring to approach her mother, who was laughing with Olive, Captain Hibbert, and Lord Dungory. Waltz after waltz had been played, and her ears reeked with their crying strain. One or two men had asked her " if they might have the pleasure ; " but she was determined to try dancing no more, and had refused them. At last, at the earnest request of Mrs. Gould, she had allowed Dr. Reed to take her in to supper. He was an earnest-eyed, stout, commonplace man, and looked some years over thirty. Alice, however, found she could get on with him better than with her other partners, and when they left the clattering supper-room, where plates were being broken and champagne being drunk by the gallon, sitting on the stairs, he talked to her till voices were heard calling for his services. A dancer had been thrown and had broken his leg. Alice saw something carried towards her, and, rushing towards May, whom she saw in the doorway, she asked for an explanation.

"Oh, nothing, nothing! he slipped down—has broken or sprained his ankle—that's all.   Why aren't you dancing? Greatest fun in the world—just beginning to get noisy—and we are going it.   Come on, Fred; come on!"

To the rowdy tune of the Posthorn polka the different couples were dashing to and fro—all a little drunk with emotion and champagne. As if fascinated, the eye followed the shoulders of a tall, florid-faced man. Doing the *deux temps*, in two or three prodigious jumps he traversed the room. His partner, a tiny creature, looked a crushed bird within the circle of his terrible arm. Like a collier labouring in a heavy sea, a county doctor lurched from side to side, overpowered by the fattest of the Miss Duffys. A thin, trim youth, with bright eyes glancing hither and thither, executed a complex step, and glided with surprising dexterity in and out, and through this rushing mad mass of light toilettes and flying coat-tails. Marks, too, of conflict were visible. Mr. Ryan had lost some portion of his garment in an obscure misunderstanding in the supper-room.   All Mr. Lynch's studs had gone, and his shirt was in a precarious state; drunken Sir Richard had not been carried out of the room before strewing the floor with his necktie and fragments of his gloves. But, in the intense excitement, these details were forgotten. The harper twanged still more violently at his strings, the fiddler rasped out the agonising tune more screechingly than ever; and as the delirium of the dance fevered this horde of well-bred people the desire to exercise their animal force grew irresistible, and they charged, intent on each other's overthrow. In the onset, the vast shoulders and the *deux temps* were especially successful. One couple had gone down splendidly before him, another had fallen over the prostrate ones; and in a moment, in positions more or less recumbent, eight people were on the floor. Fears were expressed for the tight dresses, and Violet had shown more of her thin ankles than was desirable; but the climax was not reached until a young man, whose unsteady legs forbade him this part of the fun, established himself in a safe corner, and commenced to push the people over as they passed him. This was the signal for the flight of the chaperons.

"Now come along, Miss Barton," cried Mrs. Barton, catching sight of Alice; "and will you, Lord Dungory, look after Olive?"   Lord Rosshill collected the five Honourable Miss

Gores, the Miss Brennans drew around Mrs. Scully, who, without taking the least notice of them, steered her way.

And so ended, at least so far as they were concerned, the ball given by the spinsters of the county of Galway. But the real end? On this subject much curiosity was evinced.

The secret was kept for a time, but eventually they learned that, overcome by the recollections of still pleasanter evenings spent under the hospitable roof of the Mayo bachelor, Mr. Ryan, Mr. Lynch and Sir Charles had brought in the maid-servants, and that, with jigs for waltzes, and whiskey for champagne, the gaiety had not been allowed to die until the day was well begun. Bit by bit and fragment by fragment the story was pieced together, and, in the secrecy of their bedrooms, with little smothered fits of laughter, the young ladies told each other how Sir Charles had danced with the big housemaid, how every time he did the cross over he had slapped her on the stomach; and then, with more laughter they related how she had said: "Now don't, Sir Charles, I forbid you to take such liberties." And it also became part of the story that, when they were tired of even such pleasures as these, the gentlemen had gone upstairs to where the poor man with the broken leg was lying, and had, with whiskey and song, relieved his sufferings until the Galway train rolled into Ballinasloe,

CHAPTER VI.

AFTER the ball at Ballinasloe, the county people saw very little of each other. The summer had been prolonged into autumn, but now, for whole days together, the rain came down persistently; the green pasture-lands seemed as if they were going to be washed into the brown bogs, and the blue of the Clare mountains was rarely seen through the drifting grey of the mists. But the weather rarely prevents Galway from enjoying itself; there were graver reasons for the seclusion in which the county lay buried. Mr. Forster's Coercion Bill had failed. Seven hundred people, including many members of Parliament, had been thrown into prison; wild arrests were made in every town and village; but as each fresh ring was cut, like some fabulous dragon, the Land League put forth ten, and in the humid Irish winter it grew in strength, winding itself steadily between the classes, momentarily drawing all within its power. Even hunting had ceased to be talked of. The poisoned covers, the shrieking mobs that had attended the last meets and had stoned the red horsemen into flight, were gloomily alluded to; and the good old days were remembered, with hardly a hope that their like would ever be seen again.

The air was filled with threats, murder, and rumours of many murders. Land League meetings were held in every town, in every village, and rustic orators fearlessly proclaimed the extermination of the owners of the soil. Each post brought letters marked with coffins and crossbones, or almost equally melancholy epistles from agents, declaring that the law was in abeyance, that whole armies of people assembled to prevent the bailiffs from serving their notices of eviction. Some of them had been thrown into lakes, others had been dragged out of their beds and shot in the legs, for daring to disregard the occult law that from Seventy-nine to Eighty-

94

two governed the island. It was a time of darkness and
constant alarms. It was by night that prosperous tenants
and leaseholders paid their rents; the reductions that the
League demanded often amounted to the entire balance coming
to the mortgaged landowners : and they saw themselves
deprived of their only means of existence. For how many
generations had they lived upon the taxed soil? For how
long, when other industries had failed, had they laughed and
said : "The fools ! there is nothing like the land; all else
fails, but that cannot be taken away." And now they saw
that which they had taken to be eternal, vanishing from them
even as a vapour. An entire race, a whole caste, saw themselves driven out of their soft, warm couches of idleness, and
forced into the struggle for life. The prospect appalled them ;
birds with shorn wings could not gaze more helplessly on the
high trees where they had built, as they thought, their nests
out of the reach of evil winds. What could they do with their
empty brains? What could they do with their feeble hands?
Like an avenging spirit, America rose above the horizon of
their vision, and the plunge into its shadowy arms threatened,
terrified them now, as it had terrified the famine-stricken
peasants of Forty-nine.

The landlords were divided by conflicting interests.
Those whose estates were encumbered with mortgages were
for holding out, but the majority, who had debts to meet,
found themselves forced to agree to the League's demands;
and, for fear of drawing attention on themselves individually,
they shrank from meeting in council, and declined to adopt
any common course of defence. The suddenness of the
attack and the unity of the combination took from them all
strength to resist; and, helplessly wailing by their firesides,
every morning they read aloud the articles in the *Daily Express*,
calling on the Government to pass Coercion Bills, and force
the people to pay their just debts. Would the Government
come to their assistance? This was the question that burned
in every brain; it was the pulse of every hour; and, with
avid eyes, each fragment of news was read, until at last the
interest was reversed, and the leaders of the agitation hailed
murder with less delight than the landlords, who now saw
in each fresh outrage a means of forcing the Government to
protect their jeopardised fortunes. What would Parliament
do for them when it met? was asked unceasingly; and,

listening to long lamentations and cries for help, the girls lived wearily. On their young hearts the shadow of calamity fell lightly; and they dreamed unflinchingly of their white dresses, while the island rocked with the roar of five million peasants claiming the right to own the land that they tilled.

As elsewhere, life at Brookfield was filled with forebodings. During breakfast Mrs. Barton did not cease to advise her husband as to the course he should pursue with his tenants should they refuse his last offer of twenty per cent. abatement. But, when Milord arrived, the little table was drawn forward, the glass of sherry poured out, and, just as if rents were being punctually paid, white hands were waved, and the coaxing laugh began to dissipate the gloom in which the League usually draped the morning hours. The ancient lovers sat together on the sofa, undisturbed by the recurring vision of the four policemen who faced the sweep in front of the house, or the tinkling of Mr. Barton's guitar, which was heard when the servant opened the door to announce that luncheon was ready.

Olive complained, and she often begged of her mother to leave the country. Mrs. Barton could not do this; but when Captain Hibbert returned from London she allowed him to continue his flirtation. She did so partly to give Olive an occupation, partly that she might perfect herself in the art of amusing gentlemen—an accomplishment that would be required of her when they met the Lord Kilcarney at the Castle. For Mrs. Barton had decided that her daughter was to be a marchioness; she did not doubt but the web of love that was being woven would be disentangled without difficulty when the time came; and Olive sat for hours knitting purses, working embroidered smoking-caps, and laughing and talking with Barnes. But for Alice there was nothing. On leaving school she had hoped that all jealousies would be lost in the uniting intimacies of home, and that she would live in the assurance of a sister's love. A vain dream! Worldly necessities and ambitions had torn them irrevocably apart. In the bright summer-days when the country was lovely and sweet with sunshine, when there were visits and tennis-parties, she had only seen the shadow of the dreary truth flitting by her; but now, with its face of implacable horror, it stood ever by her, with its cold eyes staring into her very soul. In the bleak winter noons, sitting with some wearying novel fallen on her knees, listening to the swishing of the long rain, or looking out on the blank snow-laden country, with its sepulchral mountains disappearing in the grey masses of cloud that the evening, like winding-sheets, slowly and silently unrolled, she realised, seeing all along the far-reaching range of consequences, that she was no more than a plain girl, whom no man would care to marry, and who would have to live without any aim or object in life, an ever-increasing burden to her people, an object of derision to her acquaintances.

For days, for weeks, for months past, all she had seen or heard had forced the girl to gaze longer and more minutely in the face of this stern fact, and in its ever-varying expression she found new cruelties; the store seemed to be inexhaustible. She was, above all, alone, terribly alone; to none could she turn for a look or a word of comfort. Her mother was alien to her in all feelings and ideas of things; her father and sister? they were very kind, but there was no use in thinking of them now. She was alone, oh! yes, terribly alone. Her heart was a desert; its solitude affrighted her, and she cried out in her anguish. Thoughts that scorched, desires she could not control, persecuted her, and so persistently that, at last, they seemed part and parcel of her habitual thought; and she was shaken with sudden and quick revulsions of feeling. Was she never to know? Was this life of weak idleness to continue for ever? These were the questions that, with a terrible intensity and unintermission of appeal, presented themselves to her mind.

To-day she had been to see Cecilia, and had come back more tired and pained than ever. The strange, passionate affection had not soothed, and the ascetic vision of life remorselessly insisted on by the cripple jarred on Alice's already overstrained feelings, till now, in her brain, fevered with loneliness and tense with natural want of love, there surged backwards and forwards, like a ghastly and unceasing dream, all the terrible allusions she had heard that day made to the long families of unmarried girls in the county, and Cecilia's pessimistic ridicule and sneers at all the joys of life. Cold and weary, she sat watching the night falling over the waste of immaculate snow.

And pallid even as the snow, the scroll that held her life's history was unfolded; and with agonised mind she strove to read the decrees of Fate. But through her gazing eyes the plain of virginal snow, flecked with the cold blue shadows of the trees, sank into her soul, bleaching it of every hope of joy; and, gathering suggestions from the surroundings, she saw a white path extending before her—a sterile way that she would have to tread—a desolate way, with no songs in its sullen air, but only sad sighs, and only stainless tears, falling, falling, ever falling—falling silently. Grey was the gloom that floated, and overworn were the spectres that passed therein; and the girl buried her face in her hands, as if to shut out the vision of the journey she would have to go. She foretasted the idleness she would have courageously to drink to the last; she foresaw the lonely death that would in the end overtake her. Her life was a grey tint, unillumined by lamp of delight or star of duty. She had not been included in the scheme of existence; there was no end for her to attain, no height for her to climb; and now, looking into the future, she could see no issue for the love and energy which throbbed within her. Must it all die? How horrible, how narrow, how indefensible, how unintelligent did the laws that guarded a young girl's life from the living touch of the world appear to her to be! and, as a prisoner will raise his arms to beat down the walls of his cell, she appealed against them all: "Give me a duty, give me a mission to perform, and I will live!" she cried despairingly; "but, oh! save me from this grey dream of idleness!" Then, her thoughts full of obtuse agony, she considered the martyrdom which was awaiting her, and from which no escape seemed possible. The scroll of the years was again unrolled before her—she saw herself growing old, amid bits of lace, faded flowers, and chattering chaperons. Those were the joys life had reserved for her; her pains would be the languors and irritations of endless idleness, and the sour sneering of girl acquaintances. She saw herself sitting amid them: the Brennans, the Duffys, the Honourable Miss Gores, and hosts of others, all waiting until someone would take pity and ask them to dance. For this, and only this, the whole system of their education had been devised. They had been dressed out in a little French, a little music, a little watercolour-painting—for this, and only this: to snigger, to cajole, to chatter to any man who would condescend to listen to them, and to gladly marry any man who would undertake to keep them. For this, and only this, did the flower-adorned bosoms swell sweetly beneath the laced corsets; for this were the white smiles that greeted the partners approaching; for this were the red laughs that cajoled behind shadowy curtains; for this were the pretty feet advanced, with the flesh seen through the open work of the stocking; for this, and only this, was the pleading azure of the adoring eyes.

And from this awful mummery in muslin there was no escape. It would continue until the comedy became tragedy; until, with aching hearts and worn faces, they would be forced aside by the crush of the younger generation; and, looking aghast in the face of their five and thirty years, read there their sentence to die, as they had lived, ignorant of life and its meaning. Oh! never to know, born never to know, condemned never to know, the one joy in which gain is forgotten! was the cry that echoed through the bleakness of the girl's heart. Black was her despair—black as the black cloud that hunted the moon. Passing, it let the white rays splinter; and, in the rapid succession of light and gloom, Alice's thoughts turned, changed, trembled, and were broken.

Oh! what a terrible cruelty is a girl's life! She with a plain face is like a seed fallen upon a rock. There she will remain to perish, while around her the green crop will grow gladly in May and April winds, and ripen to summer fulness under July and August suns. She will see her companions becoming brides, and then mothers; and, if she lives out her useless life to the end, she will see grandchildren crowding about their knees; each age will bring them new interests, while each succeeding year will rob her pitilessly of any hopes and joys she may still cling to. For her there is nothing, nothing, nothing! Her life is weak and sterile, even as the plain of moonlight-stricken snow. Like it, she will fade, will pass into a moist and sunless grave, without leaving a trace of herself on the earth—this beautiful earth, built out of and made lovely with love. Yes, built out of love—for all is love. Spring, with amorous hands, will withdraw the chaste veil of winter's maidenhood, and the world, like a bride arrayed in flowers and expectation, will be but a universal shrine, wherein is worshipped the deity. All then shall be ministrants of love. Sweet winds shall join herb and flowers, and through the purple night soft-winged moths shall carry

the desire of every plant and blossom ; in the light air the
wings of mating birds shall mingle, and upon the earth the
lowliest animals be united ; only woman is forbidden to obey
the one universal instinct, coequal with the music of the
spheres, and eternal even as it.

Then, filled with pale presentiment, the girl cried out :
" Oh ! give me life, give me love ! " and her anguish was like
the wail of the frozen bird, that wailed its thin life away in
the silent light of the stars. Alice loved her life ; and she
wished to live it sincerely, and in all its fulness. She
demanded love, it was only love that could relieve her from
the torture she was suffering—a husband had always formed
part of her thoughts. She remembered, when a child, having
once seen a pair of lovers walking with their arms about
each other. For months she had dreamed of their kisses,
striving at the same time to invent for them suitable words
and phrases ; and she reminded herself how she had always
joyed in things relating to motherhood ; how the spectacle
of a mother nursing her child had once delighted her, and how
she had looked forward to the day when she would perform
the same sweet office. But now she knew that that hope
was vain. In an hour one truth had become terribly distinct,
and, in the nightmare-terrors of her mind, strange thoughts,
thoughts of which she was ashamed, passed and mockingly
taunted her, and it required all the strength of her intelligence to regain her mental balance. Was she impure ? She
did not wish to be, but she trembled to think of her life pure
from end to end—pure as that plain of virgin snow. Then the
sorrow that rose out of her soul became part of the sorrow of
others ; and, pale and lonely as the glittering trees that raised
their faces to the sky, she saw the girls she had seen at
the ball passing stainless and sterile through the generation
of which she was but a single unit. The moon had risen out
of the clouds, and hanging like a night-lamp, blanching the
draperies of the distant woods, the land was flooded with so
divine an effulgence, that in the disordered imagination of the
girl it seemed to be the white bed of celibacy in which the
whole county was sleeping.

Yes ; all were suffering alike, all were enduring the same
white death ! Yet as her thoughts passed from the contemplation of the collective pain, and fixed themselves again on
the raw of her own individual grief, she again believed she

was the most miserable of all. For did not her companions at least hold that human life was but the hour of darkness that precedes the dawn of an eternal day—a day of glory and original light? But to her even this consolation was denied; and now, in the prostration of her ideas, she called out, though she well knew it to be impossible, to be fed at this table of thin hope. "What does it matter?" she cried; "nothing matters; and even if it be no active force in their lives, though they believe in it no more than in the flirtation of yesterday, it fills better than woolwork, or tennis-playing, or small-talk, the void of our objectless days. The duty of worshipping is an emotion if it be no more; even to the most heedless it supplies the sensation of having done something; and, to those who allow their souls to be absorbed by the myth, it supplies an adequate motive to live and to suffer pain."

But for her, who knew that life was but a pilgrimage to the worm, there was no escape; until death she would drift, a dead leaf, adown the tepid and trivial current of her life, unless—then the word marriage sighed through her thoughts. It came suddenly upon her like a gust of sweet perfume; and, through the gloom of dying and dead illusions, she dreamed of a love around which, flowerwise, two lives should twining grow, always unfolding their hopes and joys to an equal light. Nor was there in her vision any of the lascivious dependency which she daily saw taken for the highest aim. What she saw was an ideal couple, journeying with a firm step through life, sharing burdens and sorrows, that were made lighter by the sharing. Fragments of history came back to her; and, in a confused and disjointed way, she realised how men have bought women, imprisoned women, kept women as a sort of common property; but that throughout the ages they have never been considered as anything more than objects of luxury or necessity. "How then," she asked passionately, "can we be really noble and pure, while we are still decked out in innocence, virtue, and belief as ephemeral as the muslins we wear? Until we are free to think, until we are their sisters in thought, we cannot hope to become the companions, the friends, the supports of men." Alice thought clearly and directly; but, as is often the case with subjective natures, she shrank from the glare and the rough shocks of the practical contest. Although she now rebelled against social, as she had long done against religious laws, she was ready to outwardly conform to the former as to

the latter.   Having the divine power to create, and to live an
interior life, she often forgot the reality of existence, until,
with awakening hands, it shook her, as on the present occasion,
rudely from her dreams.   Light laughter was now heard
ascending the staircase, and, as Olive burst into the moon-
whitened room, she exclaimed :

"Goodness me ! Alice ; how can you remain up here all
alone, and by that smouldering fire ?   Why don't you come
downstairs ? It has been so pleasant. Papa has been humming
to himself.   He says he is quite satisfied with the first part of
the tune, but the second won't come right; and, as mamma
had a lot to say to Lord Dungory, I and Captain Hibbert sat
out in the passage together.   He was awfully nice.   He told
me that I was the prettiest girl he had ever seen, and that he
had never seen me looking so sweet.   But tell me, do tell me,
how you think this way of doing up my hair suits me ? "

"Very well, indeed ; but what else did Captain Hibbert say
to you ? "

"Well, I'll tell you something," replied Olive, suddenly
turning from the glass.   And, assuming a pose, scarcely less
affected than those of the dancing-girls by Canova, she continued : "But first promise not to tell anyone.   I don't know
what I should do if you did.   You promise ? "

"Yes, I promise."

"If you look as serious as that I shall never be able to tell
you.   It is very wicked, I know, but I couldn't help myself.
He put his arm round my waist and kissed me.   Now don't
scold, I won't be scolded," the girl said, as she watched the
cloud gathering on her sister's face.   "Oh ! you don't know how
angry I was.   I cried, I assure you I did, and I told him he
had disgraced me.   I couldn't say more than that, could I,
now ? and he promised never to do it again.   It was the first
time a man ever kissed me—I was awfully ashamed.   No one
ever attempted to kiss you, I suppose ; nor can I fancy their
trying, for your cross face would soon frighten them ; but I
can't look serious."

The words cut like a keen steel ; and, quivering with pain,
Alice said : "And did he ask you to marry him ? "

"Oh ! of course he did, but I haven't told mamma, for she
is always talking to me about Lord Kilcarney—the little
marquis, as she calls him ; but I couldn't have him. Just
fancy giving up dear Edward ! I assure you that I believe

that he would kill himself if I did. He has often told me that I am the only thing that is worth living for."

Alice looked questioningly at the silly beauty before her. She had already determined to speak to her mother about Captain Hibbert; for her good sense told her that, if in the end the girl was not intended for him, it was wrong to allow her to continue her flirtation. But, for the moment, the consideration of her own misfortunes absorbed her. Was there nothing—and all happiness seemed to lie in the balance —in marriage but a sensual gratification; and did a man seek for nothing but a beautiful body that he could kiss and enjoy? Did his desires never turn to mating with one who could sympathise with his hopes, comfort him in his fears; and united by that most profound and penetrating of all unions— that of the soul—be collaborator in life's work? If so, life were indeed a lovely thing! and, like a glad bird, the girl's heart soared through the silver skies of her dream, until the unanswerable question again struck her: "Could no man love as she did?"

All she had heard and seen said no; but, unconvinced, she, with a painful reiteration, insisted that if women did not think of men so, why should men be so degraded? Nor did her soul-searching cease at this point. The mind that had asserted its independence amid such surroundings as Alice's, that had not shrunk from following the guidance of reason, and accepting its conclusion that religion, being no truth, was to be cast aside as an idle folly, would not falter now. However repugnant it might be to her present feeling, she was ready to allow that marriage owned a material as well as a spiritual aspect, and that neither could be overlooked. Some, therefore, though their souls were as beautiful as the day, were, from purely physical causes, incapacitated from entering into the marriage-state. Cecilia was such an one! Did she, Alice, share the same fate? and, her brain throbbing with terrors as intimate and intense as the pulsing of her blood, the girl that night, straight and stark, her head buried in the pillow, asked herself if she were not proper for a husband's love; her limbs, were they not as strong and as healthy, if not as fair as her sister's? "Yes! yes!" and the darkness answered again "Yes;" but looking through the length of years, in spite of all, she saw herself for ever sleeping in celibacy.

"She knew she would never be married." It was as if

some instinct had told her. The words clashed in her ears; she forced their meaning deep into her heart—she strove to wipe away each hope as it gleamed within the mirror of her despair.

When the girls came down to breakfast Mrs. Barton left off lecturing her husband, and, as with an air of relief he stretched his embroidered-slippered feet to the fire and continued reading the *Daily Express*, she said :

"Lord Rosshill has been fired at, and only just escaped with his life."

"I am glad it was not Lord Dungory," replied Olive.

"Of course," said Mrs. Barton, slightly embarrassed ; "but Lord Rosshill is not a young man, and——"

"Neither is Lord Dungory," chimed in Olive, as she helped herself to an egg.

"I wish you would not interrupt me, Olive," said Mrs. Barton. "I was going to say that the nervous shock must be dreadful, even if one does escape with one's life from an assassin."

Then Mr. Barton read from the *Daily Express* the account of a dastardly murder in Kerry. A bailiff's house had been broken into by an armed gang, and the unfortunate man had been dragged out of bed and shot before his own door. In Meath an attempt had been made to blow up a landlord's house with dynamite ; in Queen's County shot had been fired through a diningroom window, and two large hay-yards had been maliciously burned ; in Wicklow forty head of cattle had had their tails cut off ; in Roscommon and in Galway two men, occupying farms from which tenants had been evicted, had been so seriously beaten that their lives were despaired of. This list of crimes was considered large ; but so absorbed was each family in its own private interest, that the news of the outrages committed in the East and South was received with indifference ; and it was not until Lord Rosshill's escape and the probable reductions he would make to his tenants had been fully discussed, that any reference was made to the rest of Ireland. At last Mrs. Barton said, after glancing her eye over the columns of the paper, to assure herself of the accuracy of her husband's reading :

"I wonder if all this will suffice to force the Government to pass a new Coercion Bill."

"I wish they would put me at the head of an army, ' said

Mr. Barton, whose thoughts had gone back to his picture of the "Altars of the Druids."

"Dressed in Julius Cæsar's big red cloak, on the great white horse, wouldn't papa look fine, leading the landlords against the tenants?" cried Mrs. Barton, in her winsomest manner. She treated her husband exactly as she did Milord; indeed, just as she did everybody else.

After breakfast the party separated. Mrs. Barton went to dress to receive Lord Dungory; Mr. Barton retired to his studio. In the girls' room Olive and Barnes gossiped incessantly, and the bland, soft-smiling maid ripped the body of a ball-dress, while the corn-coloured beauty trimmed a smoking-cap with yellow braid. In brief phrases she referred to, and with scornful little laughs commented on, the matrimonial prospects of different young ladies.

Captain Hibbert's name was frequently mentioned, and Alice was surprised to hear her sister say she had forbidden him ever to visit the Lawlers. At that moment the dull sound of distant firing broke the stillness of the snow.

"I took good care to make him promise not to go to this shooting-party the last time I saw him."

"And what harm was there in his going to this shooting-party?" said Alice.

"What harm? I suppose, miss, you have heard what kind of woman Mrs. Lawler is? Ask Barnes."

"You shouldn't talk in this way, Olive. We know well enough that Mrs. Lawler was not a lady before she married; but nothing can be said against her since."

"Oh! can't there, indeed? You never heard the story about her and her steward? Ask Barnes."

"Oh! don't, miss; you shouldn't really," said the maid. "What will Miss Alice think?"

"Never mind what she thinks; you tell her about the steward and all the officers from Gort."

Then Mrs. Lawler's flirtations were talked of until the bell rang for lunch. Milord was there, notwithstanding the news of the attempt made on Lord Rosshill's life; but he was obviously a little frightened, and, in spite of the waving cf white hands and the excitement of cajoling laughter, his eyes wandered occasionally in the direction of the policemen who paced the snow in the front of the house. Mrs. Barton, who looked upon herself as a kind of lotus-flower, and whose

highest aim was to make the man to whom she was talking
forget the cares of life, worked hard, but in answer to all her
allusions to knights of old and *la galanterie*, the old lord could
only say : " *L'amour est comme l'hirondelle ; quand l'heure
sonne, en dépit du danger, tous les deux partent pour les
rivages célestes.*" This was the only epigram he attempted.
Mrs. Barton, seriously alarmed, consulted her glass that
evening ; but she was not to blame. The Land League had
thrown its shadow over all, and out of that shadow no one
could lift their thoughts. It mattered little how joyously a
conversation might begin, too soon a reference was made
to Griffith's valuation, or the possibility of a new Coercion
Act.

In the course of the afternoon, however, much to the
astonishment of Milord and Mrs. Barton in the drawing-room,
and the young ladies who were sitting upstairs doing a little
needlework, a large family carriage, hung with grey trappings,
and drawn by two powerful bay horses, drove up to the hall-
door.

A gorgeous footman opened the door, and, with a momentary display of exquisite ankle, a slim young girl stepped out.
It was Violet Scully.

" I wonder," said Mrs. Barton, "that Mrs. Scully con-
descends to come out with anything less than four horses and
outriders."

" *Elle veut acheter la distinction comme elle vendait du jambon
—à faux poids,*" said Lord Dungory.

" Yes, indeed ; and to think that the woman we now receive
as an equal once sold bacon and eggs behind a counter in
Galway ! "

" No, it was not she, it was her mother."

" Well, she was hanging on to her mother's apron-strings
at the time. You may depend upon it, this visit is not for
nothing ; something's in the wind."

A moment after, looking more large and stately than
ever, Mrs. Scully sailed into the room. Mrs. Barton was
delighted to see her ; it was so good of her to come, and in
such weather as this. Then, after having refused lunch, and
referred to the snow and the horses' feet, Mrs. Scully consented to lay aside her muff and boa. The young ladies
withdrew, when the conversation turned on the state of
the county, and Lord Rosshill's fortunate escape. As they

ascended the stairs they stopped to listen to Mr. Barton, who was singing "*A che la morte.*"

"The Land League does not seem to affect Mr. Barton's spirits," said Violet; "what a beautiful voice he has!"

"Yes, and nobody designs pictures like papa; but he wouldn't study when he was young, and he says he hasn't time now on account of——"

"Now, Alice, for goodness' sake don't begin. I am sick of that Land League. It is too awful; from morning till night it is nothing but coercion and Griffith's valuation."

Violet and Alice laughed at Olive's petulance, and, opening a door, the latter said:

"This is our room, and it is the only one in the house where tenants, land, and rent are never spoken of."

"That's something to know," said Violet. "I agree with Olive; if things are bad, talking of them won't make them any better."

When the girls entered Barnes rose from her seat. She smiled encouragingly, blandly, and retreated.

"Now don't go, Barnes. Do you know Miss Scully? Violet, this is Barnes, our maid."

Violet acknowledged the introduction. There was about Barnes a false air of homeliness; but in a few moments it became apparent that her life had been spent amid muslins, confidences, and illicit conversations. Now, with motherly care she removed a tulle skirt from the table, and Violet, with quick, nervous glances, examined the room. In the middle of the floor stood the large work-table, covered with a red cloth. There was a stand with shelves, filled on one side with railway novels, on the other with worsted work, cardboard-boxes, and rags of all kinds. A canary-cage stood on the top, and the conversation was frequently interrupted by the piercing trilling of the little yellow bird. Then the pierglass was plastered with Christmas cards, and, amid robin redbreasts and babies, a photograph of Captain Hibbert caught the eye.

"You're very comfortable; I should like to come and work here with you. I wish we didn't live so far apart; one does get so tired of one's brother's company. I am sick of Fred's perpetual talk about horses; and if he isn't talking of them his conversation is so improper that I can't listen to it."

"Why, what does he say?" said Olive, glancing at Barnes, who smiled benignly in the background.

"Oh! I couldn't repeat what he says; it's too dreadful; I have to fly from him. But he's always at the Goulds' now; he and May are having a great 'case.'"

"Oh! yes, I know," said Olive; "they never left each other at our ball; don't you remember?"

"Of course I do. And what a jolly ball that was! I never amused myself so much in my life. If the balls at the Castle are as good they will do. But wasn't it sad, you know, about poor Lord Kilcarney receiving the news of his brother's murder just at that moment? I can see him now, rushing out of the room."

Violet's manner did not betoken in the least that she thought it sad, and after a pause she said:

"But you haven't shown me your dresses. I did like that one you wore at the ball."

"Yes, yes; I want to show you my cream-coloured dinner-dress; and my ruby dress, you haven't seen that either," cried Olive. "Come along, Barnes, come along." Then, stopping at the door, she turned to Alice: "Aren't you coming too?"

Alice demurred, then acceded. In the bedroom, all was in perfect order; and the pierglass was filled with the snow-white room and fragments of the snow-covered lands. Violet declared herself delighted.

"But I see you use your bedroom, too, as a sitting-room?" she said, as she glanced at the illustrations in a volume of Dickens, and threw down a volume of Shelley's poetry.

"Oh! that's this lady, here," cried Olive. "She says she cannot read in our room on account of my chattering; so she comes in here to continue her schooling. I should have thought that she had had enough of it; and she makes the place in such a mess with bits of paper. Barnes is always tidying up after her."

Alice laughed constrainedly. Taking the cream-coloured dress out of the maid's hands, Olive explained why it suited her. Violet had much to say concerning the pink trimming, and the maid referred to her late mistresses' wardrobes. The ruby dress, however, drew forth many little cries of admiration. Then an argument was started concerning the colour of hair, and, before the glass with hairpins and lithe movements of the back and loins, the girls explained their favourite coiffures.

In the meanwhile Alice stood waiting. A long silence

had fallen, and, as if struck by a sudden thought, Violet said :

"But, my goodness, Alice, you haven't opened your lips, and you haven't shown me your dresses. What's the matter ? "

"Nothing's the matter," said the girl passionately; and, speaking out of the flood of bitterness in which her soul lay, she added, "I have no dresses to show; you have seen the best."

"She is angry because we didn't look at her dresses first," exclaimed Olive ; and she ran to the door to prevent her sister from leaving the room. The interruption was a timely one, and Alice, with tears turned to laughter, said :

"Barnes will show you my dinner-frocks, but I don't think as much about what I wear as Olive does."

Violet's quick intelligence, quick as the ever-glancing eyes, understood at once the whole truth, but, with clever dissimulation, she examined and praised the black silk trimmed with red ribbons. Then allusion was made to Lord Kilcarney. Violet was clearly interested, and, as Alice noticed, she seemed specially pleased when Olive, with vain tossings of the head and vain words, strove to turn him into ridicule; and, when the girl protested that she would sooner die than accept such a little red-haired thing as that for a husband, Violet laughed delightedly.

"Anyway, you have not those faults to find with a certain officer, now stationed at Gort, who, if report speaks truly, is constantly seen riding towards Brookfield."

"Well, what harm is there in that ? " said Olive, for she did not feel quite sure in her mind if she should resent or accept the gracious insinuation.

"None whatever; I only wish such luck was mine. What with the weather, and papa's difficulties with his herds and his tenants, we haven't seen a soul for the last month. I wish a handsome young officer would come galloping up our avenue some day."

Deceived, Olive abandoned herself to the plausive charm of Violet's manner, and at different times she spoke of her flirtation, and told many little incidents concerning it—what he had said to her, how she had answered him, and how, the last time they had met, he had expressed his sorrow at being unable to call to see her until the end of the week.

" He is shooting to-day at the Lawlers'," said Violet.

" That I'm sure he's not," said Olive, with a triumphant toss of her fair head ; " for I forbade him to go there."

Violet smiled, and Olive insisted on an explanation being given.

" Well," exclaimed the girl, more bluntly than she had yet spoken, "because as we were coming here we saw him walking along one of the covers. There were a lot of gentlemen, and, just fancy, that dreadful woman, Mrs. Lawler, was shooting with them. She was marching along, just like a man, with a gun under her arm."

" I don't believe you ; you only say that to annoy me," cried Olive, trembling with passion.

" I am not in the habit of telling lies, and do not know why you should think that I would care to annoy you," Violet replied, a little too definitely ; and, unable to control her feelings any longer, Olive walked out of the room. Barnes, with black looks, folded up and put away the dresses, and Alice sought for words that would attenuate the unpleasantness of the scene. But Violet was the quicker with her tongue, and she poured out her excuses. " I am so sorry," she said, " but how could I know that she objected to Captain Hibbert's shooting at the Lawlers', or that he had promised her not to go there ? I am very sorry, indeed."

" Oh ! it doesn't matter," said Alice, hesitatingly. " You know how excitable Olive is. I don't think she cares more about Captain Hibbert than anyone else ; she was only a little piqued, you know—the surprise, and she particularly dislikes the Lawlers. Of course, it is very unpleasant for us to live so near without being able to visit them."

" Yes, I understand ; but I am very sorry. Do you know where she is gone to, for I shouldn't like to go away without seeing her ? "

" I am afraid she has shut herself up in her room. It would only make her worse to see her now ; next time you meet, she will have forgotten all about it."

Elated, but at the same time a little vexed, Violet followed Alice down to the drawing-room.

" My dear child, what a time you have been ! I thought you were never coming downstairs again," said Mrs. Scully. " Now, my dear Mrs. Barton, we really must. We shall meet again, if not before, at the Castle."

Then stout mother and thin daughter took their leave ; but the large carriage, with its sumptuous grey trappings, had not reached the crest of the hill, when, swiftly unlocking her door, Olive rushed to Barnes for sympathy.

"Oh! the spiteful little cat!" she exclaimed. "I know why she said that; she's jealous of me. You heard her say she hadn't a lover. I don't believe she saw Edward at all, but she wanted to annoy me ; don't you think so, Barnes ?"

"I'm sure she wanted to annoy you, miss. I could see it in her eyes. She has dreadful eyes—those cold, grey, glittering things, I could never trust them. And she has not a bit on her bones. Did you see that, when you were counting your petticoats, she was afraid to lift hers up ?—she was ashamed of her legs. There isn't, I'll be bound, a bit on them, and I saw her look at yours, miss."

"Did you really ?" Olive replied laughing. "I am so glad of that ; and isn't she thin ? She's like a rail; and she was always spiteful. I remember her at school. Nothing made her so angry as when anyone else was praised ; and you may be sure that that brought her here. She heard how Captain Hibbert admired me, and she came on purpose to annoy me."

"You may be sure it was that, miss," said Barnes, as she bustled about, shutting and opening a variety of cardboard boxes.

For a moment the quarrel looked as if it were going to end here ; but in Olive's brain thoughts leaped as quickly back as forward, and she startled Barnes by declaring wildly that, if Edward had broken his promise to her, she would never speak to him again.

"I don't believe that Violet would have dared to say that she saw him if it weren't true."

"Well, miss, a shooting-party's but a shooting-party, and there was a temptation, you know. A gentleman who is fond of sport !——"

"Yes; but it isn't for the shooting he is gone : 'tis for Mrs. Lawler. I know it is."

"Not it, miss. Always admitting that he is there, how could he think of Mrs. Lawler when he's always thinking of you ? And, besides, out in the snow, too. Now, I wouldn't say anything, were it fine weather, weather like we had last June, and they were giving each other meetings out in the park——"

" But what did you tell me about the steward, and how Mrs. Lawler fell in love with all the young men who come to her house ? And what did the housemaid tell you of the walking about the passages at night, and into each other's rooms ? Oh ! I must know if he's there ! "

" I'll find out in the morning, miss. The coachman is sure to know who was at the shooting-party."

" In the morning ! it will be too late then ! I must know this evening ! " exclaimed Olive, as she walked about the room, her light brain now flown with jealousy and suspicion. " I'll write him a letter," she said suddenly, " and you must get someone to take it over."

" But who can I get at this hour, miss ? Why, it is nearly seven o'clock," said Barnes, who had begun to realise the disagreeableness and danger of the adventure she was being rapidly drawn into.

" If you can't, I shall go myself," cried Olive, as she seized some paper and a pencil belonging to Alice, and sat down to write a note :

" Dear Captain Hibbert,—If you have broken your promise to me about not going to the Lawlers', I shall never be able to forgive you ! " (then, as through her perturbed mind the thought gleamed that this was perhaps a little definite, a little conclusive, she added) : " Anyhow, I wish to see you. Come at once, and explain that what I have heard about you is not true. I cannot believe it.

" Yours ever and anxiously,
" OLIVE BARTON."

" Now somebody must take this over at once to the Lawlers."

" But, miss ! really at this hour of night, too, I don't know of anyone to send. Just think, miss, what would your ma say ? "

" I don't care what mamma says. It would kill me to wait till morning ! Someone must go. Why can't you go yourself ? It isn't more than half a mile across the fields. Now, you won't refuse me, will you ? Now put on your hat, and go at once."

" And what will the Lawlers say when they hear of it, miss ? and I am sure that if Mrs. Barton ever hears of it she will——"

"No, no, she won't! for I could not do without you, Barnes. You have only to ask if Captain Hibbert is there, and, if he is there, send the letter up, and wait for an answer. Now, there's a dear! now do go at once. If you don't I shall go mad! Now say you will go; or give me the letter. Yes, give it to me, and I'll go myself. Yes, I prefer to go myself.'

CHAPTER VII.

The result of this missive was that next morning the servants whispered that someone had been about the house on the preceding evening. Alice noticed Olive's restlessness when she was not with Barnes; with knees set, and little smothered laughs and quiet glances, they sat talking for hours. There was a secret between them; and one day, unable to keep her counsel any longer, Olive told her sister what had happened. The letter that Barnes had taken across the field for her had, she declared, frightened Edward out of his senses; he had come rushing through the snow, and had spoken with her for full five minutes under her window. He loved her to distraction; and on the following day she had received a long letter, full of references to his colonel, explaining how entirely against his will and desire he had been forced to accept the invitation to go and shoot at the Lawlers'. Alice listened quietly; as if she doubted whether Captain Hibbert would have died of consumption or heartache if Olive had acted otherwise; whereat the beauty flaunted out of the room, and no attempt was made to stop her; Alice knew it would be vain to argue, and, as she sat, holding her knees with her long arms, her distress of mind was visible in her eyes; too often she was uncertain about things; and she always felt, though she could not determine what it was, that a duty was awaiting her. Now, irritated against Barnes for the hypocritical way in which she had acted, Alice sought to convince herself that the best course to follow would be to tell her mother of what had happened. Mrs. Barton's intentions were always inscrutable, but Alice could not believe that the serious turn Olive's flirtation was taking was altogether ignored. If so, what did mother mean by her allusions to the marquis, whom they were to meet at the Castle, and who, she said, would most assuredly be captured by Olive?

Then a week passed, and Captain Hibbert had been to see them four times. He had hung over Olive's shoulder as she sat at the piano, walked with her in the shrubberies, and one wet day they had spent hours together in the greenhouse. And that night Olive told her sister, as they went to bed, in broken and passionate words, how she loved him; and, wild with excitement, she confessed that he had kissed her many times. She knew it was very wrong, she had told him he was very wicked; she had threatened that she would not sit alone with him again, unless he promised to respect her. And he had promised.

Alice advised her sister quietly; but she resolved to speak to her mother of Captain Hibbert, and an occasion for so doing presented itself on the following morning. Mr. Barton was passing down the passage to his studio, Olive was racing upstairs to Barnes, Mrs. Barton had her hand on the drawing-room-door; and she looked round surprised when she saw that her daughter was following her.

"I want to speak to you, mamma."

"Come in, dear."

Alice shut the door behind her. Already the interview seemed to take an important character, and before the glass Mrs. Barton affected to arrange her hair with soft touches of the weak, white hands. The room was warm. The red-satin cushions of the basket-armchairs gleamed in the vivid lights cast by the swiftly-burning peat; and the ferns in the flower-glasses trembled and withered in the grey dimness of an uncertain Irish day.

"How bare and untidy the room looks at this season of the year; really you and Olive ought to go into the conservatory and see if you can't get some geraniums."

"Yes, mamma, I will presently; but it was about Olive that I wanted to speak," said Alice, in a strained and anxious way.

"What a bore that girl is with her serious face," thought Mrs. Barton; but, as it was her habitual policy to take things pleasantly, she laughed coaxingly, and said—

"And what has my grave-faced daughter to say—the learned keeper of the family wisdom?"

Even more than Olive's—for they were less sincere—Mrs. Barton's trivialities jarred the quiet tone of Alice's mind; already her ideas had begun to slip from her, and she to fear that she was committing an indiscretion. But at last, feeling keenly the inadequacy of her words, she said :

"Well, mamma, I wanted to ask you if Olive is going to marry Captain Hibbert ? "

It was now for Mrs Barton to look embarrassed; she had clearly not anticipated the question.

"Well, really, I don't know; nothing is arranged—I never thought about the matter. What could have made you think she was going to marry Captain Hibbert? In my opinion they are not at all suited to each other. Why do you ask me ? "

"Because I have heard you speak of Lord Kilcarney as a man you would like Olive to marry, and, if this be so, I thought I had better tell you about Captain Hibbert. I think she is very much in love with him."

"Oh ! nonsense ; it is only to kill time. A girl must amuse herself somehow."

It was on Alice's lips to ask her mother if she thought such conduct quite right, but, checking herself, she said :

"I am afraid people are talking about it, and that surely is not desirable."

The brown, the almond, the Lady Hamilton eyes, now grew for a moment almost stern ; but the mask that, independent of real sorrow or gladness, had cajoled for twenty years, did not fall—it only trembled, an effort of will replaced it—and Alice hardly guessed what was passing in her mother's mind. Mrs. Barton was sorely annoyed. The sight of the tall, puritanic girl, looking at her with her clear grey candid eyes, irritated her ; and she struggled with the knowledge that she had acted unwisely.

"But why do you come telling me these stories ? " she said.

"Why, mamma," said Alice, astonished at the question, "because I thought it right to do so."

The word "right" was unpleasant; but, recovering her temper, which for years before had never failed her, Mrs. Barton returned to her sweet little flattering manners.

"Of course, of course, my dear girl ; but you do not understand me. What I mean to say is : have you any definite reason for supposing that Olive is in love with Captain Hibbert, and that people are talking about it ? "

"I think so, mamma," said the girl, deceived by this expression of good-will. "You remember when the Scullys came here? Well, Violet was up in our room, and we were showing her our dresses; the conversation somehow turned on Captain Hibbert, and when Violet said that she had seen him that day, as they came along in the carriage, shooting with the Lawlers, Olive burst out crying and rushed out of the room. It was very awkward. Violet said she was very sorry and all that, but——"

"Yes, yes, dear; but why was Olive angry at hearing that Captain Hibbert went out shooting with the Lawlers?"

"Because, it appears, she had previously forbidden him to go there; you know, on account of Mrs. Lawler."

"And what happened then?"

"Well, that's the worst of it. I don't mean to say it was all Olive's fault; I think she must have lost her head a little, for she sent Barnes over that evening to the Lawlers' with a note, telling Captain Hibbert that he must come at once and explain. It was eleven o'clock at night, and they had a long talk through the window."

Mrs. Barton did not speak for some moments. The peat-fire was falling into masses of white ash, and she thought vaguely of putting on some more turf; then her attention was caught by the withering ferns in the flower-glasses, then by the soaking pasture-lands, then by the spiky branches of the chestnut-trees swinging against the grey dead sky.

"But tell me, Alice," she at last said, "for of course it is important that I should know—do you think that Olive is really in love with Captain Hibbert?"

"She told me, as we were going to bed the other night, mamma, that she never could care for anyone else; and—and——"

"And what, dear?"

"I don't like to betray my sister's confidence," Alice said earnestly, "but I am sure I had better tell you the truth: she told me that he had kissed her many times, yesterday afternoon, in the conservatory."

"Indeed! you did very well to let me know of this," said Mrs. Barton, becoming as earnestly inclined as her daughter Alice. "I am sorry that Olive was so foolish; I must speak to her about it. This must not occur again. I think that if you were to tell her to come down here——"

"Oh! no, mamma, Olive would know at once that I had

been speaking about her affairs; you must promise me to make only an indirect use of what I have told you."

"Of course—of course, my dear Alice; no one shall ever know what has passed between us. You can depend upon me. I will not speak to Olive till I get a favourable opportunity. And now I have to go and see after the servants. Are you going upstairs?"

On Alice, tense with the importance of the explanation, this dismissal fell not a little chillingly; but she was glad that she had been able to induce her mother to consider the matter seriously; and never did she think she had seen Mrs. Barton look so grave. Now her elbow was leaned on the mantel-board, on the hand the head was rested, and, above the gold-tinted hair, branched the blue knotted Dresden candlesticks. The fragile Wedgwood tea-service, the old silver cardcases, the Pompadour fans that filled the sandal-wood cabinets hanging between the windows, slept in a twilight as pale as the memory in which the givers lived. The givers had gone as the waves go, leaving only a few shells behind them; but from the further wall, standing on an unassailable crag, on the beach of a stormy sea, milord looked down upon this pleasant oasis.

A few minutes passed dreamily, almost unconsciously, Mrs. Barton threw two sods of turf on the fire, and resumed her thinking. Her first feeling of resentment against her eldest daughter had vanished, and she now thought solely of the difficulty she was in, and how she could best extricate herself from it. "So Olive was foolish enough to allow Captain Hibbert to kiss her in the conservatory!" Mrs. Barton murmured to herself. The morality of the question interested her profoundly. She had never allowed anyone to kiss her before she was married; and she was full of pity and presentiment for the future of a young girl who could thus compromise herself. But in Olive's love for Captain Hibbert Mrs. Barton was concerned only so far as it affected the labour and time that would have to be expended in persuading her to cease to care for him. That this was the right thing to do Mrs. Barton did not for a moment doubt. Her daughter was a beautiful girl, would probably be the belle of the season; therefore, to allow her at nineteen to marry a five-hundred-a-year captain would be, Mrs. Barton thought, to prove herself incapable, if not criminal, in the performance of the most important duty of her life. Mrs. Barton trembled when she thought of the sending of the letter: if the story were to get wind in Dublin it might wreck her hopes of the marquis. Therefore, to tell Barnes to leave the house would be fatal. Things must be managed easily, gently. Olive must be talked to, how far her heart was engaged in the matter must be found out, and she must be made to see the folly, the madness of risking her chance of winning a coronet for the sake of a beggarly five-hundred-a-year captain. And, good heavens! the chaperons: what would they say of her, Mrs. Barton, were such a thing to occur? Mrs. Barton turned from the thought in horror; and then, out of the soul of the old coquette, arose, full-fledged the chaperon, the satellite whose light and glory is dependent on that of the fixed star around which she invitingly revolves.

At this moment Olive, her hands filled with ferns, bounced into the room.

"Oh! here you are, mamma! Alice told me you wanted a few ferns and flowers to make the room look a little tidy. She sent me out to the greenhouse for them."

"I hope you haven't got you feet wet, my dear; if you have, you had better go up at once and change," said Mrs. Barton.

Olive was now more than ever like her father. Her shoulders had grown wider, and the blonde head and scarlet lips had gained a summer brilliance and beauty.

"No, I am not wet," she said, looking down at her boots; "it is not raining; but if it were Alice would send me out all the same."

"Where is she now?"

"Up in her room reading, I suppose; she never stirs out of it. I never saw such a girl in my life. I thought when we came home from school the last time that we would be better friends; but, do you know what I think: Alice is a bit sulky. What do you think, mamma?"

To talk of Alice, to suggest that she was a little jealous, to explain the difficulty of the position she occupied, to commiserate and lavish much pity upon her was, no doubt, a fascinating subject of conversation, it had burned in the brains of mother and daughter for many months; but, too wise to compromise herself with her children, Mrs. Barton resisted the temptation to gratify a vindictiveness that ranked in her heart. She said:

"Alice has not yet found her *beau cavalier ;* we shall see when we are at the Castle if she will remain faithful to her books. I am afraid that Miss Alice will then prefer some gay, dashing young officer to her ' Marmion' and her 'Lara.'"

"I should think so, indeed. She says that the only man she cares to speak to in the county is Dr. Reed, that little frumpy fellow with his medicines. I can't understand her. I couldn't care for anyone but an officer."

This was the chance Mrs. Barton required, and she instantly availed herself of it. "The red-coat fever!" she exclaimed, waving her hands. "There is no one like officers *pour faire passer le temps.*"

"Yes, ma!" cried Olive, proud of having understood so much French; "doesn't time pass quickly with them?"

"It flies, my dear, and they fly away, and then we take up with another. They are all nice; their profession makes them that."

"But some are nicer than others; for instance, I am sure they are not all as nice as Captain Hibbert."

"Oh! indeed they are," said Mrs. Barton, laughing; "wait until we get to Dublin; you have no idea what nice men we shall meet there ; and then we shall find a lord or an earl, or perhaps a marquis, who will give a coroneted carriage to my beautiful girl to drive in."

Olive tossed her head, laughed nervously, but said nothing. Her mother looked at her admiringly, and there was love in the sweet brown deceit of the melting eyes; a hard, worldly affection, but a much warmer one than any Mrs. Barton could feel for Alice, in whom she saw nothing but failure, and in the end certain spinsterhood. After a pause she said:

"What a splendid match Lord Kilcarney would be, and where would he find a girl like my Olive to do the honours of his house?"

"Oh! mamma, I never could marry him!"

"And why not, my dear girl?"

"I don't know, he's a silly little fool ; besides, I like Captain Hibbert."

"Yes, you like Captain Hibbert, so do I; but a girl like you could not throw herself away on a five-hundred-a-year captain in the army."

"And why not, mamma?" said Olive, who had already begun to whimper; "Captain Hibbert loves me, I know, very dearly, and I like him; he is of very good family, and he has enough to support me."

The moment was a supreme one, and Mrs. Barton hesitated to strike and bring the matter to a head. Would it be better, she asked herself, to let things slide and use her influence for the future in one direction? After a brief pause she decided on the former course. She said:

"My dear child, neither your father nor myself could ever consent to see you throw yourself away on Captain Hibbert. I am afraid you have seen too much of him, and have been led away into caring for him. But take my word for it, a girl's love is only *à fleur de peau*. When you have been to a few of the Castle balls you'll soon forget all about him. Remember you are not twenty yet; it would be madness."

"Oh! mamma, I did not think you were so cruel!" exclaimed Olive—and she rushed out of the room.

Mrs. Barton made no reply, but her resolve was rapidly gaining strength in her mind: Olive's flirtation was to be brought at once to a close. Captain Hibbert she would admit no more, and the girl was in turn to be wheedled and coerced. Nor did Mrs. Barton for a moment doubt that she would succeed; she had never tasted failure; and she stayed only a moment to regret, for she was too much a woman of the world to waste time in considering her mistakes. The needs of the moment were ever present to her, and she now devoted herself entirely to the task of consoling her daughter. Barnes, too, was well instructed, and henceforth she spoke only of the earls, dukes, lords, and princes who were waiting for Olive at the Castle.

In the afternoon Mrs. Barton made her come down to the drawing-room, where woman was represented as a triumphant creature walking towards great but undetermined success over the heads and hearts of men. "*Le génie de la femme est la beauté,*" declared Milord, and again: "*Le cœur de l'homme ne peut servir que de piédestal pour l'idole.*"

"Oh! milord, milord!" said Mrs. Barton. "So in worshipping us you are idolators. I'm ashamed of you."

"Pardon, pardon, madam: *Devant un amour faux on est idolâtre, mais à l'autel d'un vrai, on est chrétien.*"

And in such lugubrious gaiety the girl grieved. Captain Hibbert had been refused admission; he had written, but his letters had been intercepted; and holding them in her hand

Mrs. Barton explained that she could not consent to such a marriage; while she dazzled the girl with visions of the honours that awaited the future Marchioness of Kilcarney. " An engaged girl is not noticed at the Castle. You don't know what nice fellows you'll meet there; have your fun out first," were the arguments most frequently put forward; and, in the excitement of breaking off Olive's engagement, even the Land League was forgotten. Distracted by girlish love and vanity, Olive hesitated many days, but at length she was persuaded to at least try to captivate the marquis before she honoured the captain with her hand. Then Mrs. Barton lost not a moment in writing to Captain Hibbert, asking him to come and see them the following day, if possible, between eleven and twelve. She wanted to speak to him on a matter which had lately come to her knowledge, and which had occasioned her a good deal of surprise.

The letter was scarcely gone when it transpired that it was on the morrow that Mr. Barton had arranged to meet his tenants. But it was impossible to countermand her appointment, and Mrs. Barton spent the evening talking to Olive of Castle and London seasons, amusement, admiration, successes carried off in the face of many disappointed rivals. Alice, too, was ordered, before she went to sleep, to say something to this effect: that it would be absurd for Olive to waste her beauty on a five-hundred-a-year captain; that she was worthy of a crowned head.

During breakfast next morning, all—Mr. Barton, perhaps, excepted—felt that momentous events were gradually nearing them. He could think of nothing but the muscles of the strained back of a dying Briton, and a Roman soldier who cut the cords that bound the white captive to the sacrificial oak. He declared that it would be no use returning to the studio until these infernal tenants were settled with, and he loitered about the drawing-room windows looking pale, picturesque, and lymphatic. His presence irritated Mrs. Barton. At times she strove to prompt the arguments that should be used to induce the tenants to accept the proffered abatement, but she could not detach her thoughts from the terrible interview she was about to go through with Captain Hibbert. She expected him to be violent; he would insist on seeing Olive: and could she depend on the girl to refuse him to his face ? The question clanged like a bell within her brain : and she watched wearily the rain dripping from the wooden edges of the verandah, and the last patches of snow melting around the roots of the chestnut-trees. At last a car was seen approaching : it was closely followed by another bearing four policemen.

"Here's your agent," exclaimed Mrs. Barton, hurriedly, "don't bring him in here ; go out and meet him, and, when you see Captain Hibbert, welcome him as cordially as you can. But don't speak to him of Olive, and don't give him time to speak to you : say you are engaged. I don't want Mr. Scully to know anything about this break-off. It is most unfortunate you did not tell me you were going to meet your tenants to-day. However, it is too late now."

"Very well, my dear, very well," said Mr. Barton, trying to find his hat. "I would, I assure you, give twenty pounds to be out of the whole thing. I cannot argue with those fellows about their rents. I think the Government ought to let us fight it out. I should be very glad to take the command of a flying column of landlords, and make a dash into Connemara. I have always thought my military genius more allied to that of Napoleon than to that of Wellington."

It was always difficult to say how far Mr. Barton believed in the extravagant remarks he was in the habit of giving utterance to. Not being devoid of humour, he perceived their absurdity, although he seemed to doubt the entire inaccuracy of what he said. And now, as he picked his way across the wet stones, his pale hair blown about in the wild wind, he presented a strange contrast with the short-set vulgar man who had just got down from the car. Mr. Scully, having lived all his life among bullocks, partook of their animality. His thick legs were encased in gaiters, and he wore a long ulster.

"How d' yer do, Barton?" he exclaimed; "d' yer know that I think things are gitting worse instid of bither. There's been another bailiff shot in Mayo, and we've had a process-server nearly beaten to death down our side of the counthry. Gad ! I was out with the Sub-Sheriff and fifty police thrying to serve notices on Lord Rosshill's estate, and we had to come back as we wint. Such blawing of horns you niver heard in yer life. The howle counthry was up, and they had a trench cut across the road as wide as a canal."

"Well, what do you think we had better do with these fellows ? do you think they will take the twenty per cent. ?"

"'Tis impossible to say. Gad ! the Lague is gittin' stronger ivery day, Barton. But they ought to take it; twenty per cent. will bring it very nearly to Griffith's."

"But if they don't take it?"

"Well, I don't know what we will do, for notices it is impossible to serve. Gad! I'll never forgit how we were pelted the other day—such firing of stones, such blawing of horns! I think you'll have to give them the thirty; but we'll thry them at twinty-foive."

"And if they won't take it?"—

"What, the thirty?—they'll take that and jumping, you needn't fear. Here they come."

Turning, the two men watched the twenty or thirty peasants who, with heads set against the wild gusts, advanced steadily up the avenue. They gave way to a horseman, and, from the drawing-room window, Mrs. Barton recognised the square-set shoulders of Captain Hibbert. After shaking hands and speaking a few words with Mr. Barton, he trotted round to the stables; and when he walked back and entered the house, in all the clean-cut elegance of military boots and trousers, the peasants lifted their hats, and the interview began.

"Now, boys," said Mr. Barton, who thought that a little familiarity would not be inappropriate, "I have asked you to meet me so that we might come to some agreement about the rents. We have known each other a long time, and my family has been on this estate I don't know for how many generations. Therefore—why, of course, I should be very sorry if we had any falling-out. I don't know much about farming, but I hear everyone say that this has been a capital year; and now! . . . well, I think I cannot do better than to make you again the same offer as I made you before, that is to say, of twenty per cent. abatement all round; that will bring your rents down to Griffith's valuation."

Mr. Barton had intended to be very impressive; but, feeling that words were betraying him, he stopped short and waited anxiously to hear what answer the peasant who had stepped forward would make. The old man began by removing a battered tall-hat, out of which fell a red handkerchief. The handkerchief was quickly thrown back into the crown, and, at an intimation from Mr. Barton, hat and handkerchief were replaced upon the white head. He then commenced:

"Now, yer honour, the rints is too high; we cannot pay the present rint, at least without a reduction. I have been a tinent on the property, and my fathers before me, for the past fifty years. And it was in forty-three that the rints was ruz—in the time of your father, the Lord have mercy on his soul !—but he had an agent who was a hard man, and he ruz the rints; and since then we have been in poverty, livin' on yaller mail, and praties, and praties that is watery ; there is no diet in them, yer honour. And if yer honour will come down and walk the lands yerself, yer wi' see I am spaking the truth—we ask nothing better than yer should walk the lands yerself. There is two acres of my land, yer honour, flooded for three months of the year, and for that land I am paying twenty-five shillings an acre. I have my receipts, paid down to the last gale-day."

And, still speaking, the old man fumbled in his pockets and produced a large pile of papers which he strove to push into Mr. Barton's hand, alluding all the while to the losses he had sustained. Two pigs had died on him, and he had lost a fine mare and foal. His loquacity was, however, cut short by a sturdy middle-aged peasant standing next him.

"And I, too, yer honour, am payin' five-and-twenty shillin's for the same flooded land. Yer honour can come down any day and see it. It is not worth to me more than fifteen shillings an acre at the bare-outside. But it could be drained, for there is a fall into the marin stream betwixt yer honour's property and the Miss Brennans'. It wouldn't cost more than forty pound, and the Miss Brennans will pay half if yer honour will pay the other."

Mr. Barton listened patiently to those peasant-like digressions while Mrs. Barton listened patiently to the Captain's fervid declarations of love. He had begun by telling her of the anguish it had caused him to have been denied, and three times running, admittance to Brookfield. One whole night he had lain awake wondering what he had done to offend them. Mrs. Barton could imagine how he had suffered, for she, he ventured to say, must have long since guessed what were his feelings for her daughter.

"We were very sorry to have been out, and it is so unusual that we should be," said Mrs. Barton, leaning forward her face insinuatingly. "But you were speaking of Olive. We say here that there is no one like *le beau capitaine*, no one so handsome, no one so nice, no one so gallant, and—and—" here Mrs. Barton laughed merrily ;—for she thought the disagreeabilities of life might be so cunningly wrapped up in sweet compliments that both could be taken together like sugared medicine—in one childlike gulp. "There is, of course, no one I should prefer to *le beau capitaine*—there is no one to whom I would confide my Olive more willingly—but, then, one must look to other things; one cannot live entirely on love, even if it be the love of a *beau capitaine*."

The last phrase was spoken with another merry little laugh, and another wave of the white hands. Nevertheless, the man's face darkened. The eyebrows were contracted, the straight white nose seemed to grow straighter, and he twirled his moustache angrily.

"I am aware, my dear Mrs. Barton, that I cannot give your daughter the position I should like to, but I am not as poor as you seem to imagine. Independent of my pay, which is two, I have five hundred a year; Miss Barton has, if I be not mistaken, some money of her own; and, as I shall get my majority within the next five years, I may say that we shall begin life upon something more than a thousand a year."

"It is true that I have led you to believe that Olive has money, but Irish money can be no longer counted upon. Were Mr. Barton to create a charge on his property, how would it be possible for him to guarantee the payment of the interest in such times as the present ? We are living on the brink of a precipice. We do not know what is, and what is not, our own. The Land League is ruining us, and the Government will not put it down; this year the tenants may pay at twenty per cent. reduction, but next year they may refuse to pay at all. Look out there ; you see they are making their own terms with Mr. Barton."

"I should be delighted to give you thirty per cent. if I could afford it," said Mr. Barton, as soon as the question of reduction, that had been lost in schemes for draining, and discussion concerning bad seasons, had been re-established, "but you must remember that I have to pay charges, and my creditors won't wait any more than yours will. If you refuse to pay your rents and I get sold out, you will have another landlord here ; you'll ruin me, but you won't do yourselves any good ; you will have some Englishman here who will make you pay your rents."

"An Englishman here !" exclaimed a peasant, "arrah ! he'll go back quicker than he came."

"Maybe he wouldn't go back at all," cried another, chuckling. "We'd make an Oirishman of him for ever."

" Begad, we'd make him wear the grane in raal earnest, and, a foine scraw it would be," said a third.

The witticism was greeted with a roar of laughter, and upon this expression of a somewhat verdant patriotism, the dispute concerning the reduction was resumed.

" Give us the land all round at the Government valuation," said a man in the middle of the group.

" Why, you are only fifteen per cent. above the valuation," cried Mr. Scully.

For a moment this seemed to create a difference of opinion among the peasants ; but the League had drawn them too firmly together to be thus easily divided. They talked amongst themselves in Irish. Then the old man said :

" We can't take less than thirty, yer honour, the Lague wouldn't let us."

" I can't give you more than twenty."

" Thin let us come on home, thin ; no use us wasting our toime here," cried a sturdy peasant, who, although he had spoken but seldom, seemed to exercise an authority over the others. With one accord they followed him, but, rushing forward, Mr. Scully seized him by the arm, saying :

" Now then, boys, come back, come back, he'll settle with you right enough if you'll listen to reason."

From the drawing-room window Mrs. Barton watched, her little selfish soul racked with dividual doubt. On one side she saw her daughter's beautiful white face becoming the prize of a penniless officer ; on the other she saw the pretty furniture, the luxurious idleness, the very silk dress on her back, being torn from them, and distributed among a crowd of Irish-speaking, pig-keeping peasants. Her eyes gleamed with hatred of them. She could see that some new and important point was being argued ; and it was with a wrench she detached her thoughts from the pantomime that was being enacted within her view, and, turning to Captain Hibbert, said :

" You see, you see what is happening ; we are, that is to say, we may be, ruined at any moment by this wicked agitation. As I have said before, there is no one I should like so much as yourself ; but, in the face of such a future, how could I consent to give you my daughter ?—that is to say, I could not unless you could settle at least a thousand a year upon her. She has been brought up in every luxury."

"That may be, Mrs. Barton. I hope to give her quite as comfortable a home as any she has been accustomed to. But a thousand a year is impossible—I haven't got it; but I can settle five hundred on her, and there's many a peeress of the realm who hasn't that. Of course five hundred a year is very little—no one feels it more than I; for had I the riches of the world, I should not consider them sufficient to create a place worthy of Olive's beauty. But love must be allowed to count for something, and I think, yes I can safely say, she will never find——"

"Yes, I know, I am sure, but it cannot be."

"Then you mean to say that you will sacrifice your daughter's happiness for the sake of a little wretched pride?"

"Why press the matter further?—why cannot we remain friends?"

"Friends! yes, I hope we shall remain friends; but I will never consent to give up Olive. She loves me, I know she does; my life is bound up in hers. No I will never consent, Mrs. Barton, to give her up, and I know she won't give me up."

"Olive has laughed and flirted with you, but it was only *pour passer le temps,* and I may as well tell you that you are mistaken when you think that she loves you."

"Olive does love me, I know she does, and I will not believe she does not—at least until she tells me so. I consider I am engaged to her, and I must beg of you, Mrs. Barton, to allow me to see her and hear from her own lips what she has to say on this matter."

With the eyes of one about to tempt fortune adventurously, like one about to play a bold card for a high stake, Mrs. Barton looked on the tall handsome man before her, and, impersonal as were her feelings, she could not but admire, for the space of one swift thought, the pale aristocratic face now alive with passion. Could she depend upon Olive to say "no" to him? The impression of the moment was that no girl would. Nevertheless, she must risk the interview. Gliding towards the door with her usual cat-like motion, she called to the girl several times. Then, as a cloud that grows bright in the sudden sunshine, the man's face glowed with delight, and a moment after, white and drooping as a flower, the girl entered. Captain Hibbert made a movement as if he were going to rush forward to meet her; she looked as if she would have opened her arms to receive him, but Mrs. Barton's words fell between them like a sword.

"Olive," she said, "I hear you are engaged to Captain Hibbert! Is it true?"

Startled in the drift of her emotions, and believing her confidence had been betrayed, the girl's first impulse was to deny the impeachment. No absolute promise of marriage had she given him, and she said:

"No, mamma, I am not engaged; did Edward, I mean Captain Hibbert, say I was engaged to him? I am sure——"

"Did you not tell me Olive, that you loved me better than anyone else? Did you not even say you could never love anyone else? If I had thought that——"

"I knew my daughter would not have engaged herself to you, Captain Hibbert, without telling me of it. As I have told you before, we all like you very much, but this marriage is impossible; and I will never consent, at least for the present, to an engagement between you."

"Olive, have you nothing to say? I will not give you up unless you tell me yourself that I must do so."

"Oh! mamma, what shall I do?" said Olive, bursting into a passionate flood of tears.

"Say what I told you to say," whispered Mrs. Barton.

"You see, Edward, that mamma won't consent, at least not for the present, to our engagement."

This was enough for Mrs. Barton's purpose, and, soothing her daughter with many words, she led her to the door. Then, confronting Captain Hibbert, she said, with something of her old wheedling manner:

"There is never any use in forcing on these violent scenes. As I have told you, there is no one I should prefer to yourself. We always say here, that there is no one like *le beau capitaine,* but, in the face of these bad times, how can I give you my daughter? And you soldiers forget so quickly. In a year's time you will have forgotten all about Olive."

"That is not true; I shall never forget her. I cannot forget her; but I will consent to wait if you will consent to our being engaged."

"No, Captain Hibbert, I think it is better not; I do not approve of those long engagements."

"Then you will forget what has passed between us, and let us be the same friends as we were before?"

" I hope we shall always remain friends ; but I do not think
for my daughter's peace of mind, it would be advisable for us
to see as much of each other as we have hitherto done. And I
hope you will promise me not to communicate with my Olive
in any way."

" Why should I enter into promises with you, Mrs. Barton,
when you decline to enter into any with me ? "

Mrs. Barton did not look as if she intended to answer this
question. The conversation had fallen, and her thoughts had
gone back to the tenants and the reduction, and Mr. Scully
was now persuading them to accept twenty-five per cent. He
talked apart, first with one, then with another. His square
bluff figure in a long coarse ulster stood out in strong relief
against the green grass and the evergreens ;—Mr. Barton,
intensely wearied, shivered in his thin studio-clothes, and
overhead the gaunt branches of the chestnuts reeled in a wild
wet wind.

" Thin it is decided yer pay at twinty-foive per cint," said
Mr. Scully.

" Then, Captain Hibbert," said Mrs. Barton a little sternly,
" I am very sorry indeed that we can't agree, but, after what
has passed between us to-day, I do not think you will be justi-
fied in again trying to see my daughter."

" Begad, sor, they were all aginst me for agraying to take
the twinty-foive," whispered the well-to-do tenant who was
talking to the agent.

" I fail to understand," said Captain Hibbert, haughtily,
" that Miss Barton said anything that would lead me to suppose
that she wished me to give her up. However, I do not see
that anything would be gained by discussing this matter
further—good morning, Mrs. Barton."

" Good morning, Captain Hibbert," and Mrs. Barton smiled
winningly as she rang the bell for the servant to show him out.
When she returned to the window the tenants were following
Mr. Scully into the rent-office, and, with a feeling of real
satisfaction she murmured to herself—

" Well, after all, nothing ever turns out as badly as we
expect it."

CHAPTER VIII.

But, although Mrs. Barton had bidden the captain away, Olive's sorrowful looks haunted the house.

A white weary profile was seen on the staircase, a sigh was heard when she left the room; and when, after hours of absence, she was sought for, she was constantly found lying at full length, crying upon her bed. Mrs. Barton began to fear seriously for her daughter's beauty.

"My dear, it distresses me to see you in this state. You really must get up; I cannot allow it. There's nothing that spoils one's good looks like unhappiness. Instead of being the belle of the season, you'll be a complete wreck. I must insist on your getting up, and trying to interest yourself in something."

"Oh! mamma, don't, don't! I wish I were dead, I am sick of everything!"

"Sick of everything?" said Mrs. Barton, laughing. "Why, my dear child, you have tasted nothing yet. Wait until we get to the Castle; you'll see what a lot of Captain Hibberts there will be after this pretty face; that's to say if you don't spoil it in the meantime with fretting."

There was an insidious magic in Mrs. Barton's laugh; it was artificial, irresistible, gleeful, birdlike as an opera by Offenbach; it was characteristic of the woman; it tempted you to look upon life lightly; it helped you to play with, to twirl your worst sorrows round your finger. Had fate favoured Mrs. Barton she might have been a royal courtezan.

Olive smiled through her tears:

"But, mamma," she said, "how can I help thinking of him? —there's nothing to do here, one never hears of anything but that horrid Land League—whether the Government will or will not help the landlords, whether Paddy So-and-so will or will not pay his rent. I am sick of it. Milord comes to see you, and Alice likes reading-books, and papa has his painting; but I have nothing since you sent Captain Hibbert away."

" Yes, yes, my beautiful Olive flower, it is a little dull for you at present, and to think that this wicked agitation should have begun the very season you were coming out ! Who could have foreseen such a thing ? But come, my pet, I cannot allow you to ruin your beautiful complexion with foolish tears ; you must get up ; unfortunately I can't have you in the drawing-room, I have to talk business with milord, but you can go out for a walk with Alice—it is not raining to-day."

" Oh ! no ; I couldn't go out to walk with Alice, it would bore me to death. She never talks about anything that interests me."

For a moment the sweet pastel-like expression of Mrs. Barton's features was lost. She foresaw the trouble this plain girl would be to chaperon. The annoyance of having to find her partners would be great, and to have her dragging after her all through the Castle season would be intolerable. And all these airs of virtue, and injured innocence, how insupportable they were ! Alice, as far as Mrs. Barton could see, was fit for nothing. Even now, instead of helping to console her sister, and win her thoughts away from Captain Hibbert, she shut herself up to read books. Such a taste for reading and moping she had never seen in a girl before—*voilà un type de vieille fille.* Whom did she take after ? Certainly not after her mother, nor yet her father. It was impossible to say whom she did take after, unless it was after her grandfather—the old frump in the white waistcoat, over the dining-room chimneypiece—who had spent his life writing histories, and whose manuscripts filled several large trunks, piled away overhead in an attic. But what was the good of thinking of the tiresome girl ? There were plenty of other thing far more important to consider, and the first thing of all was—how to make Olive forget Captain Hibbert ? On this point Mrs. Barton was not quite satisfied with the manner in which she had played her part. Olive's engagement had been broken off by too violent means, and nothing was more against her nature than (to use her own expression) to *brusquer les choses.* Early in life Mrs. Barton discovered that she could amuse men, and since then she had devoted herself assiduously to the cultivation of this talent, and the divorce between herself and her own sex was from the first complete.

She not only did not seek to please, but she made no attempt to conceal her aversion to the society of women, and her preference for those forms of entertainment where they were found in fewest numbers. Balls were, therefore, never much to her taste ; at the dinner-table she was freer, but it was on the racecourse that she reigned supreme. From the box-seat of a drag the white hands were waved, the cajoling laugh was set going ; and fashionably-dressed men, with race-glasses about their shoulders, came crowding and climbing about her like bees about their queen. Mrs. Barton had passed from flirtation to flirtation without a violent word. With a wave of her hands she had called the man she wanted; with a wave of her hands, and a tinkle of the bell-like laugh, she had dismissed him. Nothing had apparently cost her a sigh; apparently nothing had ever been denied her. Success had always been hers. But now all was going wrong. Olive was whining and crying and losing her good looks. Mr. Barton had received a threatening letter, and, in consequence, had for a week past been unable to tune his guitar; poor Lord Dungory was being bored to death by protecting policemen and proselytising daughters. Decidedly everything was going wrong. This phrase was recurrent in Mrs. Barton's thoughts as she reviewed the situation. Her head was leaned in the pose of the most plaintive of the pastels that Lord Dungory had commissioned his favourite artist to execute in imitation of the Lady Hamilton portraits. And now, his finger on his lip, like harlequin glancing after columbine, the old gentleman, who had entered on tiptoe, exclaimed :

> " *Avez vous vu, dans Barcelone*
> *Une Andalouse au sein bruni ?*
> *Pâle comme un beau soir d'Automne ;*
> *C'est ma maîtresse, ma lionne !*
> *La Marquesa d'Amalëqui.*"

Instantly the silver laugh was set a-tinkling, and, with delightful gestures, milord was led captive to the sofa. "*C'est l'aurore qui vient pour dissiper les brumes du matin,*" Mrs. Barton declared as she settled her skirts over her ankles.

> " *Qu'elle est superbe en son désordre*
> *Quand elle tombe. . . .*"

"Hush, hush !" exclaimed Mrs. Barton, bursting with laughter ; and, placing her hand (which was instantly fer-

vently kissed) upon milord's mouth, she said : " I will hear no
more of that wicked poetry."

"What! hear no more of the divine Alfred de Musset?"
milord answered, as if a little discouraged.

At this moment Alice entered. She had come from her
room to fetch a book, but, obeying an involuntary impulse,
on seeing the couple on the sofa, she tried to retreat ; and
she added to her own and their embarrassment by uttering
some ill-expressed excuses.

"My dear, don't run away like that," said Mrs. Barton ;
"don't behave like a charity-school girl ; come in. I think
you know Lord Dungory."

"Oh! this is the studious one," said milord, as he took
Alice affectionately with both hands, and drew her towards
him. "Now look at this fair brow, I am sure there is poetry
here. I was just speaking to your mother about Alfred de
Musset. He is not quite proper, it is true, for you girls ; but
oh! what passion! He is the poet of passion. I suppose you
love Byron?"

"Yes, but not so much as Shelley and Keats," said Alice,
enthusiastically, forgetting for the moment her aversion to the
speaker in the allusion to her favourite pursuit.

"The study of Shelley is the fashion of the day. You
know, I suppose, the little piece entitled ' Love's Philosophy'?
—'The fountains mingle with the river ; the river with the
ocean.' You know ' Nothing in the world is single : all things,
by a law divine, in one another's being mingle. Why not I
with thine?'"

"Oh! yes, and the ' Sensitive Plant,' is it not lovely?"

"There is your book, my dear ; you must run away now ;
I have to talk with milord about important business."

Milord looked disappointed at being thus interrupted in
his quotations ; but he allowed himself to be led back to the
sofa. "I beg your pardon for a moment," said Mrs. Barton,
whom a sudden thought had struck ; and she followed her
daughter out of the room.

"Instead of wasting your time reading all this love-poetry,
Alice, it would be much better if you would devote a little of
your time to your sister ; she is left all alone, and you know I
don't care that she should be always in Barnes' society."

"But what am I to do, mamma? I have often asked Olive
to come out with me, but she says I don't amuse her."

"I want you to win her thoughts away from that horrid man, Captain Hibbert," said Mrs. Barton, trying to conceal her vindictiveness; "she is grieving her heart out and will be a wreck before we go to Dublin. Tell her you heard at Dungory Castle that he was flirting with other girls; that he is not worth thinking about, and that the Marquis is in love with her."

"But that would be scarcely the truth, mamma," Alice replied, hesitatingly.

Mrs. Barton gave her daughter one quick look; bit her lips, and, without another word, returned to milord. Everything was decidedly going wrong; and to be annoyed by that gawk of a girl in a time like the present, was unbearable. But Mrs. Barton never allowed her temper to master her, and in two minutes all memory of Alice had passed out of her mind, and she was talking business with Lord Dungory. Many important questions had to be decided. It was known that mortgages, jointures, legacies, and debts of all kinds had reduced the Marquis's income to a minimum, and that he stood in urgent need of a little ready-money. It was known that his relations looked to an heiress to rehabilitate the family fortunes. Mrs. Barton hoped to dazzle him with Olive's beauty, but it was characteristic of her to wish to bait the hook on every side, and she hoped that a little gilding of it would silence the chorus of scorn and dissent that she knew would be raised against her, when once her plans became known. Four thousand pounds might be raised on the Brookfield property, but, if this sum could be multiplied by five, Mrs. Barton felt she would be going into the matrimonial-market armed to the teeth, and prepared to meet all comers. And, seeking the solution of this problem, milord and Mrs. Barton sat on the sofa, drawn up close together, their knees touching; he, although gracious and urbane as was his wont, seemed more than usually thoughtful; she, although as charmful and cajoling as ever, in the pauses of the conversation, allowed an expression of anxiety to cloud her bright face. Fifteen thousand pounds requires a good deal of accounting for; but, after many arguments had been advanced on either side, it was decided that she had made, within the last seven years, many successful investments. She had commenced by winning five hundred pounds at racing, and this money had been put into Mexican railways. The speculation had proved an excellent

one, and then with a few airy and casual references to Hudson
Bay, Grand Trunks, and shares in steamboats, it was thought
the creation of Olive's fortune could be satisfactorily explained
to a not too exacting society.

Three or four days after, Mrs. Barton surprised the young
ladies by visiting them in the sitting-room. Barnes was
working at the machine, Olive stood drumming her fingers
idly against the window-pane.

"Just fancy seeing you, mamma ! I was looking out for
milord ; he is a little late to-day, is he not ? " said Olive.

" I do not expect him to-day—he is suffering from a bad cold ;
this weather is dreadfully trying—but how snug you are in
your little room ; and Alice is absolutely doing needlework."

"I wonder what I am doing wrong now," thought the girl.

Barnes left the room. Mrs. Barton threw some turf upon
the fire, and she looked round. Her eyes rested on the cardboard boxes—on the bodice left upon the work-table—on the
book that Alice had laid aside. In brief phrases she spoke of
these things, evidently striving to interest herself in the girl's
occupation. At length she said :

"If the weather clears up I think we might all go for a
drive ; there is really no danger. The Land League never
has women fired at. We might go and see the Brennans.
What do you think, Olive ? "

" I don't care to go off there to see a pack of women," the
girl replied, still drumming her fingers on the window-pane.

" Now, Olive, don't answer so crossly, but come and sit
down here by me," and, to make room for her, Mrs. Barton
moved nearer to Alice. " So my beautiful Olive doesn't care
for a pack of women," said Mrs. Barton, and the room
resounded with the silver tinkling of her laughter. " Olive
does not like a pack of women ; she would prefer a handsome
young Lord, or a Duke, or an Earl."

Olive turned up her lips contemptuously, for she guessed
her mother's meaning.

" What curious lives those girls do lead, cooped up there by
themselves ; with their little periodical trip up to the Shelbourne Hotel. Of course the two young ones never could have
done much ; they never open their lips, but Gladys is a nice
girl in her way, and she has some money of her own. I
wonder she wasn't picked up."

" I should like to know who would care for her ? "

"She had a very good chance once; but she wouldn't say yes, and she wouldn't say no, and she kept him hanging after her until at last off he went and married someone else. He was a Mr. Blake.

"Oh! that was his name; and why wouldn't she marry him?"

"Well, I don't know—folly I suppose. He was of course not so young as Harry Renley, but he had two thousand a year, and he would have made her an excellent husband; kept a carriage for her, and a house in London : whereas you see she has remained Miss Brennan, goes up every year to the Shelbourne Hotel to buy dresses, and gets older and more withered every day."

"I know they lead a stupid life down here, but mightn't they go abroad and travel?" asked Alice; "they are no longer so very young."

"A woman can do nothing until she is married," Mrs. Barton answered decisively.

"But some husbands treat their wives infamously; isn't no husband better than a bad husband?"

"I don't think so," returned Mrs. Barton, and she glanced sharply at her daughter. "I would sooner have the worst husband in the world than no husband." Then settling herself like a pleader who has come to the incisive point of his argument, she continued: "A woman is absolutely nothing without a husband: if she does not wish to pass for a failure she must get a husband: and upon this all her ideas should be set. I have always found that in this life we can only hope to succeed in what we undertake by keeping our minds fixed on it and never letting it out of sight until it is attained. Keep on trying, that is my advice to all young ladies : try to make yourselves agreeable, try to learn how to amuse men. Flatter them; that is the great secret; nineteen out of twenty will believe you, and the one that doesn't can't but think it delightful. Don't waste your time thinking of your books, your painting, your accomplishments; if you were Jane Austens, George Eliots, and Rosa Bonheurs, it would be of no use if you weren't married. A husband is better than talent, better even than fortune—without a husband a woman is nothing; with a husband she may rise to any height. Marriage gives a girl liberty, gives her admiration, gives her success; a woman's whole position depends upon it. And while we are on the subject it is as well to have one's say, and I speak for you both. You, Alice, are too much inclined to shrink into the background and waste your time with those horrid books;

and you too, Olive, are behaving very foolishly, wasting your time and your complexion over a silly girlish flirtation."

"There's no use talking about that. You have forbidden him the house ; you can't do any more."

" No, Olive, all I did was to insist that he should not come running after you until you had had time to consider the sacrifices you were making for him. I have no one's interests in the world, my dear girl, but your interests. Officers are all very well to laugh, talk, and flirt with—*pour passer le temps*— but I could not allow you to throw yourself away on the first man you meet. You will meet hundreds of others quite as handsome and as nice at the Castle."

" I never could care for anyone else."

"Wait until you have seen the others. Besides what do you want ? to be engaged to him ? And I should like to know what is the use of my taking an engaged girl up to the Castle ? No one would look at you."

Olive raised her eyes in astonishment ; she had not considered the question from this point of view, and the suggestion that, if engaged, she might as well stop at home, for no one would look at her, clearly filled her with alarm.

" Whereas," said Mrs, Barton, who saw that her words had the intended effect, " if you were free you would be the belle of the season ; nothing would be thought of but you ; you would have lords, and earls, and marquesses dancing attendance on you, begging you to dance with them ; you would be spoken of in the papers, described as the new beauty and what not, and then if you were free !" Here Mrs. Barton heaved a deep sigh, and, letting her white hand fall over the arm of her chair, she seemed to abandon herself to the irrevocable decrees of destiny.

" Well, what then, mamma ? " asked Olive excitedly. " I am free, am I not ? "

" Then you could cut out the other girls, and carry off the great prize. They are all watching him ; he will go to one of you for certain. I hear that Mrs. Scully—that great, fat, common creature, who sold bacon in a shop in Galway—is thinking of him for her daughter. Of course, if you like to see Violet become a marchioness, right under your nose, you can do so.

" But what do you want me to do ? " exclaimed the coronet dazzled girl.

"Merely to think no more of Captain Hibbert. But I did not tell you;—he was very impertinent to me when I last saw him. He said he would flirt with you, as long as you would flirt with him, and that he didn't see why you shouldn't amuse yourself. That's what I want to warn you against—losing your chance of being a marchioness to help an idle young officer to wile away his time. If I were you, I would tell him, when I next saw him, that he must not think about it any more. You can put it all down to me; say that I would never hear of it; say that you couldn't think of disobeying me, but that you hope you will always remain friends. You see that's the advantage of having a mother;—poor mamma has to bear everything."

Olive made no direct answer, but she laughed nervously, and in a manner that betokened assent; and, having so far won her way, Mrs. Barton determined to conclude. But she could not invite Captain Hibbert to the house! The better plan would be to meet on neutral ground. A luncheon party at Dungory Castle instantly suggested itself; and three days after, as they drove through the park, Mrs. Barton explained to Olive, for the last time, how she should act if she wished to become the Marchioness of Kilcarney.

"Shake hands with him just as if nothing had happened, but don't enter into conversation; and after lunch I shall arrange that we all go out for a walk on the terrace. You will then pair off with him, Alice; Olive will join you. Something will be sure to occur that will give her an opportunity of saying that he must think no more about her—that I would never consent."

"Oh! mamma, it is very hard, for I can never forget him."

"Now, my dear girl, for goodness' sake don't work yourself up into a state of mind, or we may as well go back to Brookfield. What I tell you to do is right; and if you see nobody at the Castle that you like better—well, then it will be time enough. I want you to be, at least, the beauty of one season."

This argument again turned the scales. Olive laughed, but her laugh was full of the nervous excitement from which she suffered. "I shan't know what to say," she exclaimed, tossing her head, "so I hope you will help me out of my difficulty, Alice."

"I wish I could be left out of it altogether," said the girl, who was sitting with her back to the horses. "It seems to me that I am being put into a very false position!"

"Put into a false position!" said Mrs. Barton; and for a moment the melting, Greuze-like eyes hardened and flashed with golden lights. "I'll hear no more of this! If you won't do as you are told you had better go back to St. Leonards—such wicked jealousy."

"Oh, mamma!" said Alice wounded to the quick, "how can you be so unjust?" She could say no more; and her eyes filled with acute tears. Since she had left school she had experienced little but a sense of retreating within herself, to escape the blinding and filthy rain of falsehood that swept in from all sides. But now the last refuge, the last verge had been reached. To live, to think, to act as did those by whom she was surrounded was impossible. Whither to go? A broken world seemed to slide and reel beneath her feet. Why was she not like the others?—why could she not think as they did? her soul cried out in its anguish; and for the pain it caused her, she almost hated the invincible goodness of her nature. Mrs. Barton was a close observer, and, seeing her temper had betrayed her into a grave indiscretion, she said:

"I am sorry, Alice dear, for having spoken so crossly; but I am sorely tried. I really am more to be pitied than blamed; and, if you knew all, you would, I know, be the first to try to help me out of my difficulties, instead of striving to increase them."

"I would do anything to help you," exclaimed Alice, deceived by the accent of sorrow with which Mrs. Barton knew how to invest her words.

"I am sure you would, if you knew how much depends— But dry your eyes, my dear, for goodness' sake. Here we are at the door. I only want you to be with Olive when she tells Captain Hibbert that she cannot—and, now mind, Olive, you tell him plainly that he must not consider himself engaged to you."

In the meeting of the lovers Mrs. Barton scored a point. The Captain was visibly perplexed and embarrassed, whereas Olive laughed, and seemed at her ease. In the ceremonious drawing-room, patched with fragments of Indian drapery, Lady Jane and Lady Sarah sat angularly and as far from their guests as possible. The spinsters suspected that their house was being made use of as a battle-ground by Mrs.

Barton, and they were determined to resent the impertinence as far as lay in their power. But Milord continued to speak of indifferent things with urbanity and courtly gestures—and as they descended the staircase, he explained the beauty of his marble statues and his stuffed birds.

"But, Lady Jane, where is Cecilia? I hope she is not unwell?"

"Oh, no; Cecilia is quite well, thank you. But she never comes down when there is company,—she is so very sensitive. But that reminds me. She told me to tell you that she is dying to see you. You will find her waiting for you in her room when we have finished lunch."

"Cecilia is not the only person to be thought of," said Milord. "I will not allow Alice to hide herself away upstairs for the rest of the afternoon. I hear, Alice, you are a great admirer of Tennyson's Idylls. I have just received a new edition of his poems, with illustrations by Doré: charming artist, full of poetry, fancy, sweetness, imagination. Do you admire Doré, Captain Hibbert?"

The Captain declared that he admired Doré far more than the old masters, a point of taste that Milord ventured to question; and until they rose from table he spoke of his collection of Arundel prints with grace and erudition. Then they all went out to walk on the terrace. But as their feet echoed in the silence of the hall, Cecilia, in a voice tremulous with expectancy, was heard speaking:

"Alice, come upstairs; I am waiting for you." Alice made a movement as if to comply, but, stepping under the banisters, Lord Dungory said:

"Alice cannot come now, she is going out to walk with us, dear. She will see you afterwards."

"Oh! let me go to her," said Alice eagerly, for in her heart still vibrated the pain caused by Lady Sarah's pitiless remark: "Cecilia never comes down when there is company."

"There will be plenty of time to see her later on," whispered Mrs. Barton, sweetly and insidiously. "Remember what you promised me," and she pointed to Captain Hibbert, who was standing on the steps of the house, his wide decorative shoulders defined against a piece of grey sky.

In despair at her own helplessness, and with a feeling of loathing so strong that it seemed like physical sickness, Alice went forward and entered into conversation with Captain

Hibbert. Lord Dungory, Mrs. Barton, and Olive walked together; Lady Jane and Lady Sarah followed at a little distance. In this order the party proceeded down the avenue as far as the first gate; then they returned by a side walk leading through the laurels, and stood in a line facing the wind-worn tennis-ground, with its black, flowerless beds, and bleak vases of alabaster and stone. From time to time remarks anent the Land League were made; but all knew that a drama even as important as that of rent was being enacted. Olive had joined her sister, and the girls moved forward on either side of the handsome Captain; and, as a couple of shepherds directing the movements of their flock, Lord Dungory and Mrs. Barton stood watching. Suddenly her eyes met Lady Jane's. The glance exchanged was tempered in the hatred of years; it was vindictive, cruel, terrible; it shone as menacingly as if the women had drawn daggers from their skirts, and Jane, obeying a sudden impulse, broke away from her sister, and called to Captain Hibbert. Fortunately he did not hear her, and, before she could speak again, Lord Dungory said:

"Jane, now Jane, I beg of you——"

Mrs. Barton smiled a sweet smile of reply, and whispered to herself: "Do that again, my lady, and you won't have a penny to spend this year."

BOOK II.

CHAPTER I.

"Now, dear, tell me, I want to hear all about it," said Mrs. Barton, as the carriage left the steps of Dungory Castle. "What did he say?"

"Oh! mamma, mamma, I am afraid I have broken his heart," replied Olive dolorously. Then she laughed a little.

"It doesn't do a girl any harm even if it does leak out that she jilted a man; it makes the others more eager after her. But tell me, dear, I hope there was no misunderstanding; did you really tell him that it was no use, that he must think of you no more?"

"Mamma dear, don't make me go over it again, I can't, I can't; Alice heard all I said—she'll tell you."

"No, no, don't appeal to me; it's no affair of mine," exclaimed the girl more impetuously than she had intended.

"I am surprised at you, Alice; you shouldn't give way to temper in that way. Come tell me at once what happened."

The thin, grey, candid eyes of the daughter, and the brown, soft, false eyes of the mother, exchanged a long deep gaze of inquiry, and then Alice burst into an uncontrollable fit of weeping. She trembled from too much grief, and could not answer; and when she heard her mother say to Olive, "Now that the coast is clear, we can go in heart and soul for the marquess," a sense of the moral degradation, to which she had been so cruelly subjected, came upon her like the foul odours of a dirty kitchen issuing through a grating.

The time for departure was now drawing near; the day of departure had been fixed; only one more week of Galway remained to be endured. But that week hung heavier than all the rest, and the hours limped slowly away. It rained incessantly. Sheets of water, blown thitherward by winds that had travelled the Atlantic, deluged the county; grey mists trailed mournful and shapeless along the edges of the domain

143

woods, over the ridges of the tenants' holdings.   Gloom, gloom, January gloom, and yet no gloom to deaden the cries for vengeance for the assassination of landlords, of agents—for the cold-blooded torturings of bailiffs, caretakers, and other deadly deeds done in the darkness ; no gloom to hide the informer, and the peasant cruelty that fell upon defenceless cattle ; not gloom enough to stifle the lowing of the red-dripping mutilations that filled the humid darkness of the fields.

The year was drawing to its close—a year of plenty, but bitter with the memory of years of famine.   With hunger still in their eyes the peasants had risen out of their wet hovels ; they seemed to be innumerable as ants ; they filled the roadways at night, and on each Sunday, from the Land League platforms, their outcry for a higher life rattled, and rolled, and cracked, like thunder, until the very air trembled with retributive victory and doom.   " Never more shall we be driven forth to die in the bogs and ditches," was the cry that rang through the mist ; and, guarded by policemen, in their stately houses, the landlords listened, waiting for the sword of a new coercion to fall and release them from their bondage.

The meeting of Parliament in the spring would bring them this ; in the meantime, all who could, fled, resolving not to return till the law restored the power that the Land League had so rudely shaken.   Some went to England, others to France.   Mr. Barton accepted two hundred pounds from his wife and proceeded to study gargoyles and pictures in Bruges ; and, striving to forget the murders and rumours of murders that filled the papers, the girls and their mammas talked of beaux, partners, and trains, in spite of the irritating presence of the Land League agitators who stood on the plat-forms of the different stations.   The train was full of girls. Besides the Bartons, there were the Brennans : Gladys and Zoe—Emily remained at home to look after the place.   Three of the Miss Duffys were coming to the drawing-room, and four of the Honourable Miss Gores; the Goulds and Scullys made one party, and they were accompanied by the illustrious Fred.   To avoid Mrs. Barton, the Ladies Cullen had pleaded important duties.   They were to follow in a day or so.

Lord Dungory talked incessantly to Mrs. Barton.   He advised her to take a house, and warned her against spending the whole season in an hotel, but apparently without avail, for whenever the train stopped a laughing voice was heard : "Milord, *Vous n'êtes qu'un vilain misanthrope ;* we shall be very comfortable at the Shelbourne ; we shall meet all the people in Dublin there, and we can have private rooms to give dinner parties." And, hearing this, Alice congratulated herself. Her practical mind had determined to make the best of the present ordering of things. She did not expect to be admired, she knew she would find but few partners, and would have to sit neglected by her mother's side during the long Castle balls. But anything was better than to remain in Galway, where there was nothing to do but listen to Olive crying after Captain Hibbert, read accounts of dreadful murders, and watch her mother flirting with Milord. Dublin society would be at least a glimpse of the world ; and she would hear something, and see a little over the horizon of her family. She therefore looked forward with avidity to two months' life in the Shelbourne ; she thought of the surprise of new faces, and the charm of unexpected impressions. Nor was she disappointed. For, even on entering the hall, she was amused by the quick voice of the busy porter, by the sight of the piled-up luggage. The little winter-garden on the first landing, and the fountain splashing amid ferns and stone frogs, were remembered. The ladies' drawing-room she knew was on the right, and when she had taken off her hat and jacket, leaving her mother and sister talking of Mrs. Symond and Lord Kilcarney, she went there hoping to find some of the people whom she had met there before.

But for the presence of one man, the room was deserted. The usually skirt-filled ottoman stood vacantly gaping, the little chairs seemed lonely about the hearthrug, even the sofa, where sat the invalid old ladies, was unoccupied, and the perforated blinds gave the crowds that passed up and down the street a shadow-like appearance. The prospect was not inspiriting, but not knowing what else to do, Alice sat down by the fire. Presently she became conscious that the eyes of the man on the other side of the rug were fixed upon her. She looked up and was at once impressed with his appearance. It was John Harding.*

"I wonder who he is," thought Alice ; and, averting her eyes, she looked into the fire, seeing there, as in a mirror, the

---

* See " A Modern Lover," and " A Mummer's Wife."

sharp clean-cut nose, the pointed chin, the long wavy brown
hair, and the cold, close-set, keen-sighted, passionless blue eyes.
His arched insteps, silk socks, and elegant shoes were very
visible : and he shifted his long legs from time to time, as he
strove, with a stumpy bit of pencil, that would not mark, to
correct the MS. that lay upon his knees. Then Alice wondered what he was writing. She could not help thinking he
was the nicest man she had seen ; and, looking at him again,
half-curiously, half-admiringly, she lapsed into dreams of him.
He worked for some minutes laboriously, twisting his pencil
from side to side, until at last, with an exclamation of disgust,
he shut the book. Their eyes met again ; and even when
Alice, in shame, turned her face away, she felt that he was
examining her closely and intently. Would he never leave
off ? Growing nervous, and afraid of scrutiny, she made a
movement to stir the fire.

" Will you allow me ? " he said, rising from his chair, " I
beg your pardon, but, if you will allow me, I will arrange the
fire."

Alice let him have the poker. When he had knocked in
the coal-crust, and put on some fresh fuel, he said :—

" If it were not for me I do not know what would become
of this fire. I believe the old porter goes to sleep and forgets
all about it. Now and again he wakes up and makes a deal
of fuss with a shovel and a broom."

So brightly, and with such keen inflexions of voice, were
these words spoken, that Alice looked up at once surprised
and amused. She was vaguely conscious that it was not
perhaps quite the correct thing to do to enter into conversation, but before she was well aware she had answered :

" I really can't say, we only came up from Galway to-
day."

" Then you don't know the famous Shelbourne Hotel ! Oh,
it is quite an institution. All the events of life are accomplished here. People live here, and die here, and flirt here, and,
I was going to say, marry here—but hitherto the Shelbourne
marriages have resulted in break-offs—and we quarrel here ;
the friends of to-day are enemies to-morrow, and then they sit
at different ends of the room. Oh ! life in the Shelbourne is
a thing in itself, and a thing to be studied."

Alice laughed again ; and again she continued her conversation.

"I really know nothing of the Shelbourne. I was only here once before, and then only for a few days last summer, when I came home from school."

"And now you are here for the drawing-room?"

"Yes, but how did you guess that?"

"The natural course of events: a young lady leaves school, she spends four or five months at home, and then she is taken to the Lord-Lieutenant's drawing-room."

Alice remained silent. There was an accent of cynical satire in Mr. Harding's words that had suddenly jarred her feelings. He had touched a chord sharply that had long been vibrating in the darkness of her consciousness. She liked him none the better for what he had said, and for a moment longed to bring the conversation to a close. But when he spoke again she forgot her intentions, and allowed his voice to charm her.

"I think you told me," he said, "that you came up from Galway to-day; may I ask you from what side of the country?"

Another piece of impertinence. Why should he question her? and yet she answered him.

"We live near Gort—do you know Gort?"

"Oh! yes, I have been travelling for the last two months in Ireland. I spent nearly a fortnight in Galway. Lord Dungory lives near Gort. Do you know him?"

"Very well indeed, he is our nearest neighbour; we see him nearly every day. Do you know him?"

"Yes, a little. I have met him in London. If I had not been so pressed for time, I should have called upon him when I was in Galway. I passed his place, going to a land meeting —oh! you need not be alarmed; I am not a Land League organiser, or else I should not have thought of calling at Dungory Castle. Beautiful place it is, and what a pretty drive it is from there to Gort. I know the road perfectly."

"Then, do you know a place on the left-hand side of the road, about a mile and a half from Dungory Castle?"

"You mean Brookfield?"

"Yes, that is our place."

"Then you are Miss Barton?"

"Yes, I am Miss Barton; do you know father or mother?"

"No, no; but I have heard the name in Galway. I was spending a few days with one of your neighbours."

" Oh, really!" said Alice, a little embarrassed; for she knew it must have been with the Lawlers that he had been staying. At the end of a long silence, she said:

" I am afraid you have chosen a rather unfortunate time for visiting Ireland. All these terrible outrages, murders, refusals to pay rent; I wonder you have not been frightened away."

" As I do not possess a foot of land, I believe I should say 'not land enough to sod a lark,' my claim to collect rent would rest on even a slighter basis than that of the landlords; and as, with the charming inconsistency of your race, you have taken to killing each other instead of slaughtering the hated Saxon, I really feel safer in Ireland than elsewhere. Besides, I am interested in agrarian outrage and the non-payment of rent."

Alice raised an alarmed face; she looked inquiringly into Harding's expressionless eyes.

" There is no need to be frightened," he said, laughing. "I am not a Land League agitator, nor am I an American adventurer."

In a pretty and embarrassed way the girl smiled. Words rose to her lips to ask him what he was doing in Ireland; but she checked herself and looked into the fire.

He watched her curiously for a few moments, then he said, assuming an air of indifference:

" I am in Ireland for the purpose of writing a couple of review articles. When they have appeared I shall add to them, and then they will come out in book form."

" Oh! you are a writer then?" said Alice with girlish impulsiveness.

" Yes, but I write as little as I can about politics."

" What are your favourite subjects?"

" I write principally novels."

" Really!" said the girl, trembling with admiration and wonder.

During the last six months her sole companions had been books; and when, forgetful of the written pages, her fancy floated above them through pale-coloured reveries, dying light, and dusky waters, shuddering beneath scintillating skies of vanishing thought—how often, in a sweet pulsing vision, the authors: shadow-shapen forms, trailing their garments of dream: had passed before her. How often had she not longed to approach nearer, to linger within sound of their voices!

But as yet she had not thought of any of her heroes—and she had many—as living men : she had seen them only in the clear mirrors of their words ; and therefore, to this imaginative girl, the sensation of hearing suddenly that the young stranger, in whom she was already interested, was a writer of novels, was at once a little blinding and bewildering ; and she was conscious of a sort of mental overbalancing. It did not occur to her to think whether he wrote good novels or bad novels ; she was merely carried along upon a rushing sense of curiosity, of wonder. He looked strange, he spoke differently from anyone she had ever known before, she felt her being quickening.

" I suppose," he said, " you do a great deal of novel-reading in the country ? "

It astonished her to hear him speak so lightly of what she held so sacred : " Oh ! yes," she answered, with almost an accent of voluptuousness in her voice, " I spent the winter reading."

" Because there was no hunting ? " replied Harding, with a smile full of cynical weariness.

" No, I assure you, no, I do not think I should have gone out hunting even if it hadn't been stopped," said Alice, hastily ; for it vexed her not a little to see that she was considered incapable of loving a book for its own sake.

" And what do you read ? "

The tone of indifference with which the question was put was not lost upon Alice, but she was too much interested in the conversation to pay heed to it. She said :

" I read nearly all Byron, Shelley, Keats, Tennyson, and Browning. . . . I think I like him better than all the poets ! Do you know the scene at St. Praxed's ? Is it not lovely ? "

" Yes, of course, there's no doubt but that it is very fine ; but I don't know that I ever cared much for Browning. Not only the verse, but the whole mind of the man is uncouth— yes, uncouth is the word I want. He is the Carlyle of poetry."

In Alice, whose judgments had been dictated by the heart rather than the intelligence, and who knew nothing of the contrasting of ideas to make mental pictures, nor of the gleam of paradox that makes daylight in a sentence, Mr. Harding's remarks produced nearly a pained sense of losing grip ; such a feeling of inability to follow as is created by the sudden rush

of horsemen, by the soaring of a bird or balloon. Presently
he said :

"Have you ever read Carlyle ? "

"Oh, yes, I have read his 'French Revolution,' and his
"Life of Schiller," but that's all. I only came home from
school last summer, and at school we never read anything.
But I wonder if I have read anything of yours ? "

"I should not think so; my books are not supposed to be
fit reading for young ladies."

"Oh! really," and Alice looked into the fire dreadfully disconcerted. Poor Alice! after six months of loneliness and
misery in the country, amid people whom she did not understand, who did not understand her, this man was a light that
she felt she must follow, must know. But at every step she
took forward, he pushed her back. Oh! it was cruel of him.
Never had she met the author of a book before; and an invincible curiosity burned within her. She wanted him to tell her
how he thought, dreamed, and felt towards life, men, and
things; but he gave her no encouragement. At last she
screwed up courage to make one more attempt.

"I couldn't get many new books down in Galway. There
were, of course, Dickens, Thackeray, George Eliot, in the
library, but that was all. I once got a beautiful book from
Dungory Castle. I wonder if you ever read it—it is called
Madame Gervaisais. From the descriptions of Rome it almost
seems to me that I have been there."

"I know the book perfectly, but I did not know that a
Catholic girl could admire it—and you are a Catholic, I
presume ? "

"I was brought up a Catholic."

"It is one thing to be brought up a Catholic, and another
to avoid doubting."

"There can surely be no harm in doubting ? "

"Not the least; but toward which side are you ? Have
you fallen into the thorny ditch of agnosticism, or the soft
feather-bed of belief ? "

"Why do you say 'the thorns of agnosticism ' ? "

Harding laughed :—"Well, I don't know that they ever
tormented me very much, but writing gets you into an anti-
thetical way of speaking."

Alice did not understand; and being more anxious to hear
something of him than to talk about herself—not because she

was afraid to speak her opinions, but merely because his personality seemed to her of such paramount importance compared
with her own—she said :

"And do you never doubt ? "

"No, I can't say I am given much to doubting, nor do I
think the subject is any longer worthy of thought.   The
world's mind after much anxiety arrives at a conclusion, and
what sages cannot determine in one age, a child is certain
about in the next.   Thomas Aquinas was harassed with doubts
regarding the possibility of old women flying through the air
on broomsticks; nowadays were a man thus afflicted he
would be surely a fit subject for Hanwell.   The world has
lived through Christianity, as it has through a score of other
things; and Bethlehem, Nazareth, and the Dove have already
been bequeathed to the vaudevillists of the future.   But I am
afraid I shock you ? "

"No, I don't think you do; only I never heard anyone
speak in that way before—that is all."

Here the conversation came to a pause, and soon after the
presence of some ladies rendered its revival impossible.   Their
evening toilettes suggested the dinner-hour, and reminded
Alice she had to prepare for *table d'hôte;* and she went upstairs, her heart filled with Mr. Harding.   His fearless speech
was what the sea-wind and the blue and white aspects of a
distant mountain range are to the convict.   Her life seemed
suddenly to have grown larger, clearer; she felt as if the
breathing of the dawn were on her face.

All the Galway people, excepting the Honourable Misses
Gore and the Scullys—who had taken houses in town for the
season—dined at *table d'hôte.*   The Miss Duffys were, with the
famous Bertha, the terror of the *débutantes.*   The Brennans
and the Goulds sat at the same table.   May, thinking of Fred,
who had promised to come during the evening, leaned back in
her chair, looking unutterably bored.   Under a window Sir
Richard and Sir Charles were immersed in wine and discussion.
In earnest tones the latter deprecated the folly of indulging in
country love; the former, his hand on the champagne bottle,
hiccoughed, "Mu—ch better come up—up Dub—lin, yer
know, my boy.   But look, look here; I know such a nice—"
a glance round, to make sure that no lady was within earshot;
and the conversation lapsed into a still more confidential
whisper.

Mr. Ryan and Mr. Lynch ate their dinner in sullen silence, and at the other end of the long table Mr. Adair—whom it was now confidently stated Mr. Gladstone could not possibly get on without—talked incessantly to Mr. Harding. He explained the statistics he had collected concerning the peasant proprietors of France and Belgium; he unfolded his plans for the draining of Ireland, and those for the creation of national sawmills, the reclaiming of the bogs, the crushing of the Land League, the planting of beetroot, and the establishment of sugar-refineries. According to Mr. Adair, these schemes should be put forward simultaneously; and he did not allow Harding to talk to the young lady on his right until he had obtained a promise from him to read the pamphlet on the amalgamation of the unions.

When dinner was over, and the few dried oranges and tough grapes that constituted dessert had been tasted, the ladies got up, and in twos and threes retired to the ladies' sitting room. They were followed by Lord Dungory, Mr. Adair, and Mr. Harding: the other gentlemen—the baronets and Messrs. Ryan and Lynch—preferring smoke and drink, to chatter and oblique glances in the direction of ankle-concealing skirts, went up to the billiard-room. And the skirts, what an importance they took in the great sitting-room full of easy-chairs and Swiss scenery: châlets, lakes, cascades, and chamois, painted on the light-coloured walls. The big ottoman was swollen with bustled skirts; the little low seats around the fire disappeared under skirts; skirts were tucked away to hide the slippered feet, skirts were laid out along the sofas to show the elegance of the cut. Then woolwork and circulating novels were produced, and the conversation turned on marriage. Bertha being the only Dublin girl present, all were anxious to hear her speak; after a few introductory remarks, she began:—

"Oh! so you have all come up to the Castle and are going to be presented. Well, you'll find the rooms very grand, and the suppers very good, and if you know a lot of people—particularly the officers quartered here—you will find the Castle balls very amusing. The best way to do is to come to town a month before the drawing-room, and give a ball; and in that way you get to know all the men. If you haven't done that, I am afraid you won't get many partners. Even if you do get introduced, they'll only ask you to dance, and you'll never see them again. Dublin is like a racecourse, men come and speak to you and pass on. 'Tis pleasant enough if you know people, but as for marriages, there are none. I assure you I know lots of girls—and very nice girls too—who have been going out these six or seven seasons, and who have not been able to pull it off."

"And ah!" said a girl, speaking with a terrible brogue, "the worst of it is that the stock is for iver increasing, every year we are growing more and more numerous, an th' men, oh! th' men seem to be gettin' fewer. Nowadays a man won't look at you unless you have at least two thousand a year."

The crudity of this speech seemed to startle the company; and Mrs. Barton, who did not wish her daughters to be discouraged from the first, settled her skirts with a movement of disdain. Mrs. Gould pathetically declared she did not believe love to be dead in the world yet, and maintained her opinion that a nice girl could always get on. But Bertha was not easily silenced, and, being perfectly conversant with her subject, she disposed of Dublin's claims as a marriage-mart, and she continued to comment on the disappointments of girls until the appearance of Lord Dungory and Mr. Harding brought the conversation to a sudden close.

"*Une causerie de femme! que dites-vous?—je le sais—l'amour n'existe plus, et l'âme de l'homme est plus près des sens que l'âme de la femme,*" said Milord. Everyone laughed; and, with a charming movement of her skirts, Mrs. Barton made room for him to sit beside her. He introduced the novelist to Mrs. Barton, and, after a few words, he was passed on to Olive.

Alice watched with pleading eyes; but she scarcely dared to hope that Harding would speak to her again. He would be drawn, like the rest, into that vortex of blonde beauty, light laughter, gay smiles, caprice, desire of change, vain words. And why not? How could he care for a girl without much figure, and not an attractive feature in her face. . . . And yet, and yet . . . And in the circling phases and passages of her thought she lost consciousness of the scene enacted around her until she suddenly heard Harding's voice addressing her. He had at first spoken eagerly to Olive, but her white and red grimacing did not interest him, and he had taken the earliest opportunity of slipping away. Perplexed, Olive looked at her mother, and Mrs. Barton cast a glance of disdain on Harding's back. The moment was tense with feminine passion. All eyes—but above all those of the girl in red—then brightened with pleasure. The throwing of this small pebble against the omnipotence of beauty afforded much delight.

In Alice, however, the tenderness of hope tempered the more acrid sweets of triumph; and she lost herself in the individuality of the man before her. Putting aside his usual sneer, he sympathised with her, talked of life, and the meaning it seemed to him to bear; he spoke to her of the books she had read, and he told of his own; he described pictures, poems, statues in a few words; anecdotes, bitter criticisms, and serene aspirations passed, lingered, disappeared, and passed again. In a word, over the intellectual counter he flaunted samples of everything he had in stock; and the girl saw God in the literary shopboy.

He was, however, obviously interested in her; and when Milord took him away to smoke a cigar, May, who had been vainly expecting Fred the whole evening, said:

"Well, Alice, I hope you have had a nice flirtation?"

Alice blushed to the roots of her hair; but she turned pale a moment after when Mrs. Barton said, with a ripple of laughter:

"Alice's flirtations are harmless enough; they never go further than talking of a lot of books, or old newspapers."

But Alice and Harding were instantly forgotten when Bertha Duffy declared that, very possibly, there would be no Drawing-room held that year. Murder was more common in Dublin than in the country; and the Lord Lieutenant dared not stir a yard without an escort of soldiers. Consolation was, however, found in Mrs. Gould's remark, that if the Castle were blown up with dynamite the conspirators would probably choose the day of the Levée rather than that on which the Drawing-room was held, but to this the girl in red answered that that would be only out of the frying-pan into the fire, for all possibilities of marriage would then be for ever at an end. The conversation, however, languished; eyes were raised from wool-work and novel in gentle consideration, and said, as plainly as eyes could, "There's no use wasting our time talking here; no more men will come in to-night." And about half-past ten a movement of retiring was made; but the entrance of a tall young man, in evening dress, arrested it.

Bowing to the girl in red, he went to the piano and sang

two love songs. Then she who had been shunned on the plea of vulgarity became at once an object of interest, and was eagerly questioned concerning the young singer. He had spoken a few words to her yesterday afternoon. He had come from London to sing at Lady So-and-so's concert, and had achieved so great a success there that he had been persuaded to stay on for another concert. From a distant sofa an old lady declared him to be Signor Parisina, the composer of the lovely songs that everybody had heard of. The girl in red preferred his high, Bertha Duffy liked his low notes, and both agreed he had no middle notes at all. Then his compositions were passionately discussed. Gladys Brennan allowed that his melodies were pretty, but insisted that they were inadequately harmonised—an opinion she attempted to modify on hearing that he had taken the prize for harmony at Milan. The old lady on the distant sofa gave some details of the young man's life. He was going to marry a lady much older than himself, and one who sang excruciatingly out of tune.

" In tune, or out of tune, I should like to know who will care for him or his songs once he's married," said Mrs. Barton ; and this conclave of ladies bowed their heads in silent acquiescence.

CHAPTER II.

"Now, my dear Alice, do make haste; it is most important that we should arrive early. Lord Kilcarney is going to be there; and the moment he comes into the room he'll be surrounded. That old cat, Lady Georgina, will introduce every girl in the place to him; nothing would please her so much as to prevent him from getting near Olive."

Lady Georgina Stapleton was Lord Dungory's sister. She too, hated Mrs. Barton, but being poor—Milord used to call himself the milch cow—she found herself, like the Ladies Cullen, occasionally obliged to smile upon and extend a welcoming hand to the family enemy. When Mrs. Barton came for the Castle season a little pressure was put upon Lady Georgina to obtain invitations from the Chamberlain; the ladies exchanged visits and there the matter ended. Nor had Mrs. Barton ever taken the trouble to conceal her abhorrence of the house in Merrion Square—and some of the hard things she had said when standing on a box-seat of a drag at the Punchestown races, pouring silvery laughter into Milord's infatuated ears, had travelled back and found a lasting resting-place in his sister's wrathful memory.

But a woman is never vulnerable until she is bringing out her daughters; and in these days when girls are a drug in the market, the struggle for existence becomes terribly intense for her. She fears every look, she trembles under every word; she finds herself cringing before the weakest. Until then the usual shafts directed against her virtue fall harmlessly on either side, but now they glance from the marriage buckler and strike the daughter in full heart. In the ball-room as in the forest, the female is most easily assailed when guarding her young, and nowhere in the whole animal kingdom is this fact so well exemplified as in Dublin Castle.

Mrs. Barton was too clever not to feel conscious of her
156

weakness; and as much as she could regret anything, she now regretted the persistency with which she had roused the enmity of women. For the first time she began to recognise their power, and she remembered that there were not ten, not seven, not five upon whom she could count for one single word of sympathy or defence. All, for spite and self-interest, would strive to separate Olive from Lord Kilcarney. The quarry was a ten-antlered stag; but even now, before the beast had broken cover, she felt that the terrible huntswomen, with a loud cracking of whips, would drive her from the trail. Her own marriage had been decided quickly: an unexpected opportunity had presented itself, and she had seized it. But in the great matrimonial hunts women have to hunt in packs. At the death they may fight among themselves, and the slyest will carry off the prey; but to ensure a kill at the commencement of the chase a certain *esprit de corps* is necessary, or in the coverts and hidden turns of fashionable life the quarry will slip away unperceived. And now whether she should, or should not enter into the army of the *élite*, Mrs. Barton was still undecided. It was a difficult question. Personally she believed in individual effort; but, it being the girls' first season, she feared it might be "remarked" if they were seen nowhere but at the Castle. It would be as well to show Olive off in some few drawing-rooms; and if the odious women made themselves too disagreeable, well, she could withdraw and give dinner-parties in a private room at the Shelbourne. There they would have Lord Kilcarney all to themselves, and he was what they wanted.

During the season in Dublin it is found convenient to give teas: the young ladies have to be introduced to the men they will meet afterwards at the Castle. These gatherings take place at five o'clock in the afternoon; and as Mrs. Barton passed along the streets on her way to Lady Georgina's, she reflected on the appearance of the town. Its present animation she declared could not be taken as in the least representative of the normal condition of things. Once the Castle season ended, all would lapse into the usual state of torpor and indifference.

"I assure you, my dears, we are all on the brink of ruin, we are dancing on the edge of a precipice. In flying from Galway we thought we had fled from the Land League; but I was talking to Lord Dungory this morning, and he says that the

city is undermined, that a network of conspiracy is spread all
over the place.   He says there are assassins waiting and watching night and day to kill the Lord Lieutenant, and that there
are so many plots hatching for the blowing up of the Castle,
that even now it is doubtful if it will be considered safe to hold
a Drawing-room."

"Oh! Mamma, I think I should die, if there were to be no
Drawing-room."

"Of course there'll be a Drawing-room; but it only shows
what a terrible state things must be in that such rumours
should be put forth.   The shopkeepers are complaining dreadfully.   Mrs. Symond says she has to give three years' credit.
You see lots of people have shut up their houses; I am afraid
there will not be many parties; it is all the fault of that wicked
Land League, and the Government won't put it down, nor yet
the Pope.   What's the use in our subscribing to his Church if
he'll do nothing for us?"

The weary, the woebegone, the threadbare streets—yes,
threadbare conveys the moral idea of Dublin in 1882.
Stephen's Green, recently embellished by a wealthy nobleman
with gravel walks, mounds and ponds, looked like a school-
treat set out for the entertainment of charity children.   And
melancholy Merrion Square! broken pavements, unpainted
hall-doors, rusty area railings, meagre outside curs hidden
almost out of sight in the deep gutters—how infinitely pitiful!

The Dublin streets stare the vacant and helpless stare of a
beggar selling matches on a doorstep, and the feeble cries for
amusement are like those of the child beneath the ragged
shawl for the red gleam of a passing soldier's coat.   On either
side of you, there is a bawling ignorance or plaintive decay.
Look at the houses!   Like crones in borrowed bonnets some
are fashionable with flowers in the rotting window frames—
others languish in silly cheerfulness like women living on the
proceeds of the pawnshop; others—those with brass-plates on
the doors—are evil smelling as the prescriptions of the threadbare doctor, bald as the bill of costs of the servile attorney.
And the souls of the Dubliners blend and harmonise with
their connatural surroundings.

We are in a land of echoes and shadows.   Lying,
mincing, grimacing—careless of all but the pleasures of
scandal and marriage, trailing their ignorance, arrogantly
the poor shades go by.   Gossip and waltz tunes are all

that they know. Is there a girl or young man in Dublin who has read a play of Shakespeare, a novel of Balzac, a poem of Shelley? Is there one who could say for certain that Leonardo da Vinci was neither comic-singer nor patriot?—No. Like children, the young and the old, run hither and thither, seeking in Liddell oblivion of the Land League. Catholic in name, they curse the Pope for not helping them in their affliction; moralists by tradition, they accept at their parties women who parade their lovers to the town from the top of a tramcar. In Dublin there is baptism in tea and communion in a cutlet.

We are in a land of echoes and shadows. Smirking, pretending, grimacing, the poor shades go by, waving a mock-English banner over a waxwork show: policemen and bailiffs in front, landlords and agents behind, time-servers, Castle hirelings, panderers and worse on the box; nodding the while their dollish cardboard heads, and distributing to an angry populace, on either side, much bran and brogue. Shadows, echoes, and nothing more. See the girls! How their London fashions sit upon them; how they strive to strut and lisp like those they saw last year in Hyde Park. See the young men —the Castle bureaucrats—how they splutter their recollections of English plays, English scenes, English noblemen. See the pot-hatted Gigmen of the Kildare Street Club! The green flags of the League are passing; the cries of a new Ireland awaken the dormant air; but the Gigmen foam at their windows and spit out mongrel curses on the land that refuses to call them Irishmen.

"The country is going to the devil!" cries one.

"Oh! that brute Gladstone!" moans a second.

"Are you going to Lady Georgina's tea, this afternoon?" asks a third.

"Of course; the whole club is to be there, I believe."

Notwithstanding her limited income, Lady Georgina was a person of taste. Her stair-carpets were neither worn nor dusty, but fresh and red, and, on the first landing a conservatory full of red and white camellias struck vibrating notes of colour.

"This is considered to be the most artistic house in Dublin," said Mrs. Barton, as the servant showed them upstairs.

"How lovely the camellias look," said Olive.

"And now, Alice, mind, none of your Liberalism in this house, or you will ruin your sister's chances."

Lady Georgina wore a wig, or her hair was arranged so as to look like one. Fifty years had rubbed away much of her youthful ugliness; and, in the delicate twilight of her rooms, her aristocratic bearing might be mistaken for good looks. Now, as she bent over her tea-table, the aristocratic grace of her figure was drawn across the narrow width of grey daylight, which divided the handsome curtains. In accordance with the latest London craze, the walls were sprinkled with Dresden and Wedgwood teacups, placed upon red velvet *étagères*. The sofas were luxurious, and each recess was beautifully composed with statues, and screens in crewel work—Lady Georgina was a celebrated needlewoman. She was now begging Lord Kilcarney to assist her at a charity bazaar; and from over the cream-jug she launched an indignant and comprehensive glance at Olive as a place was made for her next to him. Few people had as yet arrived: but when Harding was announced, Mrs. Barton whispered:

"Here's your friend, Alice; don't miss your chance."

Then every moment bevies of girls came in and were accommodated with seats, and if possible with young men. Teacups were sent down to be washed, and the young men were passed from group to group. The young ladies smiled and looked delightful, and spoke of dancing and tennis until, replying to an imperative glance from their chaperons, from time to time they rose to leave: but obeying a look of supplication from their hostess the young men remained.

Lord Kilcarney had been hunted desperately around screens and over every ottoman in the room; and Lady Georgina had proved her good will in proportion to the amount of assistance she had accorded to her friends in the chase. Long ago he had been forced away from Olive. Mrs. Barton endured with stoical indifference the scowls of her hostess; but at length, compelled to recognise that none of the accidents attendant on the handing of teacups or the moving of chairs would bring him back, she rose to take her leave. The little Marquis was on his feet in a moment, and, shaking hands with her effusively, he promised to call to see them at the Shelbourne. A glance went round; and of Mrs. Barton's triumph there could be no doubt.

*   *   *   *   *   *

Hours went, hours of anticipation, of broken dreams; hours filled with calls for "Mamma," with injunctions not to forget this thing and that; nervous, fragile hours, whose skirts trailed in remembrances, in condemnatory criticisms of young men; hours overweighted with rendezvous and visits; hours embittered by regrets at having missed Lord Kilcarney the day he called at the Shelbourne.

But the day above all other days was assuredly that when they paid their first visit to Mrs. Symond. The drive, how long it was! The cab, how it slipped sideways along the tram-lines! At last it stopped, and the women squeezed themselves out. A very narrow staircase covered with oilcloth. The portal to the temple of Hymen was bare, and as bland as an introduction in good society. There was no wrinkle in the tightly-stretched floorcloth; and the prim lay figures exhibited morning dresses in eternally ladylike attitudes. The walls were lined with tall wardrobes, and the rustling of silver paper was as continuous as the murmur of a fountain.

"Oh! how do you do, Mrs. Barton? We have been expecting you for the last two or three days. I will run upstairs and tell Mrs. Symond that you are here; she will be so glad to see you."

"That is Miss Cooper!" explained Mrs. Barton. "Everyone knows her; she has been with Mrs. Symond many years. And, as for dear Mrs. Symond, there is no one like her."

To this sympathetic dressmaker all fashionable hips and bosoms were confided, and all high-bred griefs and scandals; and when the giggling Countess left, the sighing Marchioness was received with genial sympathy. Mrs. Symond was a thin woman with long features, and a mild and affable manner. The moment she appeared at the door Mrs. Barton rushed forward, and the women kissed each other profusely.

"And how do you do, dear Mrs. Barton, and how well you are looking, and the young ladies? I see Miss Olive has improved since she was in Dublin." (In an audible whisper) "Everyone is talking about her. There is no doubt but that she'll be the belle of the season." (In a still audible, but lower tone of voice.) "But tell me, is it true that——"

"Now, now, now!" said Mrs. Barton, drowning her words in cascades of silvery laughter, "I know nothing of what you're saying; ha! ha! ha! no, no—I assure you. I will not——"

Then, as soon as the ladies had recovered their composure, a few questions were asked about her Excellency, the prospects of the Castle season, and the fashions of the year.

"And now tell me," said Mrs. Barton, "what pretty things have you that would make up nicely for trains?"

"Trains, Mrs. Barton? We have some sweet things that would make up beautifully for trains. Miss Cooper, will you kindly fetch over that case of silks that we had over yesterday from Paris?"

"The young ladies must be, of course, in white; for Miss Olive I should like, I think, snowdrops; for you, Mrs. Barton, I am uncertain which of two designs I shall recommend. Now this is a perfectly regal material."

With words of compliment and solicitation, the black-dressed assistant displayed the armouries of Venus—armouries filled with the deep blue of midnight, with the faint tints of dawn, with strange flowers and birds, with moths, and moons, and stars. Lengths of white silk clear as the notes of violins playing in a minor key; white poplin falling into folds statuesque as the bass of a fugue by Bach; yards of ruby velvet, rich as an air from Verdi played on the piano; tender green velvet, pastoral as hautboys heard beneath trees in a fair Arcadian vale; blue turquoise faille Française fanciful as the tinkling of a guitar twanged by a Watteau shepherd; gold brocade, sumptuous as organ tones swelling through the jewelled twilight of a nave; scarves and trains of mid-night-blue profound as the harmonic snoring of a bassoon; golden daffodils violent as the sound of a cornet; bouquets of pink roses and daisies, charmful and pure as the notes of a flute; white faille, soft draperies of tulle, garlands of white lilac, sprays of white heather, delicate and resonant as the treble voices of children singing carols in dewy English woods; berthas, flounces, plumes, stomachers, lappets, veils, frivolous as the strains of a German waltz played on Liddell's band.

An hour passed, but the difficulty of deciding if Olive's dress should be composed of silk or Irish poplin was very great, for determined that all should be humiliated Mrs. Barton laid her plans amid designs for night and morning; birds fluttering through leafy trees, birds drowsing on bending boughs, and butterflies folding their wings. At a critical moment, however, an assistant announced that Mrs. Scully was waiting. The ladies started; desperate effort was made; rosy clouds and veils of silver tissue were spoken of; but nothing could be settled, and on the staircase the ladies had to squeeze into a corner to allow Violet and Mrs. Scully to pass.

"How do you do, Olive? How do you do, Alice? and you, Mrs. Barton, how do you do? And what are you going to wear? Have you decided on your dress?"

"Oh! That is a secret that could be told to no one; oh, not for worlds!" said Mrs. Barton.

"I'm sure it will be very beautiful," replied Mrs. Scully, with just a reminiscence of the politeness of the Galway grocery business in her voice.

"I hear you have taken a house in Fitzwilliam Square for the season?" said Mrs. Barton.

"Yes, we are very comfortable; you must come and see us. You are at the Shelbourne, I believe?"

"Come to tea with us," cried Violet. "We are always at home about five."

"We shall be delighted," returned Mrs. Barton.

Mrs. Scully's acquaintance with Mrs. Symond was of the slightest; but, knowing that claims to fashion in Dublin are judged by the intimacy you affect with the dressmaker, she shook her warmly by the hand, and addressed her as dear Mrs. Symond. To the Christian name of Helen none less than a Countess dare to aspire.

"And how well you are looking, dear Mrs. Symond; and when are you going to take your daughters to the Castle?"

"Oh, not for some time yet; my eldest is only sixteen."

Mrs. Symond had three daughters to bring out, and she hoped when her feet were set on the redoubtable ways of Cork Hill, her fashionable customers would extend to her a cordial helping hand. Mrs. Symond's was one of the myriad little schemes with which Dublin is honeycombed, and although she received Mrs. Scully's familiarities somewhat coldly, she kept her eyes fixed upon Violet. The insidious thinnesses of the girl's figure, and her gay, winsome look interested her, and as if speaking to herself she said:

"You will want something very sweet; something quite pure and lovely for Miss Scully?"

Mother and daughter were instantly all attention, and Mrs. Symond continued:

"Let me see, I have some Surat silk that would make up sweetly. Miss Cooper, will you have the kindness to fetch those rolls of Surat silk we received yesterday from Paris?"

Then beautiful as a flower harvesting, the hues and harmonies of earth, ocean, and sky fell before the ravished eyes. The white Surat silk, chaste, beautiful, delicious as that presentiment of shared happiness which fills a young girl's mind when her fancy awakens in the soft spring sunlight; the white faille Française with tulle and garlands of white lilac, delicate and only as sensuous as the first meetings of sweethearts, when the may is white in the air and the lilac is in bloom on the lawn; trains of blue sapphire broché looped with blue ostrich feathers, seductive and artificial as a boudoir plunged in a dream of Ess. bouquet; dove-coloured velvet trains adorned with tulips and tied with bows of brown and pink—temperate as the love that endures when the fiery day of passion has gone down; corsages and trains of daffodil silk, embroidered with shaded maple-leaves, impure as lamp-lit and patchouli-scented couches; trains of white velouture festooned with tulle; trails of snowdrops, icy as lips that have been bought, and cold as a life that lives in a name.

The beautiful silks hissed as they came through the hands of the assistants, cat-like the velvet footfalls of the velvet fell; it was a witches' Sabbath, and out of this terrible cauldron each was to draw her share of the world's gifts. Smiling and genial, Mrs. Symond stirred the ingredients with a yard measure; the girls came trembling, doubting, hesitating; and the anxious mothers saw what remained of their jeopardised fortunes sliding in a thin golden stream into the flaming furnace that the demon of Cork Hill blew with unintermittent breath.

Secrets, what secrets were held on the subject of the presentation dresses! The obscure Hill was bound with a white frill of anticipation. Olive's fame had gone forth. She was admitted to be the new Venus, and Lord Kilcarney was spoken of as likely to yield to her the coveted coronet. Would he marry her without so much as looking at another girl? was the question on every lip, and in the jealousy thus generated the appraisers of Violet's beauty grew bolder. Her thinness was condoned, and her refinement insisted upon. Nor were May Gould and her chances overlooked by the gossips of

Merrion Square. Her flirtation with Fred Scully was already a topic of conversation.

Alice knew she was spoken of pityingly, but she hungered little after the praise of the Dubliners, and she preferred to stay at home and talk to Harding in the ladies' drawing-room, rather than follow her mother and sister in their wild hunt after Lord Kilcarney. Through the afternoon teas of Merrion Square and Stephen's Green the chase went merrily.

CHAPTER III.

On the night of the Drawing-room, February 20th, 1882, the rain rushed along the streets—and it could be heard wildly splashing on the flagstones. A wind, too, had risen; and, threatening to tear every window from its sash, it careered in great and fearsome gusts: sky there was none, nor sight of anything save when the lightning revealed the outline of the housetops. The rattling and the crashing of the thunder was appalling; and often, behind their closely-drawn curtains, the girls trembled, and, covering their faces in their hands, forgot the article of clothing they were in search of. In their rooms all was warm and snug and gay with firelight and silk: the chaperons had whispered that warm baths were advisable, and along the passages the ladies'-maids passed hurriedly, carrying cans of hot water, sponges, and drying-sheets.

Alice and Olive slept in two rooms on the third floor, on either side of their mother; May and Mrs. Gould were on the fourth, and next to May was Fred Scully, who, under the pretext of the impossibility of his agreeing with his mother concerning the use of a latch-key, had lately moved into the hotel. May was deeply concerned in Fred's grievance; and discussing it, or the new Shelbourne scandal—the loves of the large lady and the little man at the other end of the corridor—they lingered about each other's bedroom-doors. Alice could now hear them talking as they descended the staircase together; then a burst of smothered laughter, and May came in to see her.

" Oh ! how nice you look ! "

Nothing perhaps is diviner than the emotion which calls from us praise of things wholly different from ourselves. So far is it removed from sense, so closely allied is it to the brain, that it becomes the calm will-less knowledge that Schopenhauer holds up to us as the highest ideal to be attained. And to this round, soft-limbed girl, whose white flesh burned and was alive with the wants of the flesh, there was in Alice's candid eyes—revealing as they did her natural powerlessness to do aught but live up to the practical rectitudes of life, as she conceived them to exist—that charm, that assuagement, that vision of purity, that elevation which the Catholic draws from his God-crowned altar, which the traveller breathes when, as Words-worth expresses it, the " shades of evening . . . . connect the landscape to the quiet of the sky." There is always a close and intimate, though not always an obvious analogy, between our mental and physical characteristics. It, however, was very apparent in the present instances. The soft, the melting the almost fluid eyes, the bosom large and just a little falling, the full hips, the absence of any marked point or line, the rolling roundness of every part of the body definitely announced a want of fixed principle, and a somewhat gross and sensual temperament ; whereas the bright, affectionate, but slightly hard eyes, the thin arms and straight hips and shoulders, were admirably suggestive of the clear, the fixed, the almost stern mind ; yes, a mind so well ordered that it could, and did, ex-clude all thoughts to which it could not at once accord a frank welcome.

" If you don't 'mash' Mr. Harding to-night, he will be a tough one indeed. Did I tell you I was talking to him yester-day in the ladies' drawing-room—he is very nice, but I can't quite make him out : I think he despises us all ; all but you ; about you he said all kinds of nice things : that you were so clever, and nice, and amusing. And tell me, dear," said May, in her warm, affectionate way, " do you really like him—you know what I mean ? "

May's eyes and voice were so full of significance, that to pretend to misunderstand was impossible ; and a hot feeling of resentment, almost of disgust, filled Alice's thoughts ; but mastering it, she said as quietly as she could :

" I like Mr. Harding well enough. It is very nice to have him to talk to. To spend hour after hour listening to the crowd of ignorant gossiping women who live here is too dreadful. I am sure I don't want to run down my own sex—there are plenty only too anxious to do that—but I am afraid that there is not a girl in Dublin who thinks of anything except how she is to get married."

" I don't know about that," said May, a little offended. " I suppose if you think of a man at all, you think of how he likes you."

The defiant tone in which these words were spoken was surprising; and, for a moment, Alice stood staring blankly at this superb cream-fleshed girl—superb in her dress of cream faille, her sensual beauty poetised by the long veils which hung like gossamer-webs from the coils of her copper-gleaming hair.

"I am afraid, May," she said, "that you think a great deal too much of such things. I don't say anything against Mr. Scully, but I think it right to tell you that he is considered a very dangerous young man; and I am sure it does a girl no good to be seen with him. It was he who. . . ."

"Now I will not hear you abuse Fred," cried May. "We are great friends; I like you better than any other girl, and if you value our friendship you will not speak to me again like this. I would not put up with it, no, not from my own mother."

The girl moved hastily towards the door, but Alice laid her hand on her arm, saying:

"You must not be angry, May; perhaps you are right; I should not have meddled in things that do not concern me; but then we have been so long friends that I could not help. . . ."

"I know, I know," said the girl yielding at once to the subtle cerebral charm that Alice's mien and motions so constantly brought into play. "You were speaking only for my good; but if you are friends with a person you can't stand by and hear them abused. I know people speak badly of Fred; but then people are so jealous—and they are all jealous of Fred."

Then the conversation came to a pause, and the girls examined each other's dresses. At the end of a long silence May said:

"What an extraordinary thing this Drawing-room is when one comes to think of it. Just fancy going to all this expense to be kissed by the Lord-Lieutenant: a man one never saw before. Will you feel ashamed when he kisses you?"

"Well, I don't know that I have thought much about it," said Alice, laughing. "I suppose it does not matter, it is only a ceremony, not a real kiss."

At this moment Mrs. Barton's voice was heard, calling

—" Now, Alice, Alice, where are you ? We are waiting for you—make haste, for goodness' sake; we are very late as it is."

Staircase and corridor were empty and silent. The trail of a sachet-scented petticoat could be detected on this length of Brussels carpet, the acrid vulgarity of eau de Cologne hung like a curtain before an open door, a vision of white silk gleamed for a moment as it fled from room to room : men in a strange garb—black velvet and steel buttons—furtively hurried away, tripping over their swords, and ashamed of their stockinged calves. On the first landing, about the winter-garden, a crowd of German waiters, housemaids,—billiard-players, with cigars in their teeth and cues in their hands, had collected ; underneath, in the hall, the barmaids, and old ladies, wrapped up in rugs and shawls to save them from the terrible draughts, were criticising the dresses. Olive's name was on every lip, and to see her all were breathless with expectation ; her matrimonial prospects were discussed ; and Lord Kilcarney was openly spoken of. " Ah ! here she is, there she is ! " was whispered. The head-porter, wild with excitement, shouted for Mrs. Barton's carriage; three under-porters distended huge umbrellas ; the door was opened, an immense wind tore through the hall, sending the old ladies flying back to their sitting-room, and the Bartons, holding their hair and their trains, rushed across the wet pavement and took refuge in the brougham.

" Did one ever see such weather ? " said Mrs. Barton. " I hope your hair isn't ruffled, Olive ? "

" No, mamma, I think it is all right."

Reassured, Mrs. Barton continued : " I don't think there ever was a country so hateful as Ireland. What with rain and Land League. I wonder why we live here ! Did you notice the time, Alice, as we left the hotel ? "

" Yes, mamma ; it was twenty-five minutes to ten."

"Oh ! we are very late ; we shan't be there before ten. The thing to do is to get there about half-past nine ; the Drawing-room does not begin before eleven ; but if you can get into the first lot you can stand at the entrance of Patrick's Hall, and have the pick of the men as they come through. That's the place to stand ; all the Dublin girls know that trick—I'll show you when we arrive. And you, Alice, I see your friend Harding is going to the Drawing-room. Now, if you do what

I tell you, you won't miss him ; and I do hope you won't, for to
have you hanging about my skirts the whole evening: and it
does look so bad to see a girl alone, just as if she were unable
to get a man."

While Mrs. Barton continued to advise her girls, the
carriage rolled rapidly along Stephen's Green. It had now
turned into Grafton Street; and on the steep, rain-flooded
asphalte, they narrowly escaped an accident. The coachman,
however, steadied his horses, and soon the long colonnades of
the Bank of Ireland were seen on the left. From this point
they were no longer alone, and except when a crash of thunder
drowned every other sound, the rattling of wheels was heard
behind and in front of them. Carriages came from every side :
the night was alive with flashing lamps ; a glimpse of white fur
or silk, the red-breast of a uniform, the gold of an epaulette,
were seen, and then lost a moment after in the devouring
darkness. Thinking of the block that would take place on the
quays, the coachmen whipped up their horses ; but soon the
ordering voices of the mantled and mounted policemen were
heard, and the carriages came to a full stop.

"We are very late; hundreds will pass before us," said
Mrs. Barton, despairingly, as she watched the lines of silk-
laden carriages that seemed to be passing them by. But it
was difficult to make sure of anything; and fearful of soiling
their gloves they refrained from touching the breath-misted
windows. On the glazed roof the rain pattered madly.

"Did you ever see such a pack of women ; there seems to
be nothing else ; it wouldn't be a bad joke if half of them took
the wrong turning and drove into the river instead of going to
the Castle—and for all they'll get there ! "

Olive laughed with her usual facile lightness, then the three
women screamed—and for one electric instant the city
appeared in hideous silhouette upon a chalky-white sky. A
narrow drain-like river wedged between high-stone embankments ; right along in a slight curve the perspective floats,
and a few factory chimneys close a sinister horizon of whiskey
and beer. On the left is squalor multiform and terrible. The
plaster, in huge scabs falls from the walls, and the flaring
light of a tallow candle reveals a dismantled room. You see
a huge shouldered mother, a lean-faced crone, and a squatting
tailor that poverty chains till midnight to his work-board ;
you see a couple of coarse girls, maids of all work, who smile

and call to the dripping coachmen on the boxes; and there are low shops filled with cheap cigars and tobacco, shops where old clothes rot in fetid confusion, shops exhaling the rancid odours of decaying vegetables, shops dingy with rusting iron and cracked china, shops that traffic in obscene goods and prints; shops and streets that are but a leer of malign decrepitude. And as you near the Castle the traces of the destroyer become more apparent—more foul. Beneath the upas tree the city, even to her remotest suburb, has withered; but that in the immediate shadow—Ship Street—was black, plague-spotted, pestilential, and, as a corpse, quick with the life of the worm.

Notwithstanding the terrible weather the streets were lined with vagrants, patriots, waifs, idlers of all sorts and kinds. Plenty of girls of sixteen and eighteen come out to see the "finery." Poor little things in battered bonnets and draggled skirts, who would dream upon ten shillings a week; a drunken mother striving to hush a child that dies beneath a dripping shawl; a harlot embittered by feelings of commercial resentment; troops of labourers battered and bruised with toil: you see their hang-dog faces, their thin coats, their shirts torn and revealing the beast-like hair on their chests; you see also the Irish-Americans, with their sinister faces, and broad-brimmed hats, standing scowling beneath the pale flickering gas-lamps, and, when the block brought the carriages to a standstill, sometimes no more than a foot of space separated their occupants from the crowd on the pavement's edge. Never were poverty and wealth brought into plainer proximity. In the broad glare of the carriage lights the shape of every feature, even the colour of the eyes, every glance, every detail of dress, every stain of misery were revealed to the silken exquisites who, a little frightened, strove to hide themselves within the scented shadows of their broughams: and in like manner, the bloom on every aristocratic cheek, the glitter of every diamond, the richness of every plume were visible to the avid eyes of those who stood without in the wet and the cold.

"I wish they would not stare so," said Mrs. Barton; "one would think they were a lot of hungry children looking into a sweetmeat shop. The police ought really to prevent it."

"And how wicked those men in the big hats look," said Olive, "I'm sure they would rob us if they only dared."

Alice thought of the Galway ball, with the terrible faces looking in at the window.

The garish lightning again illumined the sky, and showed the steps and the columns of a church crowded with huddled groups, and single climbing figures. The thunder rattled with a volubility so terrible that it seemed as if the heavens were speaking for the freedom-dreaming nation, now goaded and gagged with Coercion Bills. On and on the carriages rolled, now blocked under the black rain-dripping archway of the Castle yard, now delayed as they laboriously made the tour of the quadrangle. Olive doubted if her turn would ever come; but, by slow degrees, each carriage discharged its cargo of silk, and at last Mrs. Barton and her daughters found themselves in the vestibule, taking numbers for their wraps at the cloak-rooms placed on either side of the stairway.

The slender figures ascending to tiny naked shoulders, presented a piquant contrast with the huge, black Assyrian bull-like policemen, who, guarded the passage, and reduced, by contrast, to almost doll-like proportions the white creatures who went up the great stairway. Overhead an artificial plant, some twenty feet wide, spread a decorative greenness; the walls were lined with rifles; and at regular intervals, in lieu of pictures, were set stars made out of swords. There were also three suits of plate armour; and the grinning of the helmets of old time contrasted with the bearskin shrouded faces of the red guardsmen. And through all this military display the white ware tripped to the great muslin market. The air was agleam with diamonds, pearls, skin, and tulle veils. Powdered and purple-coated footmen stood, splendid in the splendour of pink calves and salmon-coloured breeches, on every landing; and as the white mass of silk pushed along the white-painted corridor, the sense of ceremony that had till then oppressed it, evaporated in the fumes of the blazing gas.

But the battle for existence did not really begin until the blue drawing-room was reached. There heat and fatigue soon put an end to all coquetting between the sexes. The beautiful silks were hidden by the crowd; only the shoulders remained, and, to appease their terrible ennui, the men gazed down the backs of the women's dresses stupidly. Shoulders were there, of all tints and shapes. Indeed, it was like a vast rosary, alive with white, pink, and cream-coloured flowers: of Maréchal Niels, Souvenir de Malmaisons, Mademoiselle Eugène Verdiers, Aimée Vibert Scandens. Sweetly turned, adolescent shoulders, blush white, smooth and even as the petals of a Marquiso

Mortemarle; the strong, commonly turned shoulders, abundant and free as the fresh rosy pink of the Anna Alinuff; the drooping white shoulders, full of falling contours as a pale Madame Lacharme; the chlorotic shoulders, deadly white, of the almost greenish shade that is found in a Princess Clementine; the pert, the dainty little shoulders, filled with warm pink shadows, pretty and compact as Countess Cecile de Chabrillant; the large heavy shoulders full of vulgar madder tints, coarse, strawberry colour, enormous as a Paul Neron; clustering white shoulders, grouped like the blossoms of an Aimée Vibert Scandens, and, just in front of me, under my eyes, the flowery, the voluptuous, the statuesque shoulders of a tall blonde woman of thirty, whose flesh is full of the exquisite peach-like tones of a Mademoiselle Eugène Verdier, blooming in all its pride of summer loveliness.

To make way for this enormous crowd, the Louis XV. sofas and armchairs had been pushed against the walls. Large blue fans outspread ornamented every corner. Chandeliers of exquisite fragility, covered with crystal balls, hung against the blue silk curtains, with which the long line of windows on the right were draped; and in the gold mirrors on the left, all rutilant with quick flames, and the white slimnesses of the wax candles, a blurred and grotesque picture of the flesh-flowers below was reflected.

An hour passed wearily, and in this beautiful drawing-room humanity suffered in all its natural impudence. Momentarily the air grew hotter and more silicious; the brain ached with the dusty odour of poudre de ris, and the many acidities of evaporating perfume; the sugary sweetness of the blondes, the salt flavours of the brunettes, and this allegro movement of odours was interrupted suddenly by the garlicky andante, deep as the pedal notes of an organ, that the perspiring arms of a fat chaperon slowly exhaled.

At last there was a move forwards, and a sigh of relief, a grunt of satisfaction, broke from the oppressed creatures : but a line of guardsmen was pressing from behind, and the women were thrown hither and thither into the arms and on to the backs of soldiers, police officers, county inspectors and castle underlings. Now a lady turns pale, and whispers to her husband that she is going to faint; now a young girl's petticoats have become entangled in the moving mass of legs ! She cries aloud for help : her brother expostulates with those around. He is scarcely heeded.

The heart sickens in the crush. How curious the faces seem ! Here are a few silhouettes. Look at the tall woman of fifty with a hooked-nose and orange hair ; she peeps over that shoulder and tries to keep within view of her daughter ; next to her is a fat man with an eyebrow and an eyeglass ; there is a waistless lady with red hair ; her daughter—a tiny thing—has inherited the mother's red hair. A little to the right is a bald head that the heat has turned to crimson ; and you see the sallow man with the foxy beard, and the tiny little old woman, who looks as if she were down a well, so entirely is she lost between four tall men ; you see that male profile ? how distinct it comes out against the pillar ! By your side a weak girl is being driven along by a couple of police officers : very pitifully she holds up her train with both hands.

But the struggle grows still more violent when it becomes evident that the guardsmen are about to bring down the bar and stop further exit ; and begging a florid-faced attorney to unloose his sword, which had become entangled in her dress, Mrs. Barton called on her daughter, and slipping under the raised arms, they found themselves suddenly in a square, sombre room, full of a rich, brown twilight. In one corner there was a bureau, where an attendant served out blank cards ; in another the white plumes nodded against the red glare that came from the throne-room, whence Liddell's band was heard playing waltz tunes, and the stentorian tones of the chamberlain's voice called the ladies' names.

" Have you got your cards ? " said Mrs. Barton.

" I have got mine," said Olive.

" And I have got mine," said Alice.

" Well, you know what to do ? You give your card to the aide-de-camp, he passes it on and spreads out your train, and you walk right to His Excellency ; he kisses you on both cheeks, you courtesy, and, at the far door, two aides-de-camp pick up your train and place it on your arm."

The girls continued to advance, experiencing the while the nerve atrophy, the systolic emotion of communicants, who when the bell rings, approach the altar rails to receive God within their mouths.

The massive, the low-hanging, the opulently twisted gold candelabra, the smooth lustre of the marble columns are

evocative of the persuasive grandeur of a cathedral; and, deep
in the darkness of the pen, a vast congregation of peeresses
and judges watch the ceremony in devout collectiveness.
How symmetrical is the place! A red, a well-trimmed
bouquet of guardsmen has been set in the middle of the
Turkey-carpet; around the throne a semicircle of red coats
has been drawn, and above it flow the veils, the tulle, the
skirts of the ladies of honour—they seem like white clouds
dreaming on a bank of scarlet poppies—and the long
sad legs, clad in maroon-coloured breeches, is the Lord-
Lieutenant, the teeth and the diamonds on his right is Her
Excellency. And now a lingering survival of the terrible
Droit de Seigneur—diminished and attenuated, but still circulating through our modern years—this ceremony, a pale ghost
of its former self, is performed; and, having received a kiss
on either cheek, the *débutantes* are free to seek their bridal
beds in Patrick's Hall.

"Miss Olive Barton, presented by Mrs. Barton!" shouted
the chamberlain. Olive abandoned her train to the aides-de-
camp; she saw their bent backs, felt their nimble fingers
exhibiting this dress whereon Mrs. Barton and Mrs. Symond
had for days been expending all the poetry of their natures.
What white wonder, what manifold marvel of art! Dress of
snow satin, skirt quite plain in front. Bodice and train of white
poplin; the latter wrought with patterns representing night
and morning: a morning made of silver leaves with silver birds
fluttering through leafy trees, butterflies sporting among them,
and over all a sunrise worked in gold and silver thread; then
on the left side the same sun sank amid rosy clouds, and there
butterflies slept with folded wing, and there birds roosted on
bending boughs; veils of silver tissue softened the edges of the
train, and silver-stars gleamed in the corn-coloured hair, and
the long hands, gloved with white undressed kid, carried a
silver fan. She was adorably beautiful and adorably pale; and
like some wonderful white bird of downy plumage she sailed
through the red glare, along the scarlet line, unto the weary-
looking man in maroon breeches. He kissed her on both
cheeks; she courtesied to the vice-regal lips, and passed away
to the further door, where her train was caught up and handed
to her by two aides-de-camp.

Notwithstanding the automatic precision of the ceremonials,
eager looks passed between the ladies of honour standing on

the estrade. Even the superb bouquet of red coats placed in the middle of the floor, animated by one desire, turned its sixteen heads to gaze after the wonderful vision of blonde beauty that had come—that had gone. Mrs. Barton experienced an instant thrill of triumph, and her train was spread out by the aides-de-camp. In the composition of her dress she had given free range to her somewhat florid taste. The front was brocade, laid upon a ground of grey-pink, shot with orange, and the effect was such as is seen when the sun hangs behind a lowering grey cloud, tinged with pink. On this were wonderful soft-coloured flowers, yellow melting into pink, green fading to madder-like tints. The bodice and the train were of gold-brown velvet that matched the gold-brown of the hair. Mrs. Barton was transformed from the usual Romney portrait to one by Sir Peter Lely : and when she made her courtesy, Her Excellency's face contracted, and the ladies of honour whispered, " The harm she does her daughters . . . I wonder. . . ."

" Miss Violet Scully, presented by Mrs. Scully," shouted the chamberlain.

There was an admixture of curiosity in the admiration accorded to Violet. Hers was not the plain appealing of Olive's Greek statue-like beauty ; it was rather the hectic erethism of painters and sculptors in a period preceding the apogee of an art. She was a statuette in biscuit after a design by Andrea Mantegna. But the traces of this exquisite atavism were now almost concealed in the supreme modernity of her attire. From the tiny waist trailed yards of white faille française, trimmed with tulle ruchings, frecked as a meadow with faintly-tinted daisies ; the hips were engarlanded with daisies, and the flowers melted and bloomed amid snows of faille and tulle.

The Lord Lieutenant kissed her, and so warmly that Her Excellency looked up surprised, but her annoyance was lost in the crashing of the thunder which at that moment broke in terrific claps over their heads. Everyone thought instinctively of dynamite, and it was some time before even the voluptuous strains of Liddell's band could calm their inquietude. Nevertheless the chamberlain continued to shout :

" Lady Sarah Cullen, Lady Jane Cullen, Mrs. Scully, presented by Lady Sarah Cullen." Then came a batch of people whom no one knew, and in the midst of these the aides-de-camp allowed Alice to pass. Even in the trying ordeal of submitting to His Excellency's lips she preserved her grave, candid demeanour. She was prettily dressed. A train of white faille trimmed with sprays of white heather and tulle, the petticoat being beautifully arranged with folded draperies of crêpe de Chine.

A number of ladies had collected in the further ante-room; and, in lines, they stood watching the effluent tide of satin and silk discharging its volume into the spaces of Patrick's Hall. Mrs. Barton and Olive were there.

"I wish Alice would make haste and not keep us waiting. I suppose she has got behind a whole crowd of people. Here are the Scullys, let's hide; they don't know a creature and will hang on us."

Olive and Mrs. Barton tried to slip out of sight, but they were too late, and a moment after, looking immense in a train and corsage of Lyons velvet, Mrs. Scully came up and accosted them.

"And how do you do, Mrs. Barton?" she said, with a desperate effort to make herself agreeable; "I must congratulate you; everyone is admiring your dress; I assure you your train looked perfectly regal."

"I am so glad you like it," replied Mrs. Barton; "but what do you think of Olive? Do you like her dress?"

"Oh, Olive has no need of my praises. If I were not afraid of making her too vain I would tell her that all Dublin is talking of her. Indeed, I heard a gentleman say—a gentleman who, I believe, writes for the papers—that she will be in the *World* or *Truth* next week as the belle of the season. None of the other young ladies will have a chance with her."

"Oh, I don't know about that," exclaimed Mrs. Barton, laughing merrily, "have you not got your Violet? whom, by the way, you have transformed into a beautiful daisy. It will be, perhaps, not the Rose nor the Olive that will carry off the prize, but the daisy."

Violet glanced sharply at Mrs. Barton; and there was hate in the glance; for, although her mother did not, she understood well what was meant by the allusion to the daisy, the humblest of the earth's flowers.

The appearance, however, of Lord Kilcarney brought the conversation to a close; and not knowing how to address him Olive laughed beautifully from behind her silver fan. They

entered Patrick's Hall. There Lord Dungory, Lord Rosshill,
and others were waiting to receive Mrs. Barton. Establishing
herself where she could be seen; and dealing out pearly laughs
and winsome compliments to her court, she watched Olive,
who, according to orders, had taken Lord Kilcarney to sit on
the highest of the series of benches that lined one side of the
room. It was a double triumph, and for a moment Mrs.
Barton felt as if she held Dublin under her satin shoe. Alice
was her only trouble! she had slipped behind the file of white
women, who, with eyes liquid with invitation, crowded about
the doorway hoping to seize the men as they came through.
What would she do with this gawk of a girl?—but soon even
this difficulty was solved, for Harding came up and asked her
if he might take her to get an ice.

"How absurd we look dressed up in this way," said
Harding; "look at that attorney and the court sword. It
would be just as logical to stick a quill pen behind the ear of
a fat pig."

"Well, the sword; I confess I don't see much meaning in
that, but the rest of the dress is well enough. I don't see
why one style of dress should be more absurd than another;
unless it is because it is not the fashion."

"Yes, but that is just the reason; just fancy dressing
oneself up in the costume of a bygone time."

"And is everything that is not the fashion ridiculous?"
Alice asked, somewhat earnestly.

"Ah! there, I fancy, you have the best of the argument.
Waiter, a strawberry ice: but did you say you would have
strawberry?"

"I don't think I did, for I prefer lemon."

They were in an immense hall. The centre of the ceiling
was filled with an oval picture, representing St. Patrick
receiving Pagans into the true faith. The walls were white
painted, the panels were gold-listed. There were pillars at
both ends of the room; and in a top gallery, behind a curtain
of evergreen plants, Liddell's orchestra continued to pour an
uninterrupted flood of waltz melody upon the sea of satin,
silk, poplin, and velvet that surged around the buffet, angrily
demanding cream ices, champagne, and claret cup. Every
moment the crowd grew denser, and the red coats of the
Guards, and the black corded jackets of the Rifles stained like
spots of ink and blood the lugubrious pallor of the background.

A few young men looked elegant and shapely in the velvet and stockings of Court dress. One of these was Fred Scully. He was with May, who, the moment she caught sight of Alice, made frantic efforts to reach her.

"My dear, did anyone ever look so nice ! You are as sweet —well a little sweeter—than you generally are ! How do you do, Mr. Harding. And tell me, Alice, what do you think of my dress ? "

May was in cream faille with ruchings of tulle. A beautiful piece of white lilac nestled upon her right breast. She was all white, save the furnace of her hair. She drew herself up for Alice to see her; and Harding watched Fred, who was lost in sensual contemplation.

"You are very nice, May, and I think the white sets off your hair to advantage."

"Well, good-bye dear, Fred and I are going into the next room ; one is so pushed about here, but there are nice large velvet sofas there where one can sit and talk. I advise you to come."

Alice felt Harding had read through May; but he said nothing, and, thanking him inwardly for his silence, they passed from the glare of Patrick's Hall into the reposing shadows of rich velvet and sombre hangings. In amorous attitudes, women leaned over the sofas, talking to men in uniform, and two strange-looking creatures, in long garments, walked up and down the room. They were Dons from Trinity, and they argued earnestly with Mr. Adair.

"He is one of the lights of your county, is he not ? " said Harding, indicating Mr. Adair.

"Oh, yes," replied Alice, "he took honours and a gold medal at Trinity College."

"I know he did, and is not a capacity for passing competitive examinations the best proof of a man's incapacity for everything else ? "

"Do you know him ? "

"Yes, a little. He wears his University laurels at forty, builds parish schools, and frightens his neighbours with the liberality of his opinions and the rectitude of his life."

"But have you seen his pamphlets on the amalgamation of the poor houses ? " said Alice, astonished at the slight consideration afforded to the rural genius.

"I have heard of them. It appears he is going in for

politics; but his politics will be on a par with his saw-mill, and his farmyard in concrete. Mr. Adair is a well-known person. Every county in England, Ireland, and Scotland, possesses and is proud of its Mr. Adair."

Alice wondered for some moments in silence; and when suddenly her thoughts detached themselves she said: "Have you been writing a great deal? We did not see you in the ladies' drawing-room."

"I was very busy all the morning. I had two articles to write for one of my papers and some books to review."

"How nice it must be to have a duty to perform every day; to have always an occupation to which you can turn with pleasure."

"I do not know that I look upon my ink-bottle as an eternal haven of bliss. Still, I would sooner contribute articles to daily and weekly papers than sit in the Kildare Street Club, drinking glasses of sherry. Having nothing to do must be a terrible occupation, and one difficult to fulfil with dignity and honour. But," he added, as if a sudden thought had struck him, "you must have a great deal of time on your hands; why don't you do some writing?"

"Oh, what should I write about?" said Alice, blushing a little, but pleased at the compliment paid to her.

"I suppose the right and proper thing for a young lady to write is a novel. Did you ever try to write a story?"

"No, not since I was at school. I used to write stories there, and read them to the girls, and . . . ."

"And what?"

"Oh, nothing; it seems so absurd of me to talk to you about such things; you will only laugh at me just as you did at Mr. Adair."

"No, I assure you, I am very loyal to my friends."

"Friends! we have only known each other a week."

"I should have thought that friendship was a question of sympathy, and not one of time: but I will withdraw the word."

"Oh, no, I did not mean that—I am sure I am very glad . . . ."

"Very well, then, we will be friends; and now tell me what you were going to say."

"I have forgotten—what was I saying?"

"You were telling me about something you had written at school."

"Oh, yes, I remember. I did a little play for the girls to act just before we left.'"

"What was it about—what was it called?"

"It was not original—it was an adaptation of Tennyson's ballad of King Cophetua. You know Miss Gould; she played the King, and Miss Scully, she played the beggar-maid. But, of course, the whole thing was very childish."

"I don't know about that. You certainly ought to try to do something when you go back to Galway. If you will send me an article or a short story I will tell you what I think of it, and see what can be done with it. I am going back to London in about ten days."

"So soon!"

Harding had not time to answer, for at this moment a figure in knee-breeches and flesh-coloured stockings was seen waving a wand at the far end of the room. He was the usher clearing the way for the Vice-regal procession.

The first to appear were the A.D.C.s. They were followed by the Medical Department, by the Private Secretary, the Military Private Secretary, the Assistant Under Secretaries, by the Gentlemen in Waiting, the Master of the Horse, the Dean of the Chapel Royal, the Chamberlain, the Gentleman Usher, the Comptroller, the State Steward, walking with a wand, like a doge in an opera bouffe; then came another secretary, and another band of the underlings who swarm about this mock court like flies about a choice pile of excrement. Then came a heavy-built, red-bearded man, and he carried, as one might a baby, a huge gilt sword in his fat hands. He was followed by their Excellencies. The long maroon-coloured breeches preserved their usual disconsolateness, the teeth and diamonds retained their splendour, and the train—many yards of azure blue richest Duchesse satin, embroidered with large bouquets of silver lily of the valley, and trimmed with plumes of azure blue ostrich feathers, and bunches of silver coral— was upheld by two tiny children who tottered beneath its enormous weight. Then another batch of A.D.C.s in Waiting, the ladies of the Vice-regal family : their Excellencies' guests and the ladies in attendance—placed according to their personal precedence—brought up the rear of the procession. And with all the gravity of a funeral the *cortége* passes between the ranks of the women : their naked shoulders are the mourners, their skirts are the cerecloths that enwrap this poor ghost of

royalty: criminal-like, its living ears filled with the dirges
the skies are ringing, it passes down the long room, returning
to its gruesome throne, a throne that is an open bier, a throne
that is even now its eternal sepulchre of shame.

"Does not real, actual life sometimes appear to you, Miss
Barton, more distorted and unreal than the wildest midnight
dream? I know it does to me. The spectacle we have just
witnessed was a part of the ages that believed in the godhead
of Christ and the divine right of Kings; but it seems to me
utterly bewildering that such barbarities should be permitted
to loiter about the portals of this age of reason."

"But what has Christianity to do with the procession that
has just passed?"

"Everything; a nation cannot be republican as long as it is
Christian. Republicanism is common sense; Christianity is
faith, and faith is the power of believing what you know is not
true; and Christ and the Viceroy share the crutch between
them. Were it not for faith do you think a mock court 'that
an earthquake rocks and swings' could go promenading about
in that ludicrous fashion?"

"I'm not sure that it is faith that enables them to prome-
nade the state sword about. It seems to me more that power
of living in the present time which most people possess to such
an extraordinary degree."

"Perhaps you are right," and Harding glanced at Alice in
surprise.

The conversation drifted back to literature; they talked for
ten minutes, and then Alice suggested that it was time she
should return to Mrs. Barton. Patrick's Hall was still
crowded, and champagne corks exploded through the babbling
of the voices. The squadron of distressed damsels had not
deserted their favourite corner, and they waited about the
pillars like cabs on a stand. The more knowing—the five-
season girls—plied their tricks hither and thither, passing, on
trumped-up excuses, from chaperon to chaperon. At this
hour a middle-aged married doctor would be welcomed; all
were desirous of being seen, if only for a moment, on the arm
of a man. Mrs. Barton's triumph was Cæsarean. More than
half-a-dozen old lords and one young man listened to her
bewitching laugh, and were fed on the brown flashing gold of
her eyes. Milord and Rosshill had been pushed aside: and,
apart, each sought to convince the other that he was going to

ıeave town by the evening mail. Well in view of everyone, Olive had spent an hour with Lord Kilcarney. He had just brought her back to Mrs. Barton. At a little distance the poor Scullys stood waiting. They knew no one, even the Bartons had given them a very cold shoulder. Mrs. Gould, in an old black velvet dress, wondered why all the nice girls did not get married, and from time to time she plaintively questioned the passers by if they had seen May. Violet's sharp face had grown sharper. She knew she could do something if she only got a chance. But would she get a chance? The Ladies Cullen, their plank-like shoulders bound in grey frisé velvet and steel, were talking to her. Suddenly Lady Sarah bowed to Lord Kilcarney, and the bow said, "Come here!" Leaving Olive he approached. A moment after he was introduced to Violet. Her thin face lit up as if from a light within; a grey cloud dimmed the light of Mrs. Barton's golden eyes, and when she saw *Him* in the vestibule helping the Scullys on with their wraps, she shuddered as if struck with a blast of icy wind.

CHAPTER IV.

"Dungory Castle, Gort,
"Co. Galway.

"MY DEAREST ALICE,—I was so delighted to hear from you; it was very good of you to write to me. I was deeply interested in your description of the Dublin festivities, and must try and tell you all the news.

"Everybody here is talking of Olive and Lord Kilcarney. It is said that he proposed to her at the Drawing-room. Is this true? I hope so, for she seems to have set her heart on the match. But she is a great deal too nice for him. They say that when he is in London he does nothing but go about from bar-room to bar-room drinking brandies and sodas. It is also said that he used to spend much of his time with actresses. I hope these stories are false, but I cannot help thinking. . . . Well, we have often talked over these things, and you know what my opinions of men are. I hope I am not doing wrong in speaking like this; but a piece of news has reached me that forces my thoughts back into the old ways—ways that I know you have often reproved me for letting my mind wander in. In a word, darling Alice, I hear that you are very much taken up with a Mr. Harding, a writer, or painter, or something of that sort. Now, will you promise to write and tell me if this be true? I would sooner know the worst at once—hear that you love him madly, passionately, as I believe some women love men. But you, who are so nice, so good, so beautiful, you could not love a man thus. I cannot think you could—I will not think you do. I have been crying all the morning, crying bitterly; horrible thoughts have forced themselves on my mind. I have seen (but it was not true though it seemed so clear; visions are not always true) this man kissing you! Oh! Alice, let me warn you, let me beg of you to think well before you abandon yourself to a man's power, to a man's love. It is a vile and degrading thing. How women can endure it

I don't know; the thought fills me with horror. Women are pure, men are obscene animals. Their love is our degradation. Love! a nice name they give it. How can a sentiment that is merely a gratification of the lowest passions be love? And that is all they seek; I know it; in their heart of hearts they despise us.

" But you, Alice; you who are so noble, so pure, so lofty-minded, you would not soil yourself by giving way to such a sentiment. Write! you will write, and tell me that what I saw in vision was a lie, an abominable lie! Nay, you do not love Mr. Harding. You will not marry him; surely you will not. Oh! to be left here alone, never to see you again—I could not bear it, I should die. You will not leave me to die, Alice, dear, you will not; write and tell me you will not. And what grieves me doubly is that it must seem to you, dear, that I am only thinking of myself. I am not; I think of you, I wish to save you from what must be a life of misery and, worse still, of degradation; for every man is a degradation when he approaches a woman. I know you couldn't bear up against this; you are too refined, too pure—I can sympathise with you. I know, poor little cripple though I be, the horrors of married life. I know what men are—you smile your own kind, sweet smile; I see it as I write; but you are wrong: I know nothing of men in particular, but I know what the sex is—I know nothing of individuals, but I know what life is. I express myself badly, but you guess what I mean. The very fact of being forced to live apart has helped me to realise how horrible life is, and how the passions of men make it vile and abominable. All their tender little words and attentions are but lust in disguise. I hate them! I could whip, I could beat, I would torture them; and when I had done my worst I should not have done enough to punish them for the wrongs they have done to my sex.

" I know, Alice, dear, I am writing violently, that I am letting my temper get the better of me, and this is very wrong; you have often told me it is very wrong; but I cannot help it, my darling, when I think of the danger you are in. I cannot tell you how, but I do know you are in danger; something, some instinct has put me in communication with you: there are moments when I see you, yes, see you sitting by that man—I see you now:—the scene is a long blue Drawing-room all aglow with gold mirrors and wax candles—he is sitting

by you, I see you smiling upon him—my blood boils, Alice
—I fear I am going mad; my head drops on the table, and I
strive to shut out the odious sight, but I cannot, I cannot, I
cannot. . . . .

"I am calmer now : you will forgive me, Alice, dear ? I know
I am wrong to write to you in this way, but there are
moments when I realise things with such horrible vividness
that I am, as it were, maddened with pain. Sometimes I
awake in the night, and then I see life in all its hideous
nakedness, revealed, as it were, by a sudden flash of lightning.
Oh, it is terrible to think we are thus. Good-bye, dear, I
know you will forgive me, and I hope you will write at once,
and will not leave me in suspense : that is the worst torture.
With love to our friends Olive, May, and Violet, believe me,
darling Alice,

" Yours affectionately,
"CECILIA CULLEN."

Alice read steadily, word by word; then she let the letter
and her hands fall on her lap; and, engrossed in the picture it
revealed of Cecilia's obscured and perturbed mind, she forgot
the imminent happiness that played, that flashed like a sun-
beam about her. It was a sweet and radiant delight to dream
that Harding loved her; but she knew he did not love her:
still, why should she force the knife into her soul, and, turning
from it, she looked into the gloomy and distorting mirror that
Cecilia held menacingly to her : and very sinister life and love
seemed therein. "And to live in eternal communion with
such a picture," thought the girl; "and if it be a true reflection ! "

She shuddered. "But no ; things are only as we choose to
see them ;" and, on strong bright wings, her thoughts rose out
of the abyss into which they had been, for a moment, forced
to gaze; and through all the terrors of original ignorance her
confidence in humanity remained unshaken. Is not a good
man—and there are good men—of all knowable things the
highest ? Then why should we turn away from the highest
good ? Thus Alice reasoned—she who denied the Bethlehem
man-god, and was content to accept this poor miserable terrene
life of ours as the end of all consciousness, while Cecilia, she
who cried out angrily against the flesh, as if it were a foul and
leprous thing, bowed in complete humbleness of spirit before

that most human of all gods—human even unto bastardy—
that a foolish world has accepted as divine.

How various and how intricate are the questions with which
we find ourselves confronted in the course of any cerebral
investigation! How curiously mental characteristics stop
short where you would expect to find a long continuity! how
mysteriously they wander from their natal lines into crooked
devious ways, and then, suddenly, how they come flowing back
in a great stream, differing absolutely in colour and current,
from the source from which they started! And yet, if these
apparent contradictions were to be pursued closely through the
deeps of the night of creation, each could be demonstrated as
logical as any theorem in Euclid, either by heredity, or by
accidental variations of the physical nature, which in turn react
upon the brain. But here we must be brief; and in our
diagnosis of the origin of the mind of the writer of the letter,
and that of the reader, it will be only necessary to call attention
to the fundamental and main lines on which each brain was
constructed.

Alice Barton's power to judge between right and wrong,
her love of sentiment, her collectedness, yes, I will say her
reasoned collectedness were, as has been already partially shown,
the consequence of the passivity of the life and nature of her
grandfather (the historian); her power of will, and her clear,
concise intelligence were inherited from her mother, and these
qualities being placed in a perfectly healthy subject, a subject
in whom every organ functioned admirably, the result was a
mind that turned instinctively from mysticism and its adjuncts
—foolish hope and wild aspiration—to the natural duties and
interests of life, its plain and simple rectitudes as she saw
them revealed in the general history of mankind. And
Cecilia's dark and illogical mind can also be accounted for.
Her hatred of all that concerned sexual passion was consequent
on her father's age and her mother's loathing for him during
conception and pregnancy; and then, if it be considered that
this transmitted hatred was planted and left to germinate in
a misshapen body, it will be understood how a weird love of
the spiritual, of the mystical, was the almost inevitable psychical
characteristic that a human being born under such circumstances
would possess.

Alice sat on a low chair, her feet set against the fender, and
her hands laid on Cecilia's letter. Her vision was not precise,

but there were flashes of sun in it, and her thoughts loomed
and floated away. She thought of herself, of Harding, of their
first meeting. The first time she had seen him he was sitting
in the same place and in the same chair as she was sitting in
now. She remembered the first words that had been spoken:
the scene was as clear to her as if it were etched upon her
brain; and as she mused she thought of the importance of
that event. Harding was to her what a mountain is to the
level plain. From him she now looked forward and back.
"So people say that I am in love with him! well, supposing
I were I do not know that I should feel ashamed of myself."

The reflection was an agreeable one, and in it her thoughts
floated away like red-sailed barges into the white mists that
veil with dreamy enchantment the wharves and the walls of
an ancient town. But suddenly she began to think definitely.
What did she know of him? Nothing! He was to her as
much, but no more than the author of a book in which she
was deeply interested: with this difference:—she could hear
him reply to her questions; but his answers were only like
other books, and revealed nothing of his personality. She
would have liked to have known the individual man surrounded with his individual hopes and sufferings, but of these
she knew nothing. They had talked of all things, but it
seemed to her that of the real man she had never had a
glimpse. Never did he unbend, never did he lift the mask he
wore. He was interesting, but very unhuman; and he paraded
his ideas and his sneers as the lay figures did the mail armour
on the castle stairway. She did not know if he were a good or
a bad man; she fancied he was not very good, and then she
grew angry with herself for suspecting him. Alice was very
loyal. But honest or dishonest, she was sure he could love no
one, and a bitter heart-pang brought her thoughts to a pause;
and she strove to recall his face. She could remember nothing
but the cold merciless eyes—eyes that were like the palest
blue porcelain: "Why had he been so nice if he meant no
more? But how ungrateful I am," thought the girl, and she
checked the bitter flow of reproaches that rose in her mind.

It was in the ladies' drawing-room. Two old ladies sat on
the sofa under the window, their white hair and white caps
coming out very white upon the grey Irish day. They knitted
methodically; and around the ottoman the young ladies, Gladys
and Zoe Brennan, one of the Miss Duffys, and the girl in red,

yawned over circulating novels. They longed that a man might come in—not with hope that he would interest them—but because they were accustomed to think of all time as wasted that was not spent in talking to a man.

Nor were they awakened from their languid hopes until Olive came rushing into the room with a large envelope in her hand.

"Oh, I see," she said, "you have got a letter from Cecilia. What does she say? I got one this morning from Barnes;" and, bending her head, Olive whispered in Alice's ear: "She says that everyone is talking in Galway of when I shall be a marchioness!"

"Is that the letter?" asked Alice, innocently.

"No, you silly, this is a Castle invitation."

The Brennans and the girl in red looked up.

"Ah, is it for to-night or to-morrow?" said the latter.

"For to-morrow."

"Now, I wonder if there will be one for me. Is it to dinner or to the dance?"

"To dinner."

"Ah, really . . . yes, very lucky." Her eyes fell, and her look was expressive of her deep disappointment. A dance —yes, but a dinner and a dance!

Then she continued: "Ah, the Castle treats us all very badly. I am glad sometimes when I hear the Land League abusing it. We come up here, and spend all our money on dresses, and we get nothing for it except two State balls, and it is no compliment to ask us to them—they are obliged to. But what do you think of my little coat? It is this that keeps me warm," and Miss O'Reilly held out her sealskin for the company to feel the texture. For the last three weeks she had not failed, on all occasions, to call attention to this garment— "Signor Parisina had said it was lovely." Here she sighed— Signor Parisina had left the hotel. "And I have a new dress coming home—it is all red—a cardinal silk—you know nothing but red suits me!"

"Is the hall-porter distributing the invitations?" asked Gladys Brennan. "Did he give you yours?"

"No, ours was, of course, directed to mamma; I found it in her room."

"Then perhaps" . . . Zoe did not finish the sentence, and both sisters rolled up their worsted-work preparatory to going upstairs.

In Dublin, during six weeks of the year, the arrival of these large official envelopes is watched with an eagerness that words cannot describe. These envelopes are the balm of Gilead; and the Land League, and the hopelessness of matchmaking are merged and lost for a moment in an exquisite thrill of triumph or despair. An invitation to the Castle means much. The grey-headed official who takes you down to dinner may bore you, and, at the dance, you may find yourself without a partner; but the delight of asking your friends if you may expect to meet them on such a night, of telling them afterwards of your successes, are the joys of Dublin; and armed with their invitation, the Bartons scored heavily over the Scullys and the Goulds, who were only asked to the dance.

"And what will the dinner be like, mamma?" asked Olive.

"It will be very grand. Lord Cowper does things in very good style indeed; and our names will be given in the papers. But I don't think it will amuse you, dear. All the officials have to be asked—judges, police-officers, &c. You will probably go down with some old fellow of sixty: but that can't be helped. At the dance after, we'll see the marquis."

"I told you, mamma, didn't I, that Barnes wrote that everybody in Galway said he was in love with me, and had proposed?"

"You did, dear; and it does no harm for the report to have got about, for if a thing gets very much spoken of—it forces a man to come to the point. You will wear your red tulle. I don't know that you look better in anything else."

Whatever Mrs. Barton's faults may have been, she did her duty, as she conceived it, by her daughter; and during the long dinner, through the leaves of the flowering plants, she watched her Olive anxiously. A hundred-and-twenty people were present. Mothers and eligible daughters, judges, lords, police-officers, earls, poor-law inspectors, countesses, and Castle officials. Around the great white-painted, gold-listed walls the table, in the form of a horseshoe, was spread. In the soothing light of the shaded lamps, the white glitter of the piled-up silver danced over the talking faces, and descended in silvery waves into the bosoms of the women. Salmon and purple-coloured liveries passed quickly; and in the fragrance of soup and the flavours of sherry, in the lascivious pleasing of the waltz tunes that Liddell's band poured from a top gallery, the goodly company of time-servers, panders, and others, forgot their fears of the Land League, and the doom that was now waxing to fulness.

To the girls the dinner seemed interminable, but at the "private dance" afterwards those who were known in official circles, or were fortunate enough to meet their friends, amused themselves. It took place in the Throne Room. As the guests arrived they scanned each other narrowly. People, who had known each other from childhood upwards, as they met on the landing, affected a look of surprise: "Oh! so you are here? I wonder how you got your invitation? Well, I suppose you are better than I took you to be!" Acquaintances saluted each other more cordially than was their wont: he or she who had dined at the Castle took his or her place at once among the *élite*: he or she who had come to dance was henceforth considered worthy of a bow in Grafton Street. For Dublin is a city without a conviction, without an opinion. Things are right and wrong according to the dictum of the nearest official. If it be not absolutely ill-bred to say you think this, or are inclined to take such or such a view, it is certainly more advisable to say that the Attorney-General thinks so, or that on one occasion you heard the State Steward, the Chamberlain, or any other equally distinguished underling express this or that opinion. Castle tape is worn in time of mourning and in the time of feasting. Every gigman in the Kildare Street wears it in his buttonhole, and the ladies of Merrion Square are found to be gartered with it.

Mrs. Barton's first thought was to get Olive partners. Milord and Lord Rosshill were sent hither and thither, and with such good result that the whole evening the beauty was beset with A.D.C.s. But the marquis had danced three times with Violet Scully, and Mrs. Barton vented her anger on poor Alice. The girl knew no one, nor was there time to introduce her to men. She was consequently sent off with milord to see where the marquis was hiding; and she was commissioned to tell her sister to answer thus when Lord Kilcarney asked for another dance: "I am engaged, *cher marquis*, but for you of course I shall have to throw some poor fellow over." Mrs. Barton knew not how to play a waiting game. Her tactics were always to grapple with the enemy. She was a Hannibal: she risked all to gain all. Mrs. Scully, on the contrary, watched the combat from afar —as Moltke did the German lines when they advanced upon Paris.

The Bartons were not invited to the next private dance, and they had to look forward to the State ball given on the following Monday. As they mounted the stairway Mrs. Barton said:
"You know we turn to the left this time and enter Patrick's Hall by this end; the other entrance is blocked up by the daïs; and the wall-flowers, you will find, have shifted their camp. It is considered somewhat bad form to stand about the pillars; but the great thing is to get hold of the best men. We shan't have long to wait, and then we'll move up to the daïs."

St. Patrick's Hall was now a huge democratic crush. All the little sharp glances of the "private dance," "What, you here!" were dispensed with as useless, for all were within their rights in being at the ball. They pushed, laughed, danced. They met as they would have met in Rotten Row, and they took their amusement with the impartiality of pleasure-seekers jigging and drinking in a market-place on fair-day. On either side of the hall there were ascending benches; these were filled with chaperons and *débutantes*, and over their heads the white-painted gold-listed walls were hung with garlands of evergreen oak interwoven with the celebrated silver shields, the property of the Cowper family, and in front of the curtains hanging about the daïs, the maroon legs of His Excellency, and the teeth and diamonds of Her Excellency, were seen passing to and fro, and up and down to the music of oblivion that Liddell dispensed with a flowing arm.

The darling dream of the Dubliner is to dance in this quadrille—it is the highest honour he can ever hope to attain—but, for the moment, all minds were set on the realisation of a more immediate prospect. About the pillars the three and four-season girls were drawn up in battle array; and, their eyes liquid with invitation, they sought to attract the attention of the men as they went in. The girl in red, the Brennans, the Miss Duffys led the assault; even the honourable Miss Gores were there.

"I declare Olive Barton is here!" whispered the redoubtable Bertha; "this doesn't look as if the beaux were coming forward in their hundreds. It is said that Lord Kilcarney has given her up for Violet Scully."

"I'm not a bit surprised," said the girl in red; "and, now I think of it, all the beauties come to the same end. I'll just give her a couple more Castle seasons. It is that that will pull the fine feathers out of her."

But the beauty was soon spied out by some three or four A.D.C.s; an English lord engaged her for a couple of waltzes, and, in triumph, Mrs. Barton made her way up to the daïs where she had given appointment to Lord Dungory, Lord Rosshill, and her other admirers. One of them, an old man of sixty, took Alice out for a waltz, and when it was over she was free to listen to her mother's laughter, and to watch, until her eyes ached, the whirling of white and rose tulle and the pushing of black cloth shoulders. She was not alone. She was but one of the many débutantes who, amid the chaperons, sat wearily waiting on the high benches. Some are but seventeen, and their sweet, clear eyes seem as a bright morning, full of beautiful possibilities.

Alice was beginning to see to the end, and, as the old sad thoughts came back to her, she thought of the resultless life, the life of white idleness that awaited nearly all of them. What were they but snow-flakes born to shine for a moment and then to fade, to die, to disappear, to become part of the black, the foul-smelling slough of mud below? The drama in muslin was again unfolded, and she could read each act; and there was a "curtain" at the end of each. The first was made of young, hopeful faces, the second of arid solicitation, the third of the bitter, malignant tongues of Bertha Duffy and her friend. They are talking now to a pale little martyr who has spoken to no one, who has not even a brother to take her for a walk down the room, or to the buffet for an ice.

"And are not the Castle balls very nice?" said Bertha, "and how are you amusing yourself?"

"Oh, very much indeed," replied the poor débutante.

"And is it true, Bertha," asks the fierce aunt, "you know all the news, that Mr. Jones has been transferred to another ship and has gone off to the Cape?"

"Yes, yes," replied the girl with a coarse laugh; "a nice end to her beau; and after dinnering him up the whole summer too."

Alice shuddered. Was it possible, she asked herself, that she was listening to the conversation of people who passed for, and who believed themselves to be, ladies? And to think that only a few years are required to degrade a girl full of sweetness and promise to the level of that horrible harlot-like creature with the yellow hair and wide mouth! And by what delicate degrees is the soul befouled in this drama of muslin, and how

little is there left for any use of life when, after torture and
disgrace, the soul, that was once so young, appears on the
stage for the fourth act.   Examine the meagre minds of the
Ladies Cullen and the Honourable Miss Gores, listen to their
narrow bigotries, and think that once these poor old things
were fresh, hopeful, full of aspiration.   Now if they could
rise for a moment out of their living death it would be like
the skeleton in Goya's picture, to lift the tomb and write on
the headstone : " Nada."

An hour passed, and Alice had begun to experience the
worst horrors of a Castle ball.   She was sick of pity for those
around her, and her lofty spirit resented the insult that was
offered to her sex.   At last Harding came up.   Mrs. Barton
received him with enthusiasm : she at once called his attention
to Alice, and in a way that seemed to imply " For goodness
sake take her off; thank heavens there's someone who can put
up with a plain girl."

" Have you been long here, Miss Barton ? " he said, leaning
towards her ; " I have been looking out for you, but the crowd
is so great that it is hard to find anyone."

" I think we arrived about a quarter to eleven," Alice
answered, somewhat eagerly.

Then, after a pause, Harding said :   " Will you give me this
waltz ? "   Alice assented, and, as they made their way through
the dancers, he added :   " But I believe you do not care about
dancing. If you would prefer it, we might go for a walk down
the room.   Perhaps you would like an ice ?   This is the way
to the buffet."

But Alice and Harding did not stop long there ; they were
glad to leave the heat of gas, the odour of sauces, the effer-
vescence of the wine, the detonations of champagne, the tumult
of laughter, the racing of plates, the heaving bosoms, the
glittering corsets for the peace and the pale blue refinement
of the long blue drawing-room.   How much of our sentiments
and thoughts do we gather from our surroundings; and the
shining blue of the turquoise-coloured curtains, the pale dead
blue of the Louis XV. furniture, and the exquisite fragility of
the glass chandeliers, the gold mirrors rutilant with the light
of some hundreds of tall wax candles, were illustrative of the
light dreams and delicate lassitude that filled the souls of the
women as they lay back whispering to their partners, the
crinolettes lifting the skirts over the edges of the sofas.

Here the conversation seems serious, there it is smiling, and broken by the passing and repassing of a fan.

"Only four days more of Dublin," said Harding; "I have settled, or rather the fates have settled, that I am to leave next Saturday."

"And where are you going; to London ?"

"Yes, to London. I am sorry I am leaving so soon ; but it can't be helped. I have met many nice people here—some whom I shall not be able to forget."

"You speak as if it were necessary to forget them—it is surely always better to remember."

"I shall certainly remember you. Besides, I intend to write, and you have promised to send me some of your work. There is no doubt but that I shall be able to get it published."

"It is very kind of you," said Alice, hesitatingly. "I doubt my powers of being able to do anything good enough, but I shall be very glad to hear from you."

At this moment only one thing in the world seemed to be of much real importance ; it was that the man now sitting by her side should not be utterly taken away. To know that he existed, though far from her, would be almost enough, for would he not be to her a sort of beacon-light—a light she might never reach to, but which would break the darkness she dreaded ? In no century have men been loved so implicitly by women as in the nineteenth; nor could this be otherwise, for putting aside the fact that the natural wants of love have become a nervous erethism in the struggle that a surplus population of more than two million women has created, there are psychological reasons that to-day more than ever impel women to shrink from the intellectual monotony of their sex, and to view with increasing admiration the free, the vigorous intelligence of the male. For as the gates of the harem are being broken down, and the gloom of the female mind clears, and grows keenly alive to the sensations and ideas of modern life, it becomes axiomatically sure that Woman brings a loftier reverence to the shrine of Man than she has done in any past age, seeing, as she now does, in him the incarnation of the freedom of which she is vaguely conscious and which she is perceptibly acquiring. So sets the main current that is bearing civilisation along ; but beneath the great feminine tide there is an under-current of hatred and revolt. This is

particularly observable in the leaders of the movement;
women who in the tumult of their aspirations, and their
passionate yearnings towards the new ideal, and the memory
of the abasement their sex have been in the past, and are
still being in the present, subjected to, forget the immutability
of the laws of life, and with virulent virtue and protest con-
demn love—that is to say love in the sense of sexual inter-
course—and proclaim a higher mission for woman than to be
the mother of men : and an adjuvant, unless corrected by
sanative qualities of a high order, is, of course, found in any
physical defect. But as the corporeal and incorporeal heredita-
ments of Alice Barton and Lady Cecilia Cullen were examined
fully in the beginning of this chapter, it is only necessary to
here indicate the order of ideas—the moral atmosphere of the
time—to understand the efflorescence of the two minds, and
to realise how curiously representative they are of this last
quarter of the nineteenth century.

And it was necessary to make that survey of psychical cause
and effect to appreciate the sentiments that actuated Alice in
her relationship with Harding. She loved him, but more
through the imagination than the heart. She knew he was
deceiving her, but to her he meant so much that she had not
the force of will to cast him off, and abandoned herself to the
intellectual sensualism of his society. It was this, and nothing
more. What her love might have been it is not necessary to
analyse ; in the present circumstances, it was completely merged
in the knowledge that he was, to her, light, freedom, and
instruction, and that when he left, darkness and ignorance
would again close in upon her. They had not spoken for some
moments. With a cruelty that was peculiar to him, he waited
for her to break the silence.

"And what will you do," she said, at last, "when you
return to London ? "

"You mean, what literary work shall I be engaged upon ?
I shall first of all finish off my articles on Ireland——"

"I thought they were done long ago."

"Yes, but I got an order from America—the Americans
pay very well—for a series of descriptive sketches. I shall not
be long knocking them off, and then I shall do some fiction."

"What do you call descriptive sketches ?"

"Well, my idea is to take a series of representative characters
—the landlord, the grazier, the tenant farmer, the moonlighter,

the parson, the priest—and tell their history, their manner of life, and their aims and ambitions. There are many curious and interesting things to be said—the last flicker of Protestantism, the gradual absorbing of the glebe lands, and the apparent triumph of Catholicism."

"Then you think that Catholicism is likewise doomed?"

"Of course I do. The Roman Church is shattered to its base. Christ, if you will, was a radical, but the Church of Christ was built on conservative foundations, in comparison to which those of the House of Lords are socialistic, communistic, and every other 'istic.' Now, for the first time, we see the bishops of Rome waving the red flag of revolution. If a cat has nine, superstition has ninety-nine lives; but it is hardly credible that a Church that has existed eighteen hundred years through the vivifying power of one set of principles should be able to gain a new lease of life by the recanting of all its old opinions. The priests have to get their dues, and to get them they have to mount the Land League platform. The need of the moment is the greatest need of all."

"And you think they will eventually die of the bread they are now eating?"

"Of course republicanism and common-sense will not put up with their nonsense for very long; and it is my firm belief that in fifty—say a hundred—years priests and parsons, in common with other fortune-tellers, will be prosecuted under the Vagrancy Acts."

One of the many threads that drew Alice, fascinated, towards Harding was the quick flight of his thought, and the rapid and daring way in which he expressed it. She had sufficiently mastered the old weakness of belief, and she was not shocked but only a little startled at his utterances. Now she laughed softly, amused by the wit and epigrammatic force of his conversation.

Harding was not quite sincere. He spoke with a view to effect; he desired to astonish, and, if possible, to have the girl think of him when he was gone as something quite exceptional—something she would never see again. Alice's thoughts, however, had passed from the literary souvenirs that he was pouring upon her, and she thought now of his departure, and the loneliness it would bring to her. Without seeking a transitional phrase, she raised her eyes to his and said unaffectedly:

"I am sorry you are going away : I am afraid we shall never meet again."

"Oh, yes, we shall," he replied : "you'll get married one of these days and come and live in London."

"Why should I go to live in London ?"

"Watch life as it flows and breaks about us: do you not see that man's moral temperament leads him sooner or later back to his connatural home ? And we must not confuse home with the place of our birth. There are Frenchmen born in England, Englishmen born in France. Heine was a Frenchman born in Germany—and you are a Kensingtonian. I see nothing Irish in you. Oh, you are very Kensington, and therefore you will—I do not know when or how, but assuredly as a stream goes to the river and the river to the sea, you will drift to your native place—Kensington. Your tastes will bring you there; you'll be writing novels one of these days in Kensington, I wouldn't mind betting."

"I don't like you to laugh at me."

"I assure you I am not laughing at you. Have you not promised me to try your hand at an article or two and a short story, which I am going to get published for you ?"

"Yes, I said I would try."

"And you promise to write to me ?—I shall be most interested to hear how you are getting on."

"I shall have to write to you if I send you the story."

"You might send it without a letter."

"I should not be so rude as that, And, you must not forget, you promised to give me one of your books."

"Yes, I'll bring you one to-morrow. But do you know that I have left the hotel ? There were too many people about to do much work, so I took rooms in Molesworth Street— there I can write and read undisturbed. You might come and see me."

"I should like to very much, but I don't think I could ask mother to come with me ; she is so very busy just now."

"Well, don't ask your mother to come ; you won't be afraid to come alone ?"

"I am afraid I could not do that."

"Why not ? No one will ever know anything about it."

"Very possibly, but I don't think it would be a proper thing to do—I don't think it would be a *right* thing to do."

" Right ! I thought we had ceased to believe in heaven and hell."

"Yes, but does that change anything? There are surely duties that we owe to our people, to our families. The present ordering of things may be unjust, but, as long as it exists, had we not better live in accordance with it ? "

" A very sensible answer, and I suppose you are right."

Alice looked at him in astonishment, but she was shaken too intensely in all her feelings to see that he was perfectly sincere, that his answer was that of a man who saw and felt through his intelligence and not his conscience.

The conversation had suddenly come to a pause, and the silence that intervened was full of nervous apprehension. Then it was broken by whispered words, and the abundant laughter that was seemingly used to hide the emotions that oppressed the speakers. Finally they sat down quite close to, but hidden from, Alice and Harding by a screen, and through the paper even their breathing was audible. All the dancers were gone ; there was scarcely a white skirt or black coat in the pale blueness of the room. Evidently the lovers thought they were well out of reach of eavesdroppers. Alice felt this, but before she could rise to go, Fred Scully had said—

"Now, May, I hope you won't refuse to let me come and see you in your room to-night. It would be too cruel if you did. I'll steal along the passage ; no one will hear, no one will ever know, and I'll be so very good ; I promise you I will."

" Oh, Fred, I'm afraid I can't trust you ; it would be so very wicked."

"Nothing is wicked when we really love ; besides, I only want to talk to you."

" You can talk to me here."

" Yes, but it isn't the same thing ; anyone can talk to you here. I want to show you a little poem I cut out of a newspaper to-day for you. I'll steal along the passage—no one will ever know."

" You'll promise to be very good, and you won't stop more than five minutes."

The words were spoken in low soft tones, exquisitely expressive of the overthrow of reason and the merging of all the senses in the sweet abandonment of passion.

Alice sat unable to move ; she was trembling like a bird held to a man's breast. At last, awakening with a pained look in her grey eyes, she touched Harding's hand with hers, and, laying her finger on her lips, she arose. Their footfalls made no sound on the deep soft carpet; they stole away unperceived.

"This is very terrible," she murmured, half to herself.

Harding had too much tact to answer; and, taking advantage of the appearance of Violet Scully, who came walking gaily down the room on the Marquis's arm, he said—

"Your friend Miss Scully seems to be in high spirits."

Violet exchanged smiles with Alice as she passed. The smile was one of triumph. She had waltzed three times with the Marquis, and was now going to sit out a set of quadrilles.

"What a beautiful waltz the 'Blue Danube' is!" she said, leading her admirer to where the blue fans were numerous. Upon the glistening piano stood a pot filled with white azaleas; and, in the pauses of the conversation, you heard the glass of the chandeliers tinkling gently to the vibration of the music.

"It is a beautiful waltz when I am dancing it with you."

"I am sure you say that to every girl you dance with."

"No, I should not know how to say so to anyone but you," said the little man humbly; and so instinct were the words with truth that the girl, in the violence of her emotion, fancied her heart had ceased to beat.

"But you have not known me a fortnight," she answered involuntarily.

"But that doesn't matter; the moment I saw you, I—I— liked you. It is so easy to know the people we—like; we know it at once; at least I do."

She was more self-possessed than he, but the words "Am I —am I going to be a marchioness?" throbbed like a burning bullet sunk into the very centre of her forehead. And to maintain her mental equipoise she was forced, though by doing so she felt she was jeopardising her chances, to coquette with him. After a long silence she said—

"Oh, do you think we know at first sight the people we like? Do you believe in first impressions?"

"My first and last impressions of you are always the same. All I know is, that when you are present all things are bright, beautiful, and cheering, and when you are away I don't much care what happens. Now, these Castle balls used to bore me to death last year; I used to go into a back room and fall asleep, but this year I am as lively as a kitten—I think I could go on for ever, and the Castle seems to me the most glorious place on earth. I used to hate it; I was as bad as Parnell, but not for the same reasons, of course. Now I am only afraid he will have his way, and they'll shut the whole place up. Anyhow, even if they do, I shall always look back upon this season as a very happy time."

"But you do not really think that Parnell will be allowed to have his way?" said Violet, inadvertently.

"I don't know, I don't take much interest in politics, but I believe things are going terribly to the bad. Dublin, they say, is undermined with secret societies, and the murder that was committed the other day in Sackville Street was the punishment they inflict on those whom they even remotely suspect of being informers."

"But don't you think the Government will soon be obliged to step in and put an end to all this kind of thing?"

"I don't know; I'm afraid they'll do nothing until we landlords are all irretrievably ruined."

Violet's thin face contracted. She had introduced a subject that might prevent him from ever proposing to her. She knew how terribly the Kilcarney estates were mortgaged; and, even now, as she rightly conjectured, the poor little man. was inwardly trembling at the folly it had been on his lips to speak. Three of his immediate ancestors had married penniless girls, and it was well-known that another love match would precipitate the property over that precipice known to every Irish landowner—the Encumbered Estates Court. But those exquisitely shapen temples, so exquisitely shaded with light brown tresses, that delicately moulded head—delicate as an Indian carven ivory, dispelled all shadows and fears and waxed the sole, the omnipotent and omnipresent desire of his life.

She thought not of the renunciation she was making of love and passion. Her mind was blank to all but one desire, and in the nervous sensitivity of the moment, will, conscious and unconscious, became one, and the violent emotion of expectancy produced the phenomenon of involuntary, although intelligent action. The girl obeyed an unconscious conception, that is to say an instinct, and uttered the precise words that the occasion demanded:

"But things never turn out as well or as badly as we expect them to."

This facile philosophy went like wine to the little marquis's

head. He longed to throw himself at the feet of his goddess
and thank her for the balm she had poured upon him. The
gloom of approaching ruin disappeared, and he saw nothing in
the world but a white tulle skirt, a thin foot, a thin bosom,
and a pair of bright grey eyes. Vaguely he sought for equivalent words, but loud-talking dancers passed into the room. In
arid and vulgar curiosity they stared at the couple sitting
under the azaleas; and, abashed by their looks, the marquis
broke off a flowering branch and said, stammering the while
incoherently :

" Will you keep this in memory of this evening ? "

Violet thrust the flowers into her bosom, and was about to
thank him, when an A.D.C. came up and claimed her for the
dance. Coldly she told him he was mistaken, that she was
engaged; and, taking Lord Kilcarney's arm, they made their
way in silence back to the ball-room.

On the whole, Violet was satisfied; she felt now very sure
of her marquis, and, as they approached Mrs. Scully, a quick
glance said that things were going as satisfactorily as could be
desired. Not daring to trust herself to the gossip of the
chaperons, this excellent lady sat apart, maintaining the
solitary dignity to which the Galway counter had accustomed
her ; and she received the marquis with the same smile as she
used to bestow on her best customers. He sat beside Violet.
They talked for a few minutes of the different aspects of the
ball-room, of their friends, of things that did not interest
them. Then she said winsomely, affecting an accent of
command that enchanted him :

" Now I want you to go and dance with someone else; let
me see—what do you say to Olive Barton ? If you don't, I
shall be in her mother's black books for the rest of my life.
Now go. We shall be at home to-morrow; you might come
in for tea."

The marquis declared he would be delighted, and, suffocated
with secret joy, he made his way across the room to where
Mrs. Barton was sitting. He was received with waves of the
white hands and an abundance of laughter. Mrs. Barton was
too wise to show her disappointment, and, cancelling a couple
of Olive's engagements, she sent her off to dance with him.

Violet sat by her mother, refusing all her partners; but,
when "God save the Queen" was played, she accepted Lord
Kilcarney's arm, and they pressed forward to see the Lord-

Lieutenant and Her Excellency pass down the room. Violet's eyes feasted on the bowing black coats and light toilettes, and, leaning on her escutcheon, she dreamed vividly of the following year when she would take her place amid all these noble people, and, as high as they, stand a peeress on the daïs. This moment of vision was the keenest pleasure in her life: and so ended the ball.

As the Bartons drove through the wet and forlorn streets of Dublin, Olive said:

"Did you notice, mamma, how often that beast of a girl, Violet Scully, danced with Lord Kilcarney?"

"I don't think he danced oftener with her than he did with you, dear," Mrs. Barton answered, a little wearily. "It would not look well if he remained with you the whole night." And, weary of the racket of music, wine, and gaslight, the women gazed through the misted windows. The city lay mysteriously dead—immovable and mute beneath the moon, like a starved vagrant in the last act of a melodrama.

To be alone, to lie down, to forget. She had too much to think of; to-morrow she would think of it all, but now she was tired and wanted rest. But for Alice there was no rest that night. Her brain was on fire with what she had seen and heard. It seemed to her as if she had lived through a hundred years; and, as she lay under the sheets, all the old sorrows came as a river, rushing through the darkness. She was but a poor plain girl whom no one would ever marry, a poor plain girl who saw her little hopes wrecked daily before her despairing eyes, whose fine feelings were daily brutalised by those with whom she was, and would ever be, forced to live. And to think, to know—ah! yes, to know—that the world, the fair beauteous world, with all its adventures, possibilities, and achievements, would—must—remain to her for ever a blank; and through no fault of her own, but because she was but a poor plain girl whom no one would ever think of marrying!

Seen from afar all things in nature are of equal worth; and the nearest things, when viewed with the eyes of God, are raised to those heights of tragic awe which conventionality would limit to the death of kings or patriots. The history of a nation as often lies hidden in social wrongs and domestic griefs as in the story of revolution, and if it be for the historian to narrate the one, it is for the novelist to dissect and explain the other; and who would say which is of the most vital importance—the thunder of the people against the oppression of the Castle, or the unnatural sterility, the cruel idleness of mind and body of the muslin martyrs who cover with their white skirts the shames of Cork Hill?

Alice knew well that Harding would not marry her, but the knowledge did not lessen her terror of losing him, or her fear of the lonely monotony of girl-life that would again close in upon her. And to think that never, never, never, would any door of escape be open to her! And to think that the fair world with all its adventures and aspirations would never, never be known to her, would remain the thinnest of thin dreams. And why? But unlike the night when, before the snow-drowned plain, she cried out against the silence of spinsterhood and all its manifold meanings, she now thought she would be content if things could only remain unchanged. Before, she had demanded marriage as a right, but love was then an abstract passion, now it was a distinct desire possessing for her an intrinsic value. And little as it was characteristic of her to reproach, she now reproached him. Why, oh why, had he been so kind when he must have known from the beginning that all must end! and then, suddenly as lightning sears the face of night, a burning thought of May Gould tore the veil of grief.

* * * * * *

Was there no other way to retain your lover? Was Cecilia right, and did a man care for you for nothing else?

* * * * * *

Still what matter? May, at least, was not lonely and friendless; she, at least, would know what the rest of them might never know!

These thoughts were awakened into consciousness by the action of nervous passion; and, astonished, Alice raised her head, finding within herself no will for the idea. She buried her face in the pillow as if to escape from the impure thoughts with which she was unwittingly assailed.

* * * * * *

But, oh, the punishment and the shame! Her brain reeled. Oh, the terrible drama that was being enacted! How far away? Only a few yards: only a little lath and plaster separated them. Could nothing be done to save, to avert? Alas, nothing—always the same answer: she was only a plain girl who could do nothing but endure.

CHAPTER V.

"So you couldn't manage to keep him after all, my lady? When did he leave the hotel?"

"Mr. Harding left Dublin last Monday week."

Alice wondered if her mother hated her; if she did not, it was difficult to account for the bitterness and the cruelty of her words. This was to the girl a great grief. She did not suspect that Mrs. Barton was a loving and affectionate mother, who would sacrifice herself for one child almost as readily as for the other. In each of us there are traits that the chances of life have never revealed; and though she would have sat by the bedside, even if Alice were stricken with typhoid fever, Mrs. Barton recoiled spitefully like a cat before the stern rectitudes of a nature so dissimilar from her own; and then the feline claws would appear through the soft velvet paws. Olive, on the contrary, she had fashioned according to her guise, and all the cajolery which had been employed in the last twenty years, and we know with what triumphant success, was thrust upon the girl for buckler and spear. She was now but a pale copy of her mother: all the affectation had been faithfully reproduced, but the charm of the original had evaporated like a perfume. It would be rash to say that Mrs. Barton did not see that the weapons which had proved so deadly in her hands were worthless and ineffectual in her daughter's: but twenty years of elegant harlotry had blunted her finer perceptions, and now the grossest means of pushing Olive and the marquis morally and physically into each other's arms seemed to her the best. Alice was to her but a plain girl, whose mis- fortune was that she had ever been born. This idea had grown up with Mrs. Barton, and fifteen years ago she had seen in the child's face the spinster of fifty. But since the appearance of Harding, and the manifest interest he had shown in her daughter, Mrs. Barton's convictions that Alice

would never be able to find a husband had been somewhat
shaken, and she had almost concluded that it would be as well
—for there was no knowing what men's tastes were—to give
her a chance.   Nor was the dawning fancy dispelled by the
fact that Harding had not proposed, and the cutting words
she had addressed to the girl were the result of the nervous
irritation caused by the marked attention the marquis was
paying Violet Scully.

For, like Alice, Mrs. Barton never lived long in a fool's
paradise, and she now saw that the battle was going against
her, and would most assuredly be lost unless a determined
effort was made.   And she also delayed not a moment in
owning to herself that she had committed a mistake in going
to the Shelbourne Hotel.   Had she taken a house in Mount
Street or Fitzwilliam Place, she could have had all the best
men from the barracks continually at her house.   But at the
hotel she was helpless ; there were too many people about, too
many beasts of women criticising her conduct.   Mrs. Barton
had given two-dinner-parties in a private room hired for the
occasion ; but these dinners could scarcely be called successful.
On one occasion they had seven men to dinner, and as some
half-dozen more turned in in the evening, it became necessary
to send down to the ladies' drawing-room for partners.   Bertha
Duffy and the girl in red of course responded to the call, but
they had rendered everything odious by continuous vulgarity
and brogue.   Then other mistakes had been made.   A charity
costume ball had been advertised.   It was to be held in the
Rotunda.   An imposing list of names headed the prospectus,
and it was confidently stated that all the lady patronesses would
attend.   Mrs. Barton fell into the trap, and, to her dismay,
found herself and her girls in the company of the rag, tag, and
bobtail of Catholic Dublin : Bohemian girls fabricated out of
bedcurtains, negro minstrels that an application of grease and
burnt cork had brought into a filthy existence.   And from the
single gallery that encircled this tomb-like building, the small
tradespeople looked down upon the multicoloured crowd that
strove to dance through the mud that a late Land League
meeting had left upon the floor ; and through the yellow glare
of the gas the grey dust fell steadily into the dancers' eyes and
into the sloppy tea distributed at counters placed here and
there like coffee-stands in the public street.

" I never felt so low in my life," said the lady who always

brought back an A.D.C. from the Castle, and the phrase was cited afterwards as being admirably descriptive of the fête.

When it became known that the Bartons had been present at this ball, that the beauty had been seen dancing with the young Catholic nobodies, their names were struck off the lists, and they were asked to no more private dances at the Castle. Lord Dungory was sent to interview the Chamberlain, but that official could promise nothing. Mrs. Barton's hand was therefore forced. It was obligatory upon her to have some place where she could entertain officers; the Shelbourne did not lend itself to that purpose. Mrs. Barton hired a house in Mount Street, one that possessed a polished floor admirably suited to dancing.

Then she threw off the mask, and pirate-like, regardless of the laws of chaperons, resolved to carry on the war as she thought proper. She'd have done once and for ever with those beasts of women who abused and criticised her. Henceforth she would shut her door against them all, and it would only be open to men—young men for her daughters, elderly men for herself. At four o'clock in the afternoon the entertainment began. Light refreshments, consisting of tea, claret, biscuits, and cigarettes, were laid out in the dining-room. Having partaken, the company, consisting of three colonels and some half-dozen subalterns, went up-stairs to the drawing-room. And in recognition of her flirtation with Harding, a young man replaced Alice at the piano, and for half-a-crown an hour supplied the necessary music.

Round and round the girls went, passing in turn out of the arms of an old into those of a young man, and back again. If they stayed their feet for a moment, Mrs. Barton glided across the floor, and, with insinuating gestures and intonations of voice, would beg of them to continue. She declared that it was *la grâce et la beauté*, &c. The merriment did not cease until half-past six. Some of the company then left, and some few were detained for dinner. A new pianist and fresh officers arrived about nine o'clock, and dancing was continued until one or two in the morning. To yawning subalterns the house in Mount Street seemed at first like a little paradise. The incessant dancing was considered fatiguing, but there were interludes in which claret was drunk, cigarettes smoked, and loose conversation permitted in the dining-room.

Then the dinners! Mrs. Barton's dinners are worthy of

special study.   Her circle of acquaintances being limited, the
same guests were generally found at her table.   Lord Dungory
always sat next to her.   He displayed his old-fashioned shirt-
front, his cravat, his studs, his urbanity, his French epigram.
Rosshill sat opposite him; he was thin, melancholy, aristocratic, silent, and boring.   There was a captain who, since he
had left the army, had grown to the image of a butler, and
an ashen-tinted young man who wore his arm in a sling, and
an old man who looked like a dirty and worn-out broom; and
who put his arm round the backs of the chairs. These and three
A.D.C.s made up the party.   There was very little talking,
and what there was was generally confined to asking the young
ladies if they had been to the Castle, and if they liked dancing.
Mr. Barton, who had just returned from Holland, was full of
strange views concerning Dutch art, and a still stranger plan
for defending his country in case of invasion.

The marquis was a constant, although an unwilling guest at
all these entertainments.   He would fain have refused Mrs.
Barton's hospitalities, but so pressing was she that this seemed
impossible.   There were times when he started at the postman's
knock as at the sound of a Land Leaguer's rifle.   Too frequently
his worst fears were realised.   "*Mon cher marquis*, it will give
us much pleasure if you will dine with us to-morrow night at
half-past seven."   "Dear Mrs. Barton, I regret extremely that
I am engaged for to-morrow night."   An hour later, "*Mon cher
marquis*, I am very sorry you cannot come to-morrow night, but
Thursday will suit us equally well."   What was to be done?   A
second excuse would result only in a proposal to fix a day next
week—better accept and get it over.   He must do this or send
a rude message to the effect that he was engaged for every
day he intended to dine out that season, and he lacked the
moral courage to write such a letter.   Mrs. Barton's formula for
receiving the marquis never varied.   If he arrived early he
found Olive waiting to receive him in the drawing-room.
She was always prepared with a buttonhole, which she insisted
on arranging and pinning into his coat.   Then allusion was
made to the forget-me-nots that the bouquet was sure to contain; and laughing vacantly—for laughter with Olive took the
place of conversation—she fled through the rooms, encouraging
him to pursue her.   During dinner attempts were made to
exchange a few words, but without much success.   Nor was it
until Olive pelted him with flowers, and he replied by destroying

another bouquet and applying it to the same purpose, that much progress was made towards intimacy. But this little scene was exceptional, and on all other occasions Lord Kilcarney maintained an attitude of unfaltering reserve.

Mrs. Barton was at her wits' end. Three days ago she had met him walking in Grafton Street with Violet; yesterday she had caught sight of him driving towards Fitzwilliam Place in a four-wheeler. Remembering she had a visit to pay in that neighbourhood, she gave the necessary directions to her coachman, and was rewarded by seeing the marquis's cab draw up before the Scullys' door. The mere fact that he should use a cab instead of an outside car was a subject to pause upon, but when she noticed that one of the blinds was partially drawn down, her heart sank within her. Nor did the secret of this suspicious visit long remain her exclusive property. As if revealed by those mysteriously subtle oral and visual faculties observed in savage tribes, by which they divine the approach of their enemies or their prey, two days had not elapsed before the tongue of every chaperon was tipped with the story of the four-wheeler and the half-drawn blind, but it was a distinctly latter-day instinct that had led these ladies to speak of there having been luggage piled upon the roof of this celebrated cab. Henceforth eye, ear, and nostril were open, and in the quivering ardour of the chase they scattered through the covers of Cork Hill and Merrion Square, passing from one to the other, by means of sharp yelps and barkings, every indication of the trail that came across their way. Sometimes hearkening to a voice they had confidence in, they would rally at a single point, and then an old b——, her nose in the air, her capstrings hanging lugubriously on either side of her weatherbeaten cheeks, would utter a deep and prolonged baying; then a little further on the scent was recovered, and, with sterns wagging and bristles erect, they hunted the quarry vigorously. Every moment he was expected to break—fear was even expressed that he might end by being chopped.

The Shelbourne Hotel was a favourite meet; and in the ladies' drawing-room each fresh piece of news was torn with avidity. The consumption of note-paper was terrific. Two, three, four, and even five sheets of paper were often filled with what these scavengeresses could rake out of the gutters of gossip. "Ah! me arm aches, and the sleeve of me little coat is wore; I am so eager to write it all off to me ant, that I am too impatient to wait to take it off," was the verbal form in which the girl in red explained her feelings on the subject. Bertha Duffy declared she would write no more ; that she was ruining herself in stamps. Nor were the pens of the Brennans silent; and looking over the meek shoulders on which the mantles of spinsterhood were fast descending, you read : " I hear they danced at the Castle three times together last night, . . . a friend of mine saw them sitting in Merrion Square the whole of one afternoon. . . . They say that if he marries her, that he'll be ruined. . . . The estates are terribly encumbered, . . . his family are in despair about it. . . . Violet is a very nice girl, but we all know her mother sold bacon behind a counter in Galway. . . . He never looks at Olive Barton now; this is a sad end to her beau, and after feeding him the whole season. . . . He dined there three times a week : Mrs. Barton took the house on purpose to entertain him. . . . It is said that she offered him twenty thousand pounds if he'd marry her daughter. . . The money that woman spends is immense, and no one knows where it comes from."

In these matrimonial excitements the amatories of the lady who brought the A.D.C. home from the Castle passed unheeded. The critical gaze of her friends was sorely distracted, and even the night porter forgot to report the midnight visits of her young gentlemen. May too profited largely by the present ferment of curiosity; and, unobserved, she made rendezvous with Fred Scully at the corners of this and that street, and in the hotel they passed furtively down this passage and up that pair of stairs, and when disturbed they hid behind the doors. And Mrs. Gould lived in ignorance of all this chambering folly, and spent her time either writing letters or gossiping about Lord Kilcarney in the drawing-room. And when she picked up a fragment of fresh news she lost not a moment, but put on her bonnet and carried it over to Mount Street. So assiduous was she in this self-imposed duty, that Mrs. Barton was obliged at last to close her door against this obtrusive visitor.

But one day, after a moment of intense reflection, Mrs. Barton concluded that she was losing the battle—that now, in the eleventh hour, it could only be snatched out of defeat by a bold and determined effort. Then she sat down and penned one of her admirable invitations to dinner. An hour later a note feebly pleaded a " previous engagement." Undaunted,

she sat down again and wrote : " To-morrow will suit us equally
well." The marquis yielded; and Lord Dungory was
ordered, when he found himself alone with him in the dining-
room, to lose no opportunity of insisting upon the imminent
ruin of all Irish landlords. He was especially enjoined to say
that, whatever chance of escape there was for the owners of
unencumbered properties, the doom of those who had mortgages
to pay had been sounded. Milord executed his task with con-
summate ability; and when the *grand parii* entered the
drawing-room, his thoughts were racked with horrible forebodings. The domain, woods, the pride of centuries, he saw
plundered and cut down ; lawns, pleasure-grounds, and gardens
had been distributed among peasants, and he, a miserable outcast, starved in a Belgian boarding-house. Mrs. Barton's eyes
brightened at the distressed expression of his face. The victim
was prepared for the altar; in his buttonhole he wore the
flowers, and to play the music of sacrifice Olive took her place
at the piano. Milord engaged Alice's attention ; Mrs. Barton,
like a coaxing cat, glided up to the marquis and led him into
the adjoining room.

"The season is now drawing to its close," she said winningly,
" we shall be soon returning to Galway. We shall be separating. Olive thinks there is no one like *le marquis*. I know
she likes you, but if there is no—no—if it is not to be, I
should like to tell her not to think about it any more."

The marquis felt as if the earth were gliding beneath his
feet. What could have tempted the woman to speak like this
to him ? What answer was he to make her ? He struggled
with words and thoughts that gave way, as he strove to formulate a sentence, like water beneath the arms of one drowning.

" Oh, really, Mrs. Barton," he said, stammering, speaking
like one in a dream, " you take me by surprise. I did not
expect this; you certainly are too kind. In proposing this
marriage to me, you do me an honour I did not anticipate, but
you know it is difficult off hand, for I am bound to say . . at
least I am not prepared to say that I am in love with your
daughter. . . . She is, of course, very beautiful, and no one
admires her more than I, but——"

" Olive will have twenty thousand pounds paid down on her
wedding day ; not promised, you know, but paid down ; and
in the present times I think this is more than most girls can

say. Most Irish properties are embarrassed, mortgaged," she continued, risking everything to gain everything, "and twenty thousand pounds would be a material help to most men. At my death she will have more, I——"

"Oh, Mrs. Barton, do not let us speak of that!" cried the little man.

"And why not? Does it prove that because we are practical, we do not care for a person? I quite understand that it would be impossible for you to marry without money, and that Olive will have twenty thousand paid down on her wedding day will not prevent you from being very fond of her. On the contrary, I should think——"

"Twenty thousand pounds is, of course, a great deal of money," said the little man, shrinking, terror-stricken, from a suddenly protruding glimpse of the future with which milord had previously poisoned his mind.

"Yes, indeed it is, and in these times," urged Mrs. Barton.

The weak grey eyes were cast down, abashed by the daring determination of the brown.

"Of course Olive is a beautiful girl," he said.

"And she is so fond of you . . . she is so nice and so full of affection . . ."

The situation was now tense with fear, anxiety, apprehension; and with resolute fingers Mrs. Barton tightened the chord until the required note vibrated within the moral consciousness. The poor marquis felt his strength ebbing away; he was powerless as one lying in the hot chamber of a Turkish bath. Would no one come to help him? The implacable melody of "Dream Faces," which Olive hammered out on the piano, agonised him. If she would stop for one moment he would find the words to tell her mother that he loved Violet Scully and would marry none other. But bang, bang, bang the left hand pounded the bass into his stunned ears, and the eyes that he feared were fixed upon him. He gasped for words, he felt like a drunkard who clutches the air as he reels over a precipice, and the shades of his ancestors seemed to crowd menacingly around him. He strove against his fears until a thin face with luminous eyes broke through the drifting mists like a star.

"But we have seen so little of each other," he said at last; "Miss Barton is a great beauty, I know, and nobody appreciates her beauty more than I, but I am not what you call in love with her." He deplored the feebleness of his words, and Mrs. Barton swooped upon him again.

"You do not love her because, as you say, you have seen very little of each other. We are going down to Brookfield to-morrow. We shall be very glad if you will come with us, and there you will have an opportunity of judging, of knowing her : and she is such an affectionate little thing."

Appalled, the marquis sought again for words, and he glanced at his torturer timidly, as the hare looks back on the ever-nearing hounds. Why did she pursue him, he asked, in this terrible way ? Had she gone mad ? What was he to say ? He had not the courage to answer " No " to her face. Besides, if Violet would not have him, he might as well save the family estates. If Violet refused him ! Ah, he did not care what became of him then ! He sought, and he struggled for words, for words that would save him; and, in this hour of deep tribulation, words came and they saved him.

"I have a great deal of business to attend to to-morrow. I am—that is to say, my solicitor is, raising for me a large sum of money at four per cent. On one large mortgage I am paying six per cent., therefore if I can get the money at four I shall be by some hundreds of pounds a richer man than I am at present. At the end of the week this matter will be settled. I will write to you and say when I shall be able to accept your invitation."

Mrs. Barton would have preferred to have brought the matter at once to a conclusion, but in the hesitation that ensued, the marquis, unable to withstand the strain set upon his feelings any longer, moved away from her. And in the next room, to save himself from further persecution, he engaged at once in conversation with Alice. Ten minutes after he said good-night. To get out of the light into the dark, to feel the cool wind upon his cheek, oh ! what a relief it was ! "What could have persuaded that woman to speak to me as she did ? She must be mad." He walked on as if in a dream ; the guineas she had promised him chinking dubiously through his brain. Then stopping suddenly, overcome by nerve excitement, he threw his arms in the air : his features twitched convulsively. The spasm passed; and, unconscious of all save the thoughts that held and tore him—their palpitating prey— he walked onwards. . . . Black ruin on one side, and oh ! what sweet white vision of happiness on the other ! Why was he thus tortured—why was he thus torn on the rack of such a terrible discussion? He stopped again, and his weak neck swayed plaintively. Then, in the sullen calm that followed, the thought crossed his mind:—If he only knew . . . She might refuse him; if so, he did not care what became of him. . . . He would accept the other willingly . . . But would she refuse him? That he must know at once . . . he could not return to his hotel, the uncertainty was more than he could bear. . . . If she did refuse, he would, at all events, escape the black looks of his relations. In the cowardice of the thought the weary spirit was healed, assuaged, as tired limbs might be in a bath of cool, clear water. Darkness faded, and the skies seemed to glow as if with a double dawn. Why lose a moment? It was only half-past ten—an "outside" would take him in less than two minutes to Fitzwilliam Place. Yes, he would go.

And as the car clattered he feasted on the white thin face and the grey allurements of the bright eyes. He would not think—it was paradise to banish thought.

He was shown upstairs. The ladies were alone, talking over the fire in the drawing-room. Nothing could be more propitious, but his fears returned to him, and when he strove to explain the lateness of his visit, his face had again grown suddenly haggard and worn. Violet exchanged glances, and said in looks, if not in words, "It is clear they have been hunting him pretty closely to-day."

"I must apologise," he said, "for calling on you at such an hour; I really did not think it was so late, but the fact is I was rather anxious to see . . ."

"But won't you sit down, Lord Kilcarney?" said Violet. "I assure you we never go to bed before twelve; and sometimes we sit up here until one—don't we, mamma?"

Mrs. Scully smiled jocosely, and the marquis sat down. In an instant his fate was decided. Overcome by the girl's frail sweetness, by the pellucid gaiety of her grey eyes, he surrendered; and his name and fortune fluttered into her lap, helplessly as a blown leaf. He said—

"I came to see you to-night. . . I took the liberty of calling on you at this late hour, because things had occurred that . . . well, I mean . . . you must have observed that I was attached to you. I don't know if you guessed it, but the fact is that I never cared for anyone as I do for you, and I felt I could bear with uncertainty no longer, and that I must come to-night, and ask you if you will have me."

Violet raised her eyes—" Say yes," murmured the marquis, and it seemed to him that in the words life had fallen from his lips.

" Yes," was the answer, and he clasped the thin hand she instinctively extended to him.

" Ah, how happy you have made me, I never thought such honours were in store for me," exclaimed Mrs. Scully. The discipline of years was lost in a moment; and, reverting to her long-buried self, she clasped the marquis to her agitated bosom with all the naturalness of a Galway shopgirl. Violet looked annoyed, ashamed, and Mrs. Scully, whom excitement had stripped of all her grand manners, said—

" And now, me dear children, I'll leave yeu to yerselves."

The lovers sat side by side. Violet thought of how grand it would be to be a marchioness, of her triumph over the other girls; the marquis of the long years of happiness that would —that must now be his, of the frail grace that as a bland odour seemed to float about his beloved. And now that she was his he would have her know the infinitude and the imperishability of his affection; but words were weak, and he seemed to be too far away.

" Where did you dine to-night ? " she said suddenly.

" With the Bartons."

Then he told her everything—of the proposal and the invitation to Brookfield.

" And are you going down to Galway to stay with them ? "

" Of course not. Oh, my darling, how can you ask such a question ? "

" And why not—why should you not go ? I wish you would," she added; and the light in her grey eyes was malign.

" You are joking ? you surely do not mean what you say. I thought you said you loved me."

" Yes, my dear Harry, that is the very reason. We love each other, therefore I know I can trust you."

He pressed the hand—the silken skin, the palm delicately moist—in recognition of her kind words.

" I wouldn't go for anything in the world. I hate those people. 'Pon my word, I don't think anything would tempt me to spend a week with them in the country."

" Yes, I could."

The marquis laughed—"Yes you could, you could tempt me to do anything. But why should you want me to go and spend a week with them in Galway ? "

" Because, dear, they were rude to me ; because," she added, casting down her eyes, "because they tried to buy you from me. That is why I should like to humiliate them."

The enchantment of the marquis was completed, and he said :

" What, a whole week away from you, darling ! a whole week with Mrs. Barton ! I could not endure it."

" What, not for my sake ? "

" Anything for your sake, darling." He clasped her in his arms, and then they lapsed into silence that to him was even sweteer than the kiss she had given him. Love's deepest delight is the ineffable consciousness of our own weakness. We drink the sweetened cup in its entirety when, having ceased to will, we abandon ourselves with the lethal languors of the swimmer to the vague depths of dreams.

And it was past midnight when the marquis left Fitzwilliam Place. The ladies accompanied him downstairs ; their hands helped him to his hat and coat, and at last he left, looking unutterable to-morrows as he went. Then the lock slipped back sharply, and in the low gloom, broken in one spot by the low-burning gas, the women wondered,—tense with the stricken emotion of Mary and Mary Magdalene at the door of the Sepulchre.

" Oh, mamma, mamma, mamma, I am so happy ! " the girl exclaimed, and, weeping passionately, she threw herself for rest upon Mrs. Scully's arms.

" Yes, me choild, me choild, yer have been very good, yer have made me very happy, you'll be a mairchioness. Who wid iver have thought I'd have lived to see all this honour when I served in the little shop at Galway ! "

At the mention of the shop Violet recovered her composure, and mother and daughter listened to the receding footfalls.

Like a flowering tree, a luxuriant joy bloomed in the marquis's heart ; in its fragrant shade and fresh colour his thoughts lay supinely, and a prey to all sorts of floating and fanciful imaginings, he walked onwards through the darkness. When he lifted his eyes, he saw in the lowering skies only the fair face that had led him with the invincible light of a star to the verge on which he now stood. Now his consciousness was vast and vague. Filled with silence, the street stretched before him, and the heaped evergreens of Merrion Square exhaled moist and evil-smelling airs. Even the sharp network of the leafless trees was lost in the all-blurring shadow; cats crouched through the area railings, policemen moved from their hiding corners : that was all : and the lover passed on with his dreams.

But on the north side of the Square he stopped. There were carriages, and one house was illuminated for dancing, and shades flitted across the yellow window-panes.

He remembered he had received an invitation for this very ball, and he knew that if he entered, every eye would be fixed upon him. The chaperons would ogle, wheedle, cajole ; the girls would insinuate, smirk, and tell lies to their partners if they saw the remotest chance of his asking them to dance. To dance twice with him meant fame for a week in Merrion Square. There were a few girls there who had money, many who pretended to have a great deal. The tricks of the Irish heiress are legion, and the lies of the Irish chaperon are as infinite as the sands on the shore. The marquis had suffered, but the time of peace was near, and it was an exquisite delight to know that true love and false love would soon be impotent to torture him. For soon he will possess her—her whom his heart longs for. He might have had any ; not one would have refused to come to his coronet; they would have come as readily as a light o' love to a sovereign. He might have had any of them ; he might have had Olive Barton. His face contracted; all was hateful to him now but Violet ; but he suddenly remembered how he had refused twenty thousand pounds, and before him rose the spectre of the Land League, and he started as if it had laid its cold hand upon him. Yes, he might have had twenty thousand pounds, and twenty thousand pounds would have paid off how many mortgages ! But then he wouldn't have had Violet, and life without Violet would be a living tomb!—no, no, he could not have borne it. He had done wrong, but it was not his fault; it was not his fault. And, shuddering in his glazed shoes and thin evening clothes, he pursued his way through the shadowy night.

For hours he walked onwards—here and there, he knew not whither. Often he awoke, surprised to find himself staring at something he did not see. Once he stopped to gaze at

O'Connell's Statue. This was the man who had begun the
work; it was he who had withdrawn the key-stone of the
edifice, soon to fall and crush all beneath its ruins. Then he
found himself walking to and fro beneath the colonnades of
the Bank of Ireland. Here was the silent power that protected him; but soon the buyers and sellers would be scourged
out of the temple and a new power established—a power that
would turn him a beggar upon the world. And sometimes he
was seen examining the long grey line that is Trinity College.
All this would go too. This ancient seat of wisdom and learning would perish before the triumphant and avenging peasant.
For him the country, and for him the town; and for the old
race of the Kilcarneys poverty and banishment. Shivering
with fear rather than the drizzling rain that fell, the little
marquis pursued his way. Yes, he was a ruined man. Wealth,
position, and power were slipping from him; all he possessed
in the world was that thin white face—delicate and subtile as
an Indian carven ivory. But oh, that was all his—his for ever
and ever; and, in the light of the blowing gas the weak face
was stricken with a look of ineffable passion.

Like a carrier overborne by the loads hung on either side of
his shoulders, the marquis staggered beneath balancing weights
of happiness and fear. He knew not what to think or what to
do. He could not return to his hotel; and, by turns lost in
moments of emparadised tenderness and overwhelmed in dark
and abortive despair, he walked aimlessly, listening to the wild
wandering dream with which his brain was bewildered. Twice
he had crossed the river. The glooms of Sackville Street were
filled with vague groups and single figures. There was a taint of
assassination and doom in the air. Parnell, Davitt, Dillon, and
other leaders of the Irish party had been cast into prison, and
every day and hour writs for the arrest of suspected persons were
issued by the Castle; and in return the revolt of the people became more determined and implacable. In the mist and mud of
the slums plots and counter-plots were hatched, and, breaking
their shells, they emerged like reptiles into a terrible and multiform existence; out of the slime they crawled in strange and
formless confusion, and in the twilight of nationhood they fought
the obscure and blind battle of birth. Conspiracy, and nothing
but conspiracy—conspiracy to strike the knife into the ruler,
conspiracy to shoot the informer, conspiracy to overthrow rival
conspiracy. Oaths were administered of secrecy, of vengeance.

The assassin followed his victim down darksome alleys, along the wide squares of the aristocracy; cries of murder were heard—a pistol-shot—one, two, three broke the stillness, men were seen passing, a body was found the next day, and all further knowledge of the deed was lost for ever. The brown, sullen Liffey rolls by; has it borne all away? Many a secret it holds, and a dark and mighty accomplice it seems in the crimes that now convulse men's souls. Day and night silently scavenging, its wandering water lulls echoes of oaths of bloodshed, the mirksome current reflects but a moment the livid flame of incendiarism, swiftly it bears away the body of the victim, and, sunk deep in its unfathomable mud lie the abandoned knives. Even now the marquis as he walked, deaf to all things, shrouded with sorrow and crowned with love, had heard pistol-shots and mysterious cries. But he had passed on heedless; and now he stands in the centre of O'Connell's bridge. His eyes are fixed upon the mud-stream that flows deep down in the stone embankments; and as the night deepens into the small hours of the morning his grief grows unbearable. Remorse has followed him—the dreary, unrelenting remorse of those too weak by nature for repentance. Now he remembers for the hundredth time how he has sacrificed the grand old name with all its grand associations. The shades of his ancestors crowd about: and how regretfully they seem to reproach him! At every moment the meaning of the word "ruin" grows more distinct; and in distorted vision he sees down the long succession of consequences. Since his childhood he had been told that it was his duty to restore by matrimony his ancient name to its ancient prestige and power; and he had sacrificed all for that little thin white face that he could see now shining before him—a rare, a seductive jewel. If he had never met her he would have done what was right; but, having once seen her, he could not but act as he had done. No, it was not his fault—he was not to blame. He could not have lived without her; she was life to him, and to possess life he had to accept ruin. Yes, ruin; he knows it well enough. That terrible Land League would ruin him—that terrible Land League that he could feel about him. It hovered in the air like an evil spirit, and, sooner or later, it would descend and tear and rend him as a prey. Yes, he was ruined, utterly ruined. But with twenty or thirty thousand pounds he would have been able to fight it and to conquer it;

and then, as his thoughts go back to Olive, his face falls upon his hands, and he weeps.

And the darkness grows thicker, but the man still stands on the bridge. Around him every street is deserted. On the right murder has ended for the night; on the left, towards Merrion Square, the violins have ceased to sing in the ball-rooms; and in their white beds the girls sleep their white sleep of celibacy. Passion and grief have ceased to trouble the aching heart, if not for ever, at least for awhile : the murderer's and the virgin's reality are sunk beneath a swift-rolling tide of dreams—a tide deeper than the river that flows beneath the tears of the lonely lover. All but he are at rest; and now the city sleeps; wharves, walls, and bridges are veiled and have disappeared in the fog that has crept up from the sea; the shameless squalor of the outlying streets is enwrapped in the grey mist, but over them and dark against the sky the Castle still stretches out its arms as if for some monstrous embrace.

BOOK III.

CHAPTER I.

MRS. BARTON rarely took anyone into her confidence, and her plan for the capture of the marquis was locked within her breast. Certainly not to her husband, nor yet to milord, did she think of going for advice. Her special experience of life had taught her to trust none, to be self-reliant, and never to give up hope. For as she often said, it is the last effort that wins the battle. Mrs. Barton's knowledge of the world, when it came to be analysed, was only that of the courtesan—*à fleur de peau.*

Two days after she received a note from the marquis, saying he would be glad to spend a fortnight with them at Brookfield. She read it quietly, slipped it into the pocket of the black silk that covered the unseen feet, and glided out of the room. Every detail was clear to her. They must leave Dublin to-morrow morning: they need not trouble about calling on a pack of women; but they would have all their men friends to dinner.

Mr. Barton, when he was informed of these sudden determinations, was in the act of rehearsing a song he was to sing the following day at a concert.

"But, my dear," he said, tightening one of the strings, "the public will be awfully disappointed."

"Yes, my dear, yes; I am very sorry, but I have my reasons —serious reasons; and in this world we must only do what's right."

"Then in the next world we shall be able to do everything that's wrong," said Mr. Barton, and he threw back his blonde locks with troubadour-like waves of his lymphatic hand. "I shall like the next world better than this," he added, and his wife and daughter laughed, for papa was supposed to be very naughty.

" Olive dear——"

"Oh, mamma, I wish you wouldn't call me Olive. . . .
I shall change my name. . . . Captain Talbot was chaffing
me about it yesterday ; . . . everybody chaffs me about it."

"Never mind, my dear ; it makes a subject of conversation.
But I was going to tell you that we shall have to start for
Brookfield to-morrow."

"Go to Brookfield ! I couldn't possibly leave Dublin yet a
while ; what would all my young men do—they'd die of broken
hearts l"

"It won't matter much if they do ; there aren't a dozen
worth two thousand a year each."

"No ? you are joking, mamma. And the marquis l"

"That's a secret, dear."

"Then you don't think he'll propose to me after all ; and I
gave up Edward—Captain Hibbert."

"I thought you had forgotten that horrid man's name. I
did not say, dear, that the marquis would not propose to you
—of course he will. But we must leave Dublin to-morrow—I
have serious reasons."

"Oh, mamma, I did not think you were so cruel ; to go
back to that hateful place, where there isn't a man within
seven miles of one, and where everybody talks of rents and
that odious Land League."

"Now, I will not allow my darling to cry like that," exclaimed Mrs. Barton, and she threw her arms round the girl's
shoulders. "I did not say that there wouldn't be a man
within seven miles. On the contrary, there will be someone
very nice indeed."

"What do you mean, mamma ?"

"That's a secret—that's a secret ;" and peals of rippling
laughter effectually silenced all further questioning.

Alice was told briefly that she had better come home early
that afternoon, so that she might have plenty of time to pack
her own things and help her sister with hers. Was it possible
that so soon, that at last, they were going to leave this thrice-
hateful place? Latterly it had become doubly abhorrent to
her ; at every hour, at every moment her senses of sight, feeling, and hearing were outraged. But it was all over . . . .
the words sang in her ears. What happiness, what happiness
to know she was leaving that hateful little varnished floor,
that she was to escape from those complimenting old beaux,

and the youthful rudenesses of young A.D.C.s. Not their faces would she see, nor their voices would she hear again, nor would she again feel their arms about her. At Brookfield she would be alone; she would have her books and a table to write upon. The prospect emparadised her. Yes, she would really try and do something. Yes, she had an idea. She did not know if she would be able to work it out, but she would try. The girl trembled with pleasure—she would do her best, and she would send it to Harding; he would tell her what he thought of it, and to hope to hear from him would be something to live for.

Mrs. Barton had advised Alice and Olive not to call on the Scullys; and now, as Alice stood on the doorstep, she wondered at these orders. She had hardly seen May since the night of the State ball—the night she had given Fred Scully the terrible permission to see her in her room. Alice had long determined to speak to May on this subject, but somehow the opportunity had always slipped from her; she would go to her now.

May was sitting alone in the ladies' drawing-room. Her eyes had wandered from the pages of her novel, and she stared vaguely at the passers-by who went, with umbrellas aslant, through the wet air. The tints of the red furniture were vague, and all the little velvet chairs slept in the grey trailing shadows with which the room was filled. An immense heap of coal-dust smouldered dismally in the grate.

"How do you do, May?"

"Oh, how do you do, Alice? I am so glad to see you. Come and sit near the fire. What a dreadful day."

"Yes, isn't it? Don't you find it very depressing?"

"I should think I did. I'm feeling rather out of sorts. Do you ever feel out of sorts, you know, when everything seems as if it were reflected in a darkened glass? There are times when we girls are nervous and weak, and ready to quarrel with anyone. I don't know what I wish for now; I think I should like to go back to the country."

"We are going back to-morrow morning."

"Nonsense; you don't say so; and how's that? The Castle may be over, or nearly so, but there are plenty of balls and afternoon dances. What does Olive say to going home?"

"She doesn't mind. You know mamma always said she would return immediately after the Castle balls."

"And now that it is all over, tell me what you think of the Castle. Did it come up to your expectations?"

"I don't know that I think much about the matter. I am not so fond of dancing as you are."

"Oh, goodness me, goodness me, how ill I do feel," said May, as she started and yawned in a way that betokened the nervous lassitude she was suffering from.

"Perhaps you had better see the doctor," said Alice, significantly.

"But . . . I don't know; . . . then there are other things that worry me . . . . I don't think that Fred has been as nice lately as . . . he used to be."

"What has he done?"

"Last night he promised to meet me in the Square, and he wrote to say he couldn't come, that he was forced to go and see an important customer about some horses."

"Perhaps he had."

"I dare say he had, but what of that? It does not make it any less disagreeable for me to be disappointed."

"How cross you are, May !. I came out on purpose to talk to you on this very subject. I hope you won't be angry, but I think it is my duty to tell you that people are beginning to talk about you."

"And what do they say?"

"Well, they say many unpleasant things; you know how ill-natured people are."

"Yes, but what do they say?"

"They say you are desperately in love with Fred Scully."

"Supposing I were; is there any very great harm in that?"

"I only want to put you on your guard, May dear; and since I have come here for the purpose of speaking out, I had better do so, however unpleasant it may be; and I must say that you often forget yourself when he is in the room, and by your whole manner betray your feelings. . . . You look at him . . ."

"You needn't talk. . . Now that Harding has left town, these moral reflections come very easy to you !"

Alice blushed a little; she trembled, and pursuing her advantage, May said:

"Oh, yes; I have watched you in the Castle sitting out dances; and when girls like you do butter! . . . 'Pon my word, it was painful to look at you."

"I am sure," said Alice, speaking without consideration, "that nobody could think . . . no one would dream of suspecting. . . . Mr. Harding and I talked merely of books and pictures."

"If you come here to insinuate that Fred and I are in the habit of indulging in improper conversation . . . I should not have expected this from you. I shall not stop another moment. I shall not speak with you again."

Picking up her novel, and deaf to all explanations, May walked haughtily out of the room. Alice would have given much to help; and, her heart filled with gentle disappointment, she returned home. The evening was spent in packing; and next morning at dawn, looking tired, their eyes still heavy with sleep, the Bartons breakfasted for the last time in Mount Street.

At the Broadstone they met Lord Dungory. Then, their feet and knees cosily wrapped up in furs, with copies of the *Freeman's Journal* lying on the top, they deplored the ineffectiveness of Mr. Forster's Coercion Act. Eight hundred people were in prison, and still the red shadow of murder pointed across the land. Milord read from the newspaper:

"A dastardly outrage was committed last night in the neighbourhood of Mullingar. A woman named Mary —— had some differences with her sister Bridget ——. One day, after some angry words, it appears that she left the house, and seeing a man working in a potato-field, she asked him if he could do anything to help her. He scratched his head, and, after a moment's reflection, he said he was going to meet a 'party,' and he would see what could be done: on the following day he suggested that Bridget might be removed for the sum of one pound. Mary —— could not, however, procure more than fifteen shillings, and a bargain was struck. On the night arranged for the assassination Mary wished to leave the house, not caring to see her sister shot in her presence, but Pat declared that her absence would excite suspicion. In the words of one of the murderers, the deed was accomplished 'nately and without unnecessary fuss.'"

"I wonder," said Mrs. Barton, "what those wretches will have to do before the Government will consent to suspend the Habeas Corpus Act, and place the country in the hands of the military. Do they never think of how wickedly they are behaving, and of how God will punish them when they die? Do they never think of their immortal souls?"

"L'âme du paysan se vautre dans la boue comme la mienne se plaît dans la soie."

"Dans la soie! dans la soie! oh, ce milord, ce milord!"

"Oui, madame," he added, lowering his voice, "dans le blanc paradis de ton corsage."

Three days after life at Brookfield had resumed its ordinary course. Once breakfast was over, Arthur retired to the consideration of the pectoral muscles of the ancient Briton; Milord drank his glass of sherry at half-past one, and Mrs. Barton devoted herself to the double task of amusing him and encouraging Olive with visions of future fame. Alice was therefore left definitely to herself, and without hindrance or comment was allowed to set up her writing-table, and spend as much time as she pleased in her bedroom.

She had already begun work. Several sheets of foolscap paper covered with large open handwriting lay upon the table. Upon the first page, with a line ruled beneath it, stood the title: "The Diary of a Plain Girl—Notes and Sensations." She had just laid aside her pen and was waiting for Cecilia. Suddenly footsteps were heard in the corridor.

"Oh, Alice darling, how are you? I am delighted—I am so delighted to see you. Let me kiss you, let me see you; I have been longing for you for weeks—for months."

Alice bent her face down, and Cecilia lay sobbing with joy upon her shoulder for some moments. Then, holding each other's hands, the girls stood looking through a deep and expressive silence into each other's eyes. Cecilia's eyes!—large, mellow depths of light, vague and melancholy with the yearning of the soul. You see the high shoulders; the chin and neck how curiously advanced. But little is seen but the eyes! the eyes of the deformed, deep, dreamy depths of brown, luminous with a strange weariness, that we who are normal, straight, and strong, can neither feel nor understand. The brown is now liquescent; it burns, and becomes golden with passion; it melts and softens to strange tenderness. The eyes of the deformed!— deep enigmatic eyes, never will your secret be revealed; there is a trouble that words cannot speak, but that eyes may sometimes suggest:—the melting questioning grief of the spaniel that would tell his master of his love. There was something dog-like in the lavish affection with which Cecilia welcomed her friend; and, like the dumb animal, she seemed to suffer from her inability to express her joy in words.

" I wish, Alice, I could tell you how glad I am to have you back : it seems like heaven to see you again. You look so nice, so true, so sweet, so perfect. There never was anyone so nice as you, Alice."

" Cecilia, dear, you shouldn't talk to me like that ; it is absurd. Indeed, I don't think it is quite right."

" Not quite right," replied the cripple, sadly ; " what do you mean ? Why is it wrong—why should it be wrong for me to love you ? "

" I don't mean to say that it is wrong ; you misunderstand me ; but—but . . . well, I don't know how to explain myself, but . . . ."

" I know, I know, I know," said Cecilia ; and her nervous sensitivity revealed thoughts in Alice's mind—thoughts of which Alice herself was not distinctly conscious, just as a photograph exposes irregularities in the texture of a leaf that the naked eye would not perceive.

" If Harding were to speak to you so, you would not think it wrong."

Alice coloured deeply, and she said, with a certain resoluteness in her voice, " Cecilia, I wish you would not talk to me in this way. You give me great pain."

" I am sorry if I do, but I cannot help it. I am jealous of the words that are spoken to you, of the air you breathe, of the ground you walk upon. How, then, can I help hating that man ? "

The teeth gnawed at the lips, and the eyes were shot with strange flames. Alice trembled : she was obscurely troubled. At last she said :

" I do not wish to argue this point with you, Cecilia, nor am I sure that I understand it. There is no one I like better than you, dear, but that we should be jealous of each other is absurd."

" For you perhaps, but not for me." Cecilia looked at Alice reproachfully, and at the end of a long and morose silence she said :

" You received the long letter I wrote to you about him ? "

" Yes, Cecilia, and I answered it. It seems to me very foolish to pronounce condemnatory opinion on the whole world ; and particularly for you who have seen so little of it."

" That doesn't matter. People are blinded by their passions ; but when these have worn themselves out they see the truth

in all its horrible nakedness. One of these days you'll tell me
that I am right. You have been a good deal in the world
lately; tell me if you have found it beautiful. You did not
believe me when I told you that men were vile and abominable; you said there were good men in the world . . . that
you were sure of it. . . Have you found them ? . . . Was Mr.
Harding so very perfect ? "

Alice coloured; she hesitated, and in the silence Cecilia
again divined her friend's thoughts.

" I do not know that I found the world very different from
what I expected to find it. Of course there is evil—and a
great deal of evil; and if you will fix your eyes upon it, and
brood over it, of course life seems to you only a black and
hideous thing ; but there is much good—yes, there is good
even in things evil; and if we only think of the goodness we
become happier even if we do not become better ; and I cannot
but think that the best and the most feasible mode of life is
to try to live up to the ordinary and simple laws of nature of
which we are but a part." Here Alice paused, and she sought
vainly to define her ideas. She was conscious of the truth that
conscience is no more than the indirect laws—the essence of
the laws transmitted by heredity; and had she been able to
formulate her thought she would have said, " and the ideal
life should, it seems to me, lie in the reconciliation—no, reconciliation is not the word I want ; I scarcely know how to
express myself—well, in making the two ends meet—in making
the ends of nature the ends also of what we call our conscience."

How often do we find—nay, do we not always find—that
the æsthetic and philosophic aspirations of an epoch—ideas
which we believe to have been the invention of individuals,
are but the intellectual atmosphere of that epoch breathed in
greater or less quantities by all ? Nor does the phenomenon
cease here ; for the sensitivity of some is so great that they
anticipate—obeying an unknown law of attraction—ideas not
yet in existence, but which are quickening in the womb of the
world. Wordsworth is an example of this foreseeing, fore-
feeling, forehearing. For at the time of writing the " Excursion " the influence of the German pessimists had not
penetrated into England ; Schopenhauer was an unknown
name ; and yet poet and philosopher seem but the expansion of
a single mind.

Is it therefore unnatural or even extraordinary that Alice

Barton, who is if anything a representative woman of 1885, should have, in an obscure and formless way, divined the doctrines of Eduard van Hartman, the entire and unconditional resignation of personal existence into the arms of the cosmic process? Cecilia, as has been shown, with her black hatred of life concentrated upon a loathing of the origin of existence, was but another manifestation of the same stratum of thought.

"A very poor ideal indeed, it seems to me that you set yourself—to make the best of this wretched world."

"I cannot understand what good can come of craving after the unattainable," said Alice, looking earnestly out of her grey sharp eyes.

"True beauty lies only in the unattainable," said Cecilia, lifting her eyes with that curious movement of the eyeball by which painters represent faith and mysticism. At the end of a long silence, Alice said :

"But you'll have some tea, will you not, Cecilia?"

"Yes; but do not let us go downstairs."

"Oh, no; we'll have it up here; Barnes will bring it up."

"Oh, that will be so nice."

The girls drew closer to the fire, and in its uniting warmth they looked into the ardent face of their friendship. These moments were inexpressibly delicious. They talked, at first, conscious of the appropriateness of their conversation; but soon forgetful of the more serious themes they had been discussing, questions were asked and answered, and comments passed, upon the presentations, the dresses, the crowds, upon all their acquaintances.

"It is given out, Alice dear, that Lord Kilcarney is coming down to stay at Brookfield. Is it true?"

"I have heard nothing of it. Whom did you hear it from?"

"Well, the Duffys wrote it to my sisters. The Duffys, you know, have all the Dublin news."

"What dreadful gossips they are! And the wonderful part of it is that they often tell you that things have happened long before they do happen."

"Yes; I have noticed that. They anticipate the news." The girls laughed lightly, and Cecilia continued: "But tell me, which do you think he admires most, Olive or Violet? The rumour goes that he pays Violet great attentions. The

family is, of course, wild about it. She hasn't a penny
piece, and . . . and Olive, they say, has a good deal of
money."

"I do not know."

"But you, Alice dear, I suppose you were immensely
admired. You must have been . . . . You must show me
the dress you wore . . . . You described it beautifully in your
letter. . . . You must have looked very sweet. . . . Did
everybody say so?"

"I am not sure that they did. . . . Men, you know, do not
always admire what women do."

"I should think not. Men only admire beastliness."

"Cecilia, dear, you should not talk like that; it is not nice."

Cecilia looked at Alice wistfully, and she said:

"But tell me about the presentations. I suppose there
were an immense number of people present?"

"Yes, and particularly débutantes; there were a great
number presented this year. It was considered a large
Drawing-room."

"And how are you presented? I've heard my sister speak
about it, but I never quite understood."

"The Lord Lieutenant is standing under his throne, and all
his Court are about him—your name is called out by the
Chamberlain—a couple of A.D.C.s take your train from your
arm, spread it along the floor, and you walk up to his Excellency, and he kisses you on both cheeks."

"Oh, how beastly! You mean to say, Alice, that that man
kissed you?"

"Yes, he did. But it is only a fashion, a ceremony—a
stupid one I grant you—but I can't say . . ."

"You mean to say it did not disgust you?" Then after a
pause she added, "Perhaps you wished it were Mr. Harding."

Had Cecilia not been Cecilia, Alice would have answered
differently, but disarmed by the love reflected in the luminous
eyes she said:

"I believe you do not wish to give me pain, but you can
hardly be blind to the fact that such observations are almost
meant to wound my feelings."

"Oh, Alice; no, indeed! I do not wish to give you pain
but . . . ."

At that moment Barnes brought in the tea. She set it on
a little table used for the purpose. "There is a letter for you,

miss, on the tray,' she said as she left the room ; " it came by the afternoon post."

Without answering, Alice continued to pour out the tea, but when she handed Cecilia her cup, she said, surprised at the dull sullen stare fixed upon her :

" What is the matter ? Why do you look at me like that ? "

" That letter, I am sure, is from Harding; it is a man's handwriting."

Like a lamp Alice's face was illumined. She had been expecting that letter for days.

" Oh ! give it me," she said impulsively.

" There it is ; I wouldn't touch it. I knew you liked that man ; but I did not expect to find you corresponding with him. It is shameful ; it is not worthy of you. You might have left such things to May Gould."

" Cecilia, you have no right to speak to me in that way ; you are presuming too much on our friendship."

" Oh, yes, yes ; but before you met him I could not have presumed too much upon our friendship."

" If you want to know why I wrote to Mr. Harding, I'll tell you."

" It was you who wrote to him, then ? "

" Yes, I wrote to him. Mr. Harding is, as you have heard, a literary man ; he is known to all the newspaper editors and publishers in London. He was very kind when I met him in Dublin ; he not only advised and encouraged me to write, but he offered to take anything I might send him to the editors, and try and get it accepted. I see no reason why I should not avail myself of the helping hand he extends to me."

" Oh, yes, yes, yes ; avail yourself of his assistance ; do what you like. I see it all now," cried Cecilia, and she walked wildly to and fro, her eye tinged with a strange glare. " Yes, I see it all. This room, that was once a girl's room, is now Harding's room. He is the atmosphere of the place. I was conscious of it when I entered, but now it is visible to me— that manuscript, that writing-table, that letter. Oh yes, it is Harding, all is Harding ! All I loved is gone ! . . . The whiteness, the purity, the feminacy, all is gone ! . . . The shadow of a man has fallen across our friendship ; it is blackened, it is worthless. Cruel, cruel ! Why am I thus tortured ? why do I suffer ? The one thing I thought pure is

soiled. There is neither purity nor peace in the world; the
same blackness, always the same blackness. The same horrible
passion that degrades, that disgraces, that makes animals of us!
There is no escaping from it—it is everywhere, it is eternal, it
is omnipotent. We are hemmed in on every side by vileness;
there is no escape; no, no, no; . . . my last hope is gone,
and I am alone in this horrible, this ignominious world. Oh
that I might die, for I can bear with it no longer! And we
all come, we all spring from the same abomination—vile, loathsome, detestable. Take pity, oh, take pity! let me die! Oh,
God, take pity!"

"Cecilia, Ccilia, think, I beg of you, of what you are saying." But when Alice approached and strove to raise the
deformed girl from the pillow upon which she had thrown
herself, she started up and savagely confronted her.

"Don't touch me, don't touch me!" she cried; "I cannot
bear it. What are you to me, what am I to you? It is not
with me you would care to be, but with *him*. It is not my
kiss of friendship that would console you, but his kiss of
passion that would charm you. . . . Go to him, and leave
me to die."

"Was this insanity?" and then, forgetful of the abuse that
was being showered upon her, Alice said :

"Cecilia dear, listen; I'll forgive the language you have
used toward me, for I know you do not know what you are
saying. You must be ill . . . you cannot be in your right
senses to-day, or you would not speak like that."

"Right senses!" replied the girl bitterly; "you would
soothe me, but you little dream of the poison you are dropping
on my wounds. Right senses! the words show me how much
too much I expected of you. You never understood, you are
too far removed from me in thought and feeling ever to
understand—no, your spirituality is only a delusion; you are
no better at heart than May Gould. It is the same thing :
one seeks a husband, another gratifies herself with a lover.
It is the same thing, where's the difference? It is animal
passion all the same. And that letter is full of it . . . it
must be . . . I am sure it is."

"You are very insulting, Cecilia. Where have you thrown
my letter to?"

The letter had fallen beneath the table. Alice made a
movement towards it, but, overcome by mad rage, Cecilia

caught it up and threw it into the fire. Alice rescued her letter, and then, her face full of stern indignation, she said:

"I think, Cecilia, you had better leave my room, and before you come to see me again, I shall expect to receive a written apology for the outrageous way you have behaved."

In a few days came a humble and penitent letter; Cecilia returned, her eyes full of tears, and begged to be forgiven: the girls resumed their friendship, but both were conscious that it was neither so bright nor so communicative as in the olden days. They love best to whom all is impossible but love. It was so with Cecilia, and Alice had much to live for now. Every morning she went up to her room to write, and in the evenings, deaf to silly chatter and laughter, she read thoughtfully and industriously. She read the books she had heard Harding speak of. The remembrance of the man endeared them to her, and she believed they would help to educate her better than others she might choose for herself. Her mind being simple, logical, direct—so unblinded by side-lights that it often touched, if it did not merge in, the commonplace—found, without difficulty, words that were at least the appropriate equivalents of the thoughts she wished to express: not being possessed of that supreme power of seeing more than one aspect of her subject, which is genius, her execution was facile and sure as the conception was moderate and well balanced. Her choice of subject was always healthy and practical, and she wrote short stories and a newspaper article unfalteringly: her work as it unfolded itself was an image of the writer's own integrity and good sense. And if her writings excited neither nervous surprise nor any subtle emotion, they did not provoke contempt by stupidity or vulgarity. She saw life from a normal and sensible standpoint, and her merit lay not in the peculiarity or the keenness of her vision, but in the clearness and the common sense she infused into the writing, as she would have done into any other business she might have undertaken. *Au fond*, the artistic question troubled her little, but when the first cheque came, when it fell out of the envelope into her lap, her fingers trembled, and, clutching the piece of paper, she went down to breakfast. Joy bubbled in her brain. To know that she could do something, that she would not prove a drag, a hindrance upon the wheel of life, was an effervescent delight.

"Something has happened to my learned daughter," said
Mr. Barton, and he continued his thumb-nail sketch on the
tablecloth. "What is it?" he added indolently.

Alice passed the cheque and the memorandum across the
table. "Three pounds for three articles contributed to the
—— during the month of April."

"You don't mean to say, Alice, you got three pounds for
your writing?" said Mrs. Barton.

"Yes, mother, I have, and I hope to make ten pounds
next month. Mr. Harding says he can get me lots of work."

"Ha, ha, ha!" laughed Mrs. Barton, "so my lady then,
with all her shy ways, knows how to make use of a man as well
as any of us."

Mrs. Barton, however, did not willingly wound. She saw
life from the point of view of making use of men: *voilà tout*.
And when Alice walked out of the room, Mrs. Barton felt
sorry for what she had said, and she would have gone to comfort her daughter if Olive had not, at that moment, stood in
imminent need of comfort.

"I suppose," she said, pettishly, "the letter you received
this morning is from the marquis, to say he won't be here next
Tuesday?"

It was. For as the day fixed for his arrival at Brookfield
approached, he would write to apologise, and to beg that he
might be allowed to postpone his visit to Monday week or
Wednesday fortnight. Mrs. Barton replied that they would
be very glad to see him when he found it convenient to come and
see them. She did not inquire into the reason of his abominable rudeness, she was determined to fight the battle out to the
end, and she did not dare to think that he was being prompted
by that beast of a girl, Violet Scully.

"He writes a very nice letter indeed. He says he has a
very bad cold, and does not like to show himself at Brookfield
with a red nose, but that, unless he dies in the meantime, he
will be with us on the twentieth of the month, and will—if
we'll have him—stop three weeks with us."

"I knew it was a put-off. I don't believe he admires me at
all, the little beast; and I know I shall never be a marchioness.
You made me treat poor Edward shamefully, and for no
purpose, after all."

"Now, ma chérie, you must not speak like that. Go upstairs and ask Barnes if she has heard anything lately?"

" Oh, I'm sick of Barnes ; what has she heard ? "

" She is a great friend of Lady Georgina's maid, who knows the Burkes intimately, particularly Lady Emily's maid, and Barnes got a letter from her friend the other day, saying that Lady Emily was delighted at the idea of her brother marrying you, dear, and that he thinks of nobody else, speaks of nobody else. Run up and speak to her about it."

Mrs. Barton's keenest anxiety was Captain Hibbert. She had, as we have seen, successfully drugged Olive's light brain with visions of victories and honours ; with dancing, dresses, admiration ; but now, in the tiring void of country days, the remembrance of Edward's love and devotion was inevitable. He made no attempt to renew his courtship. At Gort, within three miles, he remained silent, immovable as one of the Clare mountains. Sometimes his brown-gold moustache and square shoulders were caught sight of as he rode rapidly along the roads. He had once been seen sitting with Mrs. Lawler behind the famous cream-coloured ponies ; and it was known that he spent most of his time with her. To allude to his disgraceful conduct without wounding Olive's vanity was an art that Mrs. Barton practised daily ; and to keep the girl in spirits she induced Sir Charles, who it was reported was about to emigrate his family to the wilds of Maratoga, to come and stay with them. If she could get up a little excitement, and a rumour were to reach the marquis's ears, it might help to bring him to the point. In any case Sir Charles's attentions to Olive would keep her in humour until the great day arrived. Sir Charles was treated as every man was treated at Brookfield. He was told he was charming, delightful, fascinating ; on all occasions he was presented with bouquets ; and he was sent away in the nick of time.

Well convinced that this was her last throw, Mrs. Barton resolved to smear the hook well with the three famous baits she was accustomed to angle with. They were : dinners, flattery, and dancing. Accordingly, an order was given to the Dublin fishmonger to send them fish daily for the next three weeks, and to the pastrycook for a French cook. The store of flattery kept on the premises being illimitable, she did not trouble about that, but devoted herself to the solution of the problem of how she should obtain a constant and unfailing supply of music. Once she thought of sending up to Dublin for a professional pianist, but was obliged to abandon the idea on account of the

impossibility of devising suitable employment for him during
the morning hours. A tune or two might not come in amiss
after lunch, but to have him hanging about the shrubberies
all the morning—no, it would not do. She might ask a couple
of the Brennans or the Duffys to stay with them, but they
would be in the way, occupy the marquis's time, and go tell-
taling all over the country; no that wouldn't do either. And
Alice did play so badly! It was a wonderful thing that a girl
like her would not make some effort to amuse men—would not
do something. Once Olive was married, she (Mrs. Barton)
would try to patch up something for this gawk of a girl—
marry her to Sir Charles; excellent match it would be too—
get all the children emigrated first : and if he would not have
her, there was Sir Richard. It was said that he was quite
reformed—had given up drink. But there was no use thinking of that : for the present she would have to put up with the
girl's music, which was wretched.

Olive fell in with her mother's plans, and she angled industriously for Lord Kilcarney. She did not fail to say in or out of
season : *Il n'y a personne comme notre cher marquis,* and as the
turbot and fruit, that had arrived by the afternoon train from
Dublin, were discussed, Milord did not cease to make the most
appropriate remarks. Referring to the bouquet that she had
pinned into the marquis's buttonhole, he said :

Il y a des amants partout où il y a des oiseaux et des roses,
and again :

*Les regards des amoureux sont la lumière comme le baiser est
la vie du monde.*

After dinner no time was lost, although the marquis pleaded
fatigue, in settling Alice at the piano, and dancing began in
sober earnest. After each waltz Olive conducted him to the
dining-room ; she helped him liberally to wine, and when she
held a match to his cigarette their fingers touched. But to
find occupation for the long morning hours of her young couple
was a grave trouble to Mrs. Barton. She was determined to
make every moment of the little marquis's stay in Galway
moments of sunshine ; but mental no more than atmospheric
sunshine is to be had by the willing, and the poor little fellow
seemed to pine in his Galway cage like a moulting canary.
He submitted to all the efforts made in his behalf, but his
submission was that of a victim. After breakfast he always
attempted to escape, and if he succeeded in eluding Mrs. Barton,

he would remain for hours hidden in the laurels, enwrapped in summer meditations, the nature of which it was impossible even to conjecture. In the afternoon he spoke of the burden of his correspondence, and when the inevitable dancing was spoken of, he often excused himself on the ground of having a long letter to finish. If it were impossible for her to learn the contents of these letters, Mrs. Barton ardently desired to know to whom they were addressed. Daily she volunteered to send special messengers to the post on his account; the footman, the coachman, and pony-chaise, were in turn rejected by him.

"Thank you, Mrs. Barton, thank you, but I should like to avail myself of the chance of a constitutional."

"*La santé de notre petit marquis avant tout,*" she would exclaim with much silvery laughter and all the habitual movements of the white hands. "But what do you say: I am sure the young ladies would like a walk too?"

With a view to picturesque effect Mrs. Barton's thoughts had long been centred on a picnic. They were now within a few days of the first of May, and there was enough sunshine in the air to justify an excursion to Kinvarra Castle. It is about four miles distant; and it stands on the seashore—a rocky shore full of seaweed, and the sea flows up a long narrow bay.

Mrs. Barton applied herself diligently to the task of organisation. Having heard from Dublin of the hoax that was being played on their enemy, the Ladies Cullen consented to join the party, and they brought with them one of the Honourable Miss Gores. The Duffys and Brennans numbered their full strength, including even the famous Bertha, who was staying with her sisters on a visit. The Goulds excused themselves on account of the distance and the disturbed state of the country. Mrs. Barton found, therefore, much difficulty in maintaining the noted characteristic of her parties. Sir Richard and Sir Charles had agreed to come; Mr. Adair, Mr. Ryan, and Mr. Lynch were also present. They drove up on outside cars, and were all attended by a body-guard of policemen.

"I'm afraid we shall get nothing better than a married man, even if we get that," whispered Bertha.

Mrs. Barton was the life of the party. She flattered everyone—bank clerks and police officers—and her laughter echoed amid the groined arches. Through the mullioned windows beyond the green sea-water, the white town of

Kinvarra nestled beneath the mountains; it suggested a military movement to Mr. Barton.

"If things get any worse, we might all retire into this castle. The ladies will stand on the battlements, and I will undertake to hold the place for ever against those village ruffians."

"I do not think there will be any necessity for that," replied Mr. Adair sententiously. "I think that these last terrible outrages have awakened the Government to a sense of their responsibility. I have reason to believe that immediate steps will be taken to crush this infamous conspiracy."

When lunch was over, the party dispersed for a walk, and the usual remarks concerning Mr. Adair were made. "A very clever man, an able man. He took honours at Trinity. It is true he does not care for ladies' society, but I hear that Gladstone says he cannot do without him." Nor was the famous anecdote about Mr. Ryan, the docket, and the Galway ball omitted. Then the police officers posted their men on the different headlands, and flirtation was supposed to begin, but Olive and the marquis occupied everybody's attention, and Mrs. Barton's injudiciousness was severely commented upon.

"But there is no knowing; he may be bought off yet," said Bertha.

"They say that Alice Barton is awfully clever, that she is making a fortune by writing stories," said Gladys Brennan.

"All that's only to give herself airs. If she can't be pretty she'd be clever; she's gone off for a walk with Dr. Reed."

"If she is clever, she got her cleverness from her father," said another girl. "I don't pretend to understand painting, but he does look handsome now, that fair beard and straight nose. I call him perfectly lovely; I'd prefer him to Milord any day."

"I dare say you would, but not when you were paying the housekeeper's bills or giving your daughter a fortune," exclaimed Bertha coarsely.

Although Mrs. Barton remained strangely blind to the ridicule she excited in her friends, she was keenly alive to the fact that the marquis seemed uninfluenced by Olive's beauty, nor did the knowledge of her twenty thousand pounds appear to soften his heart. To admit defeat would, however, be vain, and under the most adverse circumstances Mrs. Barton struggled on manfully to the end. And day after day the same line of conduct was implacably adhered to. At ten o'clock he was caught and sent to play tennis or walk in the garden with Olive. The girl's feelings may be divined in the sudden twitching of the facial muscles; the man is sunk in a state of nervous lethargy, from which he makes periodic efforts to rouse himself. The sun is shining brilliantly. The laurels afford but little shade, and along the flower border two butter-flies flap their white wings in the sheeny air. The lovers had not spoken for the last five minutes: their ideas follow the butterflies fatuously. Rousing himself with a supreme effort, the marquis asked:

" Are you very fond of flowers, Miss Barton ? "

"Oh yes, I delight in them. Come to the greenhouse and I'll gather you a bouquet."

While the bouquet was being cut and prepared a few remarks were made, but when it was pinned into the button-hole another morose silence fell, and they sought in vain to disentangle themselves from its meshes.

During the marquis's stay at Brookfield there were frequent dinner parties. On May 7 Mr. Adair, Mr. Ryan, and Sir Charles, were seated beneath Mr. Barton's different versions of the " Bridal of Triermain," which he declared to possess "all the beauties of Raphael, and other beauties besides." A mag-nificent turbot was on the table. Lord Dungory had just delivered himself of a neat epigram, and Mr. Adair was ex-plaining how he would crush the Land League out of exist-ence if the Government would place him in supreme power for the space of one month. "That is all I would ask : one month to restore this island to peace and prosperity. I have always been a Liberal, but I confess that I entirely fail to understand the action the Government are taking in the present crisis. Mr. Forster's Coercion Bill was, as I always said, an absurd and ineffective measure. I have always placed my faith in Mr. Gladstone, and I refuse to believe in the existence of the Kilmainham treaty; it has, I am convinced, no existence in fact ; it is no more than a Tory device. . . . And then how do you explain the appointment of Lord Frederick Cavendish ? "

At that moment the butler entered the room with an entrée. Speaking to Mr. Barton he said :

"Very dreadful news has just been received in Gort, sir: Lord Frederick Cavendish and Mr. Burke were murdered last night in the Phœnix Park."

The knives and forks dropped clinking on the plates as the entire company looked up with white terror painted upon their faces. Mr. Adair was the first to speak:

"This is," he said, "an infamous and lying report that has been put into circulation.'. . ."

"It is, unfortunately, quite true, sir; it is in all the Sunday papers?"

"Have you got a paper?"

"Yes, sir."

A paper was handed to Mr. Adair, and he read aloud the account of the Phœnix Park murders. All eyes were fixed upon him; and when he raised his eyes from the paper, the fixity of the glances he encountered shocked him. It was one of those moments when terror seems to force the soul into the eyes, as a ray of sunlight fills dead and sullen waters with an image of the sky. No one spoke, and Mrs. Barton's hospitable board was encircled with the vague abandonment of sailors who feel the sinking vessel for the last time lifting herself for a final plunge before settling down into the deep.

Then in turn, each ejaculated a few words. Mrs. Barton said, "It is dreadful to think there are such wicked people in the world."

Mr. Adair said, "There can be no doubt but that we have arrived at the crisis; Europe will ring with the echoes of the crime."

Olive said, "I think they ought to hang Mr. Parnell; I believe it was he who drove the car."

Mr. Barton said, "The landlords and land-leaguers will have to do what I say; they will have to fight it out. Now, at their head, I believe by a series of rapid marches . . ."

"Arthur, Arthur, I beg of you," exclaimed Mrs. Barton, waving her white hand impatiently.

"We shall all have to emigrate," Sir Charles murmured reflectively.

"The law is in abeyance," said Mr. Lynch.

"Precisely," replied Milord; "and as I once said to Lord Granville, ' *Les mœurs sont les hommes, mais la loi est la raison du pays.*'"

Mr. Adair looked up; he seemed about to contest the truth

of this aphorism, but he relapsed into his consideration of Mr. Gladstone's political integrity. The conversation had fallen, but at the end of a long silence Mr. Ryan said, " Begorra, I am very glad they were murthered."

All drew back instinctively. This was too horrible, and doubt of Mr. Ryan's sanity was expressed on every face.

At last Mr. Adair said, conscious that he was expressing the feelings of the entire company, "What do you mean, sir? Have you gone mad? Do you not know that this is no fitting time for buffoonery?"

" Will ye hear me cousin out?" said Mr. Lynch.

"Begorra, I'm glad they were murthered," continued Mr. Ryan; "for if they hadn't been we'd have been—there's the long and the short of it. I know the counthry well, and I know that in six months more, without a proper Coercion Act, we'd have been burned in our beds."

The unanswerableness of Mr. Ryan's words, and the implacable certainty which forced itself into every heart, that he spoke but the truth, did not, however, make the company less inclined to oppose the utilitarian view he took of the tragedy.

Unfinished phrases . . . "Disgraceful" . . . "Shocking" . . . "Inconceivable" . . . "That anyone should say such a thing" . . . were passed round, and a disposition was shown to boycott Mr. Ryan.

Mr. Adair spoke of not sitting in the room where such opinions were expressed, but Milord was seen whispering to him, and Mrs. Barton, always anxious to calm troubled waters, suggested that "people did not mean all they said." Mr. Ryan, however, maintained through it all an attitude of stolid indifference, the indifference of a man who knows that all must come back sooner or later to his views.

And presently, although the sting remained, the memory of the wasp that had stung seemed to be lost. Milord and Mr. Adair engaged in a long and learned discussion concerning the principles of Liberalism, in the course of which many allusions were made to the new Coercion Bill, which, it was now agreed, Mr. Gladstone would, in a few days, lay before Parliament. The provisions of this bill were eagerly debated. Milord spoke of an Act that had been in force consequent on the Fenian rising in '69. Mr. Adair was of opinion that the importance of a new Coercion Act could not be over estimated; Mr. Barton

declared in favour of a military expedition—a rapid dash into
the heart of Connemara. But the conversation languished,
and in the ever-lengthening silences all found their thoughts
reverting to the idea brutally expressed by Mr. Ryan :—*Yes,
they were glad ; for if Lord Frederick Cavendish and Mr. Burke
had not been assassinated, every landowner in the country would
have been murdered.*

There was no dancing that evening; and as the night
advanced the danger of the long drive home increased in
intensity in the minds of Messrs. Lynch and Ryan. They sat
on either side of Mr. Adair, and it was finally arranged that
they should unite their police-forces, and spend the night at
his place. Sir Charles was sleeping at Brookfield ; Milord had
four policemen with him ; and as all would have to pass his
gate, he did not anticipate that even the Land League would
venture to attack thirteen armed men. Mr. Barton, who saw
the picturesque in everything, declared, when he came back,
that they looked like a caravan starting for a pilgrimage across
the desert. After a few further remarks the ladies rose to
retire, but when Mrs. Barton gave her hand to Lord Kilcarney,
he said, his voice trembling a little :

"I'm afraid I must leave you to-morrow, Mrs. Barton. I
shall have to run over to London to vote in the House of
Lords. . . . You know that. . . . ."

Mrs. Barton led the poor little man into the further corner
of the room, and making a place for him by her side, she said :

"Of course we are very sorry you are leaving—we should
like you to stop a little longer with us. . . . Is it impossible
for you . . . ?"

"I am afraid so, Mrs. Barton . . . . it is very kind of you,
but . . . ."

"It is a great pity," she answered ; "but before we part I
should like to know if you have come to any conclusion about
what I spoke to you of in Dublin. If it is not to be, I should
like to know, that I might tell the girl, so that she might not
think anything more about . . . ."

"What am I to say, what am I to do?" thought the marquis. "Oh ! why does this woman worry me? . . . How can
I tell her that I wouldn't marry her daughter for tens of
thousands of pounds?" "I think Mrs. Barton . . . I mean,
I think you will agree with me that until affairs in Ireland
grow more settled, it would be impossible for anyone to enter

into any engagements whatever. We are all on the brink of ruin."

" But twenty thousand pounds would settle a great deal."

The little marquis was conscious of annihilation, and he sought to escape Mrs. Barton as he might a piece of falling rock. With a desperate effort he said :

" Yes, Mrs. Barton, yes, I agree with you, twenty thousand pounds is a great deal of money; but I think we had better wait until the Lords have passed the new Coercion Bill—say nothing more about this—leave it an open question."

And on this eminently unsatisfactory answer the matter ended ; even Mrs. Barton saw she could not, at least for the present, continue to press it. Still she did not give up hope. "Try on to the end ; we never know that it is not the last little effort that will win the game," was the aphorism with which she consoled her daughter, and induced her to write to Lord Kilcarney. And almost daily he received from her flowers, supposed to be emblematical of the feeling she enter-tained for him ; and for these Alice was sometimes ordered to compose verses and suitable mottoes.

CHAPTER II.

BUT Lord Kilcarney's replies to these letters seldom consisted of more than a few well-chosen words, and he often allowed a week, and sometimes a fortnight, to elapse before answering at all. Olive—too vain and silly to understand the indifference with which she was treated—whined and fretted less than might have been expected. She spent a great deal of her time with Barnes, who fed her with scandal and flattery. But a storm was about to break, and in August it was known, without any possibility of a doubt, that the marquis was engaged to Violet Scully, and that their marriage was settled for the autumn.

And this marriage, and the passing of the Bill for the Prevention of Crime, were the two interests present in the mind of Irish landlordism during the summer of '82. Immediately the former event was publicly announced, every girl in Dublin ran to her writing-desk to confirm to her friends and relatives the truth of the news which for the last two months she had so resolutely anticipated. The famous Bertha, the terror of the débutantes, rushed to Brookfield, but she did not get there before the Brennans, and the result was a meeting of these families of girls in Mrs. Barton's drawing-room. Gladys was, however, the person chosen by God and herself to speak the wonderful words :

" Of course you have heard the news, Mrs. Barton ? "

" No," replied Mrs. Barton, a little nervously ; " what is it ? "

" Oh, yes, what is it ? " exclaimed Olive. " Anyone going to be married ? "

" Yes—can you guess ? "

" No ; tell me quick . . . no, do tell me. Are you going to be married ? "

Had Olive been suddenly dowered with the wit of Congreve she could not have contrived an answer that would have shielded her better from the dart that Gladys was preparing to hurl. The girl winced; and divining the truth in a moment of inspiration, Mrs. Barton said :

"Ah! I know; Lord Kilcarney is engaged to Violet Scully."

The situation was almost saved, and would have been had Olive not been present. She glanced at her mother in astonishment; and Gladys, fearing utter defeat, hurled her dart recklessly.

" Yes," she exclaimed, " and their marriage is fixed for this autumn."

" I don't believe a word of it. . . . You only say so because you think it will annoy me."

" My dear Olive, how can it annoy you? You know very well you refused him," said Mrs. Barton, risking the danger of contradiction. " Gladys is only telling us the news."

"News, indeed ; a pack of lies. . . . I know her well ; and all because she is jealous of me ; . . . because she didn't succeed in hooking the man she was after in the Shelbourne last year. I am not going to listen to her lies, if you are," and on these words Olive flaunted passionately out of the room.

" So very sorry, really," exclaimed Zoe. " We really did not know . . . indeed we did not. We could not have known that, that there was any reason why dear Olive would not like to hear that Lord Kilcarney was engaged to Violet."

" Not at all, not at all. I assure you that whatever question there may once have been, I give you my word, was broken off a long time ago ; they did not suit each other at all," said Mrs. Barton. And now that she was relieved of the presence of her young, the mother fought admirably. But in a few minutes the enemy was reinforced by the arrival of the Hon. Miss Gores.

"Oh, how do you do? I am so glad to see you," said Mrs. Barton the moment they entered the room. " Have you heard the news? all is definitely settled between the little marquis and Violet. We were all talking of it ; I am so glad for her sake, of course it is very grand to be a marchioness, but I'm afraid she'll find her coronet a poor substitute for her dinner. . . . You know what a state the property is in . . . She has married a beggar. The great thing after all, nowadays, is money."

Mrs. Barton's cunning did not save her from the error of abusing the man she had failed to catch, but she kept her enemies at bay while they drank their tea and discussed the state of Lord Kilcarney's liabilities. Nor did she herself realise the thoroughness of her humiliation and defeat till the young ladies had wished her good-bye. She stood by the window watching their carriages growing smaller as they receded through the sheep-grazed lawn of Brookfield. What was she to say to her daughter? Her step she now heard on the stairs. What falsehood would suit the occasion best? she asked herself hurriedly. Pale and trembling, Olive opened the door.

"Oh, mamma," she said, "this is terrible; what shall we do —what shall we do?"

"What's terrible, my beautiful darling?"

Olive looked through her languor and tears; and she answered, petulantly:

"Oh, you know very well I'm disgraced; he's going to marry Violet, and I shall not be a marchioness after all."

"If my beautiful darling likes she can be a duchess," replied Mrs. Barton with a silvery laugh.

"I don't understand, mamma."

"I mean that we are not entirely dependent on that wretched little marquis with his encumbered property; if he was fool enough to let himself be entrapped by that designing little beast, Violet Scully, so much the worse for him; we shall get someone far grander than he. It is never wise for a girl to settle herself off the first season she comes out."

"It is all very well to say that now, but you made me break off with dear Edward, who was ever so nice, and loved me dearly."

Mrs. Barton winced, but she answered almost immediately, "My dear, we shall get someone a great deal grander than that wretched marquis. There will be a whole crowd of English dukes and earls at the Castle next year; men who haven't a mortgage on their property, and who will all fight for the hand of my beautiful Olive. Mr. Harding, Alice's friend, will put your portrait into one of the Society papers as the Galway beauty, and then next year you may be her Grace."

"And how will they do my portrait, mamma?"

"I think you look best, darling, with your hair done up on the top of your head, in the French fashion."

"Oh! do you think so? You don't like the way I have it done in now?" said the girl; and laughing, she ran to the glass to admire herself. "Barnes said I looked sweet this morning."

As quickly as an April sky brightens, Olive passed from grief to glee; her light mind could support no idea for any length of time. Concerning Lord Kilcarney she had never entertained a single personal thought; she had been fevered with visions of rank and power;—her life had been one of nervous suspense. But now the carefully calculated future which she had learned long to regard as her own had vanished, and into the mental vacuum febrile sensations of loneliness, of emptiness, of dispossession, had suddenly rushed. She tossed her head nervously, declaring she was miserable, and often she burst out crying for no assignable cause. Mrs. Barton consoled and flattered gaily; but the sweet placid countenance was sometimes a little troubled. As the girls left the breakfast-room one morning she said, as if asking their advice:

"I have just received an invitation from Dungory Castle; they are giving a tennis party and they want us to go to lunch."

"Oh! mamma, I don't want to go," cried Olive.

"And why, my dear?"

"Oh! because everybody knows about the marquis, and I couldn't bear their sneers; those Brennans and the Duffys are sure to be there."

"Bertha's in Dublin," said Mrs. Barton, in an intonation of voice a little too expressive of relief.

"Gladys is just as bad, and then there's that horrid Zoe. Oh! I couldn't bear it."

"It will look as if we were avoiding them; they will only talk the more. I always think it is best to put a bold face on everything. Sir Charles will be there for certain; you know he admires you; if I were you I would monopolise him the whole afternoon. The old is quickly forgotten in the new flirtation."

"I couldn't, I couldn't, I really couldn't, mamma," exclaimed Olive, and she burst into tears. "I'm broken-hearted, that's what I am. I have nothing to do or to think of."

Mrs. Barton winced a little before this manifestation of hysterical feeling; but of course it did not change, nor did it alter, in any way, the light in which she habitually viewed her

own and her daughter's life.   The marquis affair had not come
off; but she had done her best, and no one can do more than
their best, and now she would do her best to get out of the
difficulty.   There could be little doubt that the Ladies Cullen
had got up the tennis party so that they might have an opportunity of sneering at her, but Milord would keep them in
check (it might be as well to tell him to threaten to put down
the school if they did not keep a guard on their tongues),
and if Olive would only put a bold face on it and captivate
Sir Charles, this very disagreeable business might blow over.
Further than this, Mrs. Barton's thoughts did not travel, but
they were clear and precise thoughts, and with much subtlety
and insinuative force she applied herself to the task of over-
coming her daughter's weakness and strengthening her in this
overthrow of vanity and self-love.   At Brookfield Milord was
more profuse than ever in French flattery; and at Dungory
Castle he had doubtless been able to arrive at a very clear
understanding with Lady Sarah and Lady Jane concerning the
future of Protestantism in the parish, for on the day of the
tennis party no allusion was made to Lord Kilcarney's visit
to Brookfield; certain references to his marriage were, of
course, inevitable, but it was only necessary to question Mr.
Adair on his views concerning the new Coercion Act, to
secure for Mrs. Barton an almost complete immunity from
feminine sarcasm.

"I do not deny," said Mr. Adair, "that the Crimes Bill
will restore tranquillity, but I confess that I can regard no
Government as satisfactory that can only govern by the
sword."

These sentiments being but only very partially appreciated
by the rest of the company, the conversation came to an
awkward pause, and Lady Jane said as she left the room :

"I do not know a more able man on a county board than
Mr. Adair.   He took honours at Trinity, and if he has not
done as much since as we expected, it is because he is too
honourable, too conscientious, to ally himself to any particular
party."

"That was always the way with Lord Dungory," suggested
Mrs. Gould.

Lady Jane bit her lip and continued, without taking notice
of the interruption :

"Now I hope Mr. Adair will not write a pamphlet, or

express himself too openly concerning the Crimes Act. The question of the day is the organisation of the Land Act, and I hear that Mr. Gladstone says it will be impossible to get on without Mr. Adair's assistance."

"Every six months it is given out that Gladstone cannot go on without him, but somehow Gladstone does manage to get on without him; and then we never hear any more about it."

Lady Jane looked angry; and all wondered at Mrs. Gould's want of tact, but at that moment the footman announced Messrs. Ryan and Lynch, and Alice asked if she might go up to see Cecilia. More visitors arrived; the Brennans, the Duffys, the five Honourable Miss Gores, and the company adjourned to the tennis ground. Mr. Lynch was anxious to have May for a partner, but she refused him somewhat pettishly, declaring at the same time that she had given up tennis, and would never touch a racquet again. Her continuous silence and dejected appearance created some surprise, and her cheeks flushed with passion when her mother said she didn't know what had come over May lately. Then obeying an impulse, May rose to her feet, and leaving the tennis players she walked across the pleasure grounds. Dungory Castle was surrounded by heavy woods and overtopping clumps of trees. As the house was neared, these were filled in with high laurel hedges and masses of rhododendron, and an opening in the branches of some large beech trees revealed a blue and beautiful aspect of the Clare mountains.

"I wonder what May is angry about?" Cecilia said to Alice as they watched the tennis playing from their window; "I suppose those horrid men are annoying her."

"I never saw her refuse to play tennis before," Alice replied demurely. And ten minutes after, some subtle desire of which she was not very conscious led her through the shrubberies towards the place where she already expected to find May. And dreaming of reconciliation, of a renewal of friendship, Alice walked through the green summer of the leaves, listening to the infinite twittering of the birds, and startled by the wood pigeons that from time to time rose boisterously out of the high branches. On a garden bench, leaning forward, her hands rested on her knees, May sat swinging her parasol from side to side, playing with the fallen leaves. When she looked up, the sunlight fell full upon her face, and Alice saw that she was crying.   But affecting not to see the tears, she said speaking rapidly :

"Oh, May dear, I have been looking for you.   The last time we . . ."

But interrupted here by a choking sob, she found herself forced to say :

"My dear May, what is the matter?   Can I do anything for you?"

"Oh, no, no; only leave me; don't question me.   I don't want anyone's help."

The ungraciousness of the words was lost in the accent of grief with which they were spoken.

"I assure you I do not wish to be inquisitive," Alice replied sorrowfully, "nor do I come to annoy you with good advice, but the last time we met we did not part good friends. . . I was merely anxious to assure you that I bore no ill-feeling, but of course, if you . . ."

"Oh, no, no," cried May; reaching and catching at Alice's arm, she pulled her down into the seat beside her; "I am awfully sorry for my rudeness to you—to you who are so good —so good.   Oh, Alice dear, you will forgive me, will you not?" and sobbing very helplessly, she threw herself into her friend's arms.

"Oh, of course I forgive you," cried Alice, deeply affected. "I had no right to lecture you in the way I did, but I meant it for the best, indeed I did."

"I know you did, but I lost my temper.   Ah, if you knew how sorely I was tried you would forgive me."

"I do forgive you, May dear ; but tell me, cannot I help you now?   You know that you can confide in me, and I will do anything in my power to help you."

"No one can help me now," said the girl, sullenly.

Alice did not speak at once, but at the end of a long silence she said :

"Does Fred Scully love you no more?"

"I do not know whether he does or not; nor does it matter much . . . he's not in Ireland . . . he's far away by this time."

"Where is he?"

"He's gone to Australia.   He wrote to me about two months ago to say that all had been decided in a few hours, and that he was to sail next morning.   He's gone out with some racehorses . . . he expects to win a lot of money . . . he'll be back again in a year."

"A year is not long to wait; you'll see him when he comes back."

"I don't think I should care to see him again. . . . Oh, you were right, Alice, to warn me against him. . . . I was foolish not to listen to you . . . but it was too late even then."

Alice trembled: she had already guessed the truth, but hoping when she knew all hope was vain, she said :

"You had better tell me, May; you know I am to be trusted."

"The truth is too horrible to tell. Can't you guess it ?"

The conversation fell, and the girls sat staring into the depths of the wood. Involuntarily their eyes followed a small bird that ran up branch after branch of a beech tree, pecking as it went. It seemed like a toy mouse, so quick and unvarying were its movements. At last May said, and very dolorously :

"Alice, I thought you were kinder; have you no word of pity ? Why tell you, why ask me to tell you ? Oh ! what a fool I was ! "

"Oh ! no, no, May, you did right to tell me. I am more sorry for you than words can express, but I did not speak because I was trying to think of some way of helping you."

"Oh ! there's no—no way of helping me, dear. There's nothing for me to do but to die." And now giving way utterly, the girl buried her face in her hands and sobbed until it seemed that she would choke in thick grief.

"Oh ! May, May dear, you must not cry like that: if any-one were to come by, what would they think ? "

"What does it matter ? Everyone will know sooner or later —I wish I were dead—dead and out of sight for ever of this miserable world."

"No, May," said Alice, thinking instinctively of the child "you must not die. Your trial is a terrible one, but people before now have got over worse. I am trying to think what can be done."

Then May raised her weeping face, and there was a light of hope in her eyes. She clasped Alice's hand. Neither spoke. The little brown bird pursued his way up and down the branches of the beech; beyond it lay the sky, and the girls, tense with little sufferings, yearned into this vision of beautiful peace.

At last Alice said, " Did you tell Mr. Scully of the trouble? . . . does he know? . . ."

" He was away, and I did not like to write it to him; his departure for Australia took me quite by surprise."

" Have you told your mother?"

"Oh no, I'd rather die than tell her; I couldn't tell her. You know what she is."

" I think she ought to be told; she would take you abroad."

"Oh no, Alice dear; it would never do to tell mamma. You know what she is, you know how she talks, she would never leave off abusing the Scullys; and then, I don't know how, but somehow everybody would get to know about it. But find it out they will, sooner or later; it is only a question of time. And I shall be disgraced; no one will ever marry me then."

Something—but something she would not have been able to explain to herself—jarred Alice's feelings in these last words. She looked at May inquiringly, then the expression of her face changed, and she said :

" No, no, May, they shall know nothing of this—at least, not if I can help it."

" But you cannot help it."

" There is one thing quite certain ; you must go away. You cannot stop in Galway."

"It is all very well talking like that, but where can I go to? A girl cannot move a yard away from home without people wanting to know where she has gone. I wish I could die; I am more miserable and unhappy than you can imagine."

Alice's eyes filled with tears. Never was the human soul more strikingly reflected in small grey eyes; the grave and exquisite kindness of a beautiful soul, and to this you must add the natural pity that every woman feels for another in the distressful period of child-bearing.

"You might go up to Dublin," she said, "and live in lodgings."

" And what excuse should I give to mother?" said May, who in her despair had not courage to deny the possibility of the plan.

" You need not tell her where you are," replied Alice; and then she hesitated, feeling keenly conscious of the deception she was practising. But her unswerving common sense coming, after a moment's reflection, to her aid, she said : "You might say that you were going to live in the convent. Go to the Mother Superior, tell her of your imminent need, beg of her, persuade her to receive and forward your letters ; and in that way, it seems to me that no one need be the wiser of what is going to happen."

The last words were spoken slowly, as if with a sense of shame at being forced to speak thus. May raised her face, now aflame with hope and joy.

"Oh, Alice, how kind of you ; how can I ever thank you ? " said the girl. Then a moment after the light died out of her face and she said :

"But how shall I live ? Who will support me ? I cannot ask mother for money without awakening suspicion."

"I think, May, I shall be able to give you almost all the money you want," replied Alice, in a hesitating and slightly embarrassed manner.

"You, Alice ? "

"But I haven't told you ; I have been writing a good deal lately for newspapers, and have made nearly twenty pounds. That will be all you will want for the present, and I shall be able, I hope, to make sufficient to keep you supplied."

May clasped her hands ; her eyes flooded with tears, and she was breathless with worship. It was a heavenly right to see Alice ; she loved the stiff staid shoulders, and the whole personality seemed to her now to be a symbol of earthly good ; and she thought vaguely of the Virgin. In Alice's face, however, there was no divine vapidity, but grand belief in this world, and faith in its ultimate perfectibility. She did not utter words of blame or reproach, they did not seem to her necessary. And it is doubtful, even if they had done so, if she could have spoken : an instinct, rather than a conscious sense of modesty, would have silenced her : she would have felt that anything she might say in reproof would be indirect praise of her own good conduct. As it was, nothing was present to her mind but one aching, throbbing thought—the thought of her friend's imminent need, and of how she (Alice Barton) might help her successfully through her trouble.

"I don't think that anyone was ever as good as you, Alice. You make me feel more ashamed of myself."

"You mustn't talk in that way, dear. I am doing only

what anyone else would do if they were called upon. But we have been sitting here a long time now, and before we go back to the tennis-ground we had better arrange what is to be done. When do you propose leaving ? "

" I had better leave at once . . . . it is seven months ago now . . . . no one suspects as yet. . . ."

" Well, then, when would you like me to send you the money ? You can have it at once if you like."

" Oh, thanks, dear ; mother will give me enough to last me a little while, and I will write to you from Dublin. You are sure no one sees your letters at Brookfield ? "

" Quite sure ; there's not the slightest danger."

As they drove home that evening, Mrs. Barton babbled about Sir Charles and his prospects of marriage, of the odious Ladies Cullen, and how the dear Milord had kept them in order ; and, tickled by the remembrances of his looks, frowns, and winks, mother and daughter waved their white hands, and laughed consumedly. Alice sitting opposite them, her back to the horses, turned to pull down the blind, that she might save her eyes from the rays of the setting sun, now lying poised like a golden shield in a rift in the amphitheatrical mountains ; every perspective and aspect came out in trenchant outline, and, in the intense reverberation of the light, rocks and bushes appeared like bronze, and the tarns of the sterile landscape like flashes of silver. But now, the blinds being down, the carriage was filled with blue shadow, and Alice set herself to think of the duties she had undertaken. She did not question the advice she had given, and she felt sure that the rev. mother, if a proper appeal were made to her common sense, would consent to conceal the girl's fault. Two months would not be long passing, but the expenses of this time would be heavy, and she, Alice, would have to meet them all. She trembled for fear she might fail to do so, and she tried to reckon them up. It would be impossible to get rooms under a pound a week, and to live, no matter how cheaply, would cost at least two pounds ; three pounds a week, four threes are twelve ! The twenty pounds would scarcely carry her over a month, she would not be well for at least two ; and then there was the doctor, the nurse, the flannels for the baby. Alice tried to calculate, thinking plainly and honestly. If a repulsive detail rose suddenly up in her mind, she did not shrink, nor was she surprised to find herself thinking of such things, she did so as a matter of course, keeping her thoughts fixed on the one object of doing her duty towards her friend. And how to do this was the problem that presented itself unceasingly for solution. She felt that somehow she would have to earn twenty pounds within the next month. Out of the *Lady's Paper*, in which "Notes and Sensations of a Plain Girl at Dublin Castle," was still running, she could not hope to make more than thirty shillings a week; a magazine had lately accepted a ten-page story worth, she fancied, about five pounds, but when they would print it and pay her was impossible to say. She could write the Editor an imploring letter, asking him to advance her the money. But even then there was another nine pounds to make up. And to do this seemed to her an impossibility. She could not ask her father or mother, she would only do so if the worst came to the worst. And if she wrote to Harding, he might, instead of helping her, give her the money out of his own pocket. But no, he couldn't do that; the fact that the articles were printed was a proof that they were paid for. Yes, she might write to him, and in the meantime she must work. She would write paragraphs, articles, short stories, and would send them to every editor in London. One out of three might turn up trumps. So Alice reasoned; and ten hours a day were spent at her writing-table. You see the white room; the two white beds, the white curtains hanging from the two brass crowns, the chimneypiece covered with tiny ornaments. and the fireplace shut in with white embroidered curtains; you see the white wall-paper freckled with small flowers, the two engravings (the Youth and Maiden swinging, the Girl carving her Lover's Name on the Beech-tree). You see the two little bookcases filled with neatly bound volumes—a few choice novels and some prayer-books : the rosaries still hanging from the holy-water fonts. You remember when you first saw this room ? Is it the same now as it was then ? Not exactly. A writing-table has been set in the window; it is covered with papers and MSS., Darwin's "Origin of Species," Matthew Arnold and James Thomson have been added to the bookshelves; Carlyle's Essays—a sixpenny edition —lies on the sofa, at the foot of the beds. And the girl herself ? You remember when you saw her in this room—the ante-room of society—for the first time. She was troubled and full of fear then, she is troubled and full of fear now; but it is not the same trouble, nor is it the same fear. Hope has beat its trembling wings, has buzzed out its trembling life, and she is

content to crawl up the false, the implacable but glittering
pane, only pausing here and there to see, to consider the fuller
life of others, knowing well she cannot change the eternal issues
of things of which she is but a fragment.   She is almost without envy ; and the clouds which now dim the bright brow are
not for her own, but her friend's affliction.   She has just
received her first letter from May, who is living in a Dublin
lodging.   It runs as follows :

                          " Gardner Street, Mountjoy Square.
   " DARLING ALICE,—
      " I have been in Dublin now more than a week.   I did not
write to you before because I wished to write to tell you that I
had done all you told me to do.   The first thing I did was to
go to the convent.   Would you believe it, the new rev. mother
is Sister Mary who we knew so well at St. Leonards ?   She has
been transferred to the branch convent in Dublin.   She was so
kind, so delighted to see me, but the sight of her dear face
awoke so many memories, so many old associations, that I burst
out crying, and it seemed to me impossible that I should ever
be able to find courage to tell her the dreadful truth.   None
will ever know what it cost me to speak the words.   They came
to me all of a sudden ; I threw myself at her feet and told her
everything.   I thought she would reproach me and speak
bitterly, but she only said, ' My poor child, I am sorry you
had not strength to resist temptation ; your trial is a
dreadful one.'   She was very, very kind.   Her face lighted up
when I spoke of you, and she said : ' Sweet girl ; she was
always an angel ; one of these days she will come back to us.
She is too good for the world.'   Then I insisted that it was
your idea that I should seek help from the convent, but she
said that it was my duty to go to my mother and tell her the
whole truth.   Oh, my darling Alice, I cannot tell you what a
terrible time I went through.   We were talking for at least
two hours, and it was only with immense difficulty that I at
last succeeded in making her understand what kind of person
poor mamma is, and how hopeless it would be to expect her to
keep any secret, even if her daughter's honour was in question.
I told her how she would run about, talking in her mild
unmeaning way of ' poor May and that shameful Mr. Scully ; '
and, at last, the rev. mother, as you prophesied she would, saw
the matter in its proper light, and she has consented to receive

all my letters, and if mother writes, to give her to understand that I am safe within the convent walls. It is awfully good of her, for I know the awful risk she is wilfully incurring so as to help me out of my trouble.

"The house I am staying in is nice enough, and the landlady seems a kind woman. The name I go by is Mrs. Brandon (you will not forget to direct your letters so), and I said that my husband was an officer, and had gone out to join his regiment in India. I have a comfortable bedroom on the third floor. There are two windows, and they look out on the street. The time seems as if it would never pass; the twelve hours of the day seem like twelve centuries. I have not even a book to read, and I never go out for fear of being seen. In the evening I put on a thick veil and go for a walk in the back streets. But I cannot go out before nine, it is not dark till then, and I cannot stop out later than ten on account of the men who speak to you. My coloured hair makes me look fast, and I am so afraid of meeting someone I know, that this short hour is as full of misery as those that preceded it. Every passer-by seems to know me, to recognise me, and I cannot help imagining that he or she will be telling my unfortunate story half an hour after in the pitiless drawing-rooms of Merrion Square. Oh, Alice darling, you are the only friend I have in the world. If it were not for you, I believe I should drown myself in the Liffey. No girl was ever so miserable as I. I cannot tell you how I feel, and you cannot imagine how forlorn it all is; and I am so ill. I am always hungry, and always sick, and always longing. Oh, these longings; you may think they are nothing, but they are dreadful. You remember how active I used to be, how I used to run about the tennis court; now I can scarcely crawl. And the strange sickening fancies; I see things in the shops that tempt me, sometimes it is a dry biscuit, sometimes a basket of strawberries, but whatever it is I stand and look at it, long for it, until weary of longing and standing with a sort of weight weighing me down, and my stays all rucking up to my neck, I crawl home. There I am all alone; and I sit in the dark on a wretched hard chair by the window; and I cry; and I watch the summer night and all the golden stars, and I cannot say what I think of during all these long and lonely hours; I only know that I cannot find energy to go to bed. And I never sleep a whole night through;

the cramp comes on so terribly that I jump up screaming.   Oh,
Alice, how I hate *him*.   When I think of it all I see how
selfish men are ; they never think of us—they only think of
themselves.   You would scarcely know me if you saw me now ;
all my complexion, you know what a pretty complexion it was,
is all red and mottled.   When you saw me a fortnight ago I
was all right : it is extraordinary what a change has come
about.   I think it was the journey, and the excitement ; there
would be no concealing the truth now.   It was lucky I left
Galway when I did.

"Mother gave me five pounds on leaving home.   My ticket
cost nearly thirty shillings, a pound went in cabs and hotel
expenses, and my breakfasts brought my bill up yesterday to
two pounds—I cannot think how, for I only pay sixteen
shillings for my room—and when it was paid I had only a few
shillings left.   Will you, therefore, send me the money you
promised, if possible, by return of post ?

"Yours affectionately,
"MAY GOULD."

The tears started to Alice's eyes as she read the letter.   She
did not consider if May might have spared her the physical
details with which her letter abounded ; she did not stay to
think of the cause, of the result ; for the moment she was
numb to ideas and sensations that were not those of humble
human pity for humble human suffering : like the waters of a
new baptism pity made her pure and whole, and the false
shame of an ancient world fell from her.   Leaning her head
on her strong well-shaped hand, she set to arranging her little
plans for her friend's help—plans that were charming for their
simplicity, their sweet homeliness.   The letter she had just
read had come by the afternoon post.   If she were to send
May the money she wrote for that evening, it would be
necessary to go into Gort to register the letter.   Gort was two
miles away ; and if she asked for the carriage her mother
might propose that the letters should be sent in by a special
messenger.   This of course was impossible, and Alice, for the
first time in her life, found herself obliged to tell a deliberate
lie.   For a moment her conscience stood at bay, but she
accepted the inevitable and told Mrs. Barton that she had
some MSS. to register, and did not care to entrust them to other
hands.   It was a consolation to know that eighteen pounds

were safely despatched, but she was bitterly unhappy, she cried bitterly;—and she wrote to Harding to ask him if he could assist her in getting rid of two articles. The fear that money might be wanting in the last and most terrible hours bound her to her desk as with a chain; and when her tired and exhausted brain ceased to formulate phrases, the picture of the lonely room, the night walks, and the suffering of the jaded girl stared her in the face with a terrible distinctness. Her only moments of gladness were when the post brought a cheque from London. Sometimes they were for a pound, sometimes for fifteen shillings. Once she received five pounds ten—it was for her story. On the 10th of September she received the following letter:—

" DARLING ALICE,—

"Thanks a thousand times for your last letter, and the money enclosed. It came in the nick of time, for I was run almost to my last penny. I did not write before, because I didn't feel in the humour to do anything. Thank goodness I'm not sick any more, though I don't know that it isn't counterbalanced by the dreadful faintness and the constant movement. Isn't it awful to sit here day after day watching myself, and knowing the only relief I shall get will be after such terrible pain? I woke up last night crying with the terror of it. Cervassi says there are cases on record of pain-less confinements, and in my best moods I think mine is to be one of them. I know it is awfully wrong to write all these things to a good girl like you, but I think talking about it is part of the complaint; and poor sinner me has no one to talk to. Do you remember my old black cashmere? I've been altering it till there's hardly a bit of the original body left; but now the skirt is adding to my troubles by getting shorter and shorter in front. It is now quite six inches off the ground, and instead of fastening it I have to pin the placket-hole and then it falls nearly right. . . Don't tell me you will send me the money to buy myself anything new, because, much as I have done, miserable degraded wretch though I be, I can yet appreciate what I am costing you in all ways, and I don't want to add to it. Only three weeks longer, and then . . . But there, I won't look forward, because I know I am going to die . . . and all the accounting for it, and everything else, will be on your shoulders. Good-bye, dear, I shan't write

again, at least not till afterwards; and if there is an after-
ward, I shall never be able to thank you properly; but still I
think it will be a weight off you. Is it so, dear? do you
wish I were dead? I know you don't. It was unkind to write
that last line: I will scratch it out. You will not be angry,
dear. I am too wretched to know what I am writing, and I
want to lie down.

"Yours affectionately,
"MAY GOULD."

Outside the air was limpid with sunlight, and the newly-
mown meadow was golden in the light of evening. The
autumn-coloured foliage of the chestnuts lay mysteriously rich
and still, harmonising in measured tones with the ruddy tints
of the dim September sunset. The country dozed as if satiated
with summer love. Heavy scents were abroad—the pungent
odours of the aftermath. A high baritone voice broke the
languid silence, and, in embroidered smoking-jacket and cap,
Mr. Barton twanged his guitar. Milord had been thrown
down amid the hay; and Mrs. Barton and Olive, with much
silvery laughter, and much waving of white hands, were
showering it upon him. The old gentleman's legs were in
the air.

Crushing the letter, Alice's hands fell on the table; she
burst into tears. But work was more vital than tears, and,
taking up her pen, she continued her story—penny journal
fiction of true love and unending happiness in the end. A
month later she received this note:

"DEAREST,—

"Just a line in pencil—I mustn't sit up—to tell you it is
all over, and all I said was, "Thank God! thank God!" over
and over again, as each pain went. It is such a relief; but I
mustn't write much. It is such a funny screwed-up looking
baby, and I don't feel any of those maternal sentiments that
you read about—at least not yet. And it always cries just
when I am longing to go to sleep. Thank you again and
again for all you have done for me and been to me. I feel
awfully weak.

"Yours affectionately,
"MAY GOULD."

CHAPTER III.

THEN Alice heard that the baby was dead, and that a little money would be required to bury it. Another effort was made; the money was sent: and the calm of the succeeding weeks was only disturbed by an uneasy desire to see May back in Galway, and hear her say that her terrible secret was over and done with for ever. One day she was startled by a quick trampling of feet in the corridor, and May rushed into the room. She threw herself into Alice's arms and kissed her with effusion, with tears. The girls looked at each other long and nervously. One was pale and over-worn, her spare figure was buttoned into a faded dress, and her hair was rolled into a plain knot. The other was superb with health, and her face was full of rose-bloom. She was handsomely dressed in green velvet, and her copper hair flamed and flashed beneath a small bonnet with mauve strings.

" Oh, Alice, how tired and pale you look ! You have been working too hard, and all for me. How can I thank you ? I shall never be able to thank you . . . but believe me, it makes me so unhappy . . . I cannot find words to tell you how grateful I am—but I am grateful, Alice . . . indeed I am."

" I am sure you are, dear. I did my best for you, it is true ; and thank heaven I succeeded, and no one knows . . . I do not think that anyone even suspects."

" No, not a soul. We managed it very well, didn't we, dear ? And the reverend mother behaved splendidly—she just took the view that you said she would, She saw that no good would come of telling mamma about me when I made her understand that if a word were said my misfortune would be belled all over the country in double-quick time. But, Alice dear, I had a terrible time of it ; two months waiting in that horrible little lodging, afraid to go out for fear someone would recognise me ; it was awful. And often I

261

hadn't enough to eat, for when you are in that state you can't eat everything, and I was afraid to spend any money. You did your best to keep me supplied, dear, good guardian angel that you are." Then the impulsive girl flung herself on Alice's shoulders, and kissed her. "But there were times when I was hard up, oh, much more hard up than you thought I was; for I didn't tell you everything: if I had you would have worried yourself into your grave. Oh, I had a frightful time of it! If one is married one is petted and consoled and encouraged, but alone in a lonely lodging—oh, it was frightful."

"And what about the poor baby?" said Alice, whose disappointment rose like an acid odour to her head.

"Oh, isn't it dreadful of me? I was forgetting all about it. The poor little thing died, as I wrote you, about ten days after it was born. I nursed it; and I was so sorry for it. I really was; but of course . . . well it seems a hard thing to say—but I don't know what I should have done with it if it had lived. Life isn't so happy, is it, even under the best of circumstances?"

Alice bit her lips. She was beset with dark and painful emotions, and words failing her, the conversation came to a sudden close. At last the nervous silence that intervened was broken by May:

"We were speaking about money. I will repay you all I owe you some day, Alice dear. I will save up all the money I can get out of mother. She is such a dear old thing, but I cannot understand her; not a penny did she send me for the first six weeks, and then she sent me £25; and it was lucky she did, for the doctor's bill was something tremendous. And I bought this dress and bonnet with what was left . . . I ought to have repaid you first thing; but I forgot it until I had ordered the dress."

"I assure you it does not matter, May; I shall never take the money from you. If I did, it would take away all the pleasure I have had in serving you."

"Oh, but I will insist, Alice dear, I could not think of such a thing. But there's no use in discussing that point until I get the money . . . . Tell me, what do you think of my bonnet?"

"I think it very nice indeed; and I never saw you looking better."

When May left the room Alice felt her despair growing thicker; it descended upon her gloomily, silently. Was this all she had worked for, was this all she had striven for? She had attained her end, but, oh, how trivial it appeared when compared with the terrible anxiety that had gone to achieve it. And, without pausing to consider if she were right, her soul revolted from accepting as an adequate result of her sufferings this somewhat gross picture of satisfaction. And is it not ever so? Does not the inevitable grossness of those who fight in the outward battle always jar the pensive sadness of others who see life from a distance as a faintly drawn landscape veiled in delicate twilight, and whose victories are won over themselves rather than over circumstances and opponents?

And in her present mood the fresh colour, the new dress and bonnet, the triumphant air, were infinitely painful and repellent to Alice. She could not rid herself of a sense of injustice done, nor could she avoid seeing that it was she, and not May, who wore the penitential garb and mien. Then life appeared to her a little as it did to Cecilia—as a libidinous monster couch- ing in a cave, with red jaws dripping with foul spume. Could Cecilia be right after all? If the elegant sanctity of cloistered nuns be the only possible life, and all joys vile except passion- less and intellectual interests . . . if . . . . Oh, if . . . "But no, no," the girl wailed out in despair. "There is no absolute right; what is right for one is not right for all. She does not feel what I feel—she does not suffer as I suffer." The old, the terrible dream, the grey fear of having been born to die without having lived, again possessed her, again laid hands upon her, held her with its cold, cruel, and strangling fingers. She shuddered. The world disappeared—was engulfed in the quick fever of the flesh; and, her teeth chattering slightly, she said, "I have my work at least," and, with her brain throbbing—a throbbing that died slowly away as the mind cleared—she wrote steadily for two hours.

And thus ended, ended as completely as if everyone con- cerned in it had been sunk in the deepest depths of the sea, May Gould's Dublin adventure. It was scarcely spoken of again, and when they met at a ball given by the officers stationed in Galway, Alice was astonished to find that she experienced no antipathy whatever towards this rich-blooded young person. "My dear guardian angel, come and sit with me in this corner; I'd sooner talk to you than anyone—we won't go

down yet awhile—we'll make the men wait." May was full
of affectionate impulses, and her outspokenness was often
inexpressibly seductive. "Now I won't let you go, dear," she
would say to her girl friends when they came to see her; "we
have only a leg of mutton—mother is economising—but you
must stay and eat it with us." Her charm was the ever-
varying but ever-recognisable charm that all frankly sensual
natures exercise; and when she put her arms round Alice's
waist and told her the last news of Violet and her marquis,
Alice abandoned herself to the caress and listened.

Violet's marriage and the collection of rents were now the
two subjects that possessed the heart of Galway. Rents were
being paid; and, as an old suit of clothes drawn out of its
slumber in the back of the wardrobe will come out looking
spick and span, Galway in the autumn of 1882 bloomed into
all its old freshness and vigour. The landlords cried the Land
Act was ruin, but only to conceal their joy. For they knew
that if the Government fixed their rents, the Government
would have to enforce the payment of those rents. The
Arrears Act had passed, and it would put large sums of money
into their pockets. The Land League, which Mr. Forster's
Coercion Act had failed to put down, but, as we have already
seen, had not failed to disorganise, had during the imprison-
ment of its leaders become broken up into small parties.
And these, swollen with rancorous jealousies and separate
ambitions, had, in their efforts to crush each other, almost
forgotten the existence of their common foe—landlordism, and
great wrongs had been committed. The burden of terror had
slipped from the landlords' shoulders on to the peasantry. All
who had private grievances had taken advantage of these
seasons of lawlessness to avenge them. No one could trust his
next-door neighbour. Armed gangs demanding money broke
into the cottages by night. It had become plain to all that
rent-paying was preferable to an occult, an ever-imminent
danger from which none could make sure of defending themselves. Therefore the Crimes Bill, wisely and judiciously
administered by Lord Spencer, came an equal blessing to all,
and the lurid phantom of the League vanished; yes, vanished
suddenly as a card up the sleeve of a skilful conjurer.

The harvest had been plentiful, stock of all kinds was in
great demand, a craze for money-making had set in; none
could afford to run the risk of having his cattle houghed, an

in a moment—literally in six weeks—all the colossal machinery,
so far-reaching in its consequences, tumbled into a dust so fine
that the winds of autumn seemed to have carried it away.
Peasants and landlords rubbed their eyes, stared aghast, and
then, laughing like people awakening from a nightmare, they
resumed their ordinary occupations. The change was as
marvellous as any transformation-scene. People thought
differently, spoke differently, acted differently; stock was
bought and sold without restrictions of any kind; carriages
filled with pink-dressed young ladies traversed the country,
and the training of horses occupied every manly and many a
female mind. The stoning of the hounds, the poisoning of
the covers, were only remembered as an ugly dream; in a trice
the gentry disbanded their black-coated bodyguards, and
resumed their own red coats. Mr. Scully summed up the
situation when he said, " Rents paid, cattle high, Land League
dead." He might have added, "And my daughter's going to
marry a marquis." Mrs. Barton wondered he did not, but
Mr. Scully was a man of business, and he never interfered
with his womenfolk.

Mrs. Barton had, indeed, thought of dismissing him from the
agency, but after much consideration she had decided that this
bit of revenge would keep, and would be employed with greater
effect later on. For the present it was clear to her that she
would have to pretend that she had never gone in for Lord
Kilcarney, and make Violet Scully a handsome present. To
do this was disagreeable, and it was, if possible, still more
galling to listen with a smiling face to all the different accounts
of the wedding with which Mrs. Barton was afflicted. Mrs.
Gould was the chief torturer. All letters concerning the *event*
she forwarded to Brookfield. She was full of information concerning the bitterness with which the family viewed the
match, she had a store of racy anecdotes of how the Ladies
Burke had received Mrs. Scully, and she could furnish the
latest details of a recently-resuscitated legend. For it was
now formally asserted, and with all due emphasis, that thirty
years ago the late marquis had entered a grocer's shop in
Galway to buy a pound of tea for an importuning beggar:
"And what do you think my dear?—it was Mrs. Scully who
served it out to him." And when somebody, it never was
known who, but it was said to have been Olive, suggested
that it was all fate, for Violet had played the beggar-maid to

King Cophetua, the brain-excitement grew acute as that
attendant on solemn rites,—and, overcome with mysticity, the
women lay prone before the coincidence.

At such stories Mrs. Barton laughed bewitchingly; but Mrs.
Gould's mission in life was neither to soothe troubled waters
nor to fan raging fires, she merely propagated gossip industriously. Her information might be dubious, but it was always
abundant; and if her words were sometimes as balm, they
were sometimes as poison. She is now declaring that the
Kilcarney estates will still yield two thousand a year to the
young couple to live upon; a grey cloud steals over Mrs.
Barton's face, but Mrs. Gould continues ruthlessly:

"And Kilcarney Castle!" She would read from a letter she
had received only that morning from a cousin of hers. "There
are three avenues and five staircases, and six towers;" and
the three avenues, the five staircases, and the six towers
passioned the county of Galway for more than a month.

But, although the foremost, Mrs. Gould was not the only
news-depôt in the county. Everyone had arranged with their
Dublin friends for a constant supply of the latest details, and
during the winter months the letters fell like rain; and they
were circulated like magazines. The Brennans, the Duffys,
the Ladies Cullen were in constant communication. An on-
dit about a wedding present was sufficient cause for a visit;
a scrap of information concerning the bridesmaids took in
the female mind the importance that the fixing of a judicial
rent did in the male. The orchestra of praise was gradually
working up to a crescendo. The riches that awaited the bride
were shrieked forth by the fiddle-like voices of the Brennans
and Duffys, and, trumpeting loudly, the Ladies Cullen announced news from the peerage. For, besides the Marquis's
immediate relatives, Violet would be connected with an infinite
number of grand people; a duke, it was whispered, was among
the number. Lord So-and-so had presented her with one of
the finest pearl necklaces that money could buy, and the
Marquis of So-and-so with a tiara of diamonds, and Earls of
This and That with sets of Sèvres china. There were bracelets,
oriental vases, dressing-cases, card-cases, fans; and all the corres-
pondents spoke rapturously of a marble group of clustering
doves.

Then there was the trousseau. Everybody brought fresh
details; picturesque descriptions of the trimmings of the

morning gowns were given, and elaborate accounts in technical language were forwarded of the evening toilettes—toilettes that she would wear in Roman society, for it was understood that the bride and bridegroom would proceed direct to Italy. Nothing was omitted. There were to be so many pairs of embroidered slippers, so many embroidered pocket-handkerchiefs—mention was even made of the lace-trimmed chemises and drawers *en batiste*, with a blue ribbon above the knee.

The letters continued to fall like rain, and the country lived in a state of nervous irritation. The pale cheeks of Lord Rosshill's seven daughters waxed a hectic red; the Ladies Cullen grew more angular, and smiled and cawed more cruelly; Mrs. Barton, the Brennans, and Duffys cackled more warmly and continuously; and Bertha, the terror of the *débutantes*, beat the big drum more furiously than ever. The postscripts to her letters were particularly terrible: "And to think that the grocer's daughter should come in for all this honour. It is she who will turn up her nose at us at the Castle next year." "Ah, had I known what was going to happen it is I who would have pulled the fine feathers out of her." Day after day, week after week, the agony was protracted, until every heart grew weary of the strain put upon it and sighed for relief. But it was impossible to leave off thinking and talking; and the various accounts of orange-blossoms and the brides-maids, that in an incessant postal stream were poured during the month of January into Galway, seemed to provoke rather than abate the marriage fever. The subject was inexhaustible, and little else was spoken of until it was time to pack up trunks and prepare for the Castle season. The bride, it was stated, would be present at the second Drawing-room in March.

Nevertheless Alice noticed that the gladness of last year was gone out of their hearts; none expected much, and all remembered a little of the disappointments they had suffered. A little of the book had been read; the lines of white girls standing about the pillars in Patrick's Hall, the empty waltz tunes and the long hours passed with their chaperons were terrible souvenirs to pause upon. Still they must fight on to the last, there is no going back—there is nothing for them to go back to. There is no hope in life for them but the vague hope of a husband. So they keep on to the last, becoming gradually more spiteful and puerile, their ideas of life and things growing gradually narrower, until, in their thirty-fifth or

fortieth year, they fall into the autumn heaps, to lie there
forgotten, or to be blown hither or thither by every wind
that blows—poor old women who have never lived at all.

Two of Lord Rosshill's daughters had determined to try
their luck again, and a third was undecided; the Ladies
Cullen said that they had their school to attend to and
could not leave Galway; poverty compelled the Brennans
and Duffys to remain at home. Alice would willingly have
done the same, but, tempted by the thin chance that she
might meet with Harding, she yielded to her mother's per-
suasions. But in this she was disappointed, and she found
Dublin more lamentable and soul-wearying than ever. It
presented no new feature. The same absence of conviction,
the same noisy gossiping, and inability to see over the horizon
of Merrion Square, the same servile adoration of officialism,
the same meanness committed to secure an invitation to the
Castle, the same sing-song waltz tunes, the same miserable,
mocking, melancholy, muslin hours were endured by the same
white martyrs. The marchioness passes down the room, and
their eyes glisten with envy and their lips suck greedily at the
probability that she will be sold up in a year. But the present
is the present, and she enjoys it. She will sometimes acknow-
ledge acquaintanceship with her old schoolfellows; and with
the Bartons she is especially affable; she has fought and beaten
them;—she can afford to be generous, and she often dines with
them in Mount Street.

And if the Castle remained unchanged, Mount Street lost
nothing of its original aspect. Experience had apparently
taught Mrs. Barton nothing; she knew but one set of tricks—
if they failed she repeated them : she was guided by the indubi-
tableness of instinct rather than by the more wandering light
that is reason. Mr. Barton, who it was feared might talk of
painting, and so distract the attention from more serious
matters, was left in Galway, and amid eight or nine men collected here, there, and everywhere out of the hotels and barrack-
rooms, the three ladies sat down to dinner. Mrs. Barton, who
could have talked to twenty men, and have kept them amused,
was severely handicapped by the presence of her daughters.
Olive, at the best of times, could do little more than laugh; and
as Alice never had anything to say to the people she met at
her mother's house, the silences that hung over the Mount
Street dinner-table were funereal in intensity and length.

From time to time questions were asked relating to the Castle, the weather, and the theatre.

Therefore beyond the fact that neither Lord Kilcarney nor Mr. Harding was present, the girls passed their second season in the same manner as their first. *Les deux pièces de résistance* at Mount Street were a dissipated young English lord and a gouty old Irish distiller; and Mrs. Barton was making every effort to secure one of these. A pianist was ordered to attend regularly at four o'clock. And now if Alice was relieved of the duty of spelling through the doleful strains of "Dream Faces," she was forced to go round and round with the distiller until an extra glass of port forced the old gentleman to beg mercy of Mrs. Barton. At one o'clock in the morning the young lord used to enter the Kildare Street Club extenuated. But not much way was made with either, and when one returned to London and the other to a sick-bed, Olive abandoned herself to a series of flirtations. At the Castle she danced with all who asked her, and she sat out dances in the darkest corners of the most distant rooms with every officer stationed in Dublin. Mrs. Barton never refused an invitation to any dance, no matter how low, and in all the obscure "afternoons" in Mount Street and Pembroke Street Olive's blonde cameo-like face was seen laughing with every paltry official of Cork Hill and the gewgaw gig-men of Kildare Street.

In May the Bartons went abroad. Then followed the interminable series of flirtations with foreign titles. French Counts, Spanish Dukes, Russian Princes, Swedish noblemen of all kinds, and a goodly number of English refugees with irreproachable neckties and a taste for baccarat. And in the balmy gardens of Ostend and Boulogne, jubilant with June and the overture of Masaniello, Milord and Mrs. Barton walked in front, talking and laughing gracefully. Olive chose him who flattered her the most outrageously; and Alice strove hard to talk to the least objectionable of the men she was brought in contact with. Amid these specious talkers there were a few who reminded her of Mr. Harding, and she hoped later on to be able to turn her present experiences to account. There was, of course, much dining at cafés and dining at the casinos, and evening walks along the dark shore. Alice often feared for her sister, but the girl's vanity and lightheadedness were her safeguards, and she returned to Galway only a little wearied by the long chase after amusement.

The soft Irish summer is pleasant after the glare of foreign towns. Now all the mountain perspectives are veiled in haze, in Ireland an unfailing promise of a continuance of fair weather, and the country lies green-dozing in the silvery light. You know it all ! The rickety stone walls and the herds of cattle, the deep curved lines of the plantations of the domain lands, the long streaks of brown bog, the flashing tarns of bog-water, and the ruined cottage. For Alice there was much charm in these familiar signs ; and, although she did not approve of—although she would not care ever to meet them again—the people she had met at Ostend and Dieppe had interested her. They were at least neither so narrow-minded nor so ignorant as the Dubliners; and from them, although not in a great and effective way, she had picked up ideas of the variety of life, and now with these ideas germinating in her, a time of quiet, a time for reading and thinking, came after the noise of casinos and the glitter of fireworks as a welcome change. The liberty she had enjoyed, the sense it had brought with it that she was neither a doll nor a victim, had rendered her singularly happy. The plot of a new story was singing in her head, the characters flitted before her eyes, and to think of them, or to tell Cecilia of them, was a pleasure sufficient for all her daily desire. Olive, too, was glad. The sunlight has gone into her blood, and she romps with her mother and milord amid the hay, or, stretched at length, she listens to the green air of the lawn, and her dreams ripple like water along a vessel's side, and the white wake of the past bubbles and glistens behind her ; and when the life of the landscape is burnt out, and the day in dying seems to have left its soul behind, she stands watching, her thoughts curdling gently, the elliptical flight of the swallows through the gloom, and the flutter of the bats upon the dead sky.

But the evenings were long and silent, and the thoughtless brain, fed for many weeks upon noise and glitter, soon began to miss its accustomed stimulants. In the morning she sat with Barnes and tried to occupy herself with a little fancy-work, but the mechanical action of the fingers it involved irritated her, and the love-stories told by the smiling maid fostered the nerve-atrophy from which the girl suffered. And all the quick febrile revulsions of feeling were manifested in sudden twitchings of the face, and abrupt movements of the limbs. Mrs. Barton was keenly alive to what was passing in her daughter's mind, and she insisted on Olive's accompanying her to the tennis parties with which the county teemed. Sir Charles, Mr. Adair, and even poor Sir Richard were put forward as the most eligible of men.

"It is impossible to say when the big fish will be caught; it is often the last try that brings him to land," murmured Mrs. Barton. But Olive had lost courage, and could fix her thoughts on no one. And, often when they returned home, she would retire to her room to have a good cry. One evening Alice found her lying on her bed sobbing bitterly.

"Oh, Olive," exclaimed Alice, "what is the matter with you? What are you crying about in that way?"

"Leave me alone, Alice; oh, go away . . . . don't tease me, don't tease me . . . . I only want to be left alone."

"But listen, dear; can I do anything for you?"

"You! no, no, indeed you can't . . . . I only want to be left alone; that isn't much to ask . . . . I am so miserable, so unhappy; I wish I were dead."

"Dead?"

"Yes, dead; what's the use of living when I know that I shall be an old maid? . . . . We shall all be old maids. . . . What's the use of being pretty, either, when Violet, bag of bones that she is, got the marquis after all? . . . . I have been out two seasons now, and nothing has come of all the trying. And yet I was the belle of the season, wasn't I, Alice?" And now, looking more than ever like a cameo Niobe, Olive stared at her sister piteously. "Oh, yes, Alice, I know I shall be an old maid; and isn't it dreadful, and I the belle of the season? It makes me so unhappy . . . . no one ever heard of the belle (and I was the belle not of one but of two seasons) remaining an old maid. . . . I can understand a lot of ugly things not getting married, but I——"

Alice smiled, and half ironically she asked herself if Olive really suffered. No heart-pang was reflected in those blue mindless eyes; there was no heart to wound: only a little foolish vanity had been bruised.

"And to think," cried this whimpering beauty, when Alice had seen her successfully through a flood of hysterical tears, "that I was silly enough to give up dear Edward. . . . I am punished for it now . . . . indeed I am; and it was very

wicked of me—it was a great sin. I broke his heart. But
you know, Alice dear, that it was all mamma's fault; she
urged me on; and you know how I refused, how I resisted
her. . . . Didn't I resist—tell me? You know, and why
won't you say that I did resist?"

"You did, indeed, Olive; but you must not distress yourself, or you will make yourself ill."

"Yes, perhaps you are right, there's nothing makes one look
so ugly as crying . . . . and if I lost my looks and met
Edward he might not care for me . . . . he'd be disappointed,
I mean—but I haven't lost my looks; I am just as pretty as
I was when I came out first. Am I not, Alice?"

"Indeed you are, dear."

"You don't think I have gone off a bit—now do tell me?
and I want to ask you what you think of my hair in a fringe;
Papa says it isn't classical, but that's nonsense. I wish I
knew how Edward would like me to wear it."

"But you mustn't think of him, Olive dear; you know
mother would never hear of it."

"I can't help thinking of him. . . . And now I will tell you
something, Alice, if you promise me on your word of honour
not to scold me, and, above all, not to tell mamma."

"I promise."

"Well, the other day I was walking at the end of the lawn
feeling so very miserable. You don't know how miserable I
feel; you are never miserable, for you think of nothing but
your books. Well, mind you have given me your word not to
tell anyone . . . I saw Captain Hibbert riding along the road,
and when he saw me he stopped his horse and kissed his hand
to me."

"And what did you do?"

"I don't know what I did . . . he called me, and then I
saw Milord coming along the road, and I fled; but, oh, isn't it
cruel of mamma to have forbidden Edward to come and see us?
and he loves me as much as ever, I know he does."

This was not the moment to advise her sister against
clandestine meetings with Captain Hibbert; she was sobbing
violently, and Alice had to assure her again and again that no
one who had been the belle of the season had ever remained
an old maid. But Alice (having well in mind the fate that
had befallen May Gould) grew not a little alarmed when,
in the course of next week, she suddenly noticed that Olive

was in the habit of going out for long walks alone: and that she invariably returned in a state of high spirits, all the languor and weariness seeming to have fallen from her.

Alice once thought of following her sister. She watched her open the wicket-gate and walk across the meadows towards the Lawler domain. There was a bypath there leading to the highroad, but the delicacy of their position in relation to the owners prevented the Bartons from ever making use of it. Nor did Alice fail to notice that about the same time, Barnes, on the pretence of arranging the room for the evening, would strive to drive her from her writing-table, and beds were made and unmade, dresses were taken out of the wardrobe, and importuning conversations were begun. But, taking no heed of the officious maid, Alice, her thoughts tense with anxiety, sat at her window watching the slender figure of the girl growing dim in the dying light. Once she did not return until it was quite dark, and, reproaching herself bitterly for having remained so long silent, Alice walked across the pleasure-grounds to meet her.

"What, you here?" cried Olive, surprised at finding her sister waiting for her at the wicket. She was out of breath; she had evidently been running.

"Yes, Olive, I was anxious to speak to you—you must know that it is very wrong to meet Captain Hibbert,—and in the secrecy of a wood!"

"Who told you I had been to meet Captain Hibbert? I suppose you have been following me?"

"No, Olive, I have not, and you have no right to accuse me of such meanness. I have not been following you, but I cannot help putting two and two together. You told me something of this once before, and since then you have scarcely missed an evening."

"Well, I don't see any harm in meeting Edward; he is going to marry me."

"Going to marry you?"

"Yes, going to marry me; is there anything so very extraordinary in that? . . . . Mamma had no right to break off the match, and I am not going to remain an old maid."

"And have you told mother about this?"

"No, where's the use, since she won't hear of it?"

"And are you going to run away with Captain Hibbert?"

"Run away with him!" exclaimed Olive, laughing strangely. "No, of course I am not."

"And how are you to marry him if you don't tell mother?"

"I shall tell her when the time comes to tell her. And now, Alice dear, you will promise not to betray me, won't you? You will not speak about this to anyone, you promise me? if you did I know I should go mad or kill myself."

"But when will you tell mother of your resolution to marry Captain Hibbert?"

"Tell her? I'll tell her to-morrow if you like; that is to say if you will give me your word of honour not to speak to her about my meeting Edward in the Lawler Wood."

Afterwards Alice often wondered at her dulness in not guessing the truth. But at the time it did not occur to her that Olive might have made arrangements to elope with Captain Hibbert; and, on the understanding that all was to be explained on the following day, she promised to keep her sister's secret.

CHAPTER IV.

LORD DUNGORY dined at Brookfield that evening. He noticed that Olive was nervous and restless, and he reminded her of what a French poet had said on the subject of beauty. But she only turned her fair head impatiently, and a little later on when her mother spoke to her she burst into tears. Nor was she as easily consoled as usual, and she did not become calm until Mrs. Barton suggested that her dear child was ill, and that she would go upstairs and put her to bed. Then, looking a little alarmed, Olive declared she was quite well, but she passionately begged to be left alone. As they left the dining-room she attempted to slip away; Alice made a movement as if to follow her, but Mrs. Barton said:

"Leave her to herself, Alice; she would rather be left alone. She has overstrained her nerves, that is all."

Olive heard these words with a singular satisfaction, and as she ascended the stairs from the first landing her heart beat less violently. On the threshold of her room she paused to listen for the drawing-room door to shut. Through the silent house the lock sounded sharply.

"I hope none of them will come upstairs bothering after me," the girl murmured to herself; "if they do I shall go mad." And standing in the middle of the floor she looked round the room vacantly, unable to collect her thoughts. The wardrobe was on her right, and, seeing herself in the glass, she wondered if she were looking well. Her eyes wandered from her face to her shoulders, and hence to her feet. Going over to the toilette-table she sought amid her boots, and having selected a strong pair, she commenced to button them. Her back was turned to the door, and at the slightest sound she started into an upright position and seized the hair-brushes. Once or twice the stairs creaked, and she felt something would occur to stop her. Her heart was beating so violently that she thought she was going to be ill ; and she almost burst out crying because she could not make up her mind if she should put on a hat and travelling-shawl, or run down to the wood as she was, to meet the Captain. "He will surely," she thought, "have something in the carriage to put around me, but he may bring the dog-cart, and it looks very cold, very cold . . . But if Alice or mamma saw me coming downstairs with a shawl on, they would at once suspect something, and I should never be able to get away . . . I wonder what time it is . . . I promised to meet Edward at nine, he will of course wait for me, but what time is it? . . . We dined at half-past seven . . . we were an hour at dinner, half-past eight, and I have been ten minutes here . . . It must be nearly nine now . . . and it will take me ten minutes to get to the corner of the road . . . The house is quiet now."

On the top of the stairs the girl listened. Nothing could be heard but the occasional tinkling of a guitar, and the high notes of a baritone voice singing *Il Balen.*

Olive ran down a few steps, but at that moment heavy foot-steps and a jingling of glasses announced that the butler was carrying glasses from the dining-room to the pantry. "When will he cease, when will he cease; will he hang about that passage all night?" the girl asked herself tremblingly ; and so cruel, so poignant had her suspense become, that had it been prolonged much further her overwrought nerves would have given way, and she would have lapsed into a fit of hysterics. But the tray full of glasses she had heard jingling were now being washed, and the irritative butler did not stir forth again. This was Olive's opportunity. From the proximity of the drawing-room to the hall-door it was impossible for her to open it without being heard ; the kitchen-door was equally, even more, dangerous, and she could hear the servants stirring in the passages ; there was no safe way of getting out of the house unseen, except through the dining-room.

The candles were lighted, the crumbs were still on the table-cloth ; passing behind the red curtain she unlocked the French window, and a moment she shivered in the keen wind that was blowing.

It was almost as bright as day   A September moon soared like a bird above the dark woods ; here indicated sharply, with the ebony leaves of the high branches stamped on the clear sky, to the right and left floating away in grey and mazy lines that melted and disappeared in the blue elusive distance. The house lay log-like in the white glow, and the chestnut-trees threw back shadows upon the sward.

There was an icy stillness in the air, and the pale high moon seemed so lonely that instinctively the girl shrank from her resolution. But her thoughts were febrile and weak, and a moment after she was peering from behind a buttress, wondering if the drawing-room blinds were down, and she might pass the windows without being seen. In a broken and fragmentary way the various aspects of the journey that lay before her were anticipated: as she ran across the garden swards she saw the post-horses galloping in front of her; as her nervous fingers strove to unfasten the wicket, she thought of the railway-carriage; and as she passed under the great dark trunks of the chestnut-trees she dreamed of Edward's arm that would soon be cast protectingly around her, and his face, softer than the leafy shadows above her, would be leaned upon her, and his eyes filled with a brighter light than the moon's would look down into hers.

The white meadow that she crossed so swiftly gleamed like the sea, and the cows loomed through the greyness like peaceful apparitions. But the dark wood with its sepulchral fir-tops and mysteriously-spreading beech-trees was full of formless terror, and once the girl screamed as the birds flew with an awful sound through the dark undergrowth. A gloomy wood by night has terrors for the bravest, and it was only the certainty that she was leaving girl-life—chaperons, waltz-tunes, and bitter sneering, for ever—that gave courage to proceed. A bit of mossgrown wall, a singularly-shaped holly-bush, a white stone, took fantastic and supernatural appearances, and once she stopped, paralysed with fear, before the grotesque shadow that a dead tree threw over an unexpected glade. A strange bird rose from the bare branches, and at that moment her dress was caught by a bramble, and, when her shriek tore the dark stillness, a hundred wings flew through the pallor of the waning moon.

At the end of this glade there was a paling and a stile that Olive would have to cross, and she could now hear, as she ran forward, the needles of the silver firs rustling with a pricking sound in the wind. The heavy branches stretched from either side, and Olive thought when she had passed this dernful alley she would have nothing more to fear; and she ran on blindly until she almost fell in the arms of someone whom she instantly believed to be Edward.

"Oh! Edward, Edward, I am nearly dead with fright!" she exclaimed.

"I am not Edward," a woman answered. Olive started a step backwards; she would have fainted, but at the moment the words were spoken Mrs. Lawler's face was revealed in a beam of weak light that fell through a vista in the branches.

"Who are you? Let me pass."

"Who am I? You know well enough; we haven't been neighbours for fifteen years without knowing each other by sight. So you are going to run away with Captain Hibbert!"

"Oh, Mrs. Lawler, let me pass . . . . I am in a great hurry, I cannot wait; and you won't say anything about meeting me in the wood, will you?"

"Let you pass, indeed . . . and what do you think I came here for? Oh, I know all about it—all about the corner of the road, and the carriage and post-horses! a very nice little plan and very nicely arranged, but I'm afraid it won't come off —at least, not to-night."

"Oh, won't it, and why?" cried Olive, clasping her hands. "Then it was Edward who sent you to meet me, to tell me that—that . . . What has happened?"

"Sent me to tell you!" . . . Whom do you take me for? Is it for a . . . well, a nice piece of cheek! I carry your messages? Well, I never!"

"Then what did you come here for—how did you know? . . ."

"How did I know? That's my business. What did I come here for? What do you think? Why, to prevent you from going off with Teddy."

"With Teddy!"

"Yes, with Teddy. Do you think no one calls him Teddy but yourself?"

Then Olive understood, and, with her teeth clenched she said, "No, it isn't true; it is a lie; I will not believe it. . . . Let me pass. . . . What business have you to detain me?—what right have you to speak to me? We don't know you. . . no one knows you: you are a bad woman whom no one will know."

"A bad woman! I like that—and from you. And what do you want to be, why are you running away from home?

Why, to be what I was. . . . We're all alike, the same blood runs in our veins, and when the devil is in us we must have sweethearts, get them how we may: the airs and graces come on after; they are only so much trimming."

"How dare you insult me, you bad woman! Let me pass; I don't know what you mean."

"Oh yes, you do. You think Teddy will take you off to Paris, and spoon you and take you out; but he won't, at least not to-night. I shan't give him up so easily as you think, my lady."

"Give him up! What is he to you? How dare you speak so of my future husband? Captain Hibbert only loves me, he has often told me so."

"Loves nobody but you! I suppose you think that he never kissed, or spooned, or took anyone on his knee but you . . . Well, I suppose at twenty we'd believe anything a man told us; and we always think we are getting the first of it when we are only getting someone else's leavings. But it isn't for chicks of girls like you that a man cares, it isn't to you a man comes for the love he wants; your kisses are very skim-milk indeed. It is in our arms that they learn what passion is; it is we who teach them the words of love that they murmur afterwards in your ears."

The form here is nineteenth century, but the spirit is eternal; and, looking on Mrs. Lawler, drawn up to her full height, her opera-cloak white and vague beneath the light of a pale moon, it was easy to associate her and her aims with the dignity of a heroine of a Greek drama. The women looked at each other in silence, and both heard the needles shaken through the darkness above them. Mrs. Lawler stood by the stile, her hand was laid on the paling. At last Olive said:

"Let me pass. I will not listen to you any longer; nor do I believe a word you have said. We all know what you are; you are a bad woman whom no one will visit. Let me pass," and pushing passionately forward she attempted to cross the stile. Then Mrs. Lawler took her by the shoulder and threw her roughly back. She fell heavily to the ground.

"Now you had better get up and go home," said Mrs. Lawler, and she approached the prostrate girl. "I didn't mean to hurt you; but you shan't elope with Teddy if I can prevent it. Why don't you get up?"

"Oh! my leg, my leg; you have broken my leg!"

"Let me help you up."

"Don't touch me, you vile creature," said Olive attempting to rise; but the moment she put her right foot to the ground she shrieked with pain, and fell again.

"Well, if you are going to take it in that way, you may remain where you are, and I can't go and ring them up at Brookfield. I don't think there will be much eloping done to-night, so farewell."

. . . . .

Many and passionate were the efforts Olive made to rise, but the pain was too piercing, and, unable to reach the paling, she lay on the wet ground moaning, and listening between her moans for hours to the mysterious noises and still more mysterious silences of the night. The moon rose higher and higher, and, wan and pale as the girl's face, floated over the tall firs; and the fantastic shadow of the dead tree turned and turned until it became lost in other shadows; and the bird of prey came back with a loud clapping of wings, and it roosted till dawn on the topmost branch.

CHAPTER V.

ABOUT ten o'clock on the night of Olive's elopement, Alice knocked tremblingly at her mother's door.

"Mother," she said, "Olive is not in her room, nor yet in the house; I have looked for her everywhere."

"She is downstairs with her father in the studio," said Mrs. Barton; and, signing to her daughter to be silent, she led her out of hearing of Barnes, who was folding and putting some dresses away in the wardrobe.

"I have been down to the studio," Alice replied in a whisper.

"Then I am afraid she has run away with Captain Hibbert. But we shall gain nothing by sending men out with lanterns and making a fuss; by this time she is well on her way to Dublin. She might have done better than Captain Hibbert, but she might also have done worse. She will write to us in a few days to tell us that she is married, and to beg of us to forgive her."

And that night Mrs. Barton slept even more happily, with her mind more completely at rest, than usual; whereas Alice, fevered with doubt and apprehension, lay awake. At seven o'clock she was at her window, watching the grey morning splinter into sunlight over the quiet fields. But suddenly all vaporous thoughts of Olive and her lover were crushed into silence, and, paralysed with fear, Alice watched the gamekeeper coming towards the house with a woman in his arms. The suspicion that her sister might have been killed in an agrarian outrage gripped her heart like an iron hand. She ran downstairs, and, rushing across the gravel, opened the wicket-gate. Olive was moaning with pain, but her moans were a sweet reassurance in Alice's ears, and without attempting to understand the man's story of how Miss Olive had sprained her ankle in crossing the stile in their wood, and how he had found her as he was going his rounds, she gave the man five shillings, thanked him, and sent him away. Barnes and the butler then carried Olive upstairs, and in the midst of much confusion Mr. Barton rode down the avenue in quest of Dr. Reed—galloped down the avenue, his pale hair blowing in the breeze.

"I wish you had come straight to me," said Mrs. Barton to Alice, as soon as Barnes had left the room. "We'd have got her upstairs between us, and then we might have told any story we liked about her illness."

"But the Lawlers' gamekeeper would know all about it."

"Ah, yes, that's true. I never heard of anything so unfortunate in my life. An elopement is never very respectable, but an elopement that does not succeed, when the girl comes home again is just as bad as . . . . I cannot think how Olive could have managed to meet Captain Hibbert and arrange all this business, without my finding it out. I feel sure she must have had the assistance of a third party. I feel certain that all this is Barnes' doing. I am beginning to hate that woman, with her perpetual smile, but it won't do to send her away now; we must wait." And on these words Mrs. Barton approached the bed.

Shaken with sudden fits of shivering, and her teeth chattering, Olive lay staring blindly at her mother and sister. Her eyes were expressive at once of fear and pain.

"And now, my own darling, will you tell me how all this happened?"

"Oh, not now, mother, not now . . . I don't know; I couldn't help it. . . . You mustn't scold me, I feel too ill to bear it."

"I am not thinking of scolding you, dearest, and you need not tell me anything you do not like. . . . I know you were going to run away with Captain Hibbert, and met with an accident crossing the stile in the Lawler Wood."

"Oh, yes, yes; I met that horrid woman, Mrs. Lawler: she knew all about it, and was waiting for me at the stile She said lots of dreadful things to me . . . I don't remember what; that she had more right to Edward than I . . ."

"Never mind, dear; don't agitate yourself thinking of what she said . . . ."

"And then, as I tried to pass her, she pushed me and I fell, and hurt my ankle so badly that I could not get up; and she taunted me, and she said she could not help me home because we were not on visiting terms. And I lay in that dreadful wood all night. But I can't speak any more, I feel too ill; and I never wish to see Edward again . . . . the pain of my ankle is something terrible."

Mrs. Barton looked at Alice expressively, and she whispered in her ear :

"This is all Barnes' doing, but we cannot send her away . . . We must put a bold face on it, and brave it out."

Dr. Reed was announced.

"Oh, how do you do, doctor ? . . . . It was so good of you to come at once. . . . We were afraid Mr. Barton would not find you at home. I am afraid that Olive has sprained her foot badly. Last night she went out for a walk rather late in the evening, and, in endeavouring to cross a stile, she slipped and hurt herself so badly that she was unable to return home, and lay exposed for several hours to the heavy night dews. I am afraid she has caught a severe cold. . . . She has been shivering . . . ."

"Can I see her foot ?"

"Certainly. Olive, dear, will you allow Dr. Reed to see your ankle ?"

"Oh, take care, mamma ; you are hurting me !" shrieked the girl, as Mrs. Barton removed the bedclothes. At this moment a knock was heard at the door.

"Who on earth is this ?" cried Mrs. Barton. "Alice, will you go and see ? Say that I am engaged, and can attend to nothing now."

When Alice returned to the bedside she drew her mother imperatively towards the window. "Captain Hibbert is waiting in the drawing-room. He says he must see you."

At the mention of Captain Hibbert's name Mrs. Barton's admirably-governed temper showed signs of yielding : her face contracted and she bit her lips.

"You must go down and see him. Tell him that Olive is very ill and that the doctor is with her. And mind you, you must not answer any questions. Say that I cannot see him, but that I am greatly surprised at his forcing his way into my house after what has passed between us ; that I hope he will never intrude himself upon us again ; that I cannot have my daughter's life endangered, and that, if he insists on persecuting us, I shall have to write to his Colonel."

" Do you not think that father would be the person to make such explanations ? "

" You know your father could not be trusted to talk sensibly for five minutes—at least," she said, correcting herself, " on anything that did not concern painting or singing . . . But," she continued, following her daughter to the door, " on second thoughts I do not think it would be advisable to bring matters to a crisis . . . I do not know how this affair will affect Olive's chances, and if he is anxious to marry her I do not see why he should not . . . she may not be able to get any better. So you had better, I think, put him off—pretend that we are very angry, and get him to promise not to try to see or to write to Olive until, let us say, the end of the year. It will only make him more keen on her."

When Alice opened the drawing-room door Captain Hibbert rushed forward ; his soft eyes were bright with excitement, and his tall figure was thrown into a beautiful pose when he stopped.

" Oh, I beg your pardon, Miss Barton. I had expected your sister."

" My sister is very ill in bed, and the doctor is with her."

" Ill in bed ! "

" Yes, she sprained her ankle last night in attempting to cross the stile in the wood at the end of our lawn."

" Oh, that was the reason . . . then . . . Can I see your sister for a few minutes ? "

" It is quite impossible ; and my mother desires me to say that she is very surprised that you should come here. . . . . We know all about your attempt to induce Olive to leave her home."

" Then she has told you ? But if you knew how I love her you would not blame me. What else could I do ? Your mother would not let me see her, and she was very unhappy at home ; you did not know this, but I did, and if luck hadn't been against me. . . . Ah ! but what's the use in talking of luck ; luck was against me, or she would have been my wife now. And what a little thing suffices to blight a man's happiness in life ; what a little, oh, what a little ! " he said, speaking in a voice full of bitterness, and he buried his face in his hands.

Alice's eyes as she looked at him were expressive of her thoughts—they beamed at once with pity and admiration. He was but the ordinary handsome young man that in England nature seems to reproduce in everlasting stereotype. Long graceful legs, clad in tight-fitting trousers, slender hips rising architecturally to square wide shoulders, a thin strong neck and a tiny head—yes, a head so small that an artist would at once mark off eight on his sheet of double elephant. And now he lay over the back of a chair weeping like a child, in the intensity of his grief he was no longer commonplace, and as Alice looked at this superb animal thrown back in a superb abandonment of pose, her heart filled with the natural pity that the female feels always for the male in distress, and the impulse within her was to put her arms about him and console him; and then she understood her sister's passion for him, and her mind formulated it thus: " How handsome he is ! Any girl would like a man like that," And as Alice surrendered herself to those sensuous, or rather romantic feelings, her nature quickened to a sense of pleasure, and she grew gentler with him, and was glad to listen while he sobbed out his sorrows to her.

" Oh, why, " he exclaimed, " did she fall over that thrice-accursed stile ! In five minutes more we would have been locked in each other's arms, and for ever. I had a couple of the best post-horses in Gort ; they'd have taken us to Athenry in a couple of hours, and then . . . Oh ! what luck, what luck ! "

" But do you not know that Olive met Mrs. Lawler in the wood, and that it was she who . . ."

" What do you say ? . . . You don't mean to tell me that it was Mrs. Lawler who prevented Olive from meeting me ? " Then grinding his teeth he said, " Oh ! the vileness and the baseness ! So she dared do that, the beastly creature ! " and, looking a tower of athletic grace, he raised his arms, as if he would crush his enemy into the earth.

" Oh, what beasts, what devils women are," he said; " and the worst of it is that one cannot be even with them, and they know it. . . . If you only knew," he said, turning almost fiercely upon Alice, " how I loved your sister, you would pity me ; but I suppose it is all over now. Is she very ill ? "

" We don't know yet. She has sprained her ankle very badly, and is shivering terribly ; she was lying out all night in the wet wood."

He did not answer at once. He walked once or twice up and down the room, and then he said, taking Alice's hand in his, "Will you be a friend to me, Miss Barton?" He could get no further, for tears were rolling down his cheeks.

Alice looked at him tenderly; she was much touched by the manifestation of his love, and at the end of a long silence she said—

"Now, Captain Hibbert, I want you to listen to me. Don't cry any more, but listen."

"I daresay I look a great fool."

"No, indeed you do not," she answered; and then in kindly-worded phrases she told him that, at least for the present, he must not attempt to correspond with Olive. "Give me your word of honour that you will neither write nor speak to her for, let us say, six months, and I will promise to be your friend."

"I will do anything you ask me to do, but will you in return promise to write and tell me how she is getting on, and if she is in any danger?"

"I think I can promise to do that; I will write and tell you how Olive is in a few days. Now we must say good-bye; and you will not forget your promise to me, as I shall not forget mine to you."

When Alice went upstairs, Dr. Reed and Mrs. Barton were talking on the landing.

"And what do you think, doctor?" asked the anxious mother.

"It is impossible to say. She has evidently received a severe nervous shock, and this and the exposure to which she was subjected may develop into something serious. You will give her that Dover's powder to-night, and you will see that she has absolute quiet and rest. Have you got a reliable nurse?"

"Yes, the young ladies have a maid; I think Barnes can be trusted to carry out your orders, doctor."

"Oh, mamma, I hope you will allow me to nurse my sister; I should not like to leave her in charge of a servant."

"I am afraid you are not strong enough, dear."

"Oh, yes, I am; am I not strong enough, doctor?"

Dr. Reed looked for a moment steadily at Alice. "Your sister will," he said, "require a good deal of looking after. But if you will not overdo it I think you seem quite strong enough to nurse her. But you must not sit up at night with her too regularly; you must share the labour with someone."

"She will do that with me," said Mrs. Barton, speaking more kindly, Alice thought, than she had ever heard her speak before.

Then a wailing voice was heard calling to Alice.

"Go in and see what she wants, dear, but you will not encourage her to talk much; the doctor does not wish it."

The room did not look the same to Alice as it had ever looked before. Her eyes fell on the Persian rugs laid between the two white beds and the tall glass in the warbrobe where Olive wasted half-an-hour every evening, examining her beauty. Would she ever do so again? Now a broken reflection of feverish eyes and blonde hair was what remained. The white curtains of the chimneypiece had been drawn aside, a bright fire was burning, and Barnes was removing a foot-pan of hot water.

"Sit down here by me, Alice; I want to talk to you."

"The doctor has forbidden you to talk, dear; he says you must have perfect rest and quiet."

"I must talk a little to you; if I didn't I should go mad."

"Well, what is it dear?"

"I will tell you presently," said the sick girl, glancing at Barnes.

"You can tidy up the room afterwards, Barnes; Miss Olive wants to talk to me now."

"Oh, Alice, tell me," cried the girl when the servant had left the room, "I don't want to ask mamma—she won't·tell me the exact truth; but you will. Tell me what the doctor said . . . did he say I was going to die?"

"Going to die? Olive, who ever heard of such a thing? You really must not give way to such fancies."

"Well, tell me what he said."

"He said that you had received a severe nervous shock, that you had been subjected to several hours' exposure, that you must take great care of yourself, and, above all, have perfect rest and quiet, and not excite yourself and not talk."

"Is that all he said? Then he cannot know how ill I feel; perhaps I ought to see another doctor. But I don't believe anyone could do me much good. Oh, I feel wretchedly ill, and somehow I seem to know I am going to die! It would be

very horrible to die : but young girls no older than I have died
—have been cut off in the beginning of their life. And we
have seen nothing of life, only a few balls and parties. It
would be terrible to die so soon. When Violet carried off
the marquis I felt so bitterly ashamed that I thought
I would have liked to die; but not now—now I know that
Edward loves me I would not care to die ; it would be terrible
to die before I was married. Wouldn't it, Alice ? . . . . . .
But you don't answer me; did you never think about
death ? "

Then, as the thin wailing voice sank into her ears, Alice
started from her dreams, and she strove to submit her attention to her sister.

"Yes, dear, of course I have. Death is, no doubt, a very
terrible thing, but we can do no good by thinking of it."

"Oh yes, we should, Alice, for this is not the only world—
there is another and a better one ; and, as mamma says, and
as religion says, we are only here to try and get a good place
in it. You are surprised to hear me speak like this; you think
I never think of anything but the colour of a bonnet-string,
but I do."

"I am sure you do, Olive; I never doubted it ; but I wish
you would now do what the doctor orders, and refrain from
talking and exciting yourself, and try and get well. You may
then think of death and other gloomy things as much as you
like."

"You don't understand, Alice ; one can't think of death
then—one has so much else to think of ; one is so taken up
with other ideas. It is only when one is ill that one really
begins to see what life is. You have never been ill, and you
don't know how terribly near death seems to have come—
very near. Perhaps I ought to see the priest; it would
be just as well, just in case I should die. Don't you think
so ? "

"I don't think there is any more danger of your dying now
than there was a month ago, dear, and I am sure you can have
nothing on your mind that demands immediate confession,"
she said, her voice trembling a little.

"Oh yes, I have, Alice, and a very great deal ; I have been
very wicked."

"Very wicked ! "

"Well, I know you aren't pious, Alice, and perhaps you

don't believe there is harm in such things, but I do; and I know it was very wrong, and perhaps a mortal sin, to try to run away with Edward."

Alice drew a long breath.

"But I loved him so very dearly, and I was so tired of staying at home and being taken out to parties; and then everything seemed to be going wrong. For, although I was the belle of the season, I did not get as many offers of marriage as I expected. Edward was, after all, the only one who proposed to me, and I was afraid of remaining an old maid; and when you are in love with a man you forget everything . . . at least I did; and when he asked to kiss me I couldn't refuse. You will not tell anyone, Alice dear, that I told you this." Alice shook her head, and Olive continued, in spite of all that the doctor had said.

"But you don't know how lonely I feel at home; you never feel lonely, I dare say, for you only think of your books and papers, and don't realise what a disgrace it would be if I didn't marry, and after all the trouble that mamma has taken . . but I don't know what will become of me now. I am going to be dreadfully ill, and when I get well I shall be pretty no longer; I am sure I am looking wretchedly; I must see myself—fetch the glass, Alice, Alice."

All that day and night Alice remained in the sickroom. Towards morning she lay down; but every five minutes she was disturbed: suffering from intense nervousness, Olive lay whining and calling incessantly to her. And when Barnes came and suddenly raised the blinds there were shrieks of pain; and the room had to be kept darkened. Dr. Reed said that at present he could not speak with any certainty, but he ordered several inches of the pale silky hair to be cut away and a cold lotion to be applied to the forehead, and some sliced lemons were given to her to suck. She was obviously very ill. The clear blue eyes were dull, the breathing quick, the skin dry and hot; and on the following day four leeches had to be applied to her ankle. They relieved her somewhat, and, when she had taken her draught, she sank to sleep. But as the night grew denser and the silence of the house was tomb-like, Alice, who was dozing, was suddenly awakened by someone speaking wildly in her ear. Olive was delirious. Fancying herself with Edward, she cried, "Oh, take me away, dear! I am sick of home; I want to get away from all these spiteful girls . . . I know they are laughing at me because Violet cut me out with the marquis. We shall be married, shan't we, the moment we arrive in Dublin? It is horrible to be married at the registrar's, but it is better than not being married at all . . . But do you think they will catch us up? It would be dreadful to be taken back home, I could not bear it. . . Oh, do drive on; we don't seem to be moving. . . . You see that strange tree on the right, we have not passed it yet; I don't think we ever shall. Whip up that bay horse; don't you see that he is turning round, that he wants to go back? And I am sure that this is not the road; that man at the corner told you a lie. I know he was mocking at us—I saw it in his eye. . . . Look, look, Edward! Oh, look —it is papa, or Lord Dungory, I can't tell which, he will not lift his cloak." . . . Then the vision would fade from her delirious brain, and she would fancy herself in the wood, arguing once again with Mrs. Lawler. "No, what you say is not true; he never loved you; how could he? You are an old woman. . . . Let me pass—let me pass. . . . Why do you speak to me? We don't visit, we never did visit you. No; it was not at our house you met Edward. . . . You are a bad woman; and Edward shall not, he could not, think of running away with you—will you, darling? Oh! help me, help me out of this dreadful wood. I want to go home, but I cannot walk . . . and that terrible bird is still watching me, and I dare not pass that tree until you drive it away."

Now only the two beds, with their white curtains and brass crowns, loomed through the pale obscurity, broken only by the red-glowing basin where a nightlight burnt, and the long tongues of flame that the blazing peat scattered from time to time across the darkened ceiling. The solitude of the sleeping house grew momentarily more intense in Alice's brain, and she trembled as she strove to soothe her sister, and covered the hot feverish arms over with the bedclothes. But gradually the lonely hours wore themselves away, and the morning broke with all its welcome sounds of fluttering wings, and footfalls in the echoing corridors.

About eight o'clock Mrs. Barton came in. "What sort of night has Olive had?" she asked anxiously.

"Not a very quiet one; I am afraid she was a little delirious."

"Dr. Reed promised to be here early. How do you feel, dear?" Mrs. Barton asked, leaning over the bed.

"Oh, very ill; I can scarcely breathe, and I have such a pain in my side."

"Your lips look very sore, dear; do they hurt you?"—Olive only moaned dismally—and, looking anxiously at her elder daughter, she said:

"And you, too, Alice, you are not looking well; you are looking very tired. You must not sit up another night with you sister. To-night I will take your place."

"Oh, mother, no! I assure you it is a pleasure to me to nurse Olive. I am very well indeed; do not think about me."

"Indeed, I will think about you, and you must do as I tell you. I will look after Olive, and you must try and get a good night's rest. We will take it in turns to nurse her. And now come down to breakfast; a cup of hot coffee will do you all the good in the world. Barnes, you will not think of leaving Miss Olive until we come back; and, if any change occurs, ring for me immediately."

When Dr. Reed arrived, Alice was again sitting by the bedside. She rose to meet him. She noticed that he looked at her intently, but all was forgotten in the question:

"And how is our patient to-day?"

"I cannot say she is any better; she has a distressing cough, and last night I am afraid she was a little delirious."

"Ah, you say the cough is very distressing?"

"I am afraid I must call it distressing; is that a very bad sign?"

"Probably there is not much wrong, but it would be better to ascertain the condition of the patient, and then we may be able to do something to relieve her."

They approach the bed. The doctor draws a stethoscope from his pocket. From either side they aid each other, and they lift the patient into a sitting position.

"I should like to examine her chest," said the doctor, and his fingers moved to unfasten her chemise. Olive looked at him at once timidly and suspiciously.

"Don't expose me," she murmured feebly, and, notwithstanding her condition, she blushed to the roots of her flaxen hair.

"Now, Olive dear, remember it is only the doctor; let him examine you."

It was with difficulty Alice said the words. She felt her position sharply, but she mastered her sense of false shame and

then forgot it in the keen sensations of pity which the sight of
the poor sick beauty inspired.

The eyes were now but dull filmy blue, the lips were covered
with sores, and there was a circumscribed redness over the
cheekbones—not the hectic flush of phthisis, but the dusky red
that is characteristic of pneumonia. And so weak was the
patient that during the stethoscopic examination Alice had to
support her; her head fell from side to side as she was moved,
and when the doctor pressed her right side her moans were
pregnant with pain.

"Now let me see the tongue. . . . Dry and parched."

"Shall I die, doctor?" the girl asked feebly and plaintively
as she sank amidst the pillows.

"Die! no, not if you take care of yourself and do what you
are told."

"But tell me, Dr. Reed. . . . you can tell me the truth.
Is Olive dangerously ill, is her life in danger?" Alice asked
anxiously as they moved away from the bed towards the
window, towards Alice's work-table.

"She will get well if she takes care of herself; she is suffering from an acute attack of pneumonia."

"What is that?"

"Congestion of the lungs, or rather an advanced stage of it.
It is more common in men than in women, and it is the consequence of long exposure to wet and cold."

"Is it very dangerous?"

"No, not if the patient is taken great care of; and now let
me tell you that it is all-important that the temperature of
the room should not be allowed to vary. I attended a case
of it some three or four miles from here, but the damp of the
cabin was so great that it was impossible to combat the disease.
The cottage, or rather hovel, was built on the edge of a soft
spongy bog, and so wet was it that the woman had to sweep
the water every morning from the floor where it collected
in great pools. The poverty that these peasants endure is
something shocking. I am now going to visit an evicted
family, who are living in a partially-roofed shed fenced up by
the roadside. There, in the most sheltered corner, the father,
down with fever, lies shivering, with nothing to drink but cold
water, nothing to eat but a potato. The wife told me that last
week it rained so heavily that she had to get up three times in
the night to wring the sheets out."

"And why were they evicted?"

"Oh, that is a long story; but it is a singularly characteristic one. In the first place he was an idle fellow; he got into difficulties and owed his landlord three years' rent. Then he got into bad hands, and was prevented from coming to terms with his landlord. Mr. Scully, who is the agent, did his best to come to terms, but there was a lot of jobbing going on between the priest and the village grocer. It was arranged that the latter should pay off the existing debt if the landlord could be forced into letting him the farm at a 'fair rent,' that is to say, thirty per cent. reduction on the old rent. Then, in recognition of his protecting influence, the priest was to take a third of the farm off the grocer's hands, and the two were then to conjointly rack-rent poor Murphy for the remaining third portion, which he would be allowed to retain for a third of the original rent; but the National League heard of their little tricks, and now the farm is boycotted, and Murphy is dying in the ditch for the good of his *counthry*."

"I thought boycotting was ended, that the League had lost all power."

"It has and it hasn't. Sometimes a man takes a farm and keeps it in defiance of his neighbours; sometimes they hunt him out of it. It is hard to come to a conclusion, for when in one district you hear of rents being paid and boycotted farms letting freely, in another, only a few miles away, the landlords are giving reductions, and there are farms lying waste, that no one dare look at. In my opinion the fire is only smouldering, and when the Coercion Act expires the old organisation will rise up as strong and as triumphant as before. This is a time of respite for both parties."

The conversation then came to a sudden pause. Alice felt it would be out of place for her to speak her sympathies for the Nationalistic cause, and she knew it would be unfair to lead the doctor to express his. So at the end of a long silence, during which each divined the other's thoughts, she said:

"I suppose you see a great deal of the poor and the miseries they endure?"

"I have had good opportunities of studying them. Before I came here I spent ten years in the poorest district in Donegal. I am sure there wasn't a gentleman's house within fifteen miles of me."

"And did you not often feel very lonely?"

"Yes, I did, but one gets so used to solitude that to return to the world, after having lived long in the atmosphere of one's own thoughts, can only be achieved by violent and most painful victories over oneself. I cannot tell you how distracting and wearying I found society when I first came to live at Gort. The repugnance that grows on those who live alone to hearing their fellow-creatures express their ideas is very strange. It must be felt to be understood; and it is curious I have never seen the sentiment, I may call it a situation, dealt with in fiction."

"Do you ever read fiction?"

"Yes, and enjoy it. I cannot tell you how, in my little home amid the northern bogs, I used to look forward when I had finished writing, to spending an hour before going to bed with a volume of Thackeray or George Eliot."

"What were you writing?"

"A book."

"A book!" exclaimed Alice, looking suddenly pleased and astonished.

"Yes, but not a work of fiction—I am afraid I am too prosaic an individual for that—a medical work."

"And have you finished your book?"

"Yes, it is finished, and I am glad to say it is in the hands of a London publisher. We have not yet agreed about the price, but I hope and believe that, directly and indirectly, it will lead to putting me into a small London practice."

"And then you will leave us?"

"I am afraid so. There are many friends I shall miss—that I shall be very sorry to leave, but . . ."

"Oh, of course it would not do to miss such a chance."

When the doctor left, Alice proceeded to carry out his instructions concerning the patient, and, these being done, she sat down by the bedside and continued her thoughts of him with a sense of pleasure. She remembered that she had always liked him. Yes, it was a liking that dated as far back as the spinsters' ball at Ballinasloe. He was the only man there in whom she had taken the slightest interest. They were sitting together on the stairs when that poor fellow was thrown down and had his leg broken. She remembered how she had enjoyed meeting him at tennis-parties, and how often she had walked away with him from the players through the shrubberies; and above all she could not forget—it was a long sweet souvenir—the beautiful afternoon she had spent with him, sitting on the rock, the day of the picnic at Kinvarra Castle. It all seemed very strange to her, she was a little perplexed, and was only conscious of her happiness as one lying in the sun is of the pleasant blowing of the south wind. With the coming of her breath her bosom heaved, and as her dreams floated delicately before her, she thought of the doctor's eyes. They were grey, and her memory seemed filled with their bright quick glances. The rest of his face was a little vague to her. She had forgotten, or rather she had never thoroughly understood, that he was a short, thick-set, middle-aged man, that he wore mutton-chop whiskers and that his lips were overhung by a long dark moustache. His manners were those of an unpolished and somewhat commonplace man. But while she thought of his grey eyes her heart was thrilled with gladness, and as she dreamed of his lonely life of labour and his ultimate hopes of success, all her old sorrows and fears seemed to have evaporated, to have departed like chilly mists. Then suddenly and with the unexpectedness of an apparition the question presented itself, did she like him better than Harding? Alice shrank from the unpleasantness of the thought, nor did she force herself to answer it; but perhaps to escape from it, and there was a touch of cowardice in the acts, she busied herself with attending to her sister's wants.

And while Alice was thus happy, Olive lay suffering in all the dire humility of the flesh. Hourly her breathing grew shorter and more hurried, her cough more frequent, and the expectoration that accompanied it darker and thicker in colour. The beautiful eyes were now turgid and dull, the lids hung heavily over a line of filmy blue, and a thick scaly layer of bloody tenacious mucus persistently accumulated and covered the tiny and once almost jewel-like teeth. For three or four days these symptoms knew no abatement; and it was over this prostrated body, weakened and humiliated by illness, that Alice and Dr. Reed read love in each other's eyes, and it was about this poor flesh that their hands were joined as they lifted Olive out of the recumbent position she had slipped into, and built up the bowed-in pillows. And as it had once been all Olive in Brookfield, it was now all Alice; the veil seemed suddenly to have slipped from all eyes, and the exceeding worth of this plain girl was at last recognised. Nowhere

could her place be supplied. Mrs. Barton's presence at the
bedside did not soothe the sufferer; she grew restless and demanded her sister. Dr. Reed took heed of the devotion and
care that was ministered with such loving hands in the sickroom and when not attending the patient he and this straight-
souled girl, so wide in her sympathies, so deep in her love of
natural things, would often withdraw to the window-recess,
and for long half-hours stand talking there, looking at each
other from time to time with quick, with meditative, with
interested eyes. Each conversation began thus:—

"And do you think my sister is better to-day?"

"I am afraid she will not begin to show signs of any real
improvement until the ninth day. The malady must take its
course."

"Still I do not think she suffers so much as she did yesterday; I am sure her ankle is not so painful: the bran-poultices
have relieved her of much pain."

"I know nothing better for a sprain than a bran-poultice."

Then they would speak of indifferent things—of their
friends, of the state of the country, of the Land Bill, of Mr.
Barton's pictures. But, yielding to their emotion, they soon
spoke of what was uppermost in their minds—of the MSS. on
the table, of the London publisher. And the doctor, who had
latterly developed a taste for fiction, seemed to be always either
borrowing or returning a volume of Charlotte Brontë: and in
talking of the rights and wrongs of Rochester's love for Jane,
and Maggie Tulliver's for Stephen, the lovers revealed to each
other their present state of soul. One day Olive, who was
getting better, turned herself painfully in bed and watched
the group by the window—watched Alice's tall, thin, pre-
Raphaelite figure, so characteristic of her spiritual and intense
self, and the doctor's bluff shoulders and square weather-beaten
face, so characteristic of his nature, that would have been com-
mon-place were it not for its determination. Both were seen in
profile against the window. Their lips moved as Holbein's
lips seem to move. Dr. Reed's fat Holbein hand was laid on
the table; and the sick girl faded amid the white sheets like
a white rose in the snow, while her sick blue eyes stared
fadingly, in all the dim unreality of a drawing by Westall.

When the doctor went, when the sisters were alone Olive
said:

"Alice, do you like Dr. Reed? Would you marry him?"

CHAPTER VI.

HENCEFORTH Dr. Reed was constantly at Brookfield. He was there more frequently than the state of the patient demanded; and Alice felt that the attentions he was paying her would soon be noticed by the visitors. Cecilia she especially dreaded. More than once she had observed that the wistful brown eyes were fixed upon when she sat apart talking with him; and she knew how even a remote suspicion that he liked her would thrill the strange girl's heart with pain. But Cecilia said nothing; the days passed, and, feeling more at ease, Alice was beginning to allow her liking for the doctor to grow into, to become part of the nature of her mind.

One afternoon the girls were sitting alone in the bedroom. Cecilia had just come in; Alice had asked her to wait until a paragraph was finished. In the silence the pen scratched along sharply, and Alice's thoughts pursued the flying words to a close, when she was startled by an abrupt exclamation. Turning she saw the crooked girl, her hand clasped feverishly, staring wildly upwards.

"Oh! how beautiful the Prayer Book is! I pity you, Alice; how I pity you!"

"Goodness me, Cecilia, what is the matter?"

"Alas! you would not understand! But oh! if you knew the pain I suffer, the pain that is mine when I think of the sin that is yours, and the awful end that must overtake you! But you! you know nothing of the short starting sleeps, the dream-haunted vigils, the vicious demon-shapen terrors, intense, terrible, and profound, and the silences filled with the cries of the damned; and in this figuration of the judgment and the doom I see . . . but no, no, no, it is not true; it cannot be!

"Alice, listen to me; listen and let me tell you how terrible it is to know that you, my darling friend, would, were you to

297

die this moment, be damned to all eternity. Oh! it is fearsome, it is cruel; and my heart is eaten away with grief. And
the helplessness and hopelessness are so hard to bear. It is
vain to reason with you . . . one can but pray for you, and I
have prayed until my soul was sick with famine for the holy
face of God. And ah! how often in my loneliness do I cry
aloud the beautiful litany of Jesus and that of his Virgin
Mother—*Tower of Ivory, House of Gold, Ark of the Covenant*
. . . and I sing until in happy prayer I forget the wretched-
ness, the abominations of our lives, and remember only the
days when we all sang together those pure, those sinless chants
in that white, girl-like convent-church. And those dear, those
black-robed nuns. . . . I can see them. . . . the serge habits
trail in straight sculptured folds upon the pavement, they bow
their peaceful faces before the Altar . . . Alice, I am right,
you are wrong! There is no true happiness in this life unless
indeed we recognise it as a means of attaining God. The way
to Him is a long and bitter one, but He has given us prayer;
pure sparkling fountains at which we may drink, and gain
strength and courage to pursue our journey to the illimitable
prospect of peace which awaits us beyond the sun. All other
hopes and desires are vain as even I have found. They pass
and perish like things of sand, and mad and bruised with grief
we turn to God for confidence, for relief. And then, if we ask
fervidly, all shall be given to us, and in our hearts shall awake
a rapture of joy such as those who put their faith in mortal
sense shall never know; and then the mild felicities of forgive-
ness shall cool our faces like the flowing of a breath, and our
sin shall dissolve like a little cloud and be forgiven, as mine
has dissolved and is now forgotten. But you! you know not
of my sin, of my sin! Yes, Alice, I have sinned, and deeply,
for I desired more than God had willed to give me, and I
have suffered accordingly. Yes, Alice, I had desired more than
God had willed to give me, for I desired you. I desired to
possess you wholly and entirely. I was jealous of the flowers
you wore in your bosom, of everything your eyes rested upon.
I remember once, you were talking at the time to one of those
officers from Gort, your hair got entangled in the carving of
the chair; but before I could get up he had loosened it. I could
have spat in his face; I could have killed him; I hated him
for days and nights—I was very wicked. I offended God.
But I have done penance for my sin, I have conquered my

passion. Yes, I have left for ever the life of desire and have entered into that of prayer; and a mild and exquisite world is the world of prayer! There, there are no frozen morns nor fiery noons, but long pensive evenings, and all who live there are thrilled with happiness, and all who dream there dream of mansuetude and calm. And there we walk as in a garden of straight walks, seeing the happy end from afar; heedless we pass by the dark coverts of doubt and the red flowerage of too keen rejoicings. There sadness may not endure, nor is there delight nor grief nor terrifying morrows; and in the wan enchantment of our evenings we pass onwards in calm and holy procession; and our ranks are never broken save when one, with quiet emotion, steps aside to gather the tall roses of Resignation; with pale lips she kisses them, with pale hands weaves them into a wreath that she shall bear bloomful to the thither side of death. Yes, the flowers of Resignation are sweet to gather, and our reward shall be seventy times greater than our pain, when we, the pure, the undegraded by earthly vice and passion, on bended knees, with radiant robes flowing as water about us, shall offer the tear-starred chaplets of resignation to Him—Him who will one day come, with His Father and white attendance of Seraphim, to punish the wicked and to welcome the chosen to those high realms of Heaven where every song is a breathing perfume and every look a note of undying love. My soul is thrilled, is pierced with the long delight of contemplation; my heart is bruised, and the wine of ecstasy bubbles to my lips; the fumes of strange, keen, and unconquerable joy rise to my brain, and in uncontrollable and ever-ascending vision—vision keen and impalpable, my life reeks to thee—to thee and to God. Yes, in the mysticity of God's love, and thine, my delight shall wax and wane; in the arms of God I faint—my soul sickens, I falter, I yield myself. . . . No, Alice, no; Alice, thou who art mine, mine in eternity, I am speaking wildly, madly; you do not understand me—no, you do not understand, for you have not prayed as I have prayed; you have not spent the whole night on your knees gazing on the pale tranquillity of the skies—the home of God —and there, soaring with white and vigorous wings, I shall go when the hour comes for my spirit to tear this impeding veil of flesh, past the holy stars of Heaven, and enter an eternity of happy prayer and unapparent love. But you have not prayed, and can know nothing of the joys of prayer! They are bright and durable, while the satisfaction on the attainment of which your mind is so irrevocably set is but an ash-grey blossom that grows pale as it blooms—a degrading moment that dulls the sense and implants its festering sting."

" Cecilia! Cecilia!"

" I mean, Alice, that you must pray for faith to believe; oh, think, think of your soul; think of what you risk by your persistent denial of God, of Him who died to save your soul! Think, oh think, of that imperishable gift born to live through an eternity of happiness or of torment! Think, oh think, of what agony would be mine, if by God's most infinite grace I should be permitted to pass through the heavenly gate and from my place among the blessed should look down and see you! No, no; God in His great mercy would spare me that. But if I should hear, or feel, or somehow get to know that the long tale of Eternity's delights would to lute and lyre be ceaselessly sung without ever syllabling the sweet name of Alice! . . . Think, oh think! . . . Have you no pity?"

" Darling Cecilia, what would you wish me to do? Surely God will not punish me for not doing what He has not given me strength to do?"

" Alice, you must not speak like that; you are blaspheming your Creator. Tell me, can nothing be done to help you, to save you? Ah, if you knew the lofty hopes that were once mine, of the high ideal life I once dreamed to live with you; a pure ecstatic life untouched by any degrading passion, unassailed by any base desires! But alas! all my hopes are withered, all my love is in the dust, for no more than the rest can you hold aloof : like the rest you demand the joys and satisfactions of the flesh ; but, unlike May and Violet, you shall not live and be satisfied with them. They shall become loathsome in your eyes, they shall sicken in your sight and mind, and when the first fever of curiosity and desire has passed, you shall drink the draught in horror ; you shall long to dash down the brutal cup, your lips and mouth shall burn as with poison, and your heart shall wither within you, and your yearning soul shall call to be delivered of its uncleanness. You shall wring your hands and weep in secret, but in vain; for you will be then as a slave chained to daily and nightly degradation, and none shall be able to break your fetters but death. Now you see man's love in the fair moonlight of your imagination, but draw nearer, and its animal exhalations shall poison your nostrils, and all its foul abominations shall be revealed to you. No more than the others do you know the torture you are preparing for yourself, no more than the others do you realise the misery and the shame of the life you are choosing. My heart bleeds for you. I am sick of grief."

"Cecilia, darling Cecilia, you must not sob like that. Tell me why you are grieving, tell me what I can do; you know I love you."

"No, between you and me there is an abyss that cannot be bridged over. No, no; leave me; I do not want your sympathy. Your heart is no longer mine; it is full of base passion and vile desire; your love for that man hangs about you like an odour; to me it is a visible presence and it revolts me."

"Cecilia dear, you are excited, you do not know what you are saying . . . Were it anyone else!"

"If it were anyone else! I am no more to you than anyone else!"

"Indeed you are, Cecilia; I love you better than anyone in the world!"

"Ah! Better than anyone except him."

"What do you mean?"

"Why seek to deceive me? I know the truth, but I have prayed for grace and am prepared to bear my pain. And my pain! Oh, God! Thou, who knowest all things, Thou canst judge of its sharpness and its bitterness. Thou in thine infinite mercy hast estimated the burden and deemed it befitting to be laid upon me; and for Thy sweet sake, O Lord, I will, as bravely as may be, bear my cross to the end until I lay it one day at Thy feet, and at Thy white feet beg mercy of Thee. For Thou in Thine infinite wisdom hast taken heed of its weight and my power. Alas! not that of man nor woman, but that of a poor little cripple—a girl cripple—weak and deformed in body, but endowed with a soul capable of feeling every passing pain, and a heart in which every wandering grief may make its nest. My lot has been set about with grief and sufferings that none will ever know of; sharp keen agony, and mad sorrows that have made life to me a black, a sullen martyrdom.

"Here, none may take account of other than physical pain, but I know that the mind is capable of keener torturing than the mere flesh is ever conscious of. Ah, those terrible moments when life is revealed to me in all its natural ignominy and horror! Purblind we walk, only dimly aware of the abominations about us, and thus we are enabled to bear the agony that we call life. But there are moments, terrible moments in the middle watches of the night, when we wake to the truth, and seeing things in their fearsome, in their leprous deformity, cry aloud in our pain, cry aloud for oblivion. And then in the tumult of our despair we turn our faces to the wall and moan, and like children weep ourselves to sleep. Such a martyrdom is and shall be mine until Jesus the Redeemer comes and welcomes me into that place where there are neither tears nor laughter, and where the weary are at rest. And may that time come soon, I most humbly pray; for of peace and love there is none here for me. I have known but solitude and suffering; I have spoken and not been heard; I have loved and it has availed me nothing. Others are contented with externals, but I see the truth—the awful, the hideous, the monstrous truth. In a solitude as deep as the airless silence of the moon I live—I and the Truth. Long, too long, have we counted out together the abominable record of human life; and, as in sullen joy we traced the footmarks of man through the eternal slime, we have alternately given way to bitter exultation and blind despair; and now we are tired of both. Yes, it would seem that my heart has grown dumb. I do not long for life's joys, its pains I despise; but to live with a thousand beings, all apparently made to your own image and likeness, and to know that not one either feels or understands as you feel and understand, is unnecessary suffering; and it is lawful to confess you are not of the world's company, and to fly from it. No, Alice, no; you, no more than the rest, have understood me. I have loved you . . . well; but that is over now, and I must go hence and learn to bear the burden that Christ has given me to bear."

"But, Cecilia, I am not going to leave you: I do not understand."

"Yes, you do; you know well enough that you will marry him, and you will moreover go away with him and I shall be left alone."

"Cecilia, I assure you that he has never spoken a word of love to me; I have no reason to think that he ever thought of asking me to marry him."

"It is very clear indeed that he holds for you that sentiment which men dignify with the name of love. His blood is on fire with it ; when he looks at you . . . oh, it is horrible ! I will not think of it."

"Cecilia, for shame ! Surely it is wicked to speak like that. Surely you are sinning against your religion, which of all the religions the world has known is most human ; indeed, I may say, the most domestic. Think, do not your theories involve a condemnation of the life of Christ, and all that concerns it ? "

"Hush, Alice, hush,—that was no more than an infinitely mysterious, and an infinitely beautiful dream." As she spoke she raised her face, the light fell on the retreating temples, and the prominent eyes of the mystic were rolled upward wildly, almost convulsively.

Then Alice looked straight out of her plain, earnest eyes. She was stirred to the depths of her being with wonder, with a strange wonder in which there were mingled sensations of horror and curiosity. And, at the same time, as there are often in a violet sky vanishing touches of delicate blue so pleasantly suggestive of sunshine that they are, as it were, thoughts of happiness and pleasure, a sweet humming joy fluttered down upon her heart like wings upon a nest that was soon to grow alive with fledglings. In that moment Alice knew she was to be a wife. A soft voice cooed deliciously about her heart, but she strove not to listen. Afterwards she was ashamed of having experienced so much gladness in the presence of one whom life had crowned with much grief. At last she said :

"But, Cecilia, you must remember that marriage is a sacrament that is permitted by God."

"Marriage is a concession to the weak in spirit."

"Then do you really think it is impossible to love a man purely. And, admitting for a moment that Dr. Reed does want to marry me, do you think" (here Alice spoke with a slight hesitation in her voice) "it would be incompatible with the married state for a pure and holy affection to exist between us, a belief in each other's truth, and much firm dependence on the strength of our double life ? "

"Marriage is lawful, but for all that its passions are no whit less gross and no less detestable than those of any other form of concubinage, and he or she who would love as the angels love in heaven, who would taste the love that fills the

eternal spaces of heaven, must fly from all that is too conclusive of the earth; must not seek to make a spiritual
banquet serve for worldly meat and drink. The real and
the ideal are not one but twain, and the twain will never
turn to one. Before you, myriad brides—bright and radiant
maidens—have gone to the marriage-bed, but only to return,
as you will, abashed, defiled, and mad with the ignominy and the
shame; you, too, like them will know the truth when it is
too late. Darling, my heart is your heart, and your affections
are mine as mine are yours. I see it all. Oh God! how
clear the vision is! Listen, in horrible nightmare I have
endured . . . . yes, I have known the abominable martyrdom
which you will suffer. And now I can see it—a fearsome
monster waiting you from afar. All is dread darkness about
him, but his eyes gleam; his breath stirs the shuddering
silence. . . . Ah! it is too horrible! I will see no more.
And, darling, I can only pity you, can but hold these arms to
you for a last time. Then you will be alone, and the love I
shall send out to you will but barely reach you, and will not
help you to live. You will be alone, you will have no one by
to comfort you, to wipe away you tears, to bid you bear your
lot for Christ's most holy sake. But I shall pray, I shall pray
by day and night, for I shall know all, and you too will know
all, and in your agony your thoughts will lean to Cecilia,
to her who now seems to you no more than a strange-minded
cripple girl, to her who now seems to you but a dark-minded
cynic to whom all earthly joy is unholy and vile."

"But surely, Cecilia, you do not think all men are gross
and degraded—you do not hate your own father?"

Cecilia did not answer, but her lips curled disdainfully, and
it was easy to guess the dark and terrible thoughts that
agitated her.

"I cannot go into that question," she said abruptly; "all I
have in my heart to tell concerns the futility of material
pleasures, and the terrible future you are preparing for
yourself. I have thought long and profoundly of the meaning
of life; my deformity, forcing me to stand out of the swelling of the crowd, has given me occasion to see as from a
tower, and from my silent and lonely place I have watched
and have seen the terrible end that awaits all earthly delight—
shame, loathing, weariness. But I am not the cynic that you
declare me. I believe there are many pleasures in life, but

they are found in resignation, in calm, and never in stormful joy and violent ends. The real, the abiding gladness of this life is approached in prayer, in yearning for an ideal that cannot be ours in this life, but which we may attain in the next."

"An unattainable ideal! Of what service can it then be to us?"

"The value of an ideal lies in the fact of its unattainableness, otherwise it would be worthless and valueless to guide us, to lead us through our mortal night. And to gain power to conquer our baser passions we set our eyes upon a fair, unalterable star: in rare moments its beauty will shine upon our tired faces, and our hearts shall wax joyful, and burdens grow light upon our bending shoulders. Then we must pray. Prayer is a Divine cordial poured out of heaven that our souls may drink of and be refreshed; prayer is a flower fallen from heaven that man may cull and place it in his bosom and walk on assured of his Divine importance; and I have drunk of this cordial; I have gathered this rose and have been made strong and whole with sweet drink and immortal perfume, and may now pursue my journey to the end without fear of falling by the wayside. Life has been defeated, its thorns have been trampled under foot, and its temptations disdained. For I, even a poor girl cripple like me, have been given not only sorrows and pains to bear, but even temptations to overcome. That you do not believe, and you cannot perhaps realise, what I suffered when I saw you, my only friend, being stolen from me. Then what was loathing grew to hate, and I called upon God to curse, to kill, to relieve me of my enemy; to crush him who will degrade with his vile usage her to whom my thoughts turn as the sunflower must to the sun, her who has been to me, poor, lonely and sorrowful me, an ideal of love, of light, and of grace."

"Cecilia, darling, you shall not be alone. You shall come and live with us . . . that is to say, if what you have spoken of is to be."

"Live with you, with him! For ever in sight of your domestic affection; to become a part of it? No, I shall seek peace from you, from all too disturbing passion, in God and the hope of heaven. I shall return to that place where alone there may exist for me some small portion of earthly happiness —the Convent of the Holy Child."

" But you are not a Roman Catholic ? "

" I have always been one in sentiment, I shall now become one in God, and I shall take the veil ; and in those beautiful black robes, in that beautiful woman's church, in the silent sacramental hours, my soul shall lose consciousness of all things save of the white presence of God ; and there, when my heart has grown quieter, I shall pray for you, Alice ; and my prayers shall be heard ; and if ever you come to me, if you should ever whisper in my ear that you had learnt to believe in our Divine Lord, if you should ever kneel by me in that beautiful convent church and in our old places, and our spirits be mingled in the sweet mutuality of prayer, I should forget all past griefs, or rather I should say that for the ultimate happiness they bore, they were worth enduring."

Tears stood in Alice's eyes ; her heart was too full for words, but she took her friend in her arms and kissed her—the caress was passionately, and even violently returned.

CHAPTER VII.

A WEEK later Mrs. Barton sat waiting in her drawing-room to receive Milord. A bit of news had reached her and she was anxious to verify it. From time to time she raised her soft brown eyes to look at the clock. It was after one: consequently he would arrive in a few minutes. And as if in anticipation of his smiles the heart-shaped face was slanted in the Lady Hamilton pose; the feet were tucked neatly away beneath the black silk dress, the hands lay thereon like little white china ornaments. There was about Mrs. Barton always an air of quiet refinement; and Mrs. Barton looked more Mrs. Barton now than ever. The sweet cunning of the face was apparent in the grey Irish air that illumined the room, bringing out in aggressive distinctness the plaintive pastels, the gimcrack cabinets hung in the corners and between the windows, and over-laden with Dresden figures, French fans, ivories, and silver card-cases. Olive, looking as fragile as any toy, lay on the sofa, and the decanter of sherry on his little table was ready waiting for Milord. Suddenly the noise of wheels was heard, and a moment after the old lord entered. He was as hale and as hearty as ever; but the times had been passing him rapidly by of late, and the excessive courtliness, the expansive shirt front, the elaborate necktie with the ends hanging about, the elaborate stud were now more suggestive of high-class comedy than of real life.

"Ah, ce cher Milord, comme il est beau, comme il est parfait!" exclaimed Mrs. Barton as she led him to his chair and poured out his glass of sherry.

But there was a gloom on his face which laughter and compliments failed for a moment to dissipate—at last he said:

"Ah, Mrs. Barton, Mrs. Barton! if I had not this little retreat to take refuge in, to hide myself in, during some hours of the day, I should not be able to bear up—Brookfield has prolonged my life for . . ."

"I cannot allow such sad thoughts as these," said Mrs. Barton laughing, and waving her white hands. "Who has been teasing notre cher Milord? What have dreadful Lady Jane and terrible Lady Sarah been doing to him?"

"I shall never forget this morning, no, not if I lived to a thousand," the old gentleman murmured, plaintively. "Oh, the scenes, the scenes I have gone through! Cecilia, as I told you yesterday, has been filling the house with rosaries and holywater-fonts; Jane and Sarah have been breaking these, and the result has been tears and upbraidings. . . . Last night at dinner I don't really know what they didn't say to each other; and then the two elder ones fell upon me and declared that it was all my fault, that I ought never to have sent my daughter to a Catholic convent. I was obliged to shut myself up in the study and lock the door. Then this morning when I thought it was all over it began again worse than ever; and then in the middle of it all when Jane asked Cecilia how many Gods there were in the roll of bread she was eating if the priest were to bless it . . . a most injudicious observation, I said so at the time, and I must apologise to you, my dear Mrs. Barton for repeating it, but I am really so upset that I scarcely know what I am saying . . well, Jane had no sooner spoken than Cecilia overthrew the teacups and said she was not going to stay in the house to hear her religion insulted, and without another word she walked down to the parish priest and was baptised a Catholic; nor is that all, she returned with a scapular round her neck, a rosary about her waist, and a Pope's medal in her hand. I really thought Jane and Sarah would have fainted; indeed I am sure they would have fainted if Cecilia hadn't declared that she was going to pack up her things and return at once to St. Leonard's and become a nun. Such an announcement as this was of course far beyond fainting and . . . but no, I will not attempt to describe it, but I can assure you I was very anxious to get out of the house."

"Cecilia going to be a nun; oh, I am so glad!" exclaimed Olive. "It is far the best thing she could do, for she couldn't hope to be married."

"Olive, Olive!" said Mrs. Barton, "you should not speak so openly. We should always consider the religious prejudices of others. Of course, as Catholics we must be glad to hear of anyone joining the true Church, but we should remember that Milord is going to lose his daughter."

"I assure you my dear Mrs. Barton, I have no prejudices. I look upon all religions as equally good, but to be forced to live in a perpetual discussion in which teacups are broken, concerning scapulars, bacon and meal shops, and a school which, putting aside the question of expense, makes me hated in the neighbourhood, I regard as intolerable, and when I go home this evening I shall tell Jane that the school must be put down or carried on in a less aggressive way. I assure you I have no wish to convert the people; they are paying their rents very well now, and I think it absurd to upset them; and the fact of having received Cecilia into the Church might incline the priest very much towards us."

"And Cecilia will be so happy in that beautiful convent!" suggested Mrs. Barton.

"*C'est le génie du Catholicisme de nous débarrasser des filles laides.*"

And upon this expression of goodwill towards the Church of Rome, Cecilia's future life was discussed with much amiability. Mrs. Barton said she would make a sweet little nun; Olive declared that she would certainly go to Saint Leonard's to see her "professed," and Milord's description of Lady Sarah's and Lady Jane's ill-humour was considered irresistibly comic, and he was forced to tell the story of his woes again and again.

Soon after, the servant announced Dr. Reed, and Alice came downstairs.

Mrs. Barton was annoyed at the Doctor's visit, and she showed her annoyance by maintaining a discourteous silence.

"What can he want here every day?" she thought; "this is the third time this week he has called, and Olive is as well as ever she was. He feels her pulse and looks at her tongue and says it is a very satisfactory recovery. We all know that! I wish he'd go, and let me hear something more about Cecilia's conversion."

Dr. Reed's society manners were none of the best, and now, facing Milord's urbanity and Mrs. Barton's indifference, he sat on the edge of his chair, a picture of drawing-room misery. Alice, who knew he had come to see her, strove to make matters easy, and she industriously alluded to all

possible topics of conversation.   But without much effect ; the
Doctor evidently had something on his mind, and after an
answer had been given the conversation came to an abrupt
close.   Then she guessed that he wanted to speak to her alone ;
and in reply to a remark he had made concerning the fever
dens in Gort she said :

"I wanted to ask you a question or two about typhoid-fever,
Dr. Reed ; one of my heroines is going to die of it, and I
should like to avoid medical impossibilities.   May I show you
the passage ?"

"Certainly, Miss Barton ; I shall be delighted to give you
any assistance in my power."

When Alice left the room to fetch her manuscript, the
Doctor hurriedly bid his patient, Milord and Mrs. Barton good-
bye.   The latter said :

"Won't you wait to see Alice ?"

"I have to speak to the boy in charge of my car ; I shall
see Miss Barton as she comes downstairs."

Mrs. Barton looked as if she thought this arrangement not
a little singular, but she said nothing, and when Alice came
running downstairs with a roll of MSS. in her hand, she
attempted to explain her difficulty to the Doctor.   He made
a feeble attempt to listen to the passage she read aloud to
him ; and when their eyes met across the paper she saw he
was going to propose to her.

"Will you walk down the avenue with me ? and we will
talk of that as we go along."

Her hat was on the hall table, she took it up and in silence
walked with him out on the gravel.

"Will I put the harse up, sor ?" cried the boy from the
outside car.

"No, follow me down the avenue."

It was a wild autumn evening, full of wind and leaves.
The great green pasture lands, soaked and soddened with rain,
rolled their monotonous green turf to the verge of the blown
beech-trees, about which the rooks drifted in picturesque confusion.   Now they soared like hawks, or on straightened wings
were carried down a furious gust across the tumultuous waves
of upheaved yellow, and past the rift of cold crimson that is
tossed like a banner through the shadows of evening.

The lovers walked onwards in silence ; and, as the landscape
darkened, their lives seemed to grow brighter in the auroral

light of a new day: and the echoes of the old world sounded dim as the shuffling of the horse that tramped leisurely behind them. At last he said:

"I came here to tell you that I am going away; that I am leaving Ireland for ever. I have been able to make very satisfactory arrangements with my publisher; my book has turned out very successful indeed, and the result is that I have bought the practice I spoke to you of in Notting Hill."

"Oh, I am so glad."

"Thank you! but there is another and more important matter on which I should like to speak to you. For a long time back I had resolved to leave Ireland a sad or an entirely happy man. Which shall it be! You are the only woman I ever loved—will you be my wife?"

"Yes, I will."

Dr. Reed's face flushed with pleasure, and his eyes gleamed with delight. "Is this possible? How happy you have made me. Heaven seems to await me. But," he added sighing, "I shall not be able to give you a home like the one you are leaving; we shall have to be very economical; we shall not have more than three hundred a year to live upon. You will never be able to be satisfied with that."

"I hope, indeed—I am sure we shall get on very well; you forget that I can do something myself," she added smiling. "I have two or three orders; I do not think I am exaggerating when I say I shall be able to make two hundred a year, and that at the very least."

"Then we shall bear life's burden equally?"

"No, not quite equally, but as nearly as Nature will allow us."

Then Alice passed her arm through Dr. Reed's; and as he unfolded his plans to her, he held her hand warmly and affectionately in his: and as the twilight drifted it was wrapped like a veil about them. The rooks in great flitting flocks passed over their heads, the tempestuous crimson of the sky had been hurled further away and only the form of the grey horse, that the boy had allowed to graze, stood out distinctly in the beautiful gloom that descended upon the earth.

CHAPTER VIII.

ALICE, as she walked back to the house, was conscious of many sensations of triumph; sensations of which she was ashamed, but which she could not entirely repress. They thronged upon her rapidly—dizzily as the fumes of a strong wine. And she had to yield a little; she had to listen a little to the thoughts that sung in her ears: "Yes, I shall be married, and those girls will envy me; they who always sneered at me, who said I was a plain girl who would never be able to do anything for herself. Well, I shall be married before them after all."

And on the very first opportunity she could find, Alice told her mother that Dr. Reed had proposed to her, and that she had accepted him. Mrs. Barton said it was disgraceful, and that she would never hear of such a marriage; and when the doctor called next day she acquainted him with her views on the subject. She told him he had very improperly taken advantage of his position to make love to her daughter; she really didn't know how he could ever have arrived at the conclusion that a match was possible, and that for the future his visits must cease at Brookfield.

When Alice heard what had passed between Dr. Reed and her mother, she immediately wrote to him, expressing her regret for what had happened. She assured him that her feelings towards him would remain uninfluenced by anything that anyone might say; and she urged that as it would be very painful for her to live at home while opposing her family's wishes on such a very important question, it would be as well that the marriage should take place with the least possible delay. She took this letter down to the Post Office herself, and when she returned she entered the drawing-room and told Mrs. Barton what she had done.

"I wish you had shown me the letter before you sent it. There is nothing we need advice about so much as a letter."

"Yes, mother," replied Alice, deceived by the gentleness of Mrs. Barton's manner, "but we seemed to hold such widely different views on this matter that there did not seem to be any use in discussing it."

"Mother and daughter should never hold different views; my children's interests are my interests—what interests have I now but theirs?"

"Oh, mother, then you will consent to this marriage?"

Mrs. Barton's face always changed expression before a direct question. "My dear, I would consent to anything that would make you happy, but it seems to me impossible that you could be happy with Dr. Reed. You must remember that he is scarcely a gentleman; have you not noticed how coarse and vulgar he is? And just fancy having to put up with all that! You do not know, I mean, you do not realise what the intimacies of married life are—they are often hard to put up with, no matter who the man may be—but with one who is not a gentleman . . ."

"But, mother, Dr. Reed seems to me to be in every way a gentleman. Who is there more gentlemanly in the country? I am sure that from every point of view he is preferable to Mr. Adair or Sir Charles, or Sir Richard or Mr. Ryan, or his cousin, Mr. Lynch."

"My darling child, I would sooner see you laid in your coffin than married to either Mr. Ryan or Mr. Lynch; but that is not the question, it is, whether you had not better wait for a few years before you throw yourself away on such a man as Dr. Reed. I know that you have been greatly tried; nothing is so trying to a girl as to come out with her sister who is the belle of the season, and I must say you have borne up with a great deal of pluck and have always shown a great deal of self-restraint; and perhaps I have not been considerate enough, but I too have had my disappointments—Olive's affairs did not, as you know, turn out as well as I had expected, and to see you now marry one who is so much beneath us!"

"Mother, dear, he is not beneath us. There is no one who has got on like Dr. Reed, and he owes nothing to anyone; he has done it all by his own exertions; and now his book is a success and he has bought a London practice. No, I cannot miss this chance of settling myself in life."

"Then you do not love him, it is only for the sake of settling yourself in life that you are marrying him?"

"I respect Dr. Reed more than any man living; I bear for him a most sincere affection, and I hope to make him a good wife."

"You don't love him as you did Mr. Harding? If you will only wait you may get him. The tenants are paying their rents very well, and I am thinking of going to London in the spring."

The girl winced at the mention of Harding, but she looked into her mother's soft appealing brown eyes; and, reading clearer than she had ever read before all the adorable falseness that lay therein, she answered:

"I do not want to marry Mr. Harding; I am engaged to Dr. Reed and I do not intend to give him up."

This answer was given so firmly that Mrs. Barton lost her temper for a moment and she said:

"And do you really know what this Dr. Reed originally was? Do you know that his father kept a small shop in the village of Out—— and that the man you are thinking of marrying was educated at the National School, and that he used to run there without shoes or stockings. Lord Dungory is dining here to-night; he knows all about Dr. Reed's antecedents, and I am sure he will be horrified when he hears that you are thinking of marrying him."

"I cannot recognise Lord Dungory's right to advise me on any course I may choose to take, and I hope he will have the good taste to refrain from speaking to me of my marriage."

"What do you mean? How dare you speak to me like that, you impertinent girl!"

"I am not impertinent, mother, and I hope I shall never be impertinent to you; but I am now in my twenty-fifth year, and if I am ever to judge for myself, I must do so now."

Alice was curiously surprised by her own words; it seemed to her that it was some strange woman, and not herself—not the old self with whom she was intimately acquainted, who was speaking. Life is full of these epoch-marking moments. We have all at some given time experienced the sensation of finding ourselves either stronger or weaker than we had ever before known ourselves to be; Alice now for the first time felt that she was speaking and acting in her own individual right; and the knowledge as it thrilled through her consciousness was almost a physical pleasure. But notwithstanding the certitude that never left her of the propriety of her conduct, and the equally ever-present sentiment of the happiness that awaited her, she suffered much during the next ten days, and she was frequently in tears. Cecilia's grief—she had started for St. Leonard's without coming to wish her good-bye—and the cruel sneers, insinuations of all kinds against her and against Dr. Reed, which Mrs. Barton never missed an occasion of using, wounded the girl so deeply, that it was only at the rarest intervals that she left her room—when she walked to the post with a letter, when the luncheon or dinner-bell rang. Why she should be thus persecuted, Alice was unable to determine ; and why her family did not hail with delight this chance of getting rid of a plain girl, whose prospects were limited, was difficult to say ; nor could the girl arrive at any notion of the pleasure or profit it might be to anyone that she should waste her life amid chaperons and gossip, instead of taking her part in the world's work. And yet this seemed to be Mrs. Barton's inscrutable idea of what was right to do ; and she did not hesitate to threaten that she would neither attend herself, nor allow Mr. Barton to attend the ceremony ; and that Alice might meet Dr. Reed at the corner of the road, and be married as best she could. Alice appealed to her father against this decision, but she soon had to renounce the hope of obtaining any definite answer. He had been previously told that if he attempted any interference, his supply of paints, brushes, canvases, and guitar-strings would be cut off, and, as he was at present deeply engaged on a new picture of Julius Cæsar overturning the altars of the Druids, he hesitated before the alternatives offered to him. He spoke with much affection : he regretted that Alice could not see her way to marrying someone whom her mother could approve ! He explained the difficulties of his position, and the necessity of his turning something out —seeing what he really could do before the close of the year. Alice was bitterly disappointed, but she bore her disappointment bravely, and she wrote to Dr. Reed, telling him what had occurred, and proposing to meet him on a certain day at the Parish Church, where Father Shannon would marry them ; and, that if he refused, they would proceed to Dublin, and be married at the Registry Office. In a way Alice would have preferred this latter course, but her good sense warned her against the uselessness of offering any too violent opposition to the opinions of the world. And so it was arranged; and sad, weary and wretched, Alice lingered through the last few days of the life that had always been to her one of humiliation, and which now towards its close had quieted to one of intense pain. Thus, all had been settled, and the last few sands of girl-life were slipping through the inverted glass, and disappearing into the obscure void of the past. The Brennans had promised to meet her in the chapel, and one day as she was sitting by her window, she saw May in all the glory of her copper hair, drive a tandem up to the door. This girl, a little too corpulent, threw the reins to the groom, and rushed to her friend.

"And how do you do, Alice, and how well you are looking, and how pleased I am to see you. . . I would have come before, only my leader was coughing and I could not take him out. . . Oh, I was so wild, it is always like that; nothing is so disappointing as horses; whenever you especially require them they are laid up . . and you can't imagine the difficulty I had to get him along; I must really get another leader; he was trying to turn round the whole way . . if it hadn't been for the whip . . I took blood out of him three times running. But I know you don't care anything about horses, and I want to hear about this marriage . . I am so glad, so pleased . . but tell me, do you like him? He seems a very nice sort of man, you know, a man that would make a woman happy. . I am sure you will be happy with him, but it is dreadful to think we are going to lose you . . I shall, I know, be running over to London on purpose to see you . . but tell me, what I want to know is, do you like him? Would you believe it, I never once suspected there was anything between you?"

"Yes, my dear May," Alice replied, smiling, "I do like Edward Reed; nor do I think that I should ever like any other man half as much: I have perfect confidence in him, and where there is not confidence there cannot be love. His book has succeeded very well; he has bought a small practice in Notting Hill, which with care and industry he hopes may be worked up into a substantial business. We shall be very poor at first, but with what I shall make by writing I have no doubt but we shall be able to make both ends meet."

"Well, being both writers you will suit each other well enough, and I'm sure it will be awfully jolly to go away and live in London. I can see it all; a little suburban semi-detached house, with green Venetian blinds, a small mahogany sideboard, and a clean capped maid-servant; and in the drawing-room you won't have a piano—you don't care for music, but you'll have some basket chairs, and small book-cases, and a tea-table with tea cakes at five—oh, won't you look quiet and grave at that tea-table . . but tell me, it is all over the county that Mrs. Barton won't hear of this marriage, and that she won't allow your father to go to the chapel to give you away. It is an awful shame, and for the life of me I can't see what parents have to do with our marriage, do you?"

Without waiting for an answer, May continued the conversa-tion, and with florid vehemence she passed from one subject to another utterly disconnected without a transitional word of ex-planation. She explained how tiresome it was to sit at home of an evening listening to Mrs. Gould bemoaning the state of the country; she spoke of her terrier, and this led up to a critical examination of the good looks of several of the officers stationed at Gort; then she alluded to the last meet of the hounds, and she described the big wall she and Mrs. Manley had jumped together; a new hat and an old skirt that she had lately done up came in for a passing remark, and, with an abundance of laughter, May gave an account of a luncheon party at Lord Rosshill's; and, apparently verbatim, she told what each of the five Honourable Miss Gores had said about the marriage. Then growing suddenly serious, she said:

"It is all very well to laugh, but, when one comes to think of it, it is very sad indeed to see seven human lives wasting away, a whole family of girls eating their hearts out in blank despair, having nothing to do but to pop about from one tennis party to another, and chatter to each other or their chaperons of this girl and that who does not seem to be getting married. You are very lucky indeed, Alice—luckier than you think you are, and you are quite right to stick out and do the best you can for yourself in spite of what your people say. It is all very well for them to talk, but they don't know what we suffer: we are not all made alike, and the wants of one are not the wants of another. I daresay you never thought much about that sort of thing; but as I say, we are not all made alike. Every woman, or nearly every one, wants a husband and a home, and it is only natural she should, and if she doesn't get them the temptations she has to go through are something frightful, and if we make the slightest slip the whole world is down upon us. I can talk to you, Alice, because you know what I have gone through. . You have been a very good friend to me—had it not been for you I don't know what would have become of me. You did not reproach me, you were kind and had pity for me ; you are a sensible person and I daresay you understood that I was not entirely to blame. And I was not entirely to blame ; the circumstances we girls live under are not just—no, they are not just. We are told that we must marry a man with at least a thousand a year, or remain spinsters ; well, I should like to know where the men are who have a thousand a year, and some of us can't remain spinsters. Oh ! you are very lucky indeed to have found a husband, and to be going away to a home of your own . . I wish I were as lucky as you, Alice, indeed I do, for then there would be no excuse, and I could be a good woman."

Then May lost all control over her feelings, and she burst into a passionate flood of tears. " Oh ! Alice, Alice, I am very wicked—I am not worthy to speak to you."

" May, what do you mean ; surely you don't mean to say that you are again——"

" Oh, no ; but I am dreadfully sinful. If you knew *all* you would not speak to me : and if I died now I should go straight to *Hell !*"

" I did not know Fred Scully had come back."

" Nor has he ; it was not he."

" Who was it ? "

" Don't ask me——what does it matter ? "

" I am very sorry. . Do you love him very much ? "

" No, no ; it was an old man."   *   *   *   *   *

*   *   *   *   *   *   *   *   *   *

Alice shuddered ; her face contracted in an expression of disgust, and tears rose to her eyes. Will slipped away, and it seemed to her as if she had suddenly entered a cold, miasmal place, and the chill that sank through her flesh was such as is inhaled at the damp mouth of an earthward descending cavern, wherein dark pools lie brooding beyond the eye of day, un-silvered even by the light of a falling star. A ghoul-like terror tortured her ; and frantically she longed to shut out the vision that danced and leered through her thoughts, and that fouled with its greyness the beautiful cream and burning copper of the girl's neck and hair.

"You won't hate me too much, will you, Alice? I have made a lot of good resolutions, and they shall be kept. All is not my fault I assure you. I am determined to be a good woman yet. I wish I were going to be married like you! Then one is out of temptation. Haven't you a kind word for me? won't you kiss me and tell me you don't despise me?"

"Of course I'll kiss you, May. . . I am awfully sorry, but I am sure that one of these days—that you will be for the future——"

Alice could say no more; and the girls kissed and cried in each other's arms, and the group was a sad allegory of poor humanity's triumph, and poor humanity's more than piteous failures.

Then the girls dried their eyes and strove to speak of indifferent things, but their hearts were tense with emotion, and the conversation came to sudden and irritating closes.

At last they went downstairs, and in the hall, May showed Alice the beautiful wedding-present she had bought her, and the girl did not say that she had sold her hunter to buy it.

CHAPTER IX

AT Brookfield on the morning of the 3rd of December, '84, the rain fell persistently in the midst of a profound silence. The spike-like branches of the beech and chestnut trees stood stark in the grey air as if petrified ; for there was not wind enough to waft the falling leaf, and it fell straight as if shotted. The sheep strove to graze ; the green-painted verandah and the glass doors were lugubrious anachronisms ; and in the soaring silence and the engulfing rain there was a distinct sensation of tragedy.

Not a living thing was to be seen except the wet sheep, nor did anything stir either within or without; and the house, like a poor belated organ-woman with white head-dress and Southern earrings, looked as if it were trying to crouch, to escape, to hide itself from the merciless rain. Suddenly an outside car, one seat overturned to save the cushions from the wet, came careering up the avenue. At a glance you saw it was a post-car. There was the shaggy horse and the wild-looking driver in a long, shaggy frieze ulster. He rang the bell. The door was opened by a young woman. She was crying bitterly. Shouldering her portmanteau, the carman proceeded at once, with a piece of rope which he drew from his coat-pocket, to fasten it in front of the shaggy horse's tail. Even now, at the last moment, Alice expected the drawing-room door to open and her mother to come rushing out to wish her good-bye. But Mrs. Barton remained implacable, and after laying one more kiss on her sister's pale cheek, Alice, in a passionate flood of tears, was driven away from the home where she had known so much grief and pain. She went straight to the chapel.

In streaming macintoshes, and leaning on dripping umbrellas, she found her husband, and Gladys and Zoe Brennan waiting for her in the porch of the church. Everybody felt a little miserable, and the women strove to kiss each other's wet faces.

"Did you ever see such weather?" said Zoe.

"Is it not dreadful!" said Gladys.

"It was good of you to come," said Alice.

"It was indeed!" said the bridegroom, who felt he was obliged to say something.

"What nonsense!" said Zoe; "we were only too pleased; and if to-day be wet, to-morrow and the next and the next will be sunshine, at least for you."

And thanking Zoe inwardly for this most appropriate remark, the party ascended the church toward the altar-rails, where Father Shannon was awaiting them. Large, pompous, and arrogant, he stood on his altar-steps, and his hands were crossed over his portly stomach. On either side of him the plaster angels bowed their heads and folded their wings. Above him, the great chancel window, with its panes of green and yellow glass, jarred in an unutterable clash of colour; and the great white stare of the chalky walls, and the earthen floor with its tub of holywater, and the German prints absurdly representing the suffering of Christ, bespoke the primitive belief, the coarse superstition of which the place was an immediate symbol. Alice and the Doctor looked at each other and smiled, but their thoughts were too firmly fixed on the actual problem of their united lives to wander far in the most hidden ways of the old world's psychical extravagances. What did it matter to them what absurd usages the place they were in was put to?—they, at least, were only making use of it as they might of any other public office; the police station, where inquiries are made concerning parcels left in cabs; the Commissioner before whom an affidavit is made. And it served its purpose as well as any of the others did theirs. The priest joined their hands, Edward put the ring on Alice's finger, and the usual prayers did no harm if they did no good; and having signed their names in the register and bid good-bye to the Miss Brennans, they got into the carriage, man and wife, their feet set for ever upon one path, their interests and delights melted to one interest and one delight, their separate troubles merged into one trouble that might or might not be made lighter by the sharing: and penetrated by such thoughts they leaned back on the blue cushions of the carriage, happy, and yet a little frightened.

Rather than pass three hours waiting for a train at the little station of Ardrahan, it had been arranged to spend the time driving to Athenry; and, as the carriage rolled through the deliquefying country, the eyes of the man and the woman rested half fondly, half regretfully, and wholly pitifully on all the familiar signs and the wild landmarks, which during so many years had grown into and become part of the texture of their habitual thought; on things of which they would now have to wholly divest themselves, and remember only as the background of their younger lives. Through the streaming glass they could see the inevitable strip of bog; and the half-naked woman, her soaked petticoat clinging about her red legs, piling the wet peat into the baskets thrown across the meagre back of a starveling ass. The poor animal turned its tail to the swiftly-rolling vehicle. And further on there are low-lying swampy fields, and between them and the roadside a few miserable poplars with cabins sunk below the dung-heaps, and the meagre potato-plots lying about them; and then, as these are passed, there are green enclosures full of fattening kine, and here and there a dismantled cottage, one wall still black with the chimney's smoke, uttering to those who know the country a tale of eviction and the consequent horrors: despair, hunger, revenge, and death. And above all these, sweeping along the crests of the hills, are long lines of beautiful plantations, and, looking past the great gateways and the outlying fir-woods, between the masses of the beeches you can see the white Martello-tower-like houses of the landlords. Alice and Edward knew them all, could as they passed away from them for ever see the furniture in their rooms, catch the intonation of their voices, understand their enthusiasm for the Coercion Acts. Writs could now be served, the land-hunger was as keen as ever, and the farms of evicted tenants could be relet without difficulty or danger.

Suddenly the carriage turned up a narrow road. The coachman stopped to inquire the way, and our travellers were the unwilling witnesses of one of those scenes for which Ireland is so infamously famous—an eviction. The cabin was a fair specimen of its kind. It was built of rough stone without mortar, and through the chinks all the winds of heaven were free to wander. There was a potato-field at the back, and a mud-heap in front, and through the slush the shattered door was approached by stepping-stones. From the exterior it is easy to imagine the interior—a dark, fetid hole, smelling of smoke, potato-skins, and damp. And about this miserable tenement there were grouped a dozen policemen armed with rifles, two men in pot-hats and long ulsters, and a dozen or fifteen peasants come to watch the proceedings. An old woman of seventy had been placed for shelter beneath a hawthorn-bush; six young children clung about their shriek-ing mother; the man, with nothing but a pair of trousers and a ragged shirt to protect him from the terrible rain, stood a picture of speechless despair on the dung-heap, amid a mass of infamous bedding, and a few wooden stools that had been dragged from the house by the landlord's agents.

"Is it not terrible that human creatures should endure such misery?" exclaimed Alice.

"Yes, it is very shocking, it is horrible, let us do something for them; suppose we pay the rent for them, it cannot be much, and restore them to their miserable home. We cannot leave Ireland with such a shocking picture engraved on our minds for ever."

"Yes, yes, Edward, do pay the rent for them—it is too terrible."

The transaction was soon concluded, the man was handed a receipt, and told he might put his things back into his house. All were taken by surprise; but, when the first shock was over, uttering a wild cry, the woman, dragging her children forward, threw herself on her knees and invoked a thousand blessings on the heads of her benefactors. It was a strange sight—the old bedridden grandmother, beneath her hawthorn-bush, clasped her palsied hands; the half-naked mother and the half-naked children, the man in his tattered shirt, kneeling in line in front of their frightful hovel, in the middle of this barren Irish road, in the long wash of the rain, conscious of nothing but a wild savage feeling of gratitude, shouted forth a primitive thanksgiving for what they deemed a deliverance from evil: "May Heaven bless you, may Christ Jesus our Lord and His Holy Mother this day watch over you!"

The agents laughed coarsely. One said:—"There are plinty more of them over the hill on whom he can exercoise his charity if he should feel so disposed!"

"It would save us a dale of throuble and ixpense if he would; but to whom do we go next? Mick Flanagan! Where does he live?"

"I show you, yer honour," exclaimed half a dozen peasants, "this way, not a couple of hundred yards from here, close to the public, where we may have a drap if yer honour feels so inclined."

"And to think," said Dr. Reed reflectively, "that they are the same peasants that we once saw so firmly banded that it seemed as if nothing would ever again separate them, that nothing would ever again render them cowardly and untrue to each other; is it possible that those wretched hirelings, so ready to betray, so eager to lick the hand that smites them, are the same men whom we saw two years ago united by one thought, organised by one determination to resist the oppressor, marching firmly to nationhood? And when one thinks of the high hopes and noble ambitions that were lavished for the redemption of these base creatures, one is disposed to admit in despair the fatality of all human effort, and, hearkening to the pessimist, concede with a Mephistophelean grin that all here is vileness and degradation."

"Of humanity we must not think too much; for the present we can best serve it by learning to love each other."

Then Edward put his arm about Alice and drew her towards him. The painful incident they had just witnessed had already borne fruit; and, absorbed in the contemplation of a happiness which seemed to them immeasurable, as profound as the misery of the unfortunate people they had rescued from death, the lovers leaned back in the shadow of the carriage and listened to the ceaseless splashing of the rain which filled the ear and mingled with the cries of startled lapwings.

*　　　*　　　*　　　*

Two years and a half have passed away, and the suburban home predicted by May, when she came to bid Alice a last good-bye, arises before the reader in all its yellow paint and homely vulgarity. Here you find the ten-roomed house with all its special characteristics. Let us examine the frontage, a dining-room window looking upon a commodious area with dust and coal-holes. The drawing-room has two windows, and the slender balcony is generally set with flower-boxes. Above that come the two windows of the best bedroom belonging to Mr. and Mrs., and above that again the windows of two small rooms, respectively inhabited by the eldest son and daughter; and these are topped by the mock-Elizabethan gable which enframes the tiny window of a servant's room. Each house has a pair of trim stone pillars, the crude green of the Venetian blinds jars the cultured eye, and even the tender green of the foliage in the crescent seems as cheap and as common as if it had been bought—as everything else is in Ashbourne Crescent —at the Stores. But how much does this crescent of shrubs mean to the neighbourhood? Is it not there that the old ladies take their pugs for their constitutional walks, and is it not there that the young ladies play tennis with their gentleman acquaintances when they come home from the City on a Saturday afternoon?

In Ashbourne Crescent there is neither Dissent nor Radicalism, but general aversion to all considerations which might disturb belief in all the routine of existence, in all its temporal and spiritual aspects, as it had come amongst them. The fathers and the brothers go to the City every day at nine, the young ladies play tennis, read novels, and beg to be taken to dances at the Kensington Town Hall. On Sunday the air is alive with the clanging of bells, and in orderly procession every family proceeds to church, the fathers in all the gravity of umbrellas and prayer-books, the matrons in silk mantles and clumsy ready-made elastic-sides; the girls in all the gaiety of their summer dresses with lively bustles bobbing, the young men in frock-coats which show off their broad shoulders—from time to time they pull their tawny moustaches. Each house keeps a cook and housemaid, and on Sunday afternoons, when the skies are flushed with sunset and the outlines of this human warren grow harshly distinct—black lines upon pale red—these are seen walking arm-in-arm away towards a distant park with their young men.

To some this air of dull well-to-do-ness may seem as intolerable, as obscene in its way as the look of melancholy silliness which the Dubliners and their dirty city wear so unintermittently. One is the inevitable decay which must precede an outburst of national energy; the other is the smug optimism, that fund of materialism, on which a nation lives, and which in truth represents the bulwarks wherewith civilisation defends itself against those sempiternal storms which, like atmospheric convulsions, by destroying, renew the tired life of man. And that Ashbourne Crescent, with its bright brass knockers, its white-capped maidservant, and spotless oilcloths, will in the dim future pass away before some great tide of revolution that is now gathering strength far away, deep down and out of sight in the heart of the nation, is probable enough ; but it is certainly now, in all its cheapness and vulgarity, more than anything else representative, though the length and breadth of the land be searched, of the genius of Empire that has been glorious through the long tale that nine hundred years have to tell. Ashbourne Crescent may possibly soon be replaced by something better, but at present it commands our admiration, for it is, as has been said, more than all else, typical England. Neither ideas nor much lucidity will be found there, but much belief in the wisdom shown in the present ordering of things, and much plain sense and much honesty of purpose. Certainly if your quest be for hectic emotion and passionate impulses you would do well to turn your steps aside, you will not find them in Ashbourne Crescent ; there life flows monotonously, perhaps sometimes even a little moodily, but it is built upon a basis of honest materialism—that materialism without which the world cannot live ; which, let the word be said, is the Light of the world. Human greatness at Ashbourne Crescent is as good as it be, and it teems with all the delights of home and habit, delights that alone are assuaging, and to which even the most ardent spirits turn in the end and accept humbly and with admiration and love.

No. 31 differs a little from the rest of the houses. The paint on its walls is fresher, and there are no flowers on its balcony : the hall-door has three bells instead of the usual two, and there is a brass plate, with "Dr. Reed" engraved upon it. The cook is talking through the area-railings to the butcher-boy ; a very smart parlourmaid opens the door, and we see that the interior is as orderly, commonplace, and clean as we might expect at every house in the crescent. The floor-cloths are irreproachable, the marble-painted walls are un-adorned with a single picture. On the right is the dining-room, a mahogany table bought for five pounds in the Tottenham Court Road, a dozen chairs to match, a sideboard and a small table ; green-painted walls decorated with two engravings, one of Frith's "Railway Station," the other of Guido's "Fortune." The room is rigid and bare. Further down the passage leading to the kitchen-stairs there is a second room : this is the Doctor's consulting-room. A small bookcase filled with serious-looking volumes, a mahogany escritoire strewn with papers, letters, memoranda of all sorts. The floor is covered with a bright Brussels carpet; there are two leather armchairs, and a portrait of an admiral hangs over the fireplace.

Let us go upstairs. How bright and clean are the high marble-painted walls! and on the first landing there is a large cheaply-coloured window. The drawing-room is a double room, not divided by curtains but by stiff folding doors. The furniture is in red, and the heavy curtains that drape the windows fall from gilt cornices. In the middle of the floor there is a settee (probably a reminiscence of the Shelbourne Hotel); and on either side of the fireplace there are sofas, and about the hearthrug many armchairs to match with the rest. Above the chimneypiece there is a gilt oval mirror, worth ten pounds. The second room is Alice's study; it is there she writes her novels. A table in black wood with a pile of MSS. neatly fastened together stands in one corner; there is a bookcase just behind; its shelves are furnished with imaginative literature, such as Shelley's poems, Wordsworth's poems, Keats' poems. There are also handsome editions of Tennyson and Browning, presents from Dr. Reed to his wife. You see a little higher up the shelf a thin volume, Swinburne's "Atalanta in Calydon," and next to it is Walter Pater's Renaissance—studies in art and poetry. There are also many volumes in yellow covers, evidently French novels.

The character of the house is therefore essentially provincial, and shows that its occupants have not always lived amid the complex influences of London life, viz., is not even suburban. Nevertheless here and there traces of new artistic impulses are seen. On the mantelpiece in the larger room there are two large blue vases; on a small table stands a pot in yellow porcelain, evidently from Morris'; and on the walls there are engravings from Burne Jones. Every Thursday afternoon numbers of ladies, all of whom write novels, assemble here to drink tea and talk of their work.

It is now eleven o'clock in the morning. Alice enters her drawing-room. You see her: a tall, spare woman with kind eyes, who carries her arms stiffly. She has just finished her housekeeping, she puts down her basket of keys, and with all the beautiful movement of the young mother she takes up the crawling mass of white frock, kisses her son and settles his blue sash. And when she has talked to him for a few minutes she rings the bell for nurse : then she sits down to write.   As usual her pen runs on without a perceptible pause. Words come to her easily, but she has not finished the opening paragraph of the article she is writing when the sound of rapid footsteps attracts her attention, and Olive bursts into the room.

"Oh, Alice, how do you do? I couldn't stop at home any longer, I am sick of it."

"Couldn't stop at home any longer, Olive, what do you mean?"

"If you won't take me in, say so, and I'll go."

"My dear Olive, I shall be delighted to have you with me : but why can't you stop at home any longer—surely there is no harm in my asking?"

"Oh, I don't know; don't ask me; I am so miserable at home; I can't tell you how unhappy I am. I know I shall never be married, and the perpetual trying to make up matches is sickening.   Mamma will insist on riches, position and all that sort of thing—those kind of men don't want to get married—I am sick of going out; I won't go out any more. We never missed a tennis party last year ; we used to go sometimes ten miles to them, so eager was mamma after Captain Gibbon, and it did not come off; and then the whole country laughs."

"And who is Captain Gibbon? I never heard of him before."

"No, you don't know him : he was not in Galway in your time."

"And Captain Hibbert !   Have you heard from him since he went out to India?"

"Yes, once ; he wrote to me to say that he hoped to see me when he came home."

"And when will that be?"

"Oh, I don't know; when people go out to India one never expects to see them again."

Seeing how sore the wound was, Alice did not attempt to probe it, but strove rather to lead Olive's thoughts away from it, and gradually the sisters lapsed into talking of their acquaintances and friends, and of how life had dealt with them.

"And May, what is she doing?"

"She met with a bad accident, and has not been out hunting lately. She was riding a pounding match with Mrs. Manley across country; May's horse came to grief at a big wall, and broke several of her ribs. They say she has given up riding—now she does nothing but paint. You remember how well she used to paint at school."

" And the Brennans?"

" Oh, they go up to the Shelbourne every year, but none of them are married; and I am afraid that they must be very hard up, for their land is very highly let, and the tenants are paying no rent at all now—Ireland is worse than ever; we shall all be ruined, and they say Home Rule is certain. But I am sick of the subject."

Then the Duffys, the Honourable Miss Gores, and the many other families of unmarried girls—the poor muslin martyrs, whose sufferings were the theme of this book, were again passed in review; their failures sometimes jeeringly alluded to by Olive, but always listened to pityingly by Alice—and, talking thus of their past life, the sisters leant over the spring fire that burnt out in the grate. At the end of a long silence, Alice said:

" Well, dear, I hope you have come to live with us, or at any rate, to pay us a long visit."

THE END.

University of
Chester

DO YOU WANT TO RENEW ONLINE?

DO YOU WANT TO RESERVE YOUR OWN BOOKS?

ARE YOU STRUGGLING WITH ATHENS?

Did you know you can <u>RENEW</u> your library items via the Library Catalogue?

Did you know you can <u>RESERVE</u> library items via the Library Catalogue?

Did you know that you can now access <u>ATHENS</u> using your Novell username and password?

WANT TO KNOW MORE??

Please ask for more information
at the
Library Enquiries Desk.